Good Eats

"We should look for someone
to eat and drink with before
looking for something to
eat and drink."
////////////////////////////////////
EPICURUS

EATS 3

THE LATER YEARS

ALTON BROWN

STEWART, TABORI & CHANG

NEW YORK

CONTENTS

Woodson

Alton Brown Interviews Alton Brown
on *Good Eats 3: The Later Years*

ALTON BROWN: So . . .

ALTON BROWN: Here we are . . .

A B: Volume III.

A B: Yep.

A B: Just as heavy as Volume II . . .

A B: . . . which was heavier than Volume I.

A B: And why is that exactly?

A B: Thicker episodes, I expect.

A B: Meaning denser . . . more concentrated . . . more informative.

A B: No, meaning "thicker."

A B: So what can readers of this "thicker" third volume expect?

A B: Well, by episode 165, which is the first included here, I think we'd hit our stride. The shows in Volume I represented our formative years, Volume II portrayed a rather difficult adolescence, and now we're all grown up, if you can call playing with puppets and wanky props "grown up."

A B: But aren't those really sophisticated metaphors and parables with multiple strata of meaning?

A B: Ummm . . . Yes . . . yes they are.

A B: Was this book easier or harder to write than the earlier volumes?

A B: Much harder. Besides being thicker, the visual style of the cooking has evolved so that properly explaining the procedures without the moving visuals was really tough. So as we went back to rework the applications for written form only, there was a lot more to take into consideration.

A B: Well, let's talk about the food. Are the recipes in this book better?

A B: We don't deal in recipes, we deal in "applications." I thought we'd covered that all before.

A B: Yes, we have . . . repeatedly. I apologize.

A B: It's okay—you're nervous. I understand. Look, I would simply say that the food here is different.

A B: Okay, how is the food different?

(There's a long pause as subject thinks this over.)

A B: It's better.

(At this point the interviewer takes a deep breath and rubs his eyes.)

A B: Okay, how is it better?

A B: It's simpler, and simpler is always better. I also really like the shows that focus on common foods that people don't think about making.

A B : Cottage cheese, for instance?

A B : Exactly. And marshmallows. Other than that, the fried catfish is delightful, and I'm proud of the crockpot lasagna because it's an unorthodox approach that generates a really good dish.

A B : In looking over the book, I couldn't help but notice several unorthodox procedures—the porterhouse steak, for instance.

A B : I love that procedure because it eliminates every issue a home cook encounters when trying to get steakhouse results at home.

A B : But cooking under charcoal is a little . . .

A B : . . . weird, I know. But it gets the job done like nobody's business.

A B : What drives the reci— sorry, application development on the show?

A B : The applications have to produce tasty food, they have to prove a point, that is, some kind of scientific point, and they have to make sense. We tear every procedure down to its bare elements. Every ingredient and every step must serve a purpose or I don't want it there.

A B : Any standout moments from a cinematic standpoint?

A B : I'd say the punch show for sure. That East India Company ship was a triumph of Victorian stagecraft. The giant tempura monster attack scene is still thrilling, and I really enjoyed the sliding panel history scene from lasagna. Of course, there's the meat pie show . . .

A B : . . . the Sweeney Todd rip?

A B : I think the word you're looking for is *homage*.

A B : I'm sorry, go on.

A B : It was a lot of fun, that's all. But my favorite episode has to be "The Once and Future Fish."

A B : Your daughter was in that one, right?

A B : Yes. The episode takes place some thirty years in the future. I'm an old man and she's my granddaughter. She wore this crazy white wig, straight from manga, and I had all this latex on my face to wrinkle me up. And I wore old-man clothes and shuffled around. Seeing yourself like that can have quite an impact.

A B : And what about science models? Anything outstanding?

A B : Are you suggesting that some of them weren't?

A B : Of course not.

A B : Oatmeal.

A B : What about it?

A B : "Oat Cuisine II" has the best *Good Eats* science model ever. My attorneys aided me in a hands-on pantomime of sorts in which we explained how oats help lower "bad" cholesterol. I'm holding out for one of those early morning calls from Stockholm . . . know what I'm saying?

A B : Good luck with that. I can't help but remember that when last we spoke you said that you were going to title this volume *The Return of the King*. What happened?

A B : Well, it turns out there's already a book out with that title, so we had to punt.

A B : "The Later Years" is rather suggestive though, seeing as how not much usually comes after "later." Is this in fact the final *Good Eats* book?

A B : Well, I imagine in the years to come we'll see scholarly works written about *Good Eats*, and there will be plenty of dissertations published regarding the show's long-term effect on American culture, but these will be written by others.

A B : So you're done?

A B : In the words of Daniel Plainview, "I'm finished."

A B : Any regrets you'd like to share?

A B : I never got to do a show about snails. Just imagine what *Good Eats* coulda done with that one.

THE EPISODES

GOOD EATS | THE LATER YEARS

TORTILLAS AGAIN

EPISODE 165 | SEASON 10 | GOOD EATS

OWN WIT
BROWN!

Rarely have we followed a program concerning one particular type of food or dish with a program focusing on what to do with the leftovers, but that's exactly what "Tortillas Again" was all about. That's because when we finished "Tortilla Reform" (see Volume 2) I realized that although we'd made some pretty fine tortillas, we hadn't really done any of the things that home cooks actually do with them. And so I decided to invent some picketing protestors from Cooks Against Wasted Leftovers and a maladjusted fairy called the Mother of Culinary Invention and set about making the best tortilla-based dishes we could muster. Some fans have chastised us for not including chicken and tortilla soup in the show, but to my mind that's really about chicken soup with tortillas as garnish. Each of the applications that follow is all about the tortillas or tortilla chips.

TRIVIA My noggin was lumpy for a week after the shoot due to the repeated smacks from Widdi's wand. (I just hate Method actors.)

▷○ **Just for review:**

Tortillas are a form of Mesoamerican flatbread that can be produced from either wheat or corn flour. We've concentrated on corn tortillas, as they are more versatile and far more common in the U.S.

Tortillas are created from dough called masa, which is made from ground maize, a.k.a. "field" or "flint" corn. This type of corn is easily procured at health food stores, and even some seed-'n'-feeds (which is where bootleggers buy it for makin' corn liquor). To make the dough, the corn is soaked in an alkaline solution of water and calcium hydroxide (lime) and/or wood ash, which eases removal of the kernel's tough outer pericarp. A side effect of this process, called "nixtamalization," is an increase in the bioavailability of the grain's niacin and a mild increase in protein. It seems like a small thing, but this amplification of nutrients is quite possibly what gave early Americans the oomph to build the magnificent civilizations that Western "adventurers" later tore asunder with their cannons and pox.

Montezuma did have his revenge, though. When Cortez and his cronies took maize back to the Old World, they stuck it straight into mills and skipped the quaint old tradition of nixtamalization. As a result, millions of Europeans, particularly northern Italians, who came to depend on maize for most of their diet, ended up with pellagra, a disease caused by lack of niacin whose symptoms are most often described as the "three Ds": diarrhea, dermatitis, and dementia. Nasty stuff.

Masa, which is also used in the production of tamales, can be purchased in most megamarts as either masa harina ("corn flour") or as a wet dough that's ready to press and cook. Either of these options is superior to buying megamart tortillas, but there's yet another option.

Consider buying tortillas from a local factory. I'm always surprised at how many towns across America are home to a tortilla factory, and I've never encountered one that wasn't more than happy to sell its product right there in the lobby. Keep in mind that tortillas freeze well if left in the bag and double wrapped in aluminum foil, so you can buy in bulk. I've even found that many factories will sell you corn, nixtamal, or even *masa* dough if you want to cook your own tortillas.

Although many tortilla makers prefer to use traditional wooden rolling pins, I'm a fan of the tortilla press. Here's mine.

The tortilla applications that follow are darned tasty, but I should point out that they also serve as crucial thickeners in Good Eats Pressure Cooker Chili (episode 113, Volume 2). Fresh tortillas can also be cut into strips and used in place of noodles in our Chicken Noodle Soup from episode 91 (also in Volume 2 . . . maybe you should pick that one up—just an idea).

THE MOTHER OF CULINARY INVENTION HAS COME TO MY RESCUE . . . SORTA.

THE TORTILLA: ONCE YOU'VE MADE IT, WHAT TO DO WITH IT?

NACHO NACHO MAN

80 NACHOS

Once upon a time back in 1944 or '45, Chef Ignacio Anaya was getting ready to lock up the kitchen for the night at the Victory Club in Piedras Negras, Mexico, when three military wives from Fort Duncan, just over the border, dropped in after a long day of sightseeing and shopping. They were hungry, but Chef Anaya told them that, alas, the kitchen was closed. The damsels begged for sustenance, and Ignacio finally relented and retired to the kitchen to ponder his options. There was not much in the way of groceries, just some two-day-old tortillas, some cheese, some chiles . . . odds and ends, really. What did he make? Well, it might be helpful to point out that the definitive form of the name *Ignacio* is . . . *Nacho*.

TIDBIT Oaxaca is a white semihard cheese named after the Mexican city where it was first produced. Its easy-melting, string nature can be duplicated by part-skim mozzarella.

// SOFTWARE

80		corn tortilla chips	approximately 8 ounces
3 to 4		fresh jalapeños	thinly sliced, seeded if desired
1	small	red onion	diced
6	ounces	cheddar cheese	finely grated
6	ounces	Oaxaca cheese	finely grated
2	tablespoons	fresh oregano	finely chopped
2	cups	fresh salsa	
2	cups	sour cream	
2	cups	guacamole	

// PROCEDURE

1. Set one of the oven racks on the lowest shelf and heat the oven to 350°F.

2. Line a **half sheet pan** with **parchment paper** and set aside. Make 8 (2-inch) balls out of **aluminum foil**. Spray **3 cooling racks** with **nonstick cooking spray** and place one of the aluminum balls in each of the corners of 2 of the racks.

3. Lay one-third of the chips on one of the racks. Top each chip with a jalapeño slice and sprinkle the chips with one-third of the red onion and one-third of both of the cheeses. Repeat with the remaining chips and the other 2 racks.

4. Stack the racks on top of one another and set in the parchment-lined half sheet pan. Bake in the oven on the bottom rack for 7 minutes, or until the cheese begins to bubble. Sprinkle with the oregano. Serve immediately with the salsa, sour cream, and guacamole.

   N O T E : Depending on your heat preference, you may remove the seeds from the jalapeños or leave them intact.

THREE HUNGRY AIRMEN WIVES

MAS MASA TOTS

APPROXIMATELY 3 DOZEN TOTS

How many foods do you know of that can be cooked back to their original state? Well, with moisture and heat, tortillas—and even tortilla chips—can essentially be turned back into masa. We used this curious fact back in our chili (with an "i") show to thicken our stew by adding tortilla chips to the pressure cooker. Here we make tater tots, only with tortillas.

THIS IS MY DISHER. THERE ARE MANY LIKE IT, BUT THIS ONE IS MINE. MY DISHER IS MY BEST FRIEND...

// SOFTWARE ///

10	ounces	corn tortillas	approximately 20 (6-inch)
½	cup	whole milk	
1	large	egg	
1½	teaspoons	kosher salt	
¼	teaspoon	black pepper	freshly ground
¼	cup	onion	diced
2	tablespoons	jalapeño	minced
2	quarts	peanut oil	

// PROCEDURE ///

1. Tear the tortillas into small pieces and place in a **food processor**. Add the milk, egg, salt, and pepper. Process until a chunky paste forms and you are able to squeeze a ball together in your hand, stopping to scrape down the sides of the bowl as needed. Transfer to a **mixing bowl** and stir in the onions and jalapeños. Set aside.

2. Heat the oil in a **5-quart Dutch oven** fitted with a **deep-fry thermometer** over medium heat to 365° to 375°F.

3. Roll the dough into 1- to 1½-inch balls or scoop with a small **2-teaspoon ice cream disher**. Fry, 6 to 8 at a time, until crisp and golden brown, 2 to 3 minutes. Transfer to a **cooling rack** set over a **half sheet pan** and cool for 1 to 2 minutes before serving.

   NOTE: If using tortillas from *Good Eats 2*, decrease milk to ⅓ cup.

| 10 MINUTES MORE |---| SWEET ANTOJITOS |

For a sweet version, reduce the salt to ½ teaspoon, omit the pepper, onion, and jalapeño, and add 2 tablespoons of sugar and 1 tablespoon of orange zest. Then proceed as above.

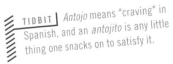

TIDBIT | *Antojo* means "craving" in Spanish, and an *antojito* is any little thing one snacks on to satisfy it.

BOWL O' BAYOU

EPISODE 166 | SEASON 10 | GOOD EATS

ON THE SET OF CAJUN CITCHEN

Gumbo is little more than a roux-thickened stew with rice, and yet to call it nothing more than a roux-thickened stew with rice is to utter culinary blasphemy, because gumbo is one of the most solidly "American" dishes there is, in that it represents at least half a dozen cultures—including the French, who supplied the roux; the Choctaw, who invented filé powder; and Africans, who contributed okra and rice (via Madagascar). The Caribbeans brought several herbs and spices to the party, and the English . . . okay, not much England in this one, which is just fine with me. Although we haven't dabbled too much in "authentic" ethnic cuisines, gumbo is heavily technique driven and much misunderstood, which makes it a fine candidate for . . .

CAJUN V. CREOLE

Although Creole cuisine (typified by classic New Orleans cuisine) embraces many of the same ingredients as Cajun cuisine, three specific points clearly indicate that gumbo is of the bayou, by the bayou, and for the bayou:

▶ It uses a dark rather than a blond roux.

▶ It is built upon oil rather than butter.

▶ There is no tomato in classic gumbo (tomatoes are a Creole addition).

TRIVIA *Cajun Citchen*, the totally made-up show that's supposedly shooting next door to *Good Eats*, is a complete goof on the excellent PBS program made for years and years by the knowledgeable and good-natured Justin Wilson, to whom I meant no disrespect.

14

Roux is French for "redhead" and refers to a mixture of flour and fat cooked to rid the flour of its raw taste and to coat each flour granule with fat so that when the roux is introduced to a liquid, typically a hot one, the flour won't clump. In classic French applications and the Creole dishes it spawned, rouxs are typically made with butter and cooked only briefly so that they are still white or perhaps "blond." In Cajun cuisine oil is used and the roux is cooked . . . and cooked . . . and cooked until it's the color of an old brick. An interesting conversion happens during this lengthy application of heat. The flavor intensifies to a roasty, toasty nuttiness reminiscent of coffee, while the thickening power, the capability of the starch inside the flour to gelatinize and thicken a liquid, is substantially reduced. That means to thicken you need more of it—or another thickener altogether.

Since the roux used in gumbo is so dang dark, it needs to get some thickening help from another source. Some folks use okra, a seed pod containing a slimy variation of mucilage that gels like a starch and can therefore thicken hot liquids quite effectively. The fact that gumbo shares more than a few letters with the West African word for okra, *guingombo*, is I think pretty clear evidence that okra and gumbo are a regular item.

But then there's gumbo filé, or "filé powder," which is ground from the leaves of the sassafras tree, the same tree whose roots have been used at various times as a medicinal cure, a tea substitute, a leather-curing agent, and a flavoring agent for root beer. But in this case it is the young leaves rather than the roots or bark that hold the power, a power that turns out to be molecular kin to the mucilage in okra. And since there's some evidence that filé was given to the Acadians by the Choctaw Indians during their southern sojourn, it may actually have thickened gumbo before okra did. So why not use both? Because that simply is not done. Ever. Just go down Louisiana way and ask around.

Filé is powerful stuff and it only takes a tablespoon to thicken a pot o' gumbo. Some Cajuns prefer to add it at the table, but I prefer to dose the pot so the flavor has time to mellow a bit.

A TASTE OF HISTORY

Back in 1755 the British forced the French population of what was then Acadia in Nova Scotia to take an oath of allegiance to the British crown, which had finagled its way into the land. Being French, they said, "We throw our rotting skunks in your general direction." What followed was an ethnic cleansing known as "the great upheaval." Six to seven thousand Acadians were forced from their homes and their land. Some were shipped to places as far away as the Falkland Islands, some were shipped back to France, others were booted into British prisons. But sixteen hundred or so made their way to Louisiana, marking the first massive immigration within the United States—or at least what was going to eventually be the United States. The region's Spanish rulers welcomed these immigrants, partly because they hoped to bolster the Catholic population of the region, and over the following decades the Acadians intermarried with locals, including members of several Native American nations. Eventually, because of a twist of the local tongue the word *Acadian* became *Cajun*.

MARDI GRAS GUYS IN FUNNY MASKS GALAVANT AROUND THE COUNTRYSIDE BEGGING FOR GUMBO INGREDIENTS.

// SOFTWARE //

4	ounces	vegetable oil	
4	ounces	all-purpose flour	
1½	pounds (31- to 50-count)	shrimp	whole, head on
2	quarts	H$_2$O	
1	cup	onion	diced
½	cup	celery	diced
½	cup	green bell pepper	diced
2	tablespoons	garlic	minced
½	cup	tomato	peeled, seeded, and chopped
1	tablespoon	kosher salt	
½	teaspoon	black pepper	freshly ground
1	teaspoon	fresh thyme	chopped
¼	teaspoon	cayenne pepper	
2		bay leaves	
½	pound	andouille sausage	cut into ½-inch pieces and browned
1	tablespoon	filé powder	

TIDBIT | The combination of onion, celery, and pepper reminiscent of a French mirepoix is referred to as the Creole Trinity or the Trinity or the Holy Trinity of Creole.

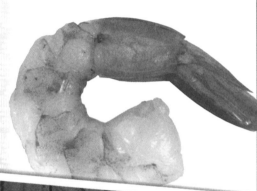

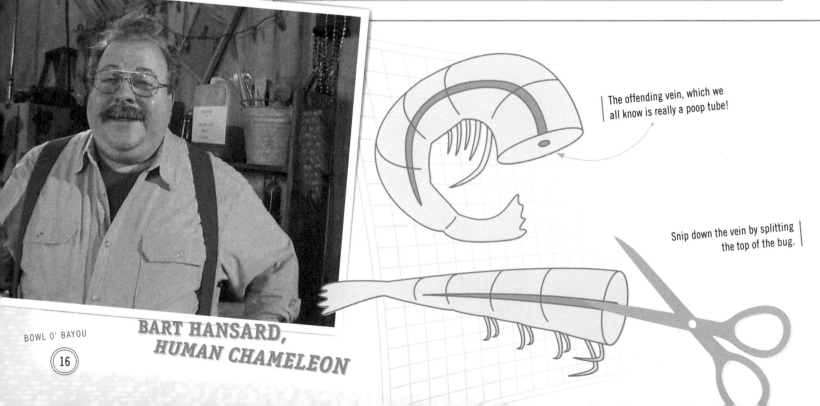

BART HANSARD,
HUMAN CHAMELEON

The offending vein, which we all know is really a poop tube!

Snip down the vein by splitting the top of the bug.

// PROCEDURE ///

1. Heat the oven to 350°F.

2. Put the oil and flour in a **5-quart cast-iron Dutch oven** and **whisk** together to combine. Place on the middle shelf of the oven, uncovered, and bake for 1½ hours, whisking 2 or 3 times.

3. While the roux is baking, de-head, peel, and devein the shrimp. Put the shrimp in a **bowl** and refrigerate. Put the heads and shells in a **4-quart saucepan** along with the 2 quarts of water, set over high heat, and bring to a boil. Decrease the heat to low and simmer for 1 hour, or until the liquid has reduced to 1 quart. Remove from the heat and strain the liquid into a **container**, discarding the solids.

4. Once the roux is done (it will be a brick red-brown), carefully remove the pot from the oven and set it over medium-high heat. Gently add the onion, celery, bell pepper, and garlic and cook, moving constantly, for 7 to 8 minutes, until the onion begins to turn translucent.

5. Add the tomato, salt, black pepper, thyme, cayenne pepper, and bay leaves and stir to combine. Gradually add the shrimp broth while whisking continuously. Decrease the heat to low, cover, and cook for 35 minutes.

6. Turn off the heat, add the shrimp and sausage, and stir to combine. Add the filé powder while stirring constantly.

7. Cover and rest for 10 minutes before serving. Serve over rice (page 183).

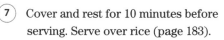
TIDBIT | The average American gulps down four pounds of shrimp each year. Too bad most of it comes from foreign waters.

BOWL O' BAYOU

17

FOWL TERRITORY

EPISODE 167 | SEASON 10 | GOOD EATS

This episode is technically about Cornish hens, but really it's all about food sanitation and keeping you and your family safe from all the nasty little microbial varmints that would like nothing more than to set up shop inside your unsuspecting innards. The birds are good—you can bank on that—but stopping the bugs is the prime directive here.

KNOWLEDGE CONCENTRATE

▷○ A Cornish or Rock game hen is defined (by the federal government, no less) as an immature chicken generally five to six weeks of age with a ready-to-cook weight of not more than two pounds that was prepared from a Cornish chicken or the progeny of a Cornish chicken crossed with another breed of chicken. The Cornish hen was first sold in 1965 by Donald John Tyson, who is often credited with crossing the Rock hen and Cornish chicken to produce the game hen. Some food historians credit Alphonsine and Jacques Makowsky of Connecticut for creating the breed some ten years before Tyson began selling it.

▷○ FOOD-BORNE ILLNESS: That's what happens when bacteria, viruses, parasites, toxins, and other microbial miscreants get into us through our food in sufficient numbers to make us sick. If we give them the chance, microbes will evade our personal space every time because they want a lot of the same things we want: warmth, moisture, nourishment, and comfort (in their case this means a reasonably neutral pH—nothing too acidic or basic). Unfortunately, many foods we target are also on their menu. However, their campaign to conquer your colon (to make no mention of your stomach, intestine, and liver, which are also very comfortable spots) can be stymied through the judicious application of the four C's: contain, clean, cook, and chill. Simple concepts all, but the trick is to apply them strategically across every phase of meal construction, from shopping to storing the leftovers.

Prevent microbes from spreading from where they might be to where they might want to go, what migration food safety folk refer to as "cross contamination."

Identify foods that are most likely to be contaminated—assume all raw meats (especially poultry and all ground meats)—and quarantine them throughout procurement and processing.

Take a cooler with ice to the market for meats, eggs, and the like so that there is no chance of juices moving from them to raw vegetables or fruits.

At home, store meat, poultry, and fish in the bottom of the fridge, preferably in a bottom drawer. Not only is this typically the coldest part of the chill chest, but also there's nothing to drip on below. Make sure raw foods and leftovers alike are refrigerated in drip-proof containment.

Use latex or vinyl gloves when working with raw poultry and meat so that you can simply pull one off to answer the phone, scratch your nose, turn on the faucet, and so on.

When grilling, make sure you don't use the same platter to bring the cooked meat back in that you used to take the raw meat out—unless you stop to wash it, of course.

Cross contamination often happens on cutting boards when raw-serve foods like lettuce follow raw meats. I have a red cutting board that is only for meats. Everything else goes on either a wooden or a white plastic board. That way there's no possible confusion.

Although bacteria can live at a wide range of temperatures, they grow and reproduce rapidly between 40° and 140°F, which is why you should always keep your refrigerator set between 35° and 38°F and your freezer below zero.[1]

Keep meat, poultry, and fish on ice for the trip from the megamart to home. Meat temperatures often rise to as high as 65°F even during a short trip. This is slap dab in the middle of the danger zone.

To quickly reduce the temperature of hot soups, stocks, and the like, divide the batch into smaller containers and set the vessels in ice water. Once they drop below 90°F or so I often drop in a couple pint-size water bottles that I keep frozen at all times. Once the liquid is good and chilled, remove the bottles and refrigerate. As for the bottles, wash them and refreeze for use another day.

For chunky foods like kabobs, burgers, or meatballs, spread them out on a half sheet pan and refrigerate or freeze them before packaging for storage.

[1] Some bugs can actually survive long stints in the freezer, so you want to be careful to cook previously frozen foods properly.

GARDEN GNOMES ARE CHEAPER THAN ACTORS (AND THEY DON'T TALK BACK).

THE FOUR C'S — CLEAN

Start with hot water and soap to thoroughly clean tools, hands, cutting boards, counters, and so on. Where meats are concerned I also sanitize.

According to the EPA, "sanitize" means to reduce bacterial presence by 99.99 percent (compared to "sterilize," which means to reduce that presence by 99.999 percent).

This is easily done with standard household items such as vinegar (bacteria hate acidity) and bleach.

Sodium hypochlorite, the active ingredient in modern bleach, is a powerful oxidizing agent capable of basically blowing up cell walls of bacteria and some viruses. And it's fairly potent stuff. A mere quarter teaspoon mixed into a cup of water (a tablespoon per gallon) would be concentrated enough to do away with most kitchen nasties. I keep it in a spritzer bottle like this . . .

. . . not only for ease of application but also because keeping it contained will make it last longer. This will remain potent for up to a week, whereas if you were to put it in an open container you'd have to replace it every single day. To use it, just spritz on any clean nonporous surface and air dry. No towel buffing necessary.

THE FOUR C'S — COOK

According to the USDA (www.fsis.usda.gov), cooking meats to the following temps will do away with any microbes hoping to hop the express train to your innards:

—— Beef, veal, and lamb steaks, roasts, and chops to 145°F.
—— All cuts of pork to 160°F.
—— Ground beef, veal, and lamb to 160°F.
—— Egg dishes and casseroles to 160°F.
—— All poultry should reach a safe minimum internal temperature of 165°F.
—— Stuffed poultry is not recommended. Cook stuffing separately to 165°F.
—— Reheat leftovers thoroughly to at least 165°F.
—— Fish should reach 145°F.
—— Bring sauces, soups, and gravies to a boil when reheating.

I will tell you right now that I do not follow these rules to the letter. I cook pork chops to about 145°F, I like my beef steaks at 135°F, and even chickens I usually stop around 155°F. I do this because I know that carryover heat is going to continue to push the temp upward even after cooking. Also I know good and well that the government has built a considerable margin of error into their numbers because salmonella actually dies at any temperature above 150°F. I do, however, religiously reheat to 165°F just to be safe.

Any of the above recommendations require the cook to own and properly operate a quality instant-read thermometer, preferably with a digital readout.

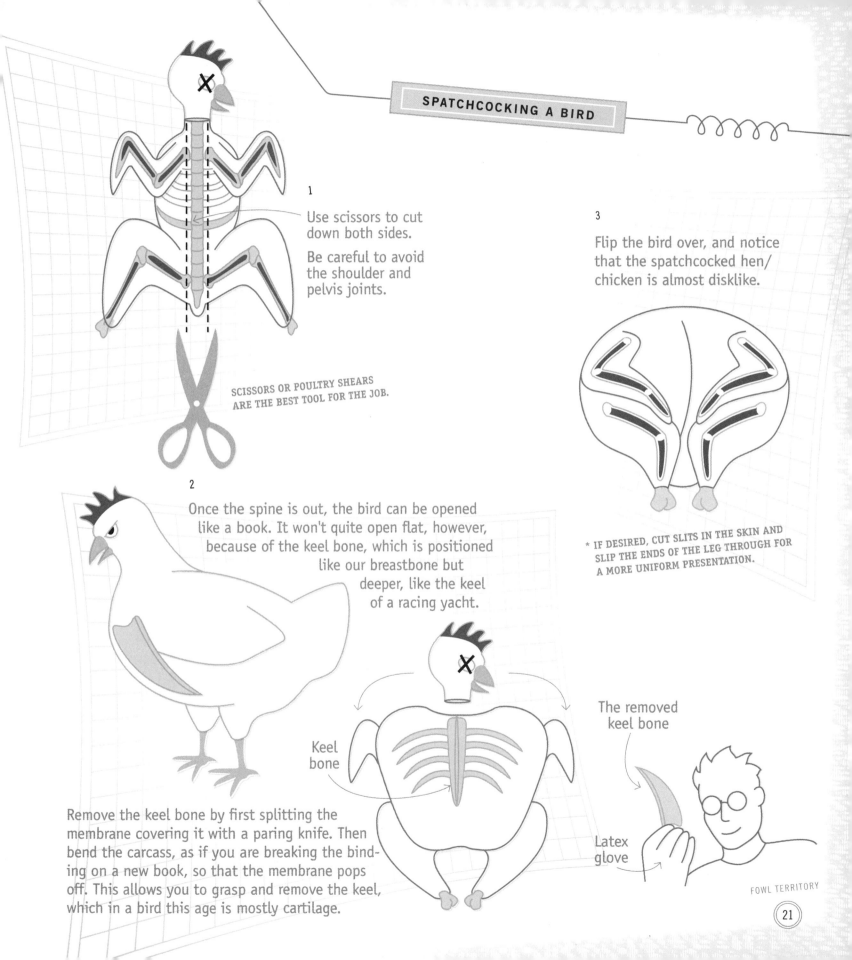

1

Use scissors to cut down both sides.

Be careful to avoid the shoulder and pelvis joints.

SCISSORS OR POULTRY SHEARS ARE THE BEST TOOL FOR THE JOB.

2

Once the spine is out, the bird can be opened like a book. It won't quite open flat, however, because of the keel bone, which is positioned like our breastbone but deeper, like the keel of a racing yacht.

Remove the keel bone by first splitting the membrane covering it with a paring knife. Then bend the carcass, as if you are breaking the binding on a new book, so that the membrane pops off. This allows you to grasp and remove the keel, which in a bird this age is mostly cartilage.

Keel bone

The removed keel bone

Latex glove

3

Flip the bird over, and notice that the spatchcocked hen/ chicken is almost disklike.

* IF DESIRED, CUT SLITS IN THE SKIN AND SLIP THE ENDS OF THE LEG THROUGH FOR A MORE UNIFORM PRESENTATION.

CORNISH GAME HEN WITH BACON AND ONIONS

4 SERVINGS

// SOFTWARE ///

2	1¼- to 1¾-pound	Cornish game hens	
	to taste	kosher salt	
	to taste	black pepper	freshly ground
4	rashers	thick-sliced bacon	cut into ½-inch pieces
20 to 24		pearl onions	frozen, defrosted

// PROCEDURE //

1. Heat the oven to 500°F. Wrap a **brick** in **aluminum foil** and put it in the oven to heat.

2. Place a hen, breast side down, on a **cutting board**. Using **scissors or poultry shears**, spatchcock the hen, following the procedure illustrated on page 21. Season on both sides with salt and pepper. Repeat with the second hen.

3. Fry the bacon in a **12-inch cast-iron skillet** over medium heat. Once crisp, remove the bacon from the skillet and set aside. Drain all but 1 tablespoon of the fat from the pan. Immediately add the two birds to the pan, skin side down. Add the onions to the pan around the edges. Top the birds with the brick and leave on the heat for 5 minutes. Transfer the pan to the oven and roast for 10 to 15 minutes, until the thigh meat reaches 170°F.

4. Remove from the oven and rest for 5 minutes before serving with the onions and bacon.

THERMOMETER TIPS:

▸ Keep the thermometer sensor clean and be sure to insert it at least ½ inch into the target food.

▸ Leave in place for at least 3 seconds before reading.

▸ Always temp the thickest part of the food.

▸ Check the calibration of your thermometer a couple times a year by temping boiling water and an ice-water slush. If they don't read 212°F and 32°F, respectively, you may have a problem.

As a personal aside, I am a huge fan of the thermometers made by the Thermopen company. And no, they don't pay me to say that.

GRILLED CURRY CORNISH GAME HENS

4 SERVINGS

// SOFTWARE

⅓	cup	vegetable oil
1	teaspoon	fennel seeds
1	teaspoon	cumin seeds
1	teaspoon	coriander seeds
½	teaspoon	mustard seeds
½	teaspoon	hot smoked paprika
⅓	cup	slivered almonds
1	teaspoon	kosher salt
2	1¼- to 1¾-pound	Cornish game hens

// PROCEDURE

1. Heat a gas grill to 500°F. Place a **brick**, wrapped in **aluminum foil**, onto the grates of the grill to heat.

2. Put the oil in a **1-quart saucepan** and place over high heat. Heat until you see ripples in the oil, but not smoke. Add the fennel, cumin, coriander, mustard seeds, and paprika. When the seeds begin to pop, remove from the heat and cool for 5 minutes. After 5 minutes, transfer the mixture to a **blender** along with the almonds and salt. Pulse until smooth, stopping to scrape down the sides of the blender if necessary.

3. Place a hen, breast side down, on a **cutting board**. Using **scissors or poultry shears**, spatchcock the hen, following the procedure illustrated on page 21. Repeat with the second hen. Place the birds in a **baking dish** and pour over the puree. Rub the puree onto the birds until roughly coated.

4. Set the birds on the middle of the grill, skin side down, and cover with the brick. Close the lid and cook for 10 minutes. If using a gas grill with multiple zones, decrease the middle flame to low. After 10 minutes, turn the birds over, replace the brick, and continue to cook until a thermometer inserted into the thigh reaches 170°F, 8 to 10 minutes. Remove to a **clean platter** and rest for 5 minutes before serving.

WASH THOSE CHICKENY HANDS!

Riddle me this, kids: What's the first step to any cooking process? I'll give you a hint: It isn't cooking. Ask the CDC, WHO, FDA, USDA, FBI, CIA, PTA, or 4H and they'll tell you that good food safety starts with proper hand washing, which can remove dirt, dead skin cells, oils, and whatnot that microbial beasties thrive on. So plenty of soap and plenty of warm water, and above all you need to take your time. Count to thirty nice and slowly before rinsing. By the way, research has shown that antibacterial soaps are no better than the regular old-fashioned kind when it comes to getting your mitts good and clean.

| Foil-wrapped brick

FRUIT TEN FROM OUTER SPACE

EPISODE 168 | SEASON 10 | GOOD EATS

ALIENS ACCIDENTALLY DELIVER POMEGRANATES TO PLANET EARTH.

Up until about ten years ago, most Americans had never even seen a pomegranate. Then, inspired by its many health benefits, a California company started cultivating them en masse in order to bottle their juice, which is considered a "superfood." Luckily, this renaissance has brought plump specimens into megamarts during the season from September to February. This episode of *Good Eats* was meant to serve as a primer for folks who might be taking home one of these strange critters for the very first time. That said, even experienced pomegranateers should be able to glean a tip or two from the following.

GRENADINE

This pomegranate syrup gets its name from the fact that the French word for pomegranate is *grenade*, which is also the French word, and our word, for this device:

Grenadine was once produced exclusively using pomegranates grown on the island of Grenada, which also makes sense. These days most modern grenadines are made with corn syrup and artificial and natural flavorings, and no actual pomegranate. That's a good argument for making our own.

Although *pomegranate* is Latin for "many-seeded apple," this gigantic berry actually contains arils, tiny sacs containing both seeds (pleasantly crunchy) and a deep vermillion juice that is uniquely sweet and astringent.

Pomegranates ripen in late fall, and a steady supply is typically available through the winter months. Although pomegranates ship fairly well, there isn't much of a market for whole fruit so don't expect to find them in the summer. (All the more reason to lay up some pomegranate syrup or molasses at Christmastime, when they're most plentiful.) Pick poms that are brightly colored and relatively blemish free. Wrinkles signify drying, so steer clear of them as well. As is true of most fruit, specimens should be heavy for their size. At home, ripe pomegranates can be kept in the fridge for up to two months.

Sprinkle arils on salads or soups, bake into muffins, stir into guacamole, enjoy atop yogurt or cottage cheese, or sauté with seafood.

These days, most pomegranate patrons are after the juice alone, and you should be able to extract about ⅓ cup of juice from a medium-size specimen. I've tried every bit and piece of juicing hardware devised by man and feel certain that the best way to juice a pomegranate is to harvest the arils, as noted below, then spin them in a blender. Strain the resulting mush to remove the seeds and you've got fresh pomegranate juice.

A single four-ounce serving of pomegranate juice contains more than twice the antioxidant power of red wine and seven times that of green tea. And if you juice your own you will also be rewarded with potent shots of calcium, iron, and vitamin C, all of which are greatly reduced during the pasteurization process all commercial juices must undergo.

IT'S A WONDER WHAT MY PROP GUYS CAN DO WITH STYROFOAM AND BALLOONS.

HARVESTING POMEGRANATE ARILS

The typical pomegranate houses four hundred to a thousand arils, each of which is anchored in a waxy exocarp. The arils must be carefully removed from their pockets lest they burst like miniature dye packs, spewing their permanent pigment all over you and everything else. To safely and efficiently harvest we must go underwater.

First take a thin slice off of each end, then score from pole to pole—don't cut all the way through the skin; that would make a mess. Just barely score the outside.

Put your pom in a bowl of clean water. Under water, just dig your thumbs in one end and split the fruit open. Depending on the make and model, the arils will either kind of fall off the interior pulp or you'll have to really work them. Either way, gently nudge them off with your fingers. That will prevent breakage as much as possible.

Since arils are filled with sugary goodness, they are dense and will therefore conveniently sink to the bottom of the bowl while the annoyingly clingy and waxy bits of exocarp float

to the surface, where they can be easily removed.

Remove the arils and strain off excess water, then move to airtight containment— either glass or plastic—and top with a moist, not wet, paper towel. Thus contained and stashed in your chill chest, these things will keep for up to two months.

POMEGRANATE SYRUP OR MOLASSES

1½ CUPS SYRUP OR 1 CUP MOLASSES

// SOFTWARE

4	cups	pomegranate juice	
½	cup	sugar	
1	tablespoon	lemon juice	freshly squeezed

TIDBIT The word *pomegranate* comes from a combination of the Latin words *pomme* ("apple") and *granate* ("seeds"). Literally translated, it means "apple full of seeds."

// PROCEDURE

FOR SYRUP:

1 Combine the pomegranate juice, sugar, and lemon juice in a **4-quart saucepan** set over medium heat. Cook, stirring occasionally, until the sugar has completely dissolved. Reduce the heat to medium-low and cook until the mixture has reduced to 1½ cups, approximately 50 minutes. It should be the consistency of syrup. Remove from the heat and cool in the saucepan for 30 minutes.

2 Transfer to a **glass jar** and cool completely before covering and storing in the refrigerator for up to 6 months.

FOR MOLASSES:

1 Place the pomegranate juice, sugar, and lemon juice in a **4-quart saucepan** set over medium heat. Cook, stirring occasionally, until the sugar has completely dissolved. Reduce the heat to medium-low and cook until the mixture has reduced to 1 cup, approximately 1 hour and 10 minutes. It should be the consistency of thick syrup. Remove from the heat and cool in the saucepan for 30 minutes.

2 Transfer to a **glass jar** and cool completely before covering and storing in the refrigerator for up to 6 months.

MY FRIENDLY, HELPFUL DUNGEON MASTER IS ALWAYS UP ON THE LATEST TECH.

GRILLED LEG OF LAMB WITH POMEGRANATE MOLASSES

6 TO 8 SERVINGS

Once you have pomegranate molasses in your possession, you'll need something to marry it with, and I can't think of a better bridegroom than grilled lamb, whose subtle gaminess is perfectly tempered by the astringency of the pom.

// SOFTWARE //

1	4- to 5-pound	boneless leg of lamb	
½	cup	Pomegranate Molasses (opposite)	plus more for serving if desired
	to taste	kosher salt	
	to taste	black pepper	freshly ground

// PROCEDURE ///

1. Heat a gas grill to 375°F, medium on most models.

2. Unroll the lamb and **brush** on all sides with the molasses. Season on all sides with salt and pepper. Reroll the lamb into a uniform package and secure with **butcher's twine**.

3. Turn off one grill burner and set the lamb over it. Cover and cook for 15 minutes, then brush with the molasses again. Turn a quarter turn and cook for another 15 minutes. Repeat the brushing and turning procedure 2 more times for a total cooking time of approximately 1 hour, or until the lamb reaches an internal temperature of 130°F.

4. Remove from the heat and rest 10 minutes before slicing and serving. Serve with additional molasses if desired.

THE KEY TO TRUSSING: NOT TOO TIGHT!

TIDBIT Some scholars believe the "apple" that Eve ate in Eden was actually a pomegranate. Considering the possible placement of Eden in the Near East, this makes sense.

◻︎◻︎◻︎◻︎ **POMEGRANATE JEL-LOW**

4 SERVINGS

I'm a huge fan of congealed desserts, and this one is my favorite. The color is intense, the flavor isn't lost in the tongue-coating action of the gelatin, and the arils provide, of course, crunch.

// SOFTWARE ///

2	cups	pomegranate juice	not from concentrate
2	envelopes	unflavored powdered gelatin	
2	tablespoons	sugar	
½	cup	pomegranate arils	

// PROCEDURE ///

1. Combine ½ cup of the pomegranate juice with the gelatin in a **medium mixing bowl**. Set aside. Bring the remaining juice and the sugar to a boil in a **small saucepan** over high heat. Remove from the heat and add to the juice-and-gelatin mixture, stirring to combine.

2. Chill until the mixture just begins to set, 30 to 40 minutes. Remove from the refrigerator and quickly stir in the arils. Spoon into a **2-cup mold** of your choice or **4 (½-cup) individual molds** and chill until set.

APPLICATION ◻︎◻︎◻︎◻︎ **TEQUILA SUNRISE**

1 SERVING

Most tequila lovers think of the Tequila Sunrise as a silly drink for people who don't actually like tequila. But believe me, homemade pomegranate syrup changes everything.

// SOFTWARE ///

		ice	
1½	ounces	tequila	
		orange juice	freshly squeezed
½	ounce	Pomegranate Syrup (page 26)	

// PROCEDURE ///

Fill a **Collins or highball glass** with ice. Add the tequila, then enough orange juice to come almost to the top of the glass. Gently pour the syrup into the glass and serve. Do not stir.

PERSEPHONE, HADES, AND THE POMEGRANATE

You no doubt recall from your high school mythology studies that Persephone, the daughter of Zeus and Demeter (goddess of earth and crops), was kidnapped by Hades, god of the underworld, an event that so distressed Demeter that she allowed famine to cover the land. Long story short, Hades is forced to let Persephone go, but just before she leaves he tricks her into eating several pomegranate arils. Since the Fates have decreed that any creature who partakes of food or drink in the underworld must remain there, Persephone must return to Hades for one season a year, forever. Thus the seasons are supposedly explained. We didn't want to leave out this tantalizing tale, but since large-scale historical reenactments tend to be pricey, we commissioned a comic book instead. Oh, and instead of the underworld, Hades lives in a spaceship. And Persephone crashes it and gets away with the pomegranate. But other than that it's the same as the original.

Corned (or "corn") beef is simply beef brisket that has been preserved either by a dry cure, or "corn," or a seasoned brine. Most Americans get their corned beef either in the form of a Reuben (the finest sandwich on earth, I declare) or on St. Patrick's Day in the form of corned beef and cabbage, which it turns out isn't very Irish even if corned beef is. In either case, we rarely make the stuff ourselves, and that's a shame because corned beef is nothing if not easy, and tasty . . .

TIDBIT | A classic Reuben sandwich is made with slices of corned beef, Swiss cheese, sauerkraut, and Russian dressing on rye bread.

The brisket is essentially the steer's breast and lies just under the chuck between the front legs. Given its location between shoulder and leg, the brisket is understandably well worked. This means it is packed with flavor—and connective tissue, which must be broken down through long, moist cooking (or smoking, as they do in Texas). The brisket is composed of two cuts: the larger, leaner "flat" cut and the triangular-shaped "point" cut. The point is only about half as big as the flat, but it's quite juicy due to a higher fat content. If you're going to the trouble of corning, I'd look for a whole brisket, but if that isn't available look for a flat with a healthy dose of marbling.

In the days before refrigeration, drying, pickling, and "corning" were the primary methods of preserving perishable foodstuffs. "Corning" refers to the ancient practice of preserving meats by rubbing them in "corn," which in this case does not refer to maize but rather small pieces of salt.[1] Thus, "corned" meat was simply a hunk of critter that had been packed in salt long enough for the salt to replace some of the moisture inside the meat, rendering it inhospitable to microorganisms.

Nitrates, typically in the form of saltpeter (potassium nitrate), were and often still are added to the "corn" because they preserve the pink color of meat and help to stave off the bacteria that can cause botulism.[2] I use saltpeter in my own corned beef but if you don't want to bother you can skip it. Just know that your corned beef will be brown rather than rosy pink. If you choose to utilize saltpeter try your local pharmacy first, but since it's a major component of rocket fuel and gunpowder, don't be surprised if you have to turn to the Internet, where you can easily procure the white powder from any number of sources.[3] By the way, many charcuterie-ists add a product called "pink salt" to their various cures, but this contains nitrites and I wouldn't touch them if you paid me.

Besides salt and saltpeter, corning mixes typically contain five or six spices, including but not limited to: pepper, clove, juniper, bay leaf, mustard seeds, and allspice.

TIDBIT | Besides cured meat and gunpowder, saltpeter is used in ice cream, toothpaste, and stump removers.

BRISKET

[1] Back in the nineteenth century, "corn" was a catchall word for anything small and granular, which is why kernels of maize became known as "corn." The word comes from the Germanic *kurnam*, meaning something the size and shape of a wheat or oat kernel.

[2] Sodium nitrite is actually a more efficient pigment fixer and botulism blocker, but it's also a carcinogen.

[3] Just search "curing meat saltpeter."

TRIVIA | Poor, poor Carolyn O'Neil. I've shoved her under the floor and in a barrel, I've put her head in a bag, I've locked her in the fridge. Yet she keeps on coming back for more.

SORRY, CAROLYN, BUT IT'S YOUR DAY IN THE BARREL!

APPLICATION ─┘┌┐┌┐└─ **CORNED BEEF**

6 TO 8 SERVINGS

This version of the classic is spicier than megamart specimens but much less salty. Gone too is that spooky slime that usually oozes out of the vacuum bag with the meat.

// SOFTWARE

2	quarts	water	
1	cup	kosher salt	
½	cup	light brown sugar	
2	tablespoons	saltpeter	(optional)
1	stick	cinnamon	broken into several pieces
1	teaspoon	mustard seeds	
1	teaspoon	whole black peppercorns	
8		whole cloves	
8		whole allspice berries	
12		whole juniper berries	
2		bay leaves	crumbled
½	teaspoon	ground ginger	
2	pounds	ice	
1	4- to 5-pound	beef brisket	trimmed
1	small	onion	quartered
1	large	carrot	coarsely chopped
1	rib	celery	coarsely chopped

// PROCEDURE

1. Put the water in a **6- to 8-quart stockpot** along with the salt, brown sugar, saltpeter, cinnamon, mustard seeds, peppercorns, cloves, allspice, juniper, bay leaves, and ginger. Cook over high heat until the salt and sugar have dissolved. Remove from the heat and stir in the ice. Refrigerate the brine until it drops below 45°F.

2. Put the brisket in a **2-gallon zip-top bag** and add the brine. Seal and lay flat inside a **drip-proof container**, cover, and refrigerate for 10 days, flipping the bag over every couple of days and checking that it isn't leaking.

3. After 10 days, discard the brine and rinse the brisket well under cool water.

4. Move the brisket to a **large pot** and add the onion, carrot, celery, and enough water to cover by 1 inch. Bring to a boil over high heat.

5. Reduce the heat to low, cover, and simmer for 2½ to 3 hours, until the meat is fork-tender. Remove from the pot and cool for 10 minutes before thinly slicing across the grain.

TIP | If long-term storage is desired, remove the spent vegetables and refrigerate the brisket in the cooking liquid, not the original brine.

CORNED BEEF AND CABBAGE

8 SERVINGS

Feasting on corned beef and cabbage on St. Paddy's Day is really more an American than an Irish tradition because most Irishmen never even saw what we think of as corned beef until they arrived in one of the metropolises of the northeastern United States. Most Irishmen would likely have preferred a traditional "bacon joint." When they couldn't find it in the States, they turned to their new Jewish neighbors, who were enjoying pickled beef brisket, which was accessible and affordable—and kosher. And so once again, what was once thought to be a traditional, indigenous dish actually hails from New York City.

// SOFTWARE

1	2- to 2½-pound	uncooked Corned Beef (opposite)	brisket should be prepared through the brining stage, but not cooked
1	tablespoon	black pepper	coarsely ground
1	teaspoon	allspice	ground
2		bay leaves	
2	teaspoons	kosher salt	
8	ounces	onion	diced
8	ounces	carrots	diced
1	pound	russet potatoes	peeled and chopped
4	ounces	celery	diced
2	pounds	cabbage	chopped

// PROCEDURE

(1) Combine the Corned Beef, pepper, allspice, bay leaves, and salt in an **8-quart pot** and add 3 quarts water. **Cover** and set over high heat. Bring to a boil, decrease the heat to low, and cook at a low simmer for 2½ hours.

(2) Add the carrots, onions, potatoes, and celery. Return to a simmer and cook, uncovered, for 15 minutes. After 15 minutes, add the cabbage and cook for an additional 15 to 20 minutes, until the potatoes and cabbage are tender. Remove the bay leaves and serve immediately.

A RABBI, A PRIEST, AND A COOK WALK INTO A BAR...

TIDBIT Any cut of beef containing the sciatic nerve and the adjoining blood vessels that run through the hindquarters is not, strictly speaking, kosher.

TIDBIT County Cork, Ireland, was once the beef-curing center of Europe.

The word *hash* comes from the French (of course) *hacher*, meaning "to slice or chop up." The dish, at least in this country, is better known as the king of leftovers. The argument could be made that the best reason for making a corned beef dinner is so that you can make hash the next day.

// SOFTWARE

3	tablespoons	unsalted butter	
1	cup	red bell pepper	finely chopped
2	cloves	garlic	minced
5	cups	Corned Beef and Cabbage (page 33)	well drained and chopped
½	teaspoon	fresh thyme	chopped
½	teaspoon	fresh oregano	chopped
¼	teaspoon	black pepper	freshly ground

// PROCEDURE

1. Melt the butter in a **12-inch cast-iron skillet** over medium heat. Add the bell pepper and cook until it begins to brown, 5 to 6 minutes.

2. Add the garlic, Corned Beef and Cabbage, thyme, oregano, and black pepper to the skillet and stir to combine. Then spread the hash evenly over the bottom of the skillet.

3. Place a **lid from a narrower pan, a heatproof plate, or a second pan** directly atop the hash and mash down lightly. Leave the lid in place and cook for 10 to 12 minutes, until browned.

4. Stir up the hash, then mash again. Cook, with the lid in place, for another 5 to 10 minutes, until browned. Serve immediately.

ESPRESS YOURSELF

There's an Italian expression, *poco ma buono*, small but good. For me this really sums up the entire Italian experience because in that country it's not about finding the biggest, the strongest, the most elaborate, or the most expensive—it's about finding, simply, "the best." (Of course, if the subject is a Lamborghini, then all of the above apply.)

Take espresso. Many would argue that it is the ultimate expression of coffee and is meant to be savored but not overdone. While in Italy it does serve as a foundation for other beverages, these beverages are still about the espresso. Here in America we go a little overboard, what with our twenty-four-ounce Big Buzz iced white chocolate double decaf mocha grande macchiato frappe with soy foam cinnamon syrup and a twist.

Luckily this sad situation can be repaired. You see, espresso is simple stuff. All you need to produce a perfect thirty-milliliter shot is nine bars of pressure to push 200°F water through a seven- to nine-gram puck of perfectly ground coffee that's been compressed with approximately forty pounds of force, all within twenty-five seconds of brew time. Sound complicated? Well, that's why for most of its existence espresso has been prepared expressly in cafés by professional baristas.

However, if we're willing to absorb a few facts, polish a little technique, pursue a bit of hardware, and obtain some quality beans, great homemade espresso is well within our reach.

TIDBIT | Subtract the foam from a latte and you have what the French call café au lait.

TIDBIT | Espresso is traditionally served in heated, half-sized cups known as demitasses or *tazzine*.

THE ITALIANS KNOW WHAT IT TAKES TO MAKE ESPRESSO, AND THANKFULLY THEY'VE LAID IT OUT FOR US WITH

THE FOUR M'S...

LA MISCELA: THE BEANS

Coffee beans aren't beans at all but rather the pits of coffee berries. There are two commercial varieties of coffee: Arabica and Robusta. Most Robusta beans find their way into big-bulk, budget blends and vending-machine coffees. Real coffee comes from Arabica beans, which are grown from Sumatra to Costa Rica, Ethiopia to Hawaii. As with wine grapes, the flavor, body, and aroma of the beans vary wildly depending on geography and climate. But nothing affects the flavor, body, and aroma of the coffee more than the roast.

Coffee beans are relatively useless until they're roasted. As the interior of the bean reaches 400°F, chemical reactions called pyrolysis take place, forcing oils to the surface of the bean and darkening the color. At this point, it is up to the roaster to stop the process at precisely the right moment to achieve the

desired flavor for that particular batch of beans. There are four basic (and generally accepted) roast levels:

Light or *cinnamon roast*: The beans are tan and dry, and a brew made from them tastes a lot like toasted grain.

Medium or *city roast*: At this point the beans are the color of milk chocolate but oil has not yet appeared on the surface. This is perhaps the best roast for tasting the subtle differences between beans from different regions and it's my personal choice for drip brewing.

Dark or *full city roast*: Now the beans are chocolate brown and starting to express a little oil. Caramel overtones start to emerge in the brew at this stage. This is my favorite for espresso, despite the fact that the next darker level is actually called . . .

Espresso, *Italian*, or *French roast*: The beans are deep mahogany and shiny with oil. Brews rendered from such beans are relatively low in acidity and contain less caffeine than brews from lesser roasts. At this point you really taste the roast, not the bean.

LA MACINAZIONE: THE GRIND

Brewing coffee is essentially a washing process whereby a solvent (water) is used to extract flavor compounds from the bean. To optimize the process, we grind the bean into small pieces, thus increasing its surface-to-mass ratio. Sounds simple, and it is—as long as we keep two things in mind:

1. Since many of the compounds we hope to capture are volatile and will therefore dissipate quickly, we need to grind immediately prior to brewing.

2. If we grind too coarsely the water will move through too quickly, leaving us with an underextracted brew. If the grind is too small we may overextract, which is just as bad.

Modern electric coffee grinders come in many forms but only two styles. Blade grinders are composed of a cup,

a small propeller, and a motor. Beans go in cup, push button, prop spins, beans smashed. This is a fantastic device for grinding spices. For coffee, not so much. Burr grinders utilize a hopper that feeds the beans into a pair of studded, nestled cones. One cone is turned by the motor while the other remains stationary. What comes out the other end is a very uniform grind.

My grinder has thirty-four grind settings, and I have found that number three is perfect for my espresso. Your particular machine may be rated completely differently. You're just going to have to tinker around and find out what works best for you and your machine.

I always brew a double shot, and that requires fourteen to seventeen grams of coffee. With some practice you'll get used to what that looks like, but until then you might as well use a digital scale.

NOT SHOT ON LOCATION

Like cotton candy, espresso exists because someone invented a *macchina* to make it. And he made that *macchina* out of desire for the great manna of the twentieth century, speed. Dateline Milan, 1901. Hoping to reduce the time his employees took for coffee breaks, manufacturer Luigi Bezzera started tinkering with a machine that used steam pressure to force water through coffee grounds, thus producing a fast—or *espresso*—coffee. Problem was, the coffee produced by his Tipo Gigante, as he called it, was so bitter that nobody wanted to drink it. In 1905 Bezzera sold his patents to Desiderio Pavoni, who improved the design and took espresso public. The next big espresso breakthrough came in 1947, when the Gaggia company delivered the first handle-actuated piston model, which gave the barista the ability to produce consistent pressure at a sub-boiling temperature, which is crucial for superior flavor. This, by the way, is where the expression "pulling" a shot came from. A decade later, an electric pump replaced the manual piston, and the modern *macchina*, capable of generating a constant nine atmospheres of pressure, was born.

Since new models are constantly being released as older ones are amended, the best thing you can do to research espresso machines is to visit a few of the many espresso sites and forums on the web. True espresso fanatics are myriad and most are highly opinionated and happy to share their knowledge and experience.

There's no such thing as a good espresso machine under $200.

Steer clear of machines that utilize premade pucks unless you really don't mind spending three to four bucks a shot, which is what it averages out to.

Heavier is better.

Old-school, lever-operated machines make great counter candy—but that's it.

Machines that use steam power to drive the water through the grounds are too hot. A proper machine will heat the water to between 195° and 202°F and use a heavy-duty pump to push that water through the grounds at nine bars of pressure.

Always take a close look at the manual, many of which are written in Italian and translated into English by Chinese manufacturers. You can imagine the hilarity that can ensue. If the manual doesn't make sense, don't buy the machine.

I have never seen a decent espresso machine in a department store, or in any of the big national kitchenwares chains. I'm not saying it couldn't happen, but I haven't seen it.

Your machine will come with a plastic tamp that looks like this:

Throw it away immediately. Then go on line and order a professional, metal tamp that will look like this:

You may also want to get yourself an indexed shot glass like this . . .

. . . so that you can properly measure your pulls. Even a quarter-ounce difference in pull volume can greatly change the flavor—and not always for the better.

The "hand" refers to the process by which we convert fourteen to seventeen grams of properly ground coffee into a tight little puck that will offer the proper resistance to the water that will be pushed through it. Forty to fifty pounds of pressure are required, and the best way to make sure you get it is to do your tamping on a bathroom scale using your new metal tamper (see above). Make sure that the coffee is level and the portafilter (the thing you're packing your puck into) is level. Set the tamper straight down on the grounds, position your arm so that it's straight up and down, then apply the pressure and twist. Lift it and give it a tap to get the grounds off the side. Tamp one more time at fifty pounds, twist, and behold: a perfect puck.

You should of course follow the instructions that came with your particular machine, but once a proper puck is packed into the portafilter and said portafilter is installed into the diffusion head assembly, if water at 200°F (give or take a degree or two) is applied at nine bars of pressure, the ideal pull time should be right at twenty-five seconds. It is only in the final moments that the much-desired coffee foam, or *crema*, will appear. But beware: Right after it forms, nasty flavors are extracted.

If we were to pull a little short—say, less than an ounce—we'd have what is called an espresso *ristretto*, or "restricted." Closer to two ounces and it would be a *lungo*, or "long." Two and a half to three ounces is a *doppio* or double. A *romano* gets a twist of lemon, and an *espresso con panna* is dressed up with a little whipped cream and cocoa. Then there is the *corretto*, which is an espresso "corrected" with a shot of grappa. (I do not recommend this first thing in the morning.)

Ristretto | Espresso | Lungo or Doppio | Espresso | Romano | Cafe Corret

VARIATIONS ON A THEME

Although I prefer my espresso with nothing but a twist of lemon, a great majority of the espresso drinks served in the United States are paired somehow with dairy, which is why most of the manufacturers of espresso machines include a frothing wand on their machines.   Milk frothing is much like whipping cream, only instead of a whisk, steam is used to whip up the bubbles. Most machine steam wands include a carburetor of sorts that helps to pull air down into the milk to assist the frothing, but true baristas rarely utilize them and I threw mine away when I unpacked the box. Good frothing technique trumps the air tube any

day. It would take several thousand words to properly explain the motion of frothing, but for some strange reason it reminds me of hula hooping, only with your wrist. It's a circular slosh with an up and down component. To get it right you need to see it live, so I suggest you visit your neighborhood coffee shop and watch a skilled barista in action.

I use whole milk, because skim just doesn't contain enough fat to foam no matter what you do. Use a cup or small pitcher (even a measuring cup) with a handle, which will protect your hand from the heat (at least 160°F) and will help you achieve the correct motion.

I prefer a small metal pitcher because when it gets too hot to hold, I know the foam is ready.

▶ 1 shot espresso + wee dollop of foam = macchiato

▶ 1 shot espresso + equal portion of steamed milk + froth = cappuccino (No self-respecting Italian would drink cappuccino after 10 a.m.)

▶ 2 shots espresso + 8 to 10 ounces steamed milk + wisp of foam = latte (This is strictly an American concoction; if you order a latte in Italy they bring you a glass of hot milk.)

It seems like in the last few years everyone with a limousine and a larynx has pumped out a CD of American standards—you know: the tunes that are supposedly ageless and unabashedly American. Yet at the very same time it seems that any and all interest in American food classics has been swept away by a flood of foreign flavors. I'm afraid that we are losing our American culinary heritage, and I just can't have that. So I took the liberty of going through two or three hundred American cookbooks and wrote down the names of about sixty dishes on note cards. I threw them up in the air, and the first one I caught got a show. And that's the true story of how spinach salad got to be on . . .

NOT ACTUAL AMISH FOLK

NOT A REAL AMISH GUY

Unlike the histories of other big American salads like the Cobb and the Waldorf, the origins of the spinach salad are hazy and vague.[1] But I believe we have only to look to our own geographical history to figure out from whence this tasty amalgamation hails. Namely, Pennsylvania.

The phrase *Pennsylvania Dutch* is actually misleading because *Dutch* is an American-ized version of *Deutsche*, so the folks we call the Amish and the Mennonite are actually of German rather than Dutch heritage.

There is a tradition in certain German communities of composing, in the springtime, a special salad of dandelions, bacon drippings, and vinegar, which is typically served with poached or hard-boiled eggs. Sound familiar? I suspect that that salad became the spinach salad. Why Pennsylvania when robust German communities sprang up in other regions, like Milwaukee and San Antonio? We'll get to that.

THE EGGS: It is impossible to make a classic spinach salad without hard-cooked eggs. Now, one might think that with eggs, fresher is always better, but when it comes to in-shell cooking, a couple of weeks in the fridge will actually help by weakening the membrane between the white, or albumin, and the shell, and that will make them a lot easier to peel once they're cooked. Notice, please, I said "cooked," not "boiled." The traditional churning cauldron of boiling water is simply too violent for egg cookery. Too much heat is transferred through the shell, and that results in rubbery whites and grainy, dark-tinged yolks. My answer: an electric kettle, which shuts off as soon as it reaches a boil.

THE BACON: The word *bacon* has different meanings depending on where you are. In Europe, bacon usually refers to one half of a fattened pig. In Ireland and Canada, bacon refers to cured meat from the loin on the back of the animal. But here in the States, we're talking about side meat taken from between rib number five and the hip bone.

It is then usually cured, usually smoked, but sometimes smoked without being cured and sometimes cured without being smoked. Bacon is available sliced into individual rashers, which come in various thicknesses, or as slab bacon, which comes in a whole *flitch*. Although it's a little tougher to find and you have to slice it up yourself, I'm a big fan of slab bacon, as the quality is typically better and I can control the thickness myself, which I like.

THE DRESSING: Besides the bacon fat, we require vinegar and mustard. *Vinegar* may mean "sour wine" in French, but it appears as often in the sweet-and-sour cuisines of Germany as it does in that of their oft-occupied neighbors to the west. Good vinegars, such as those produced via the *orleans* method, spend months in wooden barrels slowly developing. Cheap vinegars—made more quickly, from cheap wine—taste sharp, harsh, and, well . . . cheap. As for mustard, go with Dijon, which is made from crushed brown or black mustard seeds. Like other mustards, it gets its kick from a chemical reaction that occurs when the broken seeds come in contact with water. By adding either vinegar or wine to the mix, mustard makers stop the reaction in its tracks, locking the flavor in

[1] For instance, the 1962 edition of *The Joy of Cooking*, which contains instructions for skinning a squirrel, makes no mention of spinach salad whatsoever.

place forever. Mustard's microscopic particles will also help to emulsify the bacon fat and the vinegar, keeping them together after they hit the salad.

THE MUSHROOMS: Throughout the nineteenth century Pennsylvania was known for its flowers, especially carnations, which were grown in large greenhouses. In the 1890s a couple of Quaker growers decided to try to make use of the area beneath the raised carnation beds. Burlap curtains were hung and mushrooms were planted. What started as a sideline became a major industry, mostly because of the area's proximity to several large cities and to rail lines, which made fast shipment possible. And there was and is a large abundance of horse manure in the area, which is used to produce the compost that the mushrooms grow in. (But don't worry, it's pasteurized—doesn't even smell.) Today Pennsylvania is the undisputed mushroom capital of the United States.

When purchasing mushrooms, look for whole specimens free of wrinkles, bruises, or wet or soft spots. They shouldn't be spongy. As far as white button mushrooms go, the gills should always be closed. And tempting though they may be, resist presliced 'shrooms. Once it's exposed to air, the flesh of any mushroom goes downhill quickly. So anything you gain in convenience will definitely be lost in quality.

A few words about dirt: If you don't see any, then just assume your mushrooms are clean enough to use as is. If they look a little scruffy, you can give them a quick rinse under cold water. Washing will not result in a waterlogged mushroom, unless, of course, you give them a very long, leisurely soak, which you won't.

THE SPINACH: The Pennsylvania Dutch may have enjoyed dandelion salad as a rite of spring, but weeds never really got much in the way of culinary respect in this country so it makes sense that they would eventually reach for a more excepted early riser: spinach, which the twelfth-century food writer Ibn al-Awam called the prince of vegetables. Several varieties are cultivated in this country and are available both in spring and in fall: crinkly Savoy spinach; the hybrid semi-Savoy, which is one of my favorites; flat-leaf spinach, which is generally available in both the mature and the baby forms; and red-veined spinach, which looks kind of like beet greens. I find that either the Savoy or the semi-Savoy works best in the salad because the leaves don't really fall apart when they wilt and so they don't lie flat in the bowl.

You can get spinach loose (my preference), in bunches, or triple-washed in bags. I just don't trust bagged spinach, because washing accelerates decomposition, and that can be masked by the bag itself so I'll just keep the washing to myself. Look for leaves that are dark green, crisp, and free of discoloration. Spinach with slimy spots should be avoided.

Since it's usually grown in sandy soils, spinach requires a lot of washing—and I don't mean just a little shower. I mean a bath in water that is deep enough for any dislodged sand to sink down away from the leaves. Large batches may even need a change of water. After the bath, any excess surface aqua on the leaves will have to go, so you'll either have to roll this all up in a paper towel or take it for a spin.

Our last piece of software isn't exactly traditional but I do find that one small red onion, frenched (that is, cut excruciatingly thin), adds color and an earthy pungency that helps to pull the salad together.

THIS WAS ACTUALLY A SET, BUT IT LOOKS VERY REALISTIC.

YOU KNOW THE BROWN GRITTY STUFF YOU SEE ON MUSHROOMS? THAT'S NOT DIRT!

HARD-COOKED EGGS

4 HARD-COOKED EGGS, TWO FOR THE
SPINACH SALAD AND TWO FOR SNACKING

// SOFTWARE //

4	large	eggs	

// PROCEDURE //

1. Set the eggs in an **electric kettle** and cover with **water**. Turn the kettle on.

2. When the kettle clicks off, set a **timer** for 12 minutes.

3. After 12 minutes, drain the warm water and cover the eggs with cool water. When the eggs are cool enough to handle, crack and peel.

4. You can store leftover hard-cooked eggs, covered in cool water, in an **airtight container** in the chill chest for up to a week.

APPLICATION

ROAST BACON

8 SERVINGS

Bacon slabs can be on the slippery side, so I wrap the entire hunk in parchment paper before slicing. Lay it curved side up and slice with the longest, thinnest blade you possess. And yes, cut the paper, too. If it's still too floppy to manage, stash it in the freezer for an hour before dismantling. Since it splatters and crinkles in the pan, I always roast my bacon.

// SOFTWARE //

8	rashers	thick-sliced bacon	

// PROCEDURE //

1. Lay the bacon in a single layer on a **cooling rack** set in a **half sheet pan**.

2. Put the pan in a cold oven and set the temperature to 400°F. Roast the bacon for 15 to 20 minutes, or until crisp.

3. Remove the bacon from the oven and let cool on the rack for 5 minutes before crumbling. Reserve any remaining fat for salad dressing.

SPINACH SALAD WITH BACON DRESSING

4 SERVINGS

// SOFTWARE

8	ounces	young spinach	
3	tablespoons	bacon fat	
3	tablespoons	red wine vinegar	
½	teaspoon	Dijon mustard	
1	teaspoon	sugar	
	to taste	kosher salt	
	to taste	black pepper	freshly ground
1	small	red onion	thinly sliced
4	large	white mushrooms	sliced
2	large	Hard-Cooked Eggs (opposite)	
8	rashers	Roast Bacon (opposite)	

// PROCEDURE

(1) Remove the stems from the spinach and wash, drain, and dry thoroughly. Set aside.

(2) Put the bacon fat in a **large mixing bowl**, place over low heat and warm just until it begins to ripple. **Whisk** in the vinegar, mustard, and sugar. Season with a small pinch each of salt and pepper. Remove from the heat and add the spinach, onion, and mushrooms and toss to coat thoroughly. Divide the spinach among 4 plates or bowls and top with the eggs and bacon. Serve immediately.

NOTE: For a creamy dressing, remove the cooked yolks from the eggs and put them in a **large mixing bowl**. Mash with a **fork**. Whisking continuously, add the vinegar, sugar, mustard, and melted bacon fat until an emulsion is formed. Season with a pinch each of salt and pepper. Serve immediately.

HOW POPEYE GOT SO BUFF

Well, shiver me timbers, check out all these mus-culls. I yam what I yam and what I yam is ripped…in a kind of deformed and disconcerting kind of way. It is what me spinach, which is packed with iron and calcium and some of that oxalic acid, which excels the absorption of iron and calcium. I've had all I can stands, and I can't stands no more. Luckily, spinach is still an excellent source of vitamins A and K, and potassiums, and magnesiums, and coppers, and riboflavins, niacins, vitamin B6, calciums, phosphoruses, and zincs, and a little bit of the proteins, too. So kids, you gots to eat your spinach. And don't smoke!

EAT YOUR SPINACH!

MILK MADE

EPISODE 172 | SEASON 11 | GOOD EATS

TRIVIA | Confession: This was my first time . . . milking a cow.

TIDBIT | Anthropologists have suggested that lactose tolerance is mankind's most recent evolutionary mutation.

John Wayne ate steak. Of course, before he ate steak, or anything else, for that matter, he drank milk. All mammals do. Milk is, in fact, the only naturally occurring foodstuff on earth that exists solely to feed something. Think about it: The plants and animals we eat all have their own lives, and honey is technically a manufactured product. Milk is amazingly complex, chemically speaking. So much so that scientists are still attempting to unravel its mysteries. Equally enigmatic is the fact that those of us who drink milk past childhood evolved the ability to digest it when most of the planet no longer can stomach the stuff. I'd say it's high time we took a closer look at the one food that just might possess more culinary power than the mighty chicken egg: milk.

LACTOSE INTOLERANCE

One of the unique aspects of milk is its sugar lactose—a disaccharide, or double sugar, composed of one molecule each of glucose and galactose. See the bond holding the glucose and galactose molecules together? It is referred to as a beta-1, 4-glycosidic linkage. Now, when we are babies, our intestines secrete an enzyme called lactase, which breaks this bond, thus freeing the sugars. But only certain populations of northern European,

Middle Eastern, Indian, and Masai descent retain this capacity to produce this enzyme into adulthood.

So what happens when someone who doesn't produce lactase consumes milk or a milk product? The lactose heads into the colon intact, where bacteria dig in, thus producing considerable discomfort and a list of bathroom-related symptoms that just don't belong in a high-class, glossy kitchen tome such as this.

IT'S LACTOSE MAN!

DARN MY MULTI-CULTURAL HERITAGE!

44

Milk is an opaque, colloidal emulsion produced by the mammary glands of animals. It is a rich elixir of nutrients, including sugars, protein, salts, and fat, as well as vitamins, minerals, and valuable antibodies, which help protect the young critter that drinks it from getting sick.

Raw milk may be full of lovely flavor compounds, immunoglobulin, and digestive enzymes, but it can also harbor *Salmonella*, *Listeria*, *Campylobacter*, *E. coli*, and *Staphylococcus*, which is probably why almost every state in the union has some kind of law restricting the sale of raw milk. But know this: It's not the cow's fault. The problem is that the systems that get milk from "moo" to market are extremely complex. The fact that safe milk makes it to market at all is primarily due to the scientific advancements made by Louis Pasteur, who proved that bacteria can be controlled with heat. He took that discovery and put it into action by developing a process for killing pathogens in sealed containers of liquid.

Today, pasteurization can be achieved by heating to:

145°F for half an hour.

161°F for fifteen seconds.

280°F (under pressure) for two seconds.

Since time is money, faster methods mean cheaper milk prices. Problem is, the low and slow method preserves more of the original flavor and body of the milk. As you might suspect, the half-hour method is the road rarely taken.

The other process that most commercial milk goes through is homogenization. The process is simple: The milk is sprayed at high pressure through a tiny orifice, which breaks the clumps of milk fat into such tiny microglobules that they can never coalesce again. The result? Stable, homogenized—and ever so slightly boring—milk that will never separate into cream and skim milk.

Both evaporated and sweetened condensed milks have had close to 60 percent of their moisture removed. **EVAPORATED MILK** is reduced, homogenized, then fortified with various vitamins and minerals. It's then sealed in a can and sterilized, which generates some caramelization, which is why it is light brown in color. **SWEETENED CONDENSED MILK** is reduced, then mixed with an almost equal portion of sugar. The resulting goo is so sugary that it doesn't have to be sterilized for preservation, which is why it's still lily-white when it slowly, so slowly exits the can.

DID LOUIS PASTEUR REALLY USE A FLAME THROWER? I'D LIKE TO THINK SO...

TIDBIT | Cows that graze in pastures tend to give cream-colored milk. Grain-fed cows produce white milk.

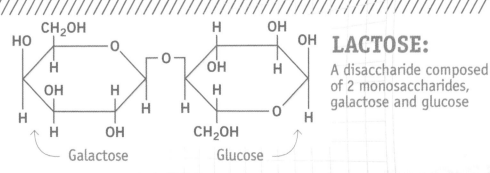

LACTOSE:

A disaccharide composed of 2 monosaccharides, galactose and glucose

Galactose   Glucose

Cake and milk: I don't know if there's a finer culinary combo on the face of the planet. In fact, about the only thing you could do to improve this scenario is to actually put the milk directly into the cake. Such a cake does exist, mostly in Latin America, and it goes by the name *tres leches*, which of course means "three milks."

// SOFTWARE //

FOR THE CAKE

		vegetable oil	for the pan
6¾	ounces	cake flour	plus extra for the pan
1	teaspoon	baking powder	
½	teaspoon	kosher salt	
4	ounces	unsalted butter	at room temperature
8	ounces	sugar	
5	large	eggs	
1½	teaspoons	vanilla extract	

FOR THE GLAZE

1	12-ounce can	evaporated milk	
1	14-ounce can	sweetened condensed milk	
1	cup	half-and-half	

FOR THE TOPPING

2	cups	heavy cream	
8	ounces	sugar	
1	teaspoon	vanilla extract	

// PROCEDURE //

MAKE THE CAKE:

1. Heat the oven to 350°F. Lightly oil and flour a **9-by-13-inch metal baking pan** and set aside.

2. **Whisk** together the cake flour, baking powder, and salt in a **medium mixing bowl** and set aside.

TIDBIT | Most manufacturers today remove milk's natural fat, then add some back based on what type of milk (1%, whole, or half-and-half) is desired.

3. Put the butter in the bowl of a **stand mixer fitted with the paddle attachment** and cream on medium speed until fluffy, approximately 1 minute. Decrease the speed to low and, with the mixer still running, gradually add the sugar over 1 minute. Stop to scrape down the sides of the bowl if necessary.

4. Add the eggs one at a time and mix to thoroughly combine. Add the vanilla and mix to combine. Add the flour mixture to the batter in 3 batches and mix just until combined.

5. Spread the batter evenly in the prepared pan. (This will appear to be a very small amount of batter.) Bake on the middle rack of the oven for 20 to 25 minutes, until the cake is lightly golden and reaches an internal temperature of 200°F.

6. Remove the pan to a **cooling rack** and cool for 30 minutes. Poke the top of the cake all over with a **skewer or fork**.

MAKE THE GLAZE:

7. **Whisk** together the evaporated milk, sweetened condensed milk, and half-and-half in a **1-quart measuring cup** (or other large pour-friendly vessel). Pour the glaze over the cake. Refrigerate the cake overnight.

MAKE THE TOPPING:

8. Put the cream, sugar, and vanilla in the bowl of a **stand mixer fitted with the whisk attachment** and whisk on low speed until it forms soft peaks. Increase the speed to medium and whip until thick. Spread the topping over the cake and chill until ready to serve.

APPROXIMATELY 1 CUP

TIDBIT | The alkalinity of the baking soda prevents the milk from curdling and promotes browning in the *dulce de leche*.

Lactose is not as sweet on the tongue as sucrose, which can be a very good thing. For proof, we turn to another milky marvel from south of the border. *Dulce de leche*, which translates (loosely) to "milk jam," probably evolved not as a confection but as a way of preserving milk without refrigeration in tropical climes. Whatever the reason for its existence, it's a delicious syrup, as thick as caramel but better, if you ask me.

// SOFTWARE ///

1	quart	whole milk	
12	ounces	sugar	approximately 1½ cups
1		vanilla bean	split and scraped
½	teaspoon	baking soda	

// PROCEDURE ///

1. Combine the milk, sugar, and vanilla bean and seeds in a **4-quart saucepan** and place over medium heat. Bring to a simmer, stirring occasionally, until the sugar has dissolved.

2. Once the sugar has dissolved, add the baking soda and stir to combine. Reduce the heat to low and cook, uncovered, at a bare simmer. Stir occasionally, but do not reincorporate the foam that appears on the top of the mixture. Continue to cook for 1 hour.

3. Remove the vanilla bean after 1 hour and continue to cook until the mixture is a dark caramel color and has reduced to about 1 cup, 1½ to 2 hours. Strain the mixture through a **fine-mesh strainer**. Store in the refrigerator in an **airtight container** for up to a month.

GUESS EVERYBODY LIKES CHICKEN...

TIDBIT | Milk from your own cows is protected under Section 256 of the food code!

TIDBIT | A century ago the average cow gave 1,700 quarts of milk a year. Modern cows produce more than 8,200 quarts.

QUICK COTTAGE CHEESE

APPROXIMATELY 2 CUPS

TIDBIT Milk is good for putting out the fire of spicy foods, thanks to casein, which cleanses burning taste buds.

In case you've ever wondered, "curds and whey" refers to two of milk's most powerful proteins, casein and whey, one of which readily coagulates, the other of which doesn't. We usually call it cottage cheese and it's so easy to make you've gotta wonder why anyone would buy it.

// **SOFTWARE** ///

1	gallon	pasteurized skim milk	
¾	cup	white vinegar	
1½	teaspoons	kosher salt	
½	cup	half-and-half or heavy cream	

Making your own cottage cheese: It's cheap, fun, tasty, and just a little bit disturbing.

// **PROCEDURE** ///

1. Pour the milk into a **large saucepan** and place over medium heat. Heat to 120°F. Remove from the heat and gently pour in the vinegar. Stir slowly for 1 to 2 minutes. The curd will separate from the whey. Cover and set aside at room temperature for 30 minutes.

2. Pour the mixture into a **colander** lined with a **tea towel** and drain for 5 minutes.

3. Gather up the edges of the towel and rinse under cold water for 3 to 5 minutes, until the curd is completely cooled, squeezing and moving the mixture the whole time.

4. Once cooled, squeeze as dry as possible and transfer to a **mixing bowl**. Add the salt and stir to combine, breaking up the curd into bite-size pieces as you go. If not serving right away, transfer to an **airtight container** and store in the refrigerator. Add the half-and-half just prior to serving.

Little Miss Muffet
sat on her tuffet,
eating her curds and whey.
Along came a spider
and terrified Little
  Miss Muffet
beyond the boundaries of
  sanity.

THE BEST PART OF MY JOB—GETTING TO WORK WITH MY DAUGHTER!

PRETZEL LOGIC

EPISODE 173 | SEASON 11 | GOOD EATS

Once upon a time (around A.D. 610, they say), a kindly monk in Aosta, in the Italian Alps, decided that the good children of the town who had properly learned their prayers deserved a special treat. Unable to come up with any great ideas himself, he wandered into the monastery kitchen, where he spied a scrap of yeast dough that oddly resembled the folded arms of a praying child. (Back then, folks prayed with their arms crossed. Go figure.) He sprinkled the tidbit with salt (a symbol of purity) and baked it. The creation, which he dubbed *pretiola*, or "little reward," was a big hit.

These days, most pretzels are anything but a treat. In fact I generally think of them as something you put up with as punishment for flying commercial. Granted, there are still places in the world where the pretzel gets some respect. Bavaria, for instance, and parts of Philadelphia, where they eat twelve times the national average. But if the rest of us want great pretzels (and I, for one, do), we'll have to take matters into our own hands.

KNOWLEDGE CONCENTRATE

▷○ **Soft pretzels are always made with yeast dough and are in fact very similar to bagels in both composition and construction.**

▷○ **Although there is such a thing as salt-less pretzels, called "baldies," I would suggest that they're really not pretzels at all, but rather cruel jokes perpetrated by bitter bakers. That said, not just any old salt will do on a pretzel. Now here we see an example of old-school pretzel salt. It's really nothing more than a coarse salt that's a little bit bigger than kosher salt, which is way too small for the job.**

New-school pretzel salt looks to be the same shape and size as the old-school stuff, but notice that it's wider, and it's opaque. That's because it's actually made from a bunch of tiny grains that have been compressed into a cake, and then broken up into this shape. I like this type of salt, because it looks nice, it crunches easily, and the saltiness moves evenly around the mouth. It can be found in some grocery stores, and all over the Internet. I wouldn't dream of pretzeling without it.

▷○ **Pretzels, pH, and You:** Of all the chemical concepts a cook must grasp in order to move up the ladder of culinary enlightenment, pH—that is, the concentration of hydrogen ions in the solution—is one of the toughest. This is especially true for cooks who, like myself, slept through the entirety of high school.

In a nutshell: If a solution has an equal number of positively and negatively charged hydrogen atoms, or "ions," it is said to be "neutral," which means it has a pH of 7, which, by the way, is the pH of distilled water.

As the number of positively charged atoms increases, the pH number goes down, and the solution becomes more acidic. Most of your common kitchen ingredients fall along this end of the scale, from milk at 6, to black coffee at 5, orange juice at 4, most vinegars at around 3, lemon juice at around 2, stomach acid at around 1, and below that, well, you're talking about battery acid, which is never good eats.

On the other end of the scale, from 8 to 14, are solutions higher in negatively charged hydrogen atoms. These are called "alkalis" or "bases," and there aren't too many of them in the kitchen environment. Sea water is slightly alkaline, as are egg whites, which usually have a pH of 8. Baking soda scores a 9, antacid tablets about a 10. Ammonia 11 to 11.5, bleach somewhere around 12, and then we get up to NaOH, a.k.a. lye, at 13, which is so caustic that every bottle features a funny little drawing of a skull and crossbones—and that does not mean that Johnny Depp gets a percentage of each bottle sold. It means that this stuff is very poisonous. As any *Fight Club* fan can tell you, lye is a critical ingredient in soap making. But what you may not know is that lye, oddly enough, is also critical to the production of great pretzels.

Dipping uncooked pretzels in a weak lye solution will instantly gelatinize starches on the surface of the dough, and break proteins down into small peptide chains that will brown rapidly in the oven, creating the characteristic nutty flavor and color we want, without the hardening that so often accompanies the Maillard reaction. My lawyers have stressed to me the importance of emphasizing that the mishandling of food-grade lye can result in very bad things—severe chemical burns or blindness—if you really do something stupid. I wear rubber gloves and goggles when I work with the stuff and I recommend you do the same.

However, if you really don't want to bother, we'll have to turn to baking soda. It's nowhere near as powerful as lye, but most folks do have it in the kitchen. And we may be able to boost its effectiveness with a judicious application of heat. It's certainly worth a try.

▷○ **I'm sure there are other ways to dip a pretzel, but I think this rig is pretty sweet, as it allows us to gently drop and raise the raw pretzels in and out of boiling water. If you're not willing to alter a splatter screen thusly, try a fish spatula to lift the pretzels individually.**

▷○ **The mustard plant is related to Brussels sprouts, broccoli, and cabbage, and like most members of that clan it contains some highly volatile phytochemicals, which are concentrated in the seeds. Crush these in the presence of water, and isothiocyanates are released, and that creates a very special kind of heat. What's really cool about this reaction is that it can be controlled. You see, once the seeds are ground (and mixed with water), the heat begins to build, hitting a sinus-roasting peak after about 15 minutes, depending on the mustard.**

However, this chemical reaction can be shut down at any point along the line by the introduction of an acid, like vinegar. And that's a good thing, because the flavor of the mustard peaks during this time as well.

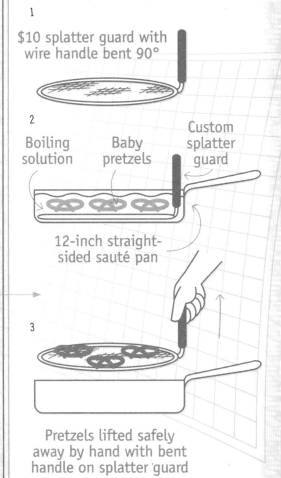

PRETZEL RIG

1

$10 splatter guard with wire handle bent 90°

2

Boiling solution

Baby pretzels

Custom splatter guard

12-inch straight-sided sauté pan

3

Pretzels lifted safely away by hand with bent handle on splatter guard

HOMEMADE SOFT PRETZELS

8 PRETZELS

// SOFTWARE ///

1½	cups	warm H$_2$O	110° to 115°F
1	tablespoon	sugar	
2	teaspoons	kosher salt	
1	envelope	active dry yeast	
22	ounces	all-purpose flour	
2	ounces	unsalted butter	melted
		vegetable oil	for the bowl and pan
10	cups	H$_2$O	
⅔	cup	baking soda	
1	large	egg yolk	beaten with 1 tablespoon H$_2$O
		pretzel salt	

TIDBIT The first American pretzel factory opened in 1861, in Lititz, Pennsylvania.

// PROCEDURE ///

1. Combine the 1½ cups warm water, the sugar, and kosher salt in the bowl of a **stand mixer** and sprinkle the yeast on top. Set aside for 5 minutes, or until the mixture foams.

2. Add the flour and butter and, using the **dough hook attachment**, mix on low speed until well combined. Change to medium speed and knead until the dough is smooth and pulls away from the side of the bowl, 4 to 5 minutes.

3. Remove the dough from the bowl, clean the bowl, then oil it well. Return the dough to the bowl, cover with **plastic wrap**, and set aside in a warm place for 50 to 55 minutes, or until the dough has doubled in size.

4. Heat the oven to 450°F. Line **2 half sheet pans** with **parchment paper** and lightly **brush** with oil. Set aside.

5. Bring the 10 cups water and the baking soda to a rolling boil in a **12-inch straight-sided sauté pan or a roasting pan** (something wide and shallow is best).

6. Meanwhile, turn the dough out onto a lightly oiled work surface and divide into 8 equal pieces. Roll out each piece of dough into a 24-inch rope. Make a U-shape with the rope, and, holding the ends of the rope, cross them over each other and press onto the bottom of the U in order to form the shape of a pretzel. Place on a half sheet pan. Repeat with the remaining pieces of dough.

7. One by one, place the pretzels in the boiling water for 30 seconds. Remove them from the water using a **large flat spatula**. Return them to the sheet pans, brush the top of each pretzel with the beaten egg yolk and water mixture, and sprinkle with pretzel salt.

8. Bake until dark golden brown in color, 12 to 14 minutes. Transfer to a **cooling rack** for at least 5 minutes before serving.

HOMEMADE HARD PRETZELS

36 PRETZEL STICKS

Although I'll go for softies every time, the planet is plenty big enough for hard pretzels too.

// SOFTWARE

1¾	cups	warm H₂O	110° to 115°F
1	tablespoon	sugar	
2	teaspoons	kosher salt	
1	envelope	active dry yeast	
22	ounces	all-purpose flour	
		vegetable oil	for the bowl and pan
1	large	egg yolk	beaten with 1 tablespoon H₂O
		pretzel salt	

// PROCEDURE

(1) Combine the water, sugar, and kosher salt in the bowl of a **stand mixer** and sprinkle the yeast on top. Set aside for 5 minutes or until the mixture begins to foam.

(2) Add the flour and, using the **dough hook attachment**, mix on low speed until well combined. Change to medium speed and knead until the dough is smooth and pulls away from the sides of the bowl, 4 to 5 minutes.

(3) Remove the dough from the bowl, clean the bowl, then oil it well. Return the dough to the bowl, cover with **plastic wrap**, and set aside in a warm place for 50 to 55 minutes, or until the dough has doubled in size.

(4) Heat the oven to 350°F. Line **4 half sheet pans** with **parchment paper** and lightly **brush** with oil. Set aside.

(5) Place enough **water** in a **roasting pan** to come one-third of the way up the sides of the pan and bring to a boil over high heat.

(6) Meanwhile, turn the dough out onto a lightly oiled work surface and divide into 1-ounce portions, approximately 36 pieces. Roll out each piece of dough into a 14- to 15-inch-long stick and place on the lined sheet pans, ¼ inch apart. Cover the dough not being used with a **slightly damp towel** to help prevent it from drying out.

(7) Gently place 6 to 8 pretzels at a time in the water for 30 seconds. Return the pretzels to the sheet pans, brush the top of each pretzel with the beaten egg yolk and water mixture, and sprinkle with pretzel salt. Bake until golden brown in color and hard, 55 to 60 minutes. Transfer to a **cooling rack** for at least 20 minutes before serving. Store in an **airtight container** for up to 1 week.

BEST MUSTARD EVER

APPROXIMATELY 1¼ CUPS

Because homemade pretzels deserve the very best.

// SOFTWARE //

¼	cup	dry mustard	
2	teaspoons	light brown sugar	
1	teaspoon	kosher salt	
½	teaspoon	ground turmeric	
¼	teaspoon	hot smoked paprika	
¼	teaspoon	garlic powder	
½	cup	sweet pickle juice	
¼	cup	H_2O	
½	cup	cider vinegar	
¼	cup	mustard seeds	

// PROCEDURE //

1. **Whisk** together the dry mustard, brown sugar, salt, turmeric, paprika, and garlic powder in a **small microwave-safe bowl**. In a separate bowl, combine the pickle juice, water, and vinegar and have them standing by.

2. Put the mustard seeds in a **spice grinder** and grind for at least 1 minute, stopping to pulse occasionally. Once ground, immediately add the mustard to the bowl with the spices and pour the liquid mixture over them. Whisk to combine.

3. Place the bowl in the **microwave oven** and heat on high for 1 minute. Remove and puree with an **immersion blender** for 1 minute. Pour into a **glass jar or container** and cool, uncovered. Once cool, cover and store in the refrigerator for up to 1 month.

TIDBIT The average American consumes 2 pounds of pretzels each year. In Philadelphia, it's more than 20 pounds.

TIDBIT In 2002, the leader of the free world passed out while choking on a pretzel.

FILMED ABOARD MY PRIVATE JET
...OK, NOT REALLY

Coconut cake: the perfect gestalt of Southern sensibility and South Sea sensation. Moist, fragrant, an infused foundation to frosting with tropical goodness, coconut cake is without a doubt my desert-island dessert. Now, as everyone knows, the best place to find top-quality cakes is a small, Southern diner or café supplied by a local "cake lady"—that is, an independent and often reclusive agent who carries on the old ways in the privacy of her home and sells the fruits of her labors to a grateful community. Cake ladies are increasingly hard to find, and so I fear the modern cook must take matters into his or her own hands (which is what *Good Eats* is about, after all).

FANS OF THE SHOW WILL REMEMBER COCO FROM "DOWN AND OUT IN PARADISE." IN THAT SHOW THE MALEVOLENT NUT NEARLY DROVE ME OVER THE EDGE.

YES, IT'S LABOR INTENSIVE.
AND YES, IT'S WORTH IT.

KNOWLEDGE CONCENTRATE

An authentic Southern coconut cake came into existence because of two factors. First, the advent of the cast-iron stove and the development of baking powder in the mid-nineteenth century made layer cakes practical. Early specimens were composed of quite thin layers sandwiched together with homemade jelly or jam and were called, surprisingly, jelly cakes.

The second factor was the import of coconuts into Southern ports from the Caribbean, which began around the same time. The coconut cake as we know it is only 150 years old, tops.

The early challenges of obtaining fresh coconut as well as the manual labor associated with grating it gave the coconut cake special-occasion status; it was something you baked for family reunions and Christmas.

Coconuts generally come in three market forms:

coconuts in the husk, which are a lot of work to harvest;

cut or immature coconuts, known for their jellylike interiors; and

mature coconuts, which have been freed of their outer husks.

The flesh or "meat" of the mature nut is firm and full flavored—perfect for cake making. When purchasing, pick nuts that seem a little heavy for their size and free of cracks and/or moldy or "crying" eyes, both of which are signs of trouble. Next, give it a shake. You should hear a good bit of liquid sloshing around in there. If you don't, it means that the nut is old. We need that liquid, so pass on lightweight (and thus dry) coconuts. Kept sealed in its shell, a nut should last anywhere from two to four months.

When Portuguese adventurers first came across coconuts in the South Seas during the fifteenth century, they looked at the indentations in the end and were reminded of the face of a *coco*, or "goblin." And so they named them, appropriately, "coconuts," even though they are not, technically, nuts but rather drupes. Alas, "cocodrupe" sounds silly.

The eyes are important to us because they are the gateways to the soul of the coconut. We need to tap through two of them in order to drain the water inside. Traditionally a mallet and an awl, nail, or ice pick would gain the careful cook admittance. But these tools seem medieval when you consider the fact that most households harbor a cordless drill of some type. A bit in the ¼- or ³⁄₁₆-inch range will do the job. Drill the two holes, then simply drain out the water and reserve for later use. Lidded up and locked in your chill chest, your coconut water should remain viable for at least a week.

To crack drained coconuts, bake them at 375°F for 15 minutes. (Always drill and drain first, lest you cause a small explosion in your oven.) The outer shell will crack in the heat and can then be pried off with a flathead screwdriver or an oyster knife. Once that's off, you still have to remove the brown husk that clings tightly to the meat. And for that, nothing beats a vegetable peeler.

As far as shredding goes, a box grater is the traditional way to go, but man, does it take a long, knuckle-busting time. Most food processors come with a grating disk, and that is by far the more efficient way to go.

COCONUT MILK is simply shredded coconut that's been steeped with an equal amount of water, then strained to remove the solids. It looks a lot like milk, hence the name. CO- CONUT CREAM, which is a whole lot harder to find, is made the same way, but with two to four times as much coconut. Whatever you do, don't confuse "coconut cream" with "cream of coconut," which is a thick, sweetened syrup commonly used in the concocting of piña coladas. They are not the same thing.

When it comes to splitting finished cake layers, I make a guide of sorts: Put a cooling rack upside down in the bottom of a half sheet pan and set the cake on the rack so that half of it is above the rim of the pan.

As to suitable cutlery, I used to use a bow saw blade from the hardware store, but it's a little on the wobbly side, so I've graduated to something a bit more stable: a serrated cake knife, which can also be used on bread or even a roast turkey. Simply lay the knife down so that both ends are resting on the rim of the pan. Place one hand on top of the cake—thumbs up and out of the way, of course—and gently saw through the cake. The cake tends to break right at the very end, so make the last few strokes particularly deli- cate. Thus bifurcated, the single cake yields two nice, even layers.

APPLICATION — COCONUT MILK

½ CUP MILK

// SOFTWARE

| 2 | ounces | freshly grated coconut | |
| ½ | cup | 2% milk | boiling |

// PROCEDURE

1. Put the coconut in a **small heatproof bowl** and pour the boiling milk over it. Stir to combine. Cover tightly and steep for 1 hour. Transfer the mixture to a **blender** and blend for 1 minute.

2. Set a **tea towel** over a **large bowl** and carefully pour the coconut mixture into it. Gather up the edges and squeeze until all of the liquid has been removed. Discard the coconut. You may use the milk immediately or store it in the refrigerator for up to 2 days.

APPLICATION — COCONUT CREAM

½ CUP CREAM

// SOFTWARE

| 4 | ounces | freshly grated coconut | |
| ½ | cup | 2% milk | boiling |

// PROCEDURE

1. Put the coconut in a **small heatproof bowl** and pour the boiling milk over it. Stir to combine. Cover tightly and steep for 1 hour. Transfer the mixture to a **blender** and blend for 1 minute.

2. Set a **tea towel** over a **large bowl** and carefully pour the coconut mixture into it. Gather up the edges and squeeze until all of the liquid has been removed. Discard the coconut. You may use the cream immediately or store it in the refrigerator for up to 2 days.

// SOFTWARE //

1½	ounces	freshly grated coconut	
4	ounces	vodka	

// PROCEDURE //

1. Combine the coconut and vodka in a **1-cup glass jar with a lid**. Place in a cool, dark place for 5 to 7 days, shaking to combine every day.

2. Pour through a **strainer** and discard the coconut. Return the vodka to a **clean jar or bottle** and store in a cool place for up to a year.

PAN-PREP ORIGAMI

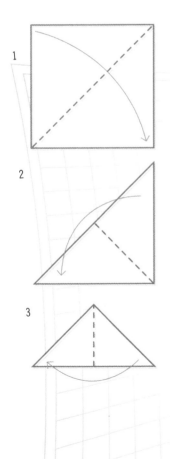

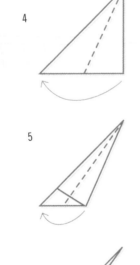

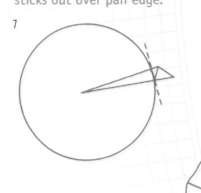

Align (folded) point of fan with center of pan and cut off whatever sticks out over pan edge.

7

8

Pan

PAN PREPARATION

Nothing's worse than dedicating two hours of your life to a layer cake, only to find you can't get the cakes out of the pan. This could be prevented if you practice proper pan-prep. My secret: parchment paper. And this is all you have to do: Fold a square of parchment in half, thusly [width-wise fold] and crease. Fold [down] again and crease. Fold yet again [down at an angle] and crease. Fold again [down at an angle the same way to make a pointy triangle] and crease. Now grab your favorite pair of shears. Line up the point of the paper with the center of the pan and snip [to the length of the radius of the pan; unfolded they roughly make a circle]. You'll now need a little lubrication. Spray the pan with nonstick cooking spray, making sure you spray the inside edges, then put the disk of parchment in the bottom and hit it one more time with the spray.

Paper round (unfolded)

Put THIS in the bottom of THIS.

COCONUT CAKE WITH SEVEN-MINUTE FROSTING

ENOUGH ICING FOR
1 (9-INCH) 2-LAYER CAKE

// SOFTWARE

FOR THE CAKE

14½	ounces	cake flour	
1½	teaspoons	baking powder	
1	teaspoon	salt	
½	cup	fresh Coconut Milk (page 58)	
½	cup	fresh Coconut Cream (page 58)	
8	ounces	unsalted butter	at room temperature
16	ounces	sugar	
1	teaspoon	Coconut Extract (page 59)	
4	large	egg whites	
⅓	cup	coconut water	

FOR THE FROSTING

3	large	egg whites	
12	ounces	sugar	
⅓	cup	coconut water	
½	teaspoon	cream of tartar	
¼	teaspoon	kosher salt	
1	teaspoon	Coconut Extract (page 59)	
½	teaspoon	vanilla extract	

TO BUILD

2	cups	freshly grated coconut	

// PROCEDURE

MAKE THE CAKE:

1. Heat the oven to 350°F. Lightly spray **2 (9-inch) cake pans** with **nonstick cooking spray**. Line the bottom of each pan with a **parchment paper circle** (see page 59). Lightly spray the parchment pieces with nonstick spray. Set aside.

2. Put the flour, baking powder, and salt into a **large mixing bowl** and **whisk** to combine.

3. Combine the Coconut Milk and Coconut Cream in a **small bowl** and set aside.

(4) Put the butter in the bowl of a **stand mixer fitted with the paddle attachment** and cream on medium speed until fluffy, approximately 1 minute. Decrease the speed to low and gradually add the sugar over 1 to 2 minutes. Once all of the sugar has been added, stop the mixer and scrape down the sides. Turn the mixer back to medium speed and continue creaming until the mixture noticeably lightens in texture and increases slightly in volume, 2 to 3 minutes. Stir in the Coconut Extract.

(5) With the mixer on low speed, add the flour mixture alternately with the milk mixture in 3 batches, ending with the milk mixture. Do not overmix.

(6) In a **separate bowl**, **whisk** the egg whites until they form stiff peaks. Fold the egg whites into the batter, just until combined. Divide the batter evenly between the pans and bang the pans on the countertop several times to remove any air and to distribute the batter evenly in the pan. Bake on the middle rack of the oven for 40 minutes, rotating the pans once about halfway through baking, or until the cakes are light golden in color and reach an internal temperature of 200°F.

(7) Cool the cakes in the pans for 10 minutes, then remove and transfer to a **cooling rack**. Once the cakes have cooled completely, split each cake across the equator to form 4 layers. Put the coconut water in a **small spritz bottle** and spray evenly onto the cut side of each layer, or brush the coconut water on with a **silicone pastry brush**. Set aside while you prepare the frosting.

MAKE THE FROSTING:

(8) Bring **1 quart water** to a boil in a **4-quart saucepan** over high heat. Decrease the heat to medium to maintain a steady simmer.

(9) Combine the egg whites, sugar, coconut water, cream of tartar, and salt in a **medium mixing bowl**. Place the bowl over the simmering water and immediately begin beating with an **electric hand mixer** set to low speed. Beat for 1 minute, then increase the speed to high and continue to beat for 5 minutes. Remove from the heat and beat in the coconut and vanilla extracts for 1 minute. Set the frosting aside for 5 minutes before using.

(10) Place approximately ¾ cup of the frosting on the first layer of cake, sprinkle with ½ cup coconut, and top with the next layer. Repeat until you reach the top layer. Frost the top and sides of the cake and sprinkle with the remaining coconut. Refrigerate for at least 30 minutes before serving.

THE HOST CONTEMPLATES THE APPROPRIATE SERVING SIZE.

SUB STANDARDS

A wise and learned man once said, "You can't always get what you want, but if you try sometimes, you might find, you get what you need." I can't think of a better credo for the kitchen. Who hasn't found oneself one egg short of an omelet, or missing a crucial ingredient the moment company arrives? The art of the substitution is just that: an art. You see, to substitute something, you really have to understand the thing you're replacing. You've got to get inside its head, look at it from every angle. Then—and only then—can you apply scientific reason, technical acumen, and ingredient savvy to turn a potential liability into an asset. And that can most certainly result in . . .

KNOWLEDGE CONCENTRATE

▷○ **The world of culinary substitutions breaks down into three categories:**

— Emergency substitutions. You need a cup of bread flour, and all you have is all-purpose. You don't have time to go to the store. What are you going to do?

— Health-related substitutions. This is any substitution that has to be made because a particular ingredient clashes with, you know, your health needs.

— Creative substitutions. These are the flights of fancy, the whims. The "I-don't-want-to-use-dill, I-want-to-use-tarragon" situations—and, you know, come to think of it, that's more willful improvisation. We'll save that for another show.

▷○ **Let's start with an easy example of a type-1, emergency substitution: You wake up early one morning to bake buttermilk biscuits, and discover, to your horror, that you're out of buttermilk. What do you do? You make buttermilk, of course.**

Let's start with what buttermilk isn't: butter and milk. In the old days, it was the milk that was left over after cream was churned into butter. These days, it is usually just skim milk that's inoculated with a bacteria that creates lactic acid, which provides some tang and thickens the product as well. In short, buttermilk provides moisture, texture, and acidity, which reacts with bases like egg whites and baking soda to produce leavening.

So, what if you go and say, "I don't have buttermilk but I want to make this recipe so I'll just use regular milk which is close enough to the same thing"? Well, if it's a soup or, say, a salad dressing, the results will certainly taste funny but you may still be able to eat it. If, however, the subject is a baked good, then the acid-base equation will be out of balance and all is doomed. Doomed, I say! Unless, of course, you acidify this milk, and that is easily done, by adding a tablespoon of lemon juice to one cup of milk. This isn't a magical way to make buttermilk, because it won't be as thick, but the amount of acidity will be about right and the application will work.

Now let's look at a typical type-2 substitution, one made for health reasons. The chocolate chip cookie—the consumption of which is considered by most Americans to be a God-given right—is off limits to those who suffer from celiac disease. That's because chocolate chip cookies contain wheat flour, and wheat flour, when agitated in the presence of water, creates gluten, and for reasons too grim to go into here, celiacs can't do gluten.

What's worse is that on *Good Eats* we make chewy chocolate chip cookies with bread flour, which contains even more of the offending proteins. So, before we attempt to fashion a replacement part, let us consider what the flour is doing there in the first place.

Starch makes up most of the volume of flour, and replacing that ought to be pretty simple. We will go with a combination approach. Brown-rice flour has a pleasant flavor, especially in applications calling for brown sugar, but it's a little on the gritty side, and tends to make for crumbly baked goods. We could smooth that out to some degree with cornstarch, but the starch in tapioca flour gelatinizes at a lower temperature than the starches in either rice flour or cornstarch, and that will help to create a pleasantly chewy tooth, not to mention a nice rise. Tapioca flour is used widely in various ethnic cuisines and is easily found at many megamarts and certainly health food stores.

Replacing the protein in flour is a little trickier. After all, protein is the rebar around which the concrete of the starch sets. Without it there is no real structure and certainly no chewiness. Luckily we can imitate this structure with a curious compound discovered back in the 1950s, when scientists at the Department of Agriculture discovered that a bacterium found on cabbage plants, *Xanthomonas campestris*, could be fermented in corn syrup to produce a polysaccharide capable of stabilizing emulsions and suspensions. When added to bread or gluten-free baked goods, this substance can add volume, viscosity, and structure, much like gluten. This miracle ingredient goes by the exotic moniker "Xanthan gum" and has been used in manufactured foods for decades. Recently, it's become more common with home cooks and is available in markets far and wide (and, yes, on the Internet).

MAKE A POWDER

Now, what if you're out of baking powder? Well, you can make that too! There are two different types of baking powder: double-acting, which releases gas twice, first when the ingredients are mixed, and again when they reach 104°F in the oven or on the griddle, and single-acting. Double-acting is pretty much impossible to formulate in the home kitchen, but single-acting is simple: 1 teaspoon cream of tartar + ½ teaspoon baking soda + ½ teaspoon cornstarch = 2 teaspoons single-acting baking powder.

TIDBIT | Tapioca is ground from cassava root, which also goes by the names "yuca" and "manioc."

SOUTHERN (FAUX-BUTTERMILK) BISCUITS

12 BISCUITS

If you have time, refrigerate the milk and lemon juice mixture for a few hours. This will allow the acid in the juice to denature some of the milk proteins, thickening the mixture a bit.

// SOFTWARE

1	cup	skim milk	
1	tablespoon	lemon juice	freshly squeezed
9¼	ounces	all-purpose flour	plus extra for rolling
4	teaspoons	baking powder	
¼	teaspoon	baking soda	
¾	teaspoon	salt	
1	ounce	unsalted butter	chilled
2	ounces	shortening	chilled

// PROCEDURE

1. Heat the oven to 450°F.

2. Combine the milk and lemon juice in a **glass measuring cup** and put it in the refrigerator.

3. **Whisk** together the flour, baking powder, baking soda, and salt in a **large mixing bowl**.

4. Using your fingertips, rub the butter and shortening into the dry ingredients until the mixture looks like crumbs. (The faster you do this, the better; you don't want the fats to melt.) Make a well in the center and pour in the chilled milk mixture. Stir just until the dough comes together. The dough will be very sticky.

5. Turn the dough out onto a floured work surface, dust the top with flour, and gently fold the dough over on itself 5 or 6 times. Press into a 1-inch-thick round. Cut out biscuits with a **2-inch round cutter**, being sure to push straight down through the dough. Place the biscuits on a **half sheet pan** so that they just touch. Re-form scrap dough, working it as little as possible, and continue cutting.

6. Bake until the biscuits are tall and light gold on top, 15 to 20 minutes.

   NOTE: Biscuits made with milk mixed with lemon juice instead of buttermilk tend to bake up with a more golden tinge due to the citric (rather than lactic) acid.

THE BISCUIT ON THE LEFT IS OUR FAUX-BUTTERMILK VERSION; THE ONE ON THE RIGHT IS THE ORIGINAL VERSION.

FAUX PEANUT SAUCE

APPROXIMATELY 2 CUPS

One of the most common food-centric allergies concerns peanuts. Unfortunately, there is no straightforward substitute for peanuts, or for peanut butter, as the flavor is simply too distinctive. However, if the issue is specifically peanuts, and other nuts are fair game, we can build a flavor profile very close to the peanut's by combining three other pastes: cashew butter, tahini, and miso. Together, these pastes do a great job of replicating the roasty-toasty flavor of peanuts.

TIDBIT | An estimated 1.5 million Americans have peanut allergies.

// SOFTWARE

¼	cup	chicken broth	
3	ounces	unsweetened coconut milk	
1	ounce	lime juice	freshly squeezed
1	ounce	soy sauce	
1	tablespoon	red miso paste[1]	
1	tablespoon	fish sauce	or 2 or 3 anchovy fillets, ground
1	tablespoon	hot sauce	
1	tablespoon	garlic	chopped
1	tablespoon	fresh ginger	chopped
¾	cup	cashew butter[2]	
¾	cup	tahini[3]	
¼	cup	fresh cilantro	chopped

// PROCEDURE

In a **food processor**, combine the broth, coconut milk, lime juice, soy sauce, miso paste, fish sauce, hot sauce, garlic, and ginger and process until smooth. Add the cashew butter and tahini and pulse to combine. Fold in the cilantro and keep refrigerated until ready to use. Serve with chicken satay, coconut shrimp, grilled meat, or even hot dogs.

[1] Miso is a fermented soybean paste that comes in several grades, from white to red to almost black. Red miso looks sort of like a deeply roasted freshly ground peanut butter.

[2] Cashew butter is available at health food stores as well as most megamarts these days.

[3] Tahini is composed of finely ground sesame seeds and is used in Middle Eastern dishes such as baba gannouj and hummus. It's usually found in the ethnic food aisle.

THE CHEWY, GLUTEN-FREE CHOCOLATE CHIP COOKIE

2 DOZEN COOKIES

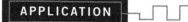

// SOFTWARE ///

8	ounces	unsalted butter	
11	ounces	brown-rice flour	
1¼	ounces	cornstarch	
½	ounce	tapioca flour	
1	teaspoon	xantham gum	
1	teaspoon	kosher salt	
1	teaspoon	baking soda	
2	ounces	sugar	
10	ounces	light brown sugar	
1	large	egg	
1	large	egg yolk	
2	tablespoons	whole milk	
1½	teaspoons	vanilla extract	
12	ounces	chocolate chips	

// PROCEDURE //

1. Melt the butter in a **heavy-bottomed medium saucepan** over low heat. Pour into the bowl of a **stand mixer**.

2. **Sift** together the rice flour, cornstarch, tapioca flour, xantham gum, salt, and baking soda into a **small bowl** and set aside.

3. Add both sugars to the bowl with the butter and, using the **paddle attachment**, cream together on medium speed for 1 minute. Add the whole egg, egg yolk, milk, and vanilla and mix until well combined. Slowly incorporate the flour mixture until thoroughly combined. Add the chocolate chips and stir to combine.

4. Chill the dough in the refrigerator until firm and cool to the touch, approximately 1 hour.

5. Heat the oven to 375°F.

6. Shape the dough into 2-ounce balls and place them on **half sheet pans** lined with **parchment paper**, 6 cookies per sheet. Bake for 14 minutes, rotating the pans after 7 minutes for even baking. Remove from the oven and cool the cookies on the pans for 2 minutes. Move the cookies to a **cooling rack** and cool completely. Store in an **airtight container**.

I'm a big fan of whole fish. They're cheaper than cut fish, they're often fresher than cut fish, and they are certainly more versatile than cut fish. But Americans are typically wary of buying anything with a face on it, so most of us have zero to zip for experience. Well, it's time for that to change. Because although steaks and fillets and loins can be good, fish in "the round" are . . .

CANDLEFISH—THE PERFECT TOUCH FOR A FORMAL TABLESCAPE.

TRIVIA | Although I've been scuba diving for years, when I showed up to dive the Ocean Voyager tank at the Georgia Aquarium, I was dismayed to discover that I'd be diving on a shore supply rather than a tank and that I'd have to walk my way across the bottom. I have to thank the dive crew at the aquarium for not letting me look like a deranged underwater zombie—which is how I felt.

▷○ Unlike a chicken or a cow, fish meat tends to be relatively uniform from tip to tail, but the musculature differs wildly depending on make and model and depends greatly on where said fish lives, its migration patterns, its diet, and so on. For instance, the grouper is a warm-water fish, and relatively slow moving, so his meat is very light and mild, and tends to overcook very quickly. Compare that to a fast-moving pelagic[1] tuna, which swims mostly in cold water, often dives very deep, and sports fatty red meat that has more in common with a steak, both in flavor and texture, than with fish. Like a steak, tuna can be cooked to temp—rare, medium, and even medium-well (if you want to ruin a perfectly good piece of fish).

▷○ Of course, most of us won't be bringing home four-hundred-pound groupers or a four-foot tuna unless we catch it ourselves. For most of us there's the fishmonger and megamart, and their things are less aversive.

Allow me to introduce one of the most versatile fin fish you will ever find: the striped bass, which, in the wild, can grow to forty pounds and beyond. Farm-raised versions typically come to market anywhere from one and a half to three pounds. This fish is firm yet flaky, sweet but not fatty. It's just a very versatile fish, and specimens farm raised in the United States are considered both healthful and sustainable.

Meet *Oncorhynchus mykiss*, a.k.a. "rainbow trout," a freshwater cousin of the salmon, which is also farm raised in the United States. Unlike a lot of carnivorous farmed fish, which consume more protein than they provide, produce large amounts of waste, and pose a threat to wild populations, trout are quite efficient at feed conversion, they don't poop too much, and they rarely escape their habitats. Best of all, they are excellent for pan cooking or planking. (Keep reading.)

Although most folks think big when it comes to whole fish, my personal favorites are rather Lilliputian. *Osmerus mordax* are more commonly known as "smelt," a name that refers to over a dozen similar species ranging in size from two inches to up to a foot and run from Labrador all the way around South America to Alaska. Other fish that fit into the oily category include mackerel and herring. Like much of the salmon family, smelt are anadromous, meaning that they live in salt water, but migrate to freshwater to spawn. When spawning time comes, they are so full of oil that the old-timers used to dry them out and use them as candles; hence the nickname "candlefish"—and no, I'm not making this up. Smelt are best when cooked simply, and since they're oily they have an affinity for the fry pan.

FISH-SCALING RIG

18-gallon (mostly) clear plastic storage bin

1

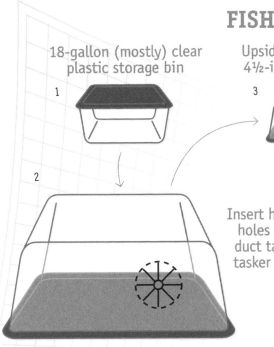

2

Drill ½-inch hole where center of large hole will be.

Then draw several 5-inch-long lines with felt-tip pen radiating out from the hole like slices of pie.

Draw the outer circumference of the circle freehand.

Using a Sawzall or coping saw, start at the hole and cut out and around, creating a laser-perfect hole.

Repeat with a second hole beside the first one.

Upside-down bin with two 4½-inch holes cut in side

3

Insert heavy rubber gloves into holes and seal in place with duct tape (world-class multitasker if ever there was one).

View from top when completed

4

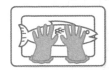

When finished, hose out scales and dump in neighbor's driveway (hee-hee).

5

Store with lid on (prevents stinkiness).

Paper towels here (helps gloves keep shape for hose-down)

I approach all whole fish as I would a big, cold, slimy cactus. Hidden among the fins one often finds spikes, some of which can be venomous. To protect myself when "breaking" fish, I wear fish-handling gloves, and I suggest you do the same.[2]

The first step when breaking fish is to use heavy scissors or shears to remove all the fins you can find except the tail, which makes a nice handle to grip during further processing.

The reason that I don't let fishmongers take the scales off my fish is that they are a very nice protective coating. Once the scales come off, the quality of the fish will start to go downhill fast. The problem is, taking them off makes a huge mess, especially if you use a scaler (a unitasker if ever there was one). I prefer to use one side of a pair of separating kitchen shears, which would already be dirty from fin cutting. To protect myself—and my neighborhood—from flying scales, I utilize a scaling box of my own ingenious design and construction.

Once the rig is constructed, simply lay your fish under it and, starting with the back of the fish facing away, start scraping back and forth, kinda like peeling a really big potato, working from the tail to the head several times. Rinse with water right in the bin, again to confine the scales, which will stick to and dry onto any surface devised by nature or man.[3]

[1] Meaning it travels great distances in open water.

[2] My favorites are made by a company called Lindy and are available at many sporting goods and tackle shops.

[3] Except Astroturf, which, it's interesting to note, cannot be gripped by octopi, either.

WHOLE STRIPED BASS

4 SERVINGS

// SOFTWARE

2	1- to 1½-pound	whole striped bass	gutted and scaled, or 1 (2- to 3-pound) specimen
3	tablespoons	olive oil	divided
1	large bunch	fresh parsley	
1	large bunch	fresh dill	
1	large	lemon	thinly sliced
1	large	onion	thinly sliced
2	tablespoons	kosher salt	
2	teaspoons	black pepper	freshly ground

TIDBIT | Farmed striped bass are a hybrid of striped and white bass and can be distinguished from wild by their broken stripes.

// PROCEDURE

1. Heat the oven to 500°F.

2. Trim the fins from the fish, rinse, and pat dry. Set aside.

3. Coat the bottom of a **roasting pan** with 1 tablespoon of the oil. Place one third of the parsley, dill, lemon, and onion in the center of the roasting pan. Make sure that the mound of aromatics is high enough to prevent the fish from touching the bottom of the pan.

4. Rub the fish inside and out with 1 tablespoon of the oil. Season inside and out with the salt and pepper and lay it on the bed of herbs. Place the second third of the aromatics into the cavity of the fish and top with the remaining third. Drizzle with the remaining 1 tablespoon oil.

5. Cover the roasting pan tightly with **aluminum foil** and roast for 30 to 35 minutes, until the fish reaches an internal temperature of 120°F. Remove from the oven and set aside to rest for 10 minutes before transferring whole to a **platter** and serving.

PLANK-GRILLED WHOLE TROUT

2 SERVINGS

// SOFTWARE //

2	1- to 2-pound	whole trout	gutted, heads and tails removed
1	tablespoon	olive oil	
1	tablespoon	kosher salt	
2	teaspoons	black pepper	freshly ground

// SPECIAL HARDWARE //

2 untreated cedar or alder planks, ¾ inch thick and 12 to 15 inches long

// PROCEDURE //

1. Soak the **planks** in cool **water** for at least 2 hours and up to overnight.

2. Heat a gas grill to 375° to 400°F.

3. **Brush** the trout, inside and out, with the oil. Season inside and out with the salt and pepper. Set the trout on the planks, belly down and open. Place the planks over indirect heat and grill for 15 to 20 minutes, until the fish reaches an internal temperature of 120°F. Remove from the grill and set aside to rest for 5 to 10 minutes before serving as is or deboning and serving.

THE TRUTH ABOUT PLANKING

Centuries ago, Native Americans in the Pacific Northwest learned to preserve fish by stretching them on cedar or alder planks, which were planted upright beside a smoldering fire. The method made up for the fact that metal grills had yet to be invented, and it infused the fish with a smoky goodness.

These days, you can walk into just about any cooking store and find a selection of cedar, alder, maple, or hickory planks, cut in the ⅜-inch-thick range. Most come two to a pack, and run anywhere from ten to fifteen dollars. Now, if that sounds a wee bit steep to you, and it certainly does to me, you can also head down to your local lumber concern and purchase a ¾- to 1-inch-thick board, and have it cut down into a bunch of planks. Just remember: Most commercial-grade lumber has been treated with preservatives, like creosote, pentachlorophenol, and/or arsenic, none of which are good eats, so you're going to want to buy furniture-grade wood that is untreated and that has also been kiln-dried. My favorite planking woods are cherry, pecan, and apple.

TIDBIT In the upper Midwest, whitefish from the Great Lakes is a favorite for planking.

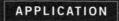
4 SERVINGS

HEALTH AND COLD-WATER FISH

When it comes to healthy eating, it's tough to beat oily, cold-water fish like salmon, sardines, mackerel, herring, and the like. Among other things, like vitamins A and D, these fish are loaded with polyunsaturated omega-3 fatty acids, which not only are good for your heart, but can actually help regulate your heartbeat, and may even stave off certain types of cancer.

// SOFTWARE //

2	pounds	smelt	about 12 (6- to 8-inch-long) fish, gutted, fins removed
½	cup	dried bread crumbs	
1	teaspoon	kosher salt	
½	teaspoon	black pepper	freshly ground
¼	cup	lemon juice	
		peanut oil	for frying

// PROCEDURE ///

1. Rinse the smelt thoroughly and pat dry. Combine the bread crumbs, salt, and pepper in a **zip-top bag**. Put the lemon juice in a **shallow dish**. Dip the smelt into the juice and then place in the bag with the dry mixture and shake until the fish are well coated.

2. Put enough oil in a **12-inch cast-iron skillet** to just cover the bottom of the pan. Set over medium-high heat until shimmering. Add the smelt to the pan, 4 or 5 at a time, being careful not to overcrowd the pan. Fry for 3 to 4 minutes per side, until lightly browned and cooked through. Serve immediately.

TIDBIT | I like to do my fish frying outside—you know, to fight the funk.

TIDBIT | Smelt take their name from the Anglo-Saxon word *smoelt*, meaning "shiny."

If there's a battle cry for foodies these days, it's "seasonality," the idea being that palate and planet alike profit when you serve up what is grown locally whenever possible, and only when it's in season. Of course, carrying through on this mission is not easy for Americans, who have grown accustomed to having a steady supply of everything, all the time. Unlike our grandparents, most of us lack the necessary canning skills to capture the seasons, and our freezers are too crammed with pizzas and popsicles for serious "puttin' up." And so, when the tidal waves of plenty crash over us in the harvesting months, the fruit piles high, and no matter how much we munch, we can't possibly munch it all. Before you know it, bacteria, yeast, and mold barge in, reducing our cornucopia to a gooey puddle. Luckily, with a little bit of know-how, some sound science, and a wee smidgen of hardware, you can comfortably contain an entire season's worth of fruity goodness. How? You dry it, of course.

KNOWLEDGE CONCENTRATE

▷○ Most ripe fruits are microbial nirvanas because they're loaded with fuel (sugar) and, above all, moisture. Plums contain 80 percent water; peaches, 89; figs, 78; strawberries, 90; apples, 84; bananas, 76; and the eponymous watermelon, 92. With proper drying, we can reduce that moisture to 10, maybe 20 percent, while inversely increasing the sugar to the point where it actually becomes a threat to microbes through increased osmotic pressure. What we need to do is make mummies of our fruit.

▷○ When it comes to dehydrating, no one has ever beat the embalmers of ancient Egypt. They knew that the key to keeping a newly deceased pharaoh or pharaoh-ette rot-free wasn't exposure to the arid climate, but, rather, proper prep. Obviously, we don't need a series of clay jars for the liver, lungs, intestines, and stomach, because fruits, thankfully, do not possess such organs. Nor do we require the use of this device, because fruits have neither brains nor noses to pull them through.

Before being wrapped in a thousand yards of linen, royal remains would be soaked in a form of sodium carbonate related to lye, called "natron," for forty days. This pulled moisture out of the, er, client, and altered the pH so that the body would be unappealing to bacteria. Although modern commercial fruit embalmers don't employ natron, they do use an equally ancient and mystical substance.

Anyone who has purchased commercially dried fruit in the United States—or red wine, for that matter—has witnessed firsthand the preservative power of sulfur, which is one of the most versatile food additives in the world because it can slow bacteria, mold, and yeast by tricking them into mistaking it for vitamin D; they pig out on the sulfur, and then, ironically, die of vitamin-D deficiency. Sulfur can also slow the rancidity of fats by halting oxidation, the rather violent process by which certain less stable molecules steal electrons from other molecules. It can also shut down the enzymatic engine that makes cut fruits turn brown.

Taking the preservative power of sulfur into your own hands is a simple, albeit stinky, proposition. The Internet is full of websites offering instruction for this sort of thing, most of which call for stacking up cooling racks or oven racks lined with the fruit, in some kind of box—outside, of course. Then you place some kind of heatproof vessel underneath, add a little food-grade sulfur, light it, and close the box for a predetermined period of time.

Or you could just dip the fruit in any number of sulfur-based solutions, the process used for most commercially dried fruit. The problem is that many folks, especially asthmatics, are prone to sulfur and sulfide allergies, which can be sudden and severe. So we need to find a substance that bacteria don't like, that contains antioxidants, and that can interrupt enzymatic action but is essentially nonallergenic.

Ascorbic acid, or vitamin C, would certainly do the job, but it is extremely bitter, even in small doses. The acetic acid in vinegar would do in a pinch, but its distinctive pungency would be as overwhelming as the vitamin C. Citric acid, on the other hand, has very little flavor, is almost as powerful an antioxidant as the ascorbic variety, and is available in powdered form in many megamarts. Of course, citric acid is also readily available in lemons.

I have a deep personal disdain for food dehydrators. It's not just that they're all unitaskers (which they are), but 99 percent of the models on the market are little more than cheap heaters attached to the back of cheap plastic boxes. At best, they cook rather than dry the fruit and at the very worst they do nothing at all.

If you're a fan of this program you no doubt remember the Blowhard 5000, which we employed to dry herbs and beef jerky. It is a simple hack, requiring only a box fan, four cellulose furnace filters, and a couple of bungee cords, all of which are easily obtained at your local hardware store.

Fruit, of course, is sticky, and it's wet, and it'll definitely bind up on those filters. I used to line the filters with big pieces of window screen, but my doctors told me, "That's not food-grade plastic" and I could, like, sprout another eye or something. Now I use mats that come from commercial dehydrators—but without the dehydrator. Go to the Internet, type in "dehydrator tray liners," and you can buy them cheaply and quickly. You're going to need six of them.

Here's a quick Blowhard assembly review:

Filter 1 goes on the fan so that the ridges would be parallel to the floor when standing upright.

The first mat of fruit goes down, another mat goes on top to trap it safely, and then another filter is positioned over that for maximum airflow.

Repeat 2 more times.

Attach 2 bungee cords to the fan, wrapping them around the filter stack. Be careful when attaching them, as once they're stretched an accidental release can knock out a couple of teeth.

Place your Blowhard someplace clean and peaceful (I use my guest shower), activate your fan (on high speed), and leave on for 42 to 48 hours depending on the humidity level of your home.[1]

Not into the Blowhard scene? You could use the oven, but most can't cruise below 170°F, and we really don't want the fruit exposed to anything over about 120°F. A bit of additional hardware will do the trick (don't worry: no assembly required).

Most hardware stores sell small portable heaters that have built-in fans. Some cost as little as twenty bucks and are actually made to go flush against the wall, which means we could just set it on the floor of the oven and dry the fruit above. I've done several batches like this, but small though it is, the fan still creates considerable heat, and if you're not very careful you'll end up with cooked fruit. And that's why I went to the pet store and purchased a "lizard rock," which is essentially a plug-in ceramic heater that creates very low heat. Couple that with a small portable clip-on fan (from the drugstore or hardware store), and you can convert any oven into a dehydrator.[2]

[1] My attorneys request that I remind you that electricity and water mix only too well and that turning on the water while the fan is in the shower could lead to a very bad day indeed.

[2] Remember to put a label on the door to remind you not to turn the oven on.

APPLICATION — DRIED FRUIT

VARIES BASED ON FRUIT

// SOFTWARE

1	cup	lemon juice	freshly squeezed
1	quart	H$_2$O	
		fruit	apples, mangoes, pears, apricots, bananas, strawberries

// SPECIAL HARDWARE

6 (14-by-14-inch) plastic dehydrator sheets, 4 paper air-conditioning filters, 1 box fan, 2 bungee cords

// PROCEDURE

1. Combine the lemon juice and water in a **large glass bowl**. Set aside until ready to use.

2. **Peel** and core the fruit. **Dice** all fruit, with the exception of strawberries, into ½-inch cubes. For strawberries, slice ⅛ inch thick. Dip the fruit into the lemon water and soak for 2 minutes. Remove and **drain** thoroughly.

3. If using the Blowhard 5000 method to dry your fruit, see the instructions on page 75. If using a commercial dehydrator, follow the manufacturer's directions. Either way, when dry, the fruit should be pliable but not sticky. You should not be able to squeeze moisture from the fruit.

4. Remove the fruit from the filters and store in an **airtight container** in a cool, dry place.

TIP | Although dried fruit can be reanimated, as it were, by simply soaking it in boiling water and juice for 10 or 15 minutes, I often find that it can be rehydrated in the target food. For instance, chopped dried fruit can be added directly to a muffin batter or a rice pilaf. I've also been known to cook fruit directly into ice cream bases, and although it can be sprinkled directly on salads, if you take the time to soak it in your vinaigrette first—well, you can see where I'm going with that.

LOOKS MORE LIKE THE GOPHER FROM *CADDYSHACK*.

So, once you have all that dried fruit, what do you do with it? Read on.

// SOFTWARE

8	ounces	dried apples, pears, and apricots[3]	
4	cups	H$_2$O	
½	cup	orange juice	freshly squeezed
4	ounces	sugar	
1		lemon	zested
1	stick	cinnamon	
1	whole	clove	

Compote works and plays well with others, including ice cream, grilled chicken or pork chops, pork tenderloin, and even toast or biscuits.

// PROCEDURE

1. Soak the dried fruit in 2 cups of the water in a **large bowl** for 1 hour.

2. Combine the remaining 2 cups water, the orange juice, sugar, and lemon zest in a **small saucepan** over medium-high heat. Add the fruit and the soaking liquid. Bring to a boil, stirring occasionally.

3. Reduce the heat to medium-low and add the cinnamon and clove. Simmer for about 40 minutes, stirring occasionally, until the fruit has softened and the mixture has thickened. Remove from the heat and set aside to cool. Remove the cinnamon and clove and discard. Serve warm or cold.

TIP | To make a nice little pocket pie, cut a few rounds of puff pastry dough, put about a tablespoon of the compote in the middle, fold it over, and seal it with a fork. Poke some holes in the top, brush with an egg wash, and bake at 375°F for 25 minutes.

[3] If using store-bought dried fruit, chop the pieces into ½-inch chunks and simmer the mixture an additional 15 to 20 minutes.

APPLICATION | TRAIL MIX

5 CUPS

// SOFTWARE

7	ounces	dried fruit	about 3 cups
5	ounces	mixed nuts	about 1 cup
3½	ounces	granola	about 1 cup

TIP | If the trail mix becomes soft overnight, your fruit was not dry enough.

// PROCEDURE

Combine the dried fruit, nuts, and granola in a **large bowl**. Store in an **airtight container** in a cool, dry place for up to 1 month.

STEW ROMANCE

Ah, the stew pot. If there's a more enduring or endearing symbol of hearth and home, I don't know what it is. From the dawn of cookery, when water simmered in animal hides stretched over campfires through the Ages of Clay, Bronze, Iron, and Steel, cooks have continually fed and fed from their stew pots. A tough hunk of mastodon here, a snaggled bit of taproot there. All rendered edible and nourishing through the combined efforts of time, heat, and water. The problem is, all that time, heat, and water tend to blur the individual notes of the ingredients into a murky monotone. If you ask me, a stew, or a culture for that matter, should be more like, well, a barbershop quartet: Each note should be distinct yet in utter harmony with the whole.

KNOWLEDGE CONCENTRATE

▷○ I don't actually stew stews. I braise them. Technically speaking, stewing involves cooking small pieces of food. Braising calls for larger cuts; this limits surface area and therefore moisture loss from the target food. Unlike stewing, which calls for submersion of the food pieces in liquid, braising calls for a relatively small amount of liquid, which, if handled properly, translates to less-watered-down flavors. Stewing is often achieved in an open vessel. Braising calls for a tightly sealed vessel, which prevents moisture loss via evaporation and helps to tenderize meat through the slight elevation in vessel pressure. More important, while stewing always calls for cooking ingredients of different natures together, braising applications often require the separation of meats and vegetables.

▷○ Although *boeuf bourguignon* from France, *Hasenpfeffer* from Germany, *wat* from Ethiopia, and *Brunswick stew* from America are all celebrated examples of "stews," my personal favorite of the species, from a flavor standpoint, is Hungarian goulash. And my favorite goulash meat is short ribs, which hail from both the chuck primal and the plate primal of the beef critter.

As you can see, ribs one through five are in the chuck area, and the ends of ribs six through twelve are in the plate. Although there isn't much meat to speak of on nine through twelve, the front plate ribs render some nice meat. But for my money, and we're not talking about a lot of money here, the chuck ribs provide the best mixture of meat, fat, and connective tissue.

○ **When it comes to buying short ribs, we have choices.**

Chuck or plate? For stew, plate is the way to go. It possesses more connective tissue, so it's better for slow cooking.

Whole, English style, or flanken cut? Whole, not surprisingly, is one whole rib with the meat cut parallel to the bone. English style is just half of that. Flanken is a cross cut that contains the meat of several different ribs. Although I'm a flanken fan, for goulash I'd stick with the standard English cut; each rib is going to weigh about a quarter of a pound. Nearly half of that weight is lost during the cooking process, so you'll want to plan on a minimum of two pieces per diner.

○ **The unctuous body and lip-smacking goodness of braised meats are made possible by a curious chemical characteristic of a particular tissue type common to all mammals. In your body, right now, there are three major types of connective tissue holding you up and together.**

First, we have elastin, represented here by a mesh of bungee cords. These fibers make up tough, gristle-y stuff like cartilage, which has very limited culinary use.

Another type of connective tissue is reticulin, represented here by a honeycomb drying rack. They are very fine, and form the outer skins of things like your lungs and kidneys and what-not. They're not good eats.

And then there is collagen, represented by this opaque plastic sheet. Our muscles, bones, tendons, and such are all held together with this stuff.

Here's the weird and wonderful part: When exposed to water and long, low heat, collagen molecules break down and rearrange into another protein structure called gelatin, which makes most glues possible as well as a host of classic desserts. The key to this magical conversion is heat control. Although many braise and stew recipes call for simmering long and low on the cook top, the truth is, even a top-notch burner makes a ring of fire, and there is no way to control a braise with a ring of fire. The oven is the tool for this job. Therein we can control the temperature and depend on the heat to come at the food from every direction. Since air conducts heat much more slowly than water, the meat will heat slowly, and that will give us maximum collagen-to-gelatin conversion without overcooking the whole.

As gelatin cools, it moves from a suspended colloidal state to a gel state, which, if the gelatin is concentrated, can be quite strong. If you've ever seen one of those brainy crime lab shows where they shoot a bullet into a big block of goo in order to attempt to match it with a weapon, the block of goo is in fact "ballistic" gelatin with a gelatin-to-water ratio of 8:1, which supposedly imitates the general density of the human body, bones and . . . stuff notwithstanding.

What's really interesting, though, is that once gelatin has reached the gel state, it takes more heat to redissolve it than it did to render it from collagen in the first place. And, believe it or not, that is a good thing.

BALLISTIC GEL— FUN FOR THE WHOLE FAMILY.

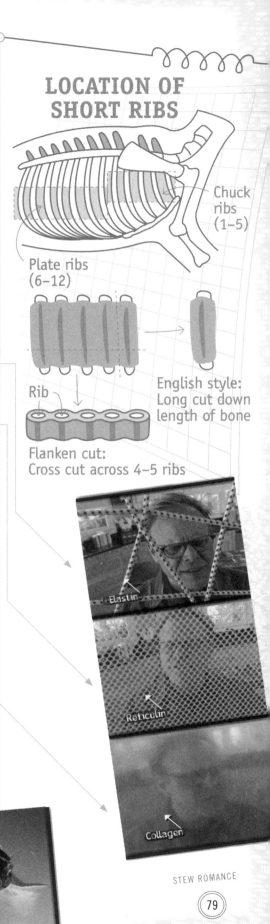

LOCATION OF SHORT RIBS

Chuck ribs (1–5)

Plate ribs (6–12)

Rib

English style: Long cut down length of bone

Flanken cut: Cross cut across 4–5 ribs

Elastin

Reticulin

Collagen

PAPRIKA

Paprika is a spice created by drying and grinding sweet peppers, such as *Capsicum annum*, into a fine powder. Native to South America, pepper plants first arrived in Hungary around the seventeenth century, courtesy of refugees of Balkan states escaping the Turks, who were actively marauding at the time. By the late eighteenth century, paprika was firmly ensconced in Hungarian cuisine.

"Hot paprika" isn't so much "chile" hot as it is simply pungent. "Sweet" paprika isn't so much "sweet" as simply not very pungent. The most commonly exported variety is called "noble sweet," although smoked varieties are gaining popularity here in the United States. Since you have to buy it in ground form, you're going to want to keep paprika very, very tightly sealed in a cool place, and you're going to want to replace it every eight months, give or take a month.

The word *stew* comes from an Old French word, *estuve*, meaning "stove" or "hot enclosure." French cooks, understanding how important it is to keep moisture in, used to seal up their dry *estuves* or *daubes* with a homemade library paste that they would chisel off when the multiday cooking was done. Since it's easily shaped, tight sealing, and a fine heat conductor, heavy-duty aluminum foil is my first choice for a braise like the one below.

// SOFTWARE ///

¼	cup	tomato paste	
¼	cup	apple cider vinegar	
1½	teaspoons	Worcestershire sauce	
1	tablespoon	paprika	
1½	teaspoons	dried herbs	any combination of thyme, oregano, and rosemary
3	pounds	English-cut short ribs	
1	tablespoon	kosher salt	plus 1 teaspoon
1	large	yellow onion	thinly sliced
1	pound	red potatoes	unpeeled, diced small
		black pepper	freshly ground
1	tablespoon	fresh parsley	chopped

// PROCEDURE ///

1. **Whisk** together the tomato paste, vinegar, Worcestershire sauce, paprika, and dried herbs in a **large bowl**. Set aside.

2. Season the short ribs with 1 tablespoon of the salt. Place a **large griddle** over medium-high heat and when a drop of water bounces off, sear the meat on the griddle until browned on all sides.

3. Remove the meat to the bowl with the paste mixture and toss to combine. Transfer to a large piece of **heavy-duty aluminum foil** and seal tightly. Put the package in a cold oven on the middle rack, and set a **metal pan** below the package. Set the oven temperature to 250°F and cook for 4 hours.

BALKAN REFUGEES ESCAPING THE TURKS BROUGHT PAPRIKA TO HUNGARY IN THE SEVENTEENTH CENTURY.

4. Remove the meat from the oven and carefully poke a hole in the pack while holding it over a **heatproof container**. Drain the liquid into the container and put it in the refrigerator to cool enough so that the fat separates from the rest of the liquid, approximately 1 hour. Transfer the liquid to the freezer until the fat cap has solidified, approximately 1 hour. Reseal the package of ribs and set aside at room temperature while the liquid is cooling.

5. Retrieve the liquid from the freezer and remove the fat cap that has formed on top. Measure out 1 tablespoon of the fat and reserve the rest for another use. Put the fat in a **large saucier** and place over medium heat. Once the fat has melted, add the onion and the remaining 1 teaspoon salt and stir to separate the onions into rings. Cook for 2 to 3 minutes, stirring occasionally. Add the potatoes along with a pinch of pepper and stir to combine. Add the liquid reserved from the meat and stir. Cover tightly and decrease the heat to low so that no heat is escaping the lid. Cook for 30 minutes, or until the potatoes are fork tender.

6. Meanwhile, cut the meat away from the bones, removing and discarding the bones and connective tissue. When the potatoes are tender, set the meat atop the vegetables. Cover and continue to cook for 10 minutes. Serve sprinkled with the parsley.

DISSOLVING ALUMINUM FOR FUN AND PROFIT . . . OKAY, JUST FUN

I know what you're thinking. You're thinking, "Cooking tomato products in aluminum is insane because the acid dissolves the metal." Well, you're right. A few little aluminum ions may slip out of their normal position. But it would take a very, very long time for that leaching to reach anything close to a toxic level: months, in fact. If you really want to see aluminum dissolve, try this.

If you cook or store something containing a lot of acid—say, tomatoes—in a steel or, better yet, cast-iron vessel, and cover it tightly with aluminum foil so that the foil is in contact with the acid, well, you're making a battery. And in no time, the aluminum will erode and pit wherever it is touching that acid. Since our braise doesn't involve two metals, which is key, I'm not the least bit concerned.

CUKE, IT IS TIME TO FULFILL YOUR DESTINY.

If you ask me, no magical metamorphosis is more spectacular than the transformation of cucumber to pickle. Now, I realize that we've walked down the pickled path before, you and I, but in that particular episode, we made fresh-packed, or processed, pickles, which counted on a stiff dose of acid and a jolt of heat to get the pickling job done. Those were good eats, to be sure, but if you want to produce honest-to-goodness dill pickles, a category made up of many subvarieties, you will have to learn to manage time, brine, bacteria, and, of course, cucumbers.

KNOWLEDGE CONCENTRATE

▷○ Behold *Cucumis sativus*, the cucumber. Cousin to gourds and melons, native of India, but much loved from Mesopotamia to Rome, where radical advancements in agriculture were achieved simply to ensure that the emperor Tiberius would have his required daily supply. When Rome fell, so too did the cucumber. Most Europeans of the day just didn't go for all that bitterness. Today we don't typically think of cucumbers as bitter fruits, but back then they contained quite a bit more cucurbitacin, a naturally accruing steroid that is almost as bitter as caffeine, which has since been bred out of the plant.

▷○ Strictly speaking, any dwarf variety of *Cucumis sativus* can be pickled. You just want to look for a few characteristics. They should be firm, with a nice rounded end. It's good to see a little stem on the bottom. Color should be dark green to mottled or striated. If they're yellow all the way across, you want to avoid them. They're probably going to have some little spines or warts, and that is fine.

▷○ Dill pickles are a lot like sauerkraut in that bacteria rather than yeast are responsible for the fermentation of the product. They will break apart the sugars in the cukes and create carbon dioxide, some alcohol, and lactic acid. This acid is extremely unfriendly to the types of bacteria that ordinarily cause spoilage, which means that lactic acid is a preservative, even if bacteria make it. Ironic, don't you think?

To run smoothly, however, this process requires a chemical control agent, which in this case is salt. Think of it as a bouncer who regulates which bacteria get into the pickles and which ones don't. There are two ways we could go about the process. If the target food is very, very small, or cut up into chunks, or shredded, like cabbage for sauerkraut, we could just pour on straight solid salt, because it would require only a relatively short fermentation period. But given the surface-to-mass ratio of cucumbers, we're better off using a premixed brine or "pickle."

Where you decide to pickle your pickles matters because it needs to be very clean and temperature stable. The contents of your crock should not be allowed to rise much above 70°F. The fermentation would still take place at higher temps, but it would be drastically slowed and that would only serve to allow other, less desirable microorganisms an opportunity to set up house. In the winter, I've actually used my garage for pickling. In summer I put my crock in a cooler, and I just add some ice to the cooler (not the crock) every day or two.

During fermentation, you will see bubbles, a sure sign that the process is under way. First, strains of bacterial storm troopers, *Leuconostoc mesenteroides*, move in and kick-start the fermentation. They can work in very salty or sugary conditions at a wide range of temperatures, but they don't create much in the way of flavor. After they've softened up the targets a bit, other species of *Lactobacillus*, related to the ones that turn milk into yogurt, go to work, creating the lactic acid that will grant our little green friends immortality—well, culinary immortality. Besides acting as a preservative, lactic acid has a much smoother and more complex flavor than the acetic acid that flavors vinegar-cured pickles.

From here on out, think of this crock as your virtual pet. It does not need to be walked or talked to or scratched behind the ears, but it will need to be skimmed of scum every day, or at least every couple of days. Most of the scum will actually be on the bag that keeps the cucumbers submerged in brine, so carefully lift it out and just dunk it right into a vessel of clean water, and the scum will wash off. Then take a spoon and look around the edges and just scrape off anything that kind of looks white and moldy. It's not actually mold, at least it shouldn't be. Every now and then it is. But usually it's just leftover stuff.

Depending on the microorganisms particular to your region, your pickles should be "mostly" fermented in six to ten days. You'll know when mostly fermented has been reached, because the bubbling will stop. At that point, you've got some choices to make.

You can move your pickles to the refrigerator, replace the bag with a loose cover such as a plate, and continue scumming, off and on, for three days. The cold will retard fermentation, leaving you with a batch of Polish or Hungarian dill pickles. If you move the pickles into a jar, then strain the juice back over them, cover, and refrigerate, you'll be able to keep them for up to two months.

On the other hand, you could just leave them in their original spot and continue scumming regularly for three to four weeks. Then you'd have yourself some true power pickles, honest-to-goodness high-octane kosher dills so sour they may turn your mouth inside out—in a good way.

In the old days, pickles were simply sealed in crocks or barrels and left alone. As much as I would like to instruct you to do just that, there's just too much chance of spoilage, and spoilage leads to sickness and sickness eventually leads to increased billings from my lawyers Itchy and Twitchy, vermin-at-law.

WHAT A CROCK!

Once upon a time, when home pickling was the norm, pickles were pickled in stone or earthenware "crocks," and to my mind they're still the best tools for the job. They block light, they're insulators, so they help to regulate temperature fluctuations, and they are utterly nonreactive, so they neither give nor receive flavors. And let's face it: They're cool-looking.

The crock pictured here came from my wife's grandmother's attic. Check out the lid. It looks like it doesn't fit, but fermentation is ideally an anaerobic process, and lids like this used to be made to keep the transforming food submerged in the brine, while still allowing gases to expand. If you possess such a vessel you should certainly use it. If not, an alternative is easily assembled.

I would suggest that if you really get into pickling, you find yourself a crock. Red Wing Pottery in Minnesota is a fine source.

MY FAVORITE PICKLE CROCK

// SOFTWARE

5½	ounces	pickling salt	
1	gallon	filtered H_2O	
3	pounds	pickling cucumbers	4 to 6 inches in length
1	tablespoon	black peppercorns	
1	tablespoon	red pepper flakes	
2	cloves	garlic	crushed
1	teaspoon	dill seed	
1	bunch	fresh dill	

TIDBIT | "Dill" pickles were developed in northern Europe, where dill is common. Some say that volatile oils in dill also help to moderate which bacteria grow in the pickle.

TIDBIT | "Kosher" dills are dill pickles that have garlic in the brine.

// PROCEDURE

1. Combine the salt and water in a **pitcher** and stir until the salt has dissolved.

2. Rinse the cucumbers thoroughly and trim off the blossom end. Set aside.

3. Put the peppercorns, pepper flakes, garlic, dill seed, and fresh dill in a **1-gallon crock**. Add the cucumbers to the crock on top of the aromatics. Pour the brine mixture over the cucumbers to completely cover them. Pour the remaining water into a **1-gallon zip-top bag** and seal. Place the bag on top of the pickles, making sure that all of them are completely submerged in the brine. Set in a cool, dry place.

4. Check the crock after 3 days. Fermentation has begun if you see bubbles rising to the top of the crock. After this, check the crock daily and skim off any scum that forms. If scum forms on the zip-top bag, rinse it off and return it to the top of the crock.

5. The fermentation is complete when the pickles taste sour and the bubbles have stopped rising; this should take 6 to 7 days. Once this happens, cover the crock loosely and place in the refrigerator for 3 days, skimming daily or as needed. Store for up to 2 months in the refrigerator, skimming as needed. If the pickles become soft or begin to take on an off odor, this is a sign of spoilage and they should be discarded.

NOTE: If the whole fermentation thing is just not where it's at for you, don't give up the pickle. You can still make what's called refrigerator pickles. Just cut your cucumbers into spears, pack them in the same brine, in jars, and stick them in the refrigerator for 3 to 4 days. You'll have the same kind of pickle that many delis serve alongside their sandwiches.

TIDBIT | Americans consume about nine pounds of pickles per person annually.

TIDBIT | The namesake of this country, Amerigo Vespucci, was once a pickle peddler.

DEEP-FRIED PICKLES

APPROXIMATELY 32 PICKLE SPEARS

// **SOFTWARE** ///

		peanut oil	
1	quart	kosher dill pickles	
1	cup	buttermilk	
2	cups	plain cornmeal	
1	tablespoon	kosher salt	

// **PROCEDURE** ///

1. Fill a **5-quart cast-iron Dutch oven** halfway with peanut oil. Set over medium-high heat and bring to 390° to 400°F on a **deep-fry thermometer**.

2. Remove the pickles from their brine and cut them into quarters lengthwise, like spears. Lay the spears on a **half sheet pan** lined with **paper towels** and pat them dry.

3. Pour the buttermilk into a **shallow dish** and mix together the cornmeal and salt in a **separate shallow dish**. Dip each pickle, one at a time, first into the buttermilk, then into the cornmeal, and then repeat. Carefully place 3 or 4 spears at a time in the hot oil and cook until golden brown, approximately 2 minutes, adjusting the heat if necessary to maintain a constant temperature of 390° to 400°F.

4. Transfer the pickles to a **cooling rack** set in a **half sheet pan** and cool for 5 minutes before eating. Season with additional salt if desired.

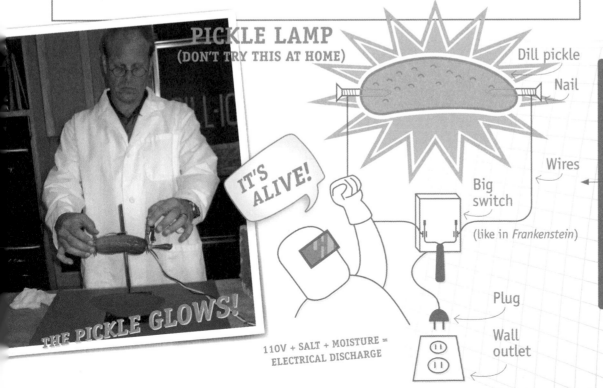

PICKLE LAMP
(DON'T TRY THIS AT HOME)

IT'S ALIVE!

THE PICKLE GLOWS!

Dill pickle

Nail

Wires

Big switch

(like in *Frankenstein*)

Plug

Wall outlet

110V + SALT + MOISTURE = ELECTRICAL DISCHARGE

PROBABLY DANGEROUS PICKLE EXPERIMENT

If your insurance is paid up and you possess some rudimentary electronic equipment and no sense of personal responsibility, you can make yourself a dill pickle lamp.

That's my experiment. But, under no circumstances should you ever, ever, ever, ever, ever attempt this experiment. It's deadly, horrible, and you shouldn't do this. Ever. But if you do, I won't tell anyone.

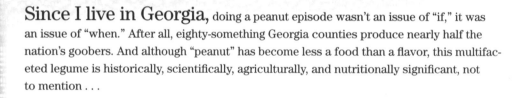

Since I live in Georgia, doing a peanut episode wasn't an issue of "if," it was an issue of "when." After all, eighty-something Georgia counties produce nearly half the nation's goobers. And although "peanut" has become less a food than a flavor, this multifaceted legume is historically, scientifically, agriculturally, and nutritionally significant, not to mention . . .

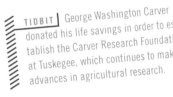

TIDBIT | George Washington Carver donated his life savings in order to establish the Carver Research Foundation at Tuskegee, which continues to make advances in agricultural research.

TRIVIA | It was about 103°F at the stadium, but B. J. Winfrey never complained about the foam peanut I made him wear—or the wool suit, for that matter.

Take a look at a peanut plant and right away you see that something is missing. Namely: peanuts. Somewhere along the line, *Arachis hypogaea* developed an effective defense against marauding critters. After the flowers are fertilized above ground, they droop down and push themselves into the soil, where their fruit matures in safety.

Following the failure of the Southern cotton crop from boll weevils in 1910, a scientist at the Tuskegee Institute penned a pamphlet titled "How to Grow the Peanut, and 105 Ways of Preparing It for Human Consumption." Its author, George Washington Carver, saved the agricultural future of the country by developing hundreds of uses for the peanut, including peanut milk, peanut shampoo, peanut flakes, peanut sausage, peanut-orange punch, chili sauce, mock chicken, mock goose, mock oyster, peanut face cream, peanut hand lotion . . . you get the point.

The peanut family is extremely diverse, on a global scale, but here in the United States four varieties dominate the marketplace.

VALENCIAS grow two to five nuts per shell. Their paper clings tenaciously to the nut, making them not so popular with roasters.

SPANISH peanuts are the smallest of all peanuts and yet they contain the highest percentage of oil.

RUNNER peanuts, which make up most of the crop in Georgia, are quite popular due to their high yields and their specific fat composition. If you bite into a candy bar with a peanut in it, odds are it's a Runner.

The VIRGINIA peanut is the peanut we think of when we bite into a peanut. The nuts themselves are gigantic (as peanuts go) and are the best for roasting and eating out of hand.

When shopping for raw shell peanuts, look for firm, hard shells with no cracks, no black moldy spots, and as little dust as possible.

After purchase, transfer raw nuts to an airtight containment unit and store in a cold, dark, dry place for up to a month. If you plan on keeping them on hand any longer, refrigerate for up to 3 months or cook and store even longer.

Nearly half the peanuts grown in this country become peanut butter, which was invented by a doctor from St. Louis. But the brown goo didn't become popular until a salesman name of C. H. Sumner sold it as health food at the 1904 World's Fair. Today, commercial peanut butter is required by law to contain at least 90 percent peanuts. In "natural peanut butter," the remaining weight is composed of peanut oil, and in some cases salt. Mass-market brands also add sugar, stabilizers, and various additives to enhance shelf life and creaminess. Most contain small amounts of hydrogenated oils as well. All good reasons to make your own. But first, a flavor-boosting roast is recommended.

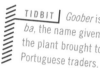

TIDBIT | America ranks third in global peanut production, after China and India. But while those countries grow most of their peanuts for oil, ours are primarily for munching.

TIDBIT | *Goober* is derived from *nguba*, the name given by West Africans to the plant brought to their continent by Portuguese traders.

NUTRITION

Peanuts are high in fiber, potassium, and the B-vitamins riboflavin and folate, which have been shown to reduce the risk of heart attacks and some birth defects. Peanuts are also high in the amino acids lysine and isoleucine, but they're lacking in tryptophan, cystine, and methionine, so if you want to create a complete protein with peanuts you need to pair them with something like wheat (can you say peanut butter sandwich?).

▭▭▭▭▭ **ROASTED PEANUTS**

APPROXIMATELY 2 POUNDS
ROASTED PEANUTS IN SHELL

// SOFTWARE //

2	pounds	peanuts (see note, below)	raw, in shell
2	tablespoons	peanut oil	
1 to 2	tablespoons	kosher salt	

// PROCEDURE //

1. Crank the oven to 350°F.

2. Wash the peanuts under cool water. Drain, pat dry, and put them in a **large bowl**. Toss with the peanut oil and salt to coat.

3. Divide the peanuts between **2 half sheet pans**, making sure to spread them out in a single layer. Roast for 30 to 35 minutes, rotating the pans halfway through cooking. Remove and cool slightly prior to devourment, as they will continue to "cook," becoming crunchy as they cool.

   N O T E : If you plan to eat the peanuts roasted right out of the shell, use Virginia or Valencia peanuts. If you're going to use the roasted peanuts to make peanut butter, use Spanish peanuts, as they have a higher oil content.

TIP | To remove the skin of shelled roasted peanuts, rub the peanuts together in your hands held over a salad spinner, allowing the peanuts and skins to fall into the bowl. When the skin has been loosened from all of the peanuts, close the salad spinner and spin until all of the skin has been separated from the peanuts.

APPLICATION ▭▭▭▭▭ **HOMEMADE PEANUT BUTTER**

APPROXIMATELY 1½ CUPS

// SOFTWARE //

15	ounces	Roasted Peanuts (above)	shelled and skinned
1	teaspoon	kosher salt	
1½	teaspoons	honey	
1½	tablespoons	peanut oil	

// PROCEDURE //

Combine the peanuts, salt, and honey in a **food processor**. Process for 1 minute. Scrape down the sides of the bowl. Place the lid back on and continue to process while slowly drizzling in the oil; process until the mixture is smooth, 1½ to 2 minutes. Store the peanut butter in an **airtight container** in the refrigerator for up to 2 months.

APPLICATION — PEANUT BUTTER PIE

10 SERVINGS

// SOFTWARE

6½	ounces	chocolate wafers	
1	tablespoon	granulated sugar	
10	tablespoons	unsalted butter	at room temperature, divided
1	batch	Homemade Peanut Butter (opposite)	
3	ounces	confectioners' sugar	
1	teaspoon	vanilla extract	
¼	cup	heavy cream	plus 1 tablespoon
2	ounces	good-quality bittersweet chocolate	

// PROCEDURE

1. Heat the oven to 350°F.

2. Combine the wafers and granulated sugar in a **food processor**. Process until the wafers are fine crumbs. Melt 6 tablespoons of the butter and drizzle it into the crumb mixture. Pulse to combine. Press this mixture into the bottom, up the sides, and just over the lip of a **9-inch metal pie pan**. Bake on the middle rack of the oven for 10 minutes. Cool completely.

3. Once the crust has cooled, put the peanut butter and the remaining 4 tablespoons butter in the **food processor**. Process for 1 minute, then add the confectioners' sugar and vanilla and process for another 1½ to 2 minutes, until smooth. Carefully spread the mixture in the pie shell and bake for 10 minutes. Remove from the oven and cool while preparing the topping.

4. Put the cream in a **heatproof bowl** and microwave on high just until simmering, approximately 30 seconds. Remove from the microwave and add the chocolate. Make sure the chocolate is completely submerged in the cream. Set aside for 2 minutes. Gently **whisk** until the chocolate is melted and combined with the cream, 2 to 3 minutes.

5. Spread the chocolate mixture over the pie and chill in the refrigerator for 1½ hours before serving.

GEORGE WASHINGTON CARVER, "MR. PEANUT"

BOILED PEANUTS

APPROXIMATELY 4 POUNDS IN SHELL
AND 2 POUNDS OUT OF SHELL

// SOFTWARE ///

2	pounds	Virginia or Valencia peanuts	raw, in shell
3	ounces	kosher salt	

// PROCEDURE ///

1. Wash the peanuts in cool water until the water runs clear. Soak in cool water for 30 minutes to loosen any remaining dirt.

2. Drain the peanuts in a colander and rinse well. Put the peanuts in a **12-quart pot** along with the salt and 3 gallons water. Stir well. Cover and cook over high heat for 4 hours (see note, below). Check the texture of the peanut at this point for doneness. When done, a boiled peanut should have a texture similar to that of a cooked dried bean. It should hold its shape, but not crunch when bitten. Add more water throughout the cooking process if needed. If necessary, continue cooking for 3 to 4 hours longer.

3. Drain the peanuts and refrigerate in an **airtight container** for up to 1 week.

NOTE: The cooking time can vary greatly depending on how fresh the peanuts are. The fresher the peanut, the less time it will take to cook.

TRIVIA | I like to use this old egg basket to rinse and soak my peanuts. I found it years ago at a junk shop. A salad spinner does the job just as well.

BOILED PEANUT SOUP

6 TO 8 SERVINGS;
APPROXIMATELY 3 QUARTS

// **SOFTWARE** ///

8	rashers	thick-sliced bacon	chopped
14	ounces	onions	chopped
6	cups	chicken broth	
22	ounces	shelled Boiled Peanuts (opposite)	
1	tablespoon	fresh thyme	chopped
3	cups	2% milk	
4	teaspoons	rice vinegar	
1½	teaspoons	kosher salt	
¼	teaspoon	ground white pepper	

// **PROCEDURE** ///

1. Set a **6-quart pot** over medium-high heat. Add the bacon and cook, stirring frequently, until the bacon is browned, 6 to 7 minutes. Remove the bacon to a **paper towel–lined plate**. Pour off all but 3 tablespoons of the bacon fat.

2. Decrease the heat to medium and add the onions to the pot. Cook, stirring occasionally, until the onion is softened and beginning to brown around the edges, approximately 6 minutes. Add the broth, peanuts, and thyme. Increase the heat to high and bring to a boil. When the mixture reaches a boil, reduce the heat to medium-low to maintain a rapid simmer. Cook until the peanuts begin to loosen from their skins and the broth is reduced by one-quarter, 20 to 25 minutes.

3. Turn off the heat and puree the mixture with an **immersion blender** until smooth. Add the milk, vinegar, salt, and white pepper and puree until combined. Turn the heat back on to medium and cook until warmed through, 5 to 7 minutes. Garnish with the bacon and serve immediately.

BEAN STALKER

Every year of my youth,

my Aunt Gert would bring a green bean casserole to the Brown family reunion, and my mom would make me eat it. Aunt Gert supposedly had a lot of money and nobody wanted to, you know . . . alienate her. I can distinctly recall the limp beans, the greasy onions, and gravy the likes of which would push H. P. Lovecraft to the brink of madness. Finally, one year I refused to eat the stuff, citing the Geneva Convention. Sure enough, the old bat left me out of her will. I boycotted all green bean casseroles from that day on, but now I'm ready to let the healing begin, starting with . . .

KNOWLEDGE CONCENTRATE

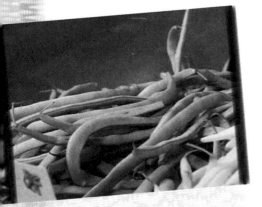

. . . the beans. With the exception of a few Old World favorites like fava beans and lentils, most of the beans that we know and love are members of the species *Phaseolus vulgaris*, which descended from one proto-bean that grew in the southern Andes thousands of years ago. How is it that one species exhibits so much diversity? The answer: maize. That's right, the grain that we know as corn is responsible for bringing us our beans. Maize has been a staple across most of Central and South America for thousands of years. It's nutritious, but lacking in crucial amino acids like lysine. Add beans to the pot, and suddenly you've got yourself a complete protein.

Once this dietary miracle became known, beans spread, evolving as they moved across the landscape and across cultures. As part of the Columbian exchange, beans traveled from the New World to the Old and back again, mutating happily all the way.

What we refer to as a "green bean" can be the unripe pod, or fruit, of over a hundred different varieties of bean, but those most often found in American megamarts (not to mention American green bean casseroles) are *Phaseolus vulgaris*, commonly referred to as either "string beans" or "snap beans." *P. vulgaris* subspecies are categorized by whether they grow on a bush (bush beans) or a pole (pole beans). As you might suspect, bush beans form bushes and pole beans climb. The pod color can be green, yellow, purple, or variegated—though, if you ask me, using purple beans in a casserole is a little creepy.

Regardless of what green beans you find, make sure that they are uniform in color. You don't want to see any blemishes, any dark spots. And when you bend them, they should snap crisply at about 90 degrees. If they don't, they're old. And if they're old, you don't want them.

Modern green beans have been bred with a little extra fiber in them to help them survive shipping and handling. But they still don't bear up in the refrigerator too well because their metabolism keeps ticking even after picking. I wouldn't give them more than three days in the chill chest, sealed tightly in a zip-top bag with all the air sucked out. Since condensation leads to rotting, always chill the beans in an open bag, then seal when well chilled.

Once upon a time, a tough bundle of fibers—kind of like green dental floss—ran up the spine of most green beans, and it had to be stripped off before said bean would snap. Luckily, the string has been bred out of most modern pods, though you may still encounter them in heirloom varieties. After a good rinse, I just hold a bundle of beans in one hand and use my thumb and forefinger to break off the stem end of each one. Then I transfer to the other hand to snap the long beans in half. Short ones I leave intact.

As far as cooking goes, I think of beans the way I do pasta. In other words, I don't ever put these in a pot of water without having at least a gallon of water at a boil, liberally seasoned with not one but two tablespoons of salt. I probably could use a smaller vessel, but all that water does two things. First, it'll bounce back to a boil quickly, which will shorten the overall cooking time. And that is good because it'll help prevent the beans from turning brown. Why?

When beans go into boiling water, something wonderful happens. Within a couple of moments, the green brightens, as oxygen, masking the chlorophyll pigment, is released into the water. As the cooking continues, cell walls within the beans soften, which is also a good thing, because it means that it'll be easier for us to get to good stuff like minerals and vitamins C and K. But there's also a downside here. As the cooking continues, acids are released, which once loose in the water will attack the chlorophyll, turning the bean a drab and dreary brown-gray. By cooking in plenty of water, these acids can be diluted and rendered powerless.

Once your beans are just tender to the tooth, drain them in a colander and put them in an ice-water bath to shut down the cooking process. Once the beans are safely chilled, you may continue with casserole construction or store them in the fridge for another 2 to 3 days.

BEAN STALKER

APPLICATION ⎍⎍⎍ **BEST-EVER GREEN BEAN CASSEROLE**

4 TO 6 SERVINGS

//SOFTWARE //

FOR THE TOPPING

2	medium	onions	thinly sliced
¼	cup	all-purpose flour	
2	tablespoons	Japanese bread crumbs	a.k.a. panko
1	teaspoon	kosher salt	

FOR THE BEANS AND SAUCE

1	tablespoon	kosher salt	
1	pound	fresh green beans	rinsed, trimmed, and halved
2	tablespoons	unsalted butter	
12	ounces	button mushrooms	
1	teaspoon	kosher salt	
½	teaspoon	black pepper	
2	cloves	garlic	minced
½	teaspoon	nutmeg	freshly ground
2	tablespoons	all-purpose flour	
1	cup	half-and-half	
1	cup	low-sodium chicken broth	

THE PANKO DIFFERENCE

Unlike most bread crumbs made on planet Earth, the makers of panko do not just crumble up dried pieces of bread. They're very secretive about how they do it, but we know it involves a yeast-risen wheat dough that is allowed to rise twice, then cooked not with heat but with an electrical current. The resulting loaf is dried and then broken up with some kind of top-secret bread-breaker-upper. The crumbs are then "screened" for size and shape. Does all this really make a difference when compared to regular bread crumbs? Heck, yes.

| Regular bread crumbs | Panko

1. Heat the oven to 475°F.

2. Make the topping: Combine the onions, flour, panko, and salt in a **large bowl** and toss to combine. Coat a **half sheet pan** with **nonstick cooking spray** and evenly spread the onions in the pan. Bake on the middle rack of the oven until golden brown, approximately 30 minutes, tossing the onions 2 or 3 times during cooking. Set aside until ready to use. Turn the oven temperature down to 400°F.

3. While the onions are cooking, make the beans and sauce: Bring **1 gallon water** and 2 tablespoons salt to a boil in an **8-quart saucepan**. Add the beans and blanch for 5 minutes. Drain in a **colander** and immediately plunge the beans into a **large bowl of ice water** to stop the cooking. Drain and set aside.

4. Melt the butter in a **12-inch cast-iron skillet** set over medium-high heat. Add the mushrooms, salt, and pepper and cook, stirring occasionally, until the mushrooms begin to release some of their liquid, 4 to 5 minutes. Add the nutmeg and garlic and cook for 1 to 2 minutes. Sprinkle the flour over the mixture and stir to combine. Cook for 1 minute. Add the broth and simmer for 1 minute. Decrease the heat to medium-low and add the half-and-half. Cook, stirring occasionally, until the mixture thickens, 6 to 8 minutes.

5. Remove from the heat and stir in one-quarter of the onions and all of the beans. Top with the remaining onions. Bake until bubbly, approximately 15 minutes. Serve immediately.

TIDBIT | Phillip Miller, an eighteenth-century gardener, was an early advocate of cooking and eating green beans in their pods.

TIDBIT | The string was first bred out of the bean by New York breeder Calvin Keeney in 1894.

THE BIRTH OF A CLASSIC

Unlike the classic dishes of most cultures, much of the American culinary canon was born of the Industrial Revolution, when American pantries were flooded with new possibilities made possible by a cavalcade of processed foods in cans, boxes, tins, jars, bottles, and envelopes.

One of the companies that sprang up during this time was a collaboration between an icebox manufacturer, Abraham Anderson, and a fruit merchant named Joseph Campbell. The Thomas Campbell Preserve Company sold canned tomatoes, vegetable soups, minced meats, things like that. In 1897, a chemist named Dr. John T. Dorrance joined the company and figured out a way to remove much of the water from soup, which meant a thirty-two-ounce can of soup could basically fit in a ten-ounce can. Such "condensed" soups became so popular that the company eventually amended its name to "Campbell's Soup." Like so many manufacturers of the period, Campbell's got into a new thing called "marketing," which meant finding ways to make American cooks dependent upon products that didn't exist just a few short years ago. One way to do this was to flood the press with recipes constructed upon the new foods. Of all the dishes born in this age, none reached greater popularity than the green bean casserole, concocted in 1955 by Campbell's kitchen head Dorcas Reilly. The recipe, which originally called for four cups of cooked, cut green beans, one can of cream of mushroom soup, some milk, some soy sauce, a dash of pepper, and canned French-fried onions, landed Reilly a spot in the Inventors Hall of Fame in 2002.

KINDA BLUE

EPISODE 182 | SEASON 11 | GOOD EATS

TRIVIA | Yes, this is a reference to the 1959 Miles Davis release, which is one of the top three jazz albums of all time.

George Carlin famously posed a query regarding the whereabouts of "the blue food." Had George picked summer blueberries in South Carolina, he'd have been able to answer his own question because those little orbs of goodness are as blue as blue gets. Or he could have just given me a call, because blueberries have been my favorite from way back. When they're in season, which is the only time I buy them, I go through a pint a day, easy. Not only are blueberries great for out-of-hand eating (I like them in cottage cheese), but their size, shape, color, and flavor also make them highly versatile and, yes . . . good eats.

TIDBIT | Native Americans called the blueberry "star-berry" due to its ruffled, five-pointed calyx.

HOMEMADE TIME MACHINE—REALLY WORKS!

The key to *Vaccinium cyanococcus* happiness is to buy locally grown product, and only during summer months. If possible, pick them yourself. Due to the relative ease of harvest, and human-size bushes, you-pick blueberry farms dot much of the countryside, at least here in the eastern United States. Regardless of whether you're picking from a patch or a produce department, always look for firm, dry, wrinkle-free specimens. Although size isn't a strong indicator of flavor, color is. Always reach for deep indigo blues coated with a light, silvery frost. The frost, which also appears on grapes and plums, is called "fruit bloom," and it serves as a natural waterproofing.

Most of the nation's blueberries hail from California, Michigan, the Carolinas, Oregon, Florida, and of course Maine, where the modern blue was invented. That's right: invented. And for that we have two people to thank.

A USDA science type by the name of Frederick Coville was researching wild blueberries. Lizzy White, who was a cranberry farmer in New Jersey, heard about Coville and contacted him with an offer that included agreeing to supply all the pickers he needed to go out in the woods and find the best and the biggest blueberries the wild had to offer. Coville took these blueberries and used them to develop a "high bush" blueberry plant that grew large berries and was easy to harvest. The first crop was picked in 1916, and the entire U.S. blueberry industry was born out of it.

Due to their size, shape, texture, and sugar content, blueberries take very well to freezing. The trick is to freeze them as quickly as possible so that the internal ice crystals that form will be small. Smaller crystals do less cellular damage, and that will result in less weepage upon thawing.[1] Simply arrange the berries in a single layer on a metal sheet pan and put them in the freezer. The metal, of course, is a conductor. It will help to move heat out of the blueberries and freeze them as quickly as possible. Once they are hard as a rock, you can move them into the storage vessel of your choice. I typically go with zip-top freezer bags, which are also easy to label.

Besides being low in calories and high in vitamin C and fiber, blueberries are considered a "super food," mostly because of their anthocyanins. Those are the pigments that give blues their hue. They also provide chart-topping antioxidant power. Antioxidants are the free radical–chomping substances that play a major role in guarding the body against a host of degenerative diseases and disorders.

Due to their intense color, flavor, and sugar level when ripe, blueberries are my favorite fruit for baking and when it comes to baking you just can't beat a buckle. If you look "buckle" up in a decent dictionary, right after the bit about the thing at the end of a belt you'll see the verb form: "to bend, warp, bulge, or collapse." Read on and you may find: "an early American form of coffee cake, usually baked with fresh fruit." Although I'm a big cobbler fan, Americans should seriously rediscover the art of the buckle.

[1] Of course, if you plan on baking with them, weeping may be what you want.

BLUEBERRY BUCKLE

1 (9-INCH) CAKE

// SOFTWARE ///

FOR THE TOPPING

3½	ounces	sugar	
1½	ounces	cake flour	
½	teaspoon	nutmeg	freshly grated
4	tablespoons	unsalted butter	cubed and chilled

FOR THE CAKE

9	ounces	cake flour	
1	teaspoon	baking powder	
½	teaspoon	kosher salt	
½	teaspoon	ground ginger	
4	tablespoons	unsalted butter	at room temperature
5¼	ounces	sugar	
1	large	egg	
½	cup	whole milk	
15	ounces	fresh blueberries	

// PROCEDURE //

MAKE THE TOPPING:

1. Combine the sugar, flour, and nutmeg in a **small bowl**. Add the butter and work into the dry ingredients, using a **fork** to combine. Continue until the mixture has a crumblike texture. Set aside.

MAKE THE CAKE:

2. Heat the oven to 375°F. Spray a **9-inch square glass baking dish** with **nonstick cooking spray** and set aside.

3. **Whisk** together the flour, baking powder, salt, and ginger in a **medium bowl**. Set aside.

4. Beat together the butter and sugar in a **stand mixer fitted with the paddle attachment** on medium speed until light and fluffy, approximately 1 minute. Add the egg and beat until well incorporated, approximately 30 seconds. Add one-third of the flour mixture and beat on low speed just until incorporated, then add one-third of the milk and beat until incorporated. Repeat, alternating flour and milk, until everything is combined. Gently stir in the blueberries and pour the mixture into the prepared baking dish.

5. Sprinkle the topping mixture over the cake. Bake on the middle rack of the oven for 35 minutes, or until golden. Cool for at least 10 minutes before serving.

TIDBIT   The first buckle recipe on record is from Elsie Masterton's 1959 *Blueberry Hill Cookbook.*

BLUEBERRY SODA

ABOUT 3 CUPS BLUEBERRY SYRUP,
ENOUGH FOR 12 GLASSES

Having given up commercial soda a while back, I've gotten into making my own. One of my favorites is Blueberry Soda, which I can make year round thanks to the fact that I freeze up bushels of blueberries when they're in season.

// SOFTWARE ///

20	ounces	fresh blueberries	rinsed and drained
2	cups	H_2O	
7	ounces	sugar	
1		lime	juiced
		carbonated H_2O	

// PROCEDURE ///

(1) Bring the blueberries and water to a boil in a **medium saucepan** over medium-high heat. Reduce the heat to low and simmer for 15 minutes.

(2) Remove from the heat and pour the mixture into a **colander** lined with **cheesecloth** that is set in a **large bowl**. Cool for 15 minutes. Gather up the edges of the cheesecloth and squeeze out as much of the liquid as possible. Discard the skin and pulp.

(3) Return the blueberry juice to the saucepan along with the sugar and lime juice. Cook over medium-high heat, stirring until the sugar is dissolved. Bring to a boil and cook for 2 minutes. Remove from the heat, transfer to a **heatproof glass container**, and place in the refrigerator, uncovered, until completely cooled.

TO SERVE:

(4) Combine ¼ cup of the blueberry syrup with 8 ounces of carbonated water and pour over ice.

Our food culture is full of delicacies that, for one reason or another, have fallen from the apex of gourmet delicacy to the nadir of poly-bad pabulum. Take, for instance, marshmallows. It's hard to believe that these factory-formed, gluey gobs, destined for flaming twigs, were originally handmade masterworks formed one at a time in the finest confectionery shops of Paris. Those marshmallows, or *pâte de guimauve*, possessed subtle flavors, beautiful textures, and heady perfumes. But no more. Years of mediocrity have deadened our palates and hardened our hearts to this magnificent manifestation. It's time for all true marshmallow lovers to rise up and take back the candy that, perhaps more than any other, qualifies as . . .

THE MARSH MALLOW*

Mini marshmallows grow from top sprouts

Full-size marshmallows ripen on lower branches

GATORS LOVE THEM!

Marshmallow fluff extracted from roots

* UM . . . NOT REALLY

A few botanical notes: We've become so separated from our traditional foodways that folks don't even remember that once upon a time, marshmallows grew on bushes. Okay, you couldn't actually pick them, but if it weren't for a plant called the "marsh mallow," there would be no marshmallows.

The marsh mallow (*Althaea officinalis*) is native to most of Europe, where it grows in salt marshes and other moist places—drainage ditches, flooded fields, and the like. The stems grow to between three and four feet in height, and the leaves are broad and about three inches long. The leaves die back in fall, signaling that the root is ripe with a form of mucilage (the slimy stuff in okra), which possesses anti-inflammatory properties. In his classic fifteenth-century cooking treatise, *De Honesta Voluptate et Valetudine* ("On Right Pleasure and Good Health"), Bartomomio Platina devotes an entire chapter to the mallow and its usual applications, most of which are medicinal—curing sore throats and urinary-tract infections, for example. Confectioners in France eventually learned how to cook down the goop and sweeten it into a formable candy that in truth most of us wouldn't recognize today as a marshmallow. That's because marshmallows don't contain marsh mallow anymore and haven't for well over a century. Instead, we use gum arabic. Although this processed extract of the acacia tree has been used to stabilize commercial marshmallows for close to a hundred years, gum arabic isn't very easy for the home cook to find. However, gelatin, a protein derived from connective tissue of cows and pigs, is, and it can do the job just fine.

In order to thicken a liquid, gelatin must dissolve into it. Dissolving requires the target liquid to be quite hot, almost boiling, but dry gelatin (which comes in both powder and sheet form) won't dissolve, even in hot liquid, unless it is soaked in a cold liquid first—a process we call "blooming." In most applications a small amount of water is used, but in many cases a small amount of whatever liquid is being thickened can be used.

Whether you're making nougats, lollipops, taffy, toffee, fudge, caramel sauce, or marshmallows, candy making is, by and large, all about controlling the concentration of sugar in syrups—that is, how much sucrose (and sometimes just glucose and fructose) is dissolved in a liquid like water. Before reliable thermometers became commonplace, generations of experimentation rendered a semi-reliable guide, called the "ball" system, which took advantage of the fact that a small amount of hot syrup, when dropped into cold water, will act in a particular way. Less concentrated syrups make threads of various textures, more concentrated versions form balls, and eventually the sugar just burns and won't make anything at all other than a mess. Luckily, we don't have to learn these stages because someone figured it all out in plain, good old-fashioned Fahrenheit degrees. And now we have very reliable thermometers. Hurray.

Water boils at 212°F at sea level. But as the water boils out of a solution, that solution becomes more concentrated and the boiling point goes up. So for marshmallows, all we have to do is boil our sugar solution until enough water leaves the pan for the remaining solution to hit 240°F. That's a snap, as long as you're in possession of a candy thermometer like this.

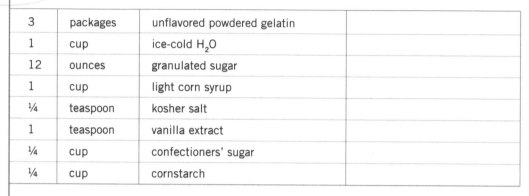

HOMEMADE MARSHMALLOWS

9 DOZEN MARSHMALLOWS OR
1½ POUNDS MINIATURE MARSHMALLOWS

// **SOFTWARE** //

3	packages	unflavored powdered gelatin	
1	cup	ice-cold H_2O	
12	ounces	granulated sugar	
1	cup	light corn syrup	
¼	teaspoon	kosher salt	
1	teaspoon	vanilla extract	
¼	cup	confectioners' sugar	
¼	cup	cornstarch	

// **PROCEDURE** //

1. Combine the gelatin with ½ cup of the cold water in the bowl of a **stand mixer**. Have the **whisk attachment** standing by.

2. Combine the remaining ½ cup water, the granulated sugar, corn syrup, and salt in a **2-quart saucepan**. Place over medium-high heat, cover, and cook for 3 to 4 minutes. Uncover, clip a **candy thermometer** onto the side of the pan, and continue to cook until the mixture reaches 240°F, 7 to 8 minutes. When the mixture reaches this temperature, immediately remove from the heat.

3. Turn the mixer fitted with the whisk attachment to low speed and, with the mixer running, slowly pour the sugar syrup down the side of the bowl into the gelatin mixture. Once you have added all of the syrup, increase the speed to high. Continue to whip until the mixture becomes very thick and is lukewarm, 12 to 15 minutes. Add the vanilla during the last minute of whipping. While the mixture is whipping, prepare the pans as follows.

FOR REGULAR MARSHMALLOWS:

4. Combine the confectioners' sugar and cornstarch in a **small bowl**. Lightly spray a **9-by-13-inch metal baking pan** with **nonstick cooking spray**. Add the sugar and cornstarch mixture and move around to completely coat the bottom and sides of the pan. Return the remaining mixture to the bowl for later use.

5. When ready, pour the marshmallow mixture into the prepared pan, using a **lightly oiled spatula** to spread it evenly. Dust the top with enough of the remaining sugar and cornstarch mixture to lightly cover. Reserve the rest for later. Set aside, uncovered, for at least 4 hours and up to overnight.

TIP | Build s'mores with Graham Crackers, page 177.

Starch

High Fructose Corn Syrup

6   Turn the marshmallows out onto a **cutting board** and cut into 1-inch squares using a **pizza wheel** dusted with the sugar and cornstarch mixture. Once cut, lightly dust all sides of each marshmallow with the remaining mixture, using additional if necessary. Store in an **airtight container** for up to 3 weeks.

FOR MINIATURE MARSHMALLOWS:

4   Combine the confectioners' sugar and cornstarch in a **small bowl**. Line **4 half sheet pans** with **parchment paper**, spray the paper with **nonstick cooking spray**, and dust with the sugar and cornstarch mixture.

5   When ready, scoop the marshmallow mixture into a **piping bag** fitted with a **½-inch round tip**. Pipe the mixture onto the prepared sheet pans lengthwise, leaving about 1 inch between the strips. Sprinkle the tops with enough of the remaining cornstarch and sugar mixture to lightly cover. Set aside, uncovered, for at least 4 hours, or up to overnight.

6   Cut into ½-inch pieces using a **pizza wheel or scissors** dusted with the sugar and cornstarch mixture. Once cut, lightly dust all sides of each marshmallow with the remaining mixture. Store in an **airtight container** for up to 1 week.

WHY CORN SYRUP?

Corn syrup is the candy maker's friend because it can prevent sucrose molecules from growing together to form big, crunchy crystals, which is what they want to do, especially in a pot that is slowly having all of its water cooked out of it. Corn syrup prevents this because it's not sucrose and can't grow crystals with it, even though it's technically made from the same stuff as sugar. How is that? Well, it all starts with corn.

Of course, no matter how delicious it is, sweet corn really isn't that sweet, because it doesn't contain that much sugar. What it contains is a lot of starch, which the human tongue simply cannot recognize. However, if we add a little acid, and perhaps a bit of heat, we can change the starch molecule into little glucoses molecules. Problem is, glucose isn't sensed as being very sweet. But if we bring a few enzymes to the party, some of the glucose will be converted to the much sweeter fructose. By dissolving the whole thing into a solution, you produce high-fructose corn syrup—which is very sweet indeed.

ANOTHER LAME MODEL, BUT A CHANCE TO LET MY DAUGHTER FLY.

THE COLONEL COOKS AGAIN!

Of course, once you've got marshmallowin' down, you'll want to spread your fluff and fly. You can use the unset fluff for fluffinutter sandwiches, you can get a bunny mold and make your version of the Easter fave, and, need I say it: s'mores. (I make mine with gorgonzola cheese between the chocolate and marshmallow: very nice, especially with a cold glass of muscat.) But if you're a Southerner, sooner or later your mind will turn to ambrosia.

Now, typically we use a very straightforward format for show applications, but since this one was worked out by Col. Boatwright, I think I'll let him tell it in his own words.

SIPPIN' ON NECTAH ALL THE LIVELONG DAY

Colonel Bob Boatwright (as Zeus): Now, everybody knows that Zeus and his cronies up on old Mount Olympus rollicked about all the livelong day, sipping on nectar and snacking on a succulent sustenance called "ambrosia." Problem is, none of the citizens of this fair and lofty land bothered to write down the recipe. So about a hundred years ago, we Southerners decided to suss it out our own selves.

// SOFTWARE

½	cup	heavy cream	
1	tablespoon	sugar	
4	ounces	sour cream	
1	cup	clementine orange segments	about 6 clementines
1	cup	chopped fresh pineapple	
1	cup	freshly grated coconut (see page 57)	
1	cup	pecans	toasted and chopped
½	cup	maraschino cherries	drained
6	ounces	Homemade Miniature Marshmallows (page 102)	

// PROCEDURE

1. Put that heavy cream in your **mixing bowl** and stick that old **whisk**-y thing on there. Slowly add the sugar. Whip that up until it looks just like a big old white fluffy cloud.

2. We're going to add the sour cream. Now, you know that no matter what this turns out to be, it's going to be some kind of delicious. So I'm going to just **stir** that on in there.

3. We're going to stir in some bits and pieces, starting with the clementine segments. Now, this here's a yuletide dish, you know, and that time of year, well, these little jewels, they just jump right up in the old grocery cart. They do. I'm serious. All right, we'll follow that up with chopped pineapple. Now, you know fresh is best, don't you? Sure you do. Same could be said of this shredded coconut. I recall the first one of these I ever did see when I was a boy. Thought my daddy dug up a Yankee cannonball when he brought that in the house. Now, I know what y'all are thinking. You want to buy the kind that comes in a bag. But you ain't gonna do it! Nope, you ain't gonna! Next, let's see here, a cup of chopped pecans—"pee-cans," "pee-cahns," I don't care how you say it—and half a cup of maraschino cherries. Have you ever seen anything so red? I suspect you have not.

4. Now for the pièce de résistance. We're going to put in three cups of homemade miniature marshmallows. Goodness me! Now, just stir that up and come on over to the icebox. Whoo, a couple of hours of chilling and this humble collection of goods has become food for the gods. Now, I know it's going to be hard, your waiting. But your patience will be rewarded, I reckon.

AMERICAN SLICER

EPISODE 184 | SEASON 11 | GOOD EATS

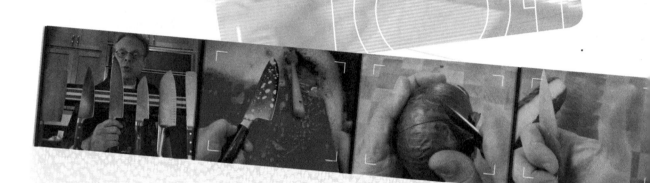

Many cooks have a favorite pan, or spoon, or whisk they really dig. But no kitchen relationship is more mystical than the one between cook and knife. Ironically, no kitchen tool is more misunderstood. With that in mind, I hope you'll read on, as this episode was (and is) intended to elevate your cutlery consciousness, to help you and your blades turn out some really . . .

TIDBIT Knives made from flint were busy slicing and dicing as early as 3000 B.C.

KNIFE ANATOMY

Point
Tip
Spine
Belly
Heel
Bolster
Return
Handle

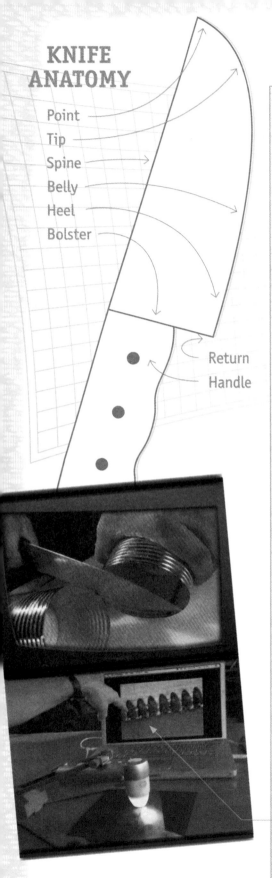

Before we get all cut-happy, let's review a little knife anatomy. We'll begin with the blade. The back is called the "spine." The point, oddly enough, is the "point." The first third of the edge back from the point is the "tip." Then you have the "belly" and, finally, the "heel." The blade then turns up toward the "handle" at the "return," into the "bolster." There may or may not be a finger guard located here.

In quality European-style knives, the blade metal continues to the end of the knife in what is called a "full tang." Most Asian-style knives have a hidden tang, which can either be long and narrow or short and stubby. No matter the style, size, or shape of the knife, these parts will be present in one form or another.

Notice that the blade tapers from the spine to the edge, and that there's a transition to another angle—a secondary belly—and the narrower that angle, the better the cut. Of course, to get this kind of angle requires the right kind of steel. And to understand steel, you've got to understand . . . baked goods. A baker can produce a chewy or crunchy crust, a firm or soft crumb, a dense or light texture, simply by varying the amounts of a relatively short list of ingredients: flour, sugar, eggs, butter, milk, baking powder, salt.

The metallurgist has a pantry too. We should review it, so that when the salespeople start throwing around big words you will be able to parry their every thrust. At its most basic, steel is iron and a little bit of carbon. Without carbon, iron is too soft to be of much use.

CHROMIUM hardens steel and, more important, adds some corrosion resistance.

MOLYBDENUM is a carbide former. When you hear the word *carbide*, think "grain": The more even and fine that grain is, the better the knife will be.

NICKEL adds toughness. Think of toughness as a kind of elasticity, allowing the edge to snap back into place if it gets smacked around. Hard metals, brittle metals, can crack, and that's not a good thing.

TUNGSTEN. This is important. Wear resistance.

VANADIUM refines the grain.

SILICON adds strength.

MANGANESE . . . Well, you get the picture.

By mixing these ingredients, you can create thousands of different steels, or alloys. Knife makers match the alloy they use to the characteristics they want their knives to have.

We've all seen the ads and infomercials for knives (we'll call them Kutzus) that can cut through tin cans to the tune of $29.99. Why would you spend a hundred dollars or more on one blade when you can clearly have an entire set of viciously sharp Kutzus for the price of a pizza dinner? I'll show you.

Let's take a look at that Kutzu edge. It is, essentially, a hacksaw. The steel is so lousy that even if it could take a real edge, which it can't, it wouldn't be able to keep it for long. So once the serrations are gone, this tool will become useless. Not that it's worth that much to begin with. Of course, if you ever need to hack a shoe in half, you'll know what to reach for.

Ladies and gentlemen, a knife is only as good as the surface upon which it glides. So let us turn our attention, for a moment, to the cutting board. There are two main issues to be considered here. First, the material. Although they are pretty, the following materials *are evil*, and your blades should never come in contact with them, ever. Let us review.

Marble? Evil. Granite? Evil. Composite countertops? Evil. Metal? Evil. Glass? Dark-Lord-of-the-Sith evil.

Where does this leave us? With three good choices, that's where:

WOOD COMPOSITE boards are nice because wood is a renewable resource, and composites can be molded and shaped into a multiplicity of configurations. Composite boards resist warping and they're not porous like standard wooden boards.

HIGH-DENSITY POLYETHYLENE boards are especially useful for raw meats. They can go into the dishwasher, and even once they're old and gouged and scratched you can still use them around the house for utility cutting and whatnot.

Most of my slicing and dicing, chiffonading, julienne-ing, brunoise-ing, and so on is done on ROCK MAPLE. Boards come either crosscut (with the grain) or endcut (across the grain), either of which cuts fast and clean. Rock maple tends to be heavy and expensive, but it remains the best cutting surface I know.

While we're at it, we should make mention of bamboo boards, which have become quite popular over the last few years. Bamboo is a grass, so it's highly renewable. But since it's a grass it's very "fibery" (yes, I know that's not a word) and it tends to grab the knife's edge a bit, slowing down the action. Bamboo boards can also split and warp, so if you buy one go for a model that's relatively heavy and thick.

One more board issue: size. This one is simple. Take your largest knife and lay it on the board diagonally, corner to corner. There needs to be at least two inches of board sticking out on either end. If there isn't, your board is too small for the knife.

The intersection where knife and cook become one is called the "grip," and which one you choose matters. A lot of folks prefer what I call the "Excalibur," which is wonderful if you're trying to hack your way through opposing forces in battle, but not so good when you're trying to mow through an onion.

Then we have what I call the "Accuser," because it's always pointing a finger at someone. And although it gives you a bit of tip control, stability is a joke. Only use this if you can easily reach your insurance card with the other hand, if you get my drift.

My grip of choice I call the "Pinch." Simply pinch the spine between your thumb and forefinger, in front of the bolster. Not only does this give you accuracy and control, but by moving the pivot point ahead of the bolster, you increase the power transfer from arm to blade.

When handling a paring knife, I like to use what's called the "Choke" grip, positioning the knife so that the blade is partly in your hand. That puts it in a good position to use the thumb to feed the food into the blade. But more on that later.

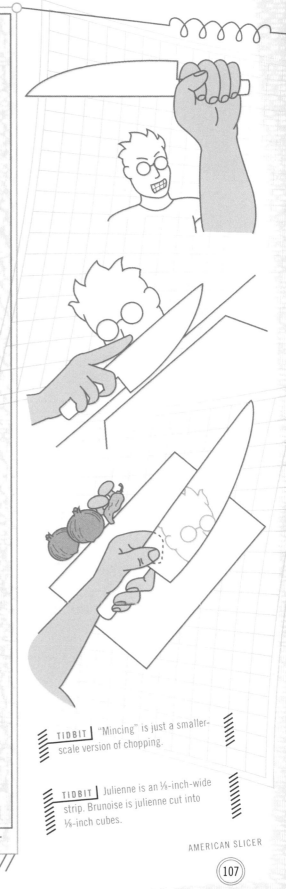

TIDBIT | "Mincing" is just a smaller-scale version of chopping.

TIDBIT | Julienne is an ⅛-inch-wide strip. Brunoise is julienne cut into ⅛-inch cubes.

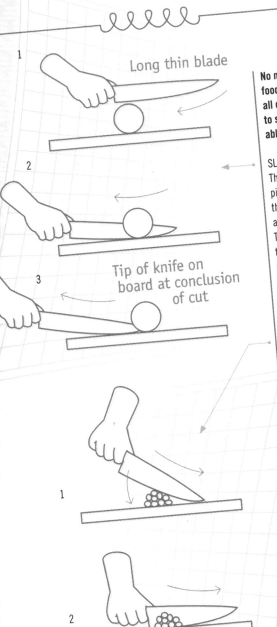

1

Long thin blade

2

3

Tip of knife on board at conclusion of cut

1

2

When chopping, the cutting motion is forward and down. The only time a straight down cut is useful is when chopping herbs or nuts. In this case, the opposing hand should be placed on the back of the spine.

No matter what shape you hope to whittle your food down to, you're going to have to use one or all of the primary cuts. That means you are going to slice, you are going to chop, and you're probably going to pare. Let's start at the top.

SLICE: To cut with a long pulling stroke. That's it. The fact that such a motion may very well produce a piece of food known as a slice is completely beside the point. Knives that call themselves "slicers" are typically long (at least ten inches) and thin. This helps to minimize back-and-forth sawing motions that can make a mess of things. The goal is a single pulling cut that begins with the heel of the blade against the food and concludes with the tip on the board. It matters not if you're cutting roast beef or rhubarb, the slicing motion is always the same.

CHOP: What a terrible word for a precision cutting operation. After all, it's the same word we use for the felling of a tree via axe. I don't like it, I tell you, but until we come up with a better verb, we're pretty much stuck with it. My definition of "chop" is a forward cutting motion in which the entire length of the blade comes in contact with the board. But the real secret here is not to think "chop," but to think "choo-choo". . .

. . ."choo-choo train," that is. Ever noticed how the side rod of an old locomotive moves, up and down and forward and back in an orbital pattern? That's exactly what you want your knife to be doing during the chopping process, and the tip of the blade should never, ever leave the board. Handled thusly, the chopping knife becomes a second-class lever. And everyone knows that a lever magnifies force, so that the chopper (that's you) can get more work done with less effort.

Notice that the hand holding the knife drives it rhythmically, but the blade itself is actually being guided by the front of the fingers on the other hand. In this configuration, with a wide knife like a chef's knife, it's very difficult to actually cut yourself, as long as the food you're cutting isn't too tall and you keep your fingertips (on the hand holding the food) folded back.

Although this is especially useful for breaking down multiple long items, like green onions or celery, chopping is also handy for herbs. Take basil, for instance. Pick yourself about a dozen leaves and then just stack them up with the largest leaf on the bottom. Roll the bundle up, place on the board seam side down, then just gently mow through the roll, using that smooth choo-choo-train motion. The French call the strips this forms a *chiffonade*, and it's a very useful technique for cutting herbs without bruising the leaves.

PARE: To trim down or reduce something in size. In practical application, it is distinct from the other cutting methods, because the cutting happens up off the board and the knife is always facing the cutter.

Back in the days before vegetable peelers, peeling was done with a paring knife. I realize that putting one of your digits right up against a blade is not a natural instinct. But this seemingly dangerous dance is an integral part of paring. The crucial detail here is that the knife and the thumb are connected to the same hand, so slicing your own thumb becomes a lot less likely (oddly enough). And if you keep your knife sharp, minimum force will be required. Remember: When you start having to force dull knives around, bad things happen.

The best part about sharpening your knife skills is that you get to eat the result. Salsa is an excellent dish for this, and if you take it a little further you'll have a fine gazpacho, an Andalusian classic that began as a simple soup of bread, oil, and garlic. Today, it's a liquid salad, and that's okay by me.

SLICER CAM

// SOFTWARE

1½	pounds	vine-ripened tomatoes	
		tomato juice	
1	cup	cucumber	peeled, seeded, and chopped
½	cup	red bell pepper	chopped
½	cup	red onion	chopped
1	small	jalapeño	seeded and minced
1	clove	garlic	
¼	cup	extra virgin olive oil	
1		lime	juiced
2	teaspoons	balsamic vinegar	
2	teaspoons	Worcestershire sauce	
1	teaspoon	kosher salt	
½	teaspoon	cumin	toasted and ground
¼	teaspoon	black pepper	freshly ground
2	tablespoons	fresh basil	cut into chiffonade

// PROCEDURE

1. Fill a **6-quart pot** halfway full of water, set over high heat, and bring to a boil.

2. Make an X with a **paring knife** on the bottom of each tomato. Drop the tomatoes into the boiling water for 15 seconds, remove, and transfer to an ice-water bath until cool enough to handle, approximately 1 minute. Remove and pat dry. Peel and halve the tomatoes. Seed the tomatoes, putting the seeds and juice in a **fine-mesh strainer** set over a **bowl or measuring cup** to catch the juice. Press as much of the juice through as possible, then add enough bottled tomato juice to bring the total to 1 cup. Chop the tomato flesh.

3. Combine the tomatoes and juice in a **large bowl**. Add the cucumber, bell pepper, onion, jalapeño, garlic, oil, lime juice, vinegar, Worcestershire sauce, salt, cumin, and black pepper and stir to combine.

4. Transfer 1½ cups of the mixture to a **blender** and puree for 15 to 20 seconds on high speed. Return the pureed mixture to the bowl and stir to combine. Cover and chill for 2 hours or up to overnight. Serve with the basil.

TIDBIT Never, ever, ever put fine cutlery in the dishwasher. The environment is too harsh for either the steel or the handles. And it's dangerous to have sharp stuff flopping around in there. Hand-wash your knives.

TRIVIA | Just in case you were wondering, yes, I did my own flying in this show but I did have a safety pilot with me. You can never be too careful about these things.

Most folks don't think of bars, pubs, or saloons as bastions of culinary creativity, but if you think about it, they are bastions of culinary comfort, and many an endearing and enduring dish has been introduced to a grateful world across a wide expanse of mahogany, tin, zinc, leather, teak, or oak. The nacho platter, loaded potato skins, stuffed mushrooms, and fried cheese sticks have all become classic bar grub, but none of these can touch the phenomenon that is "Buffalo" chicken wings, a.k.a. hot wings. The story of their creation is legend. It is said that in October 1964, one Theresa Bellissimo was getting ready to close her place, the Anchor Bar, on Main Street in Buffalo, New York, when her son and several of his college buddies dropped by. Feeding the boys on the fly became necessary, and necessity, as we all know, is the mother of invention, and what Mrs. Bellissimo is said to have invented that night is nothing short of . . .

I AM *SO NOT PUTTING* MY HAND IN THAT BOX.

THE MOTHER OF ALL CHICKENS

Pictured here is a Red Jungle fowl from Southeast Asia, the ancestor of all chickens. The Red is a ground-dwelling bird capable of flying only short distances to evade predators. They can also fly up into trees to roost. This bird is about as close to a direct link to the dinosaurs as we've got. Of course, through the ages the Red evolved and mutated, allowing for a considerable amount of genetic variety. The chicken most of us buy at the megamart is the broiler chicken, named for the way it's best cooked.

Wings are amazing structures. The ones on my airplane create lift by taking advantage of Bernoulli's principle, which states that fluids, including air, undergo a reduction of pressure as velocity increases. Since air moves over the top of the wings faster than under them, we can fly. These wings must be strong enough to handle the load of the plane, g-forces, turbulence, and whatnot, but they luckily do not have to provide propulsion. Birds' wings do, and that requires an extremely sophisticated system of joints, muscles, and ligaments, which can be tasty, yet troublesome for the cook.

A long history of laziness has devolved the chicken wing into a relatively simple structure characterized by three segments and two hinges.

Here is where the wing was cut away from the shoulder at the plant. That's the scapula bone up there. This first section is called the drumette, because of its resemblance to the drumstick. It houses the humorous bone (and no, I'm not joking). The second section, or wing flat, contains the ulna and the radius. The wing tip, or nubbin, is a wasteland, meat-wise, but can still bring flavor and body to a stock or soup.

Since there is such a high demand for breast meat in this country, wings are still relatively cheap. I would never consider cooking wings without cooking a mess of wings, so I typically purchase prewrapped party packs. Sure, you could just cut the wings off of every chicken you cook for the next year and freeze them until you have your own prewrapped party pack, but that's a little bit extreme even for me.

Being bar food, most Buffalo-style wings are deep-fried, because deep-frying is fast and tasty, and most bars that serve food have commercial fryers. I would argue, however, that deep-frying is not the best way to cook Buffalo chicken wings because they already contain enough fat to fry themselves. But that in and of itself poses a problem, because if we roast the wings in the oven at a temperature sufficient to crisp the skin, we will produce a cloud of acrid, tear-inducing smoke that will stink up the house for days. Nope, before they roast we've got to get some of that fat out, and the best way to do that (think back to our duck episode in volume 1) is steam.

I'm a fan of metal folding steamer baskets, but they're typically low-occupancy devices and the last thing I want to do when cooking wings is work in batches. The answer: the steel lotus (patent pending). Odd though it may seem, the steel lotus is a stellar polytasker. I use mine for everything from wontons to steamed buns, various vegetation, fish pieces, shrimp, and just about anything else that needs steaming.

If my intel concerning that fateful night in 1964 is correct, the original Buffalo chicken wing sauce was nothing more than a mixture of bottled hot sauce and margarine, a butter substitute named for margaric acid, a saturated fat discovered in 1813 that doesn't occur in nature. Consisting of a blend of hydrogenated vegetable oils, emulsifiers, coloring agents, vitamins, and, in some versions, a big whopping dollop of trans-fats, which we all now know to be evil, margarine is not an ingredient I keep on hand. I use butter, of course.

CHICKEN WING 2
000000
20293-1
-437.60 mm
25 mA
MRI 4 IMAGING OF W
PICK
29 Nov 2007 2
120kV
8L
R

THE STEEL LOTUS:

1. 1 (1-inch) washer
2. 1 (10- to 12-inch-long) stainless steel threaded rod
3. 8 (5/16-inch) stainless steel hex nuts
4. 3 standard steamer baskets
Additional hardware: pliers

To assemble the steel lotus, remove the handles from all three steamers by holding the nut under the steamer with the pliers and unscrewing the stem. Apply one nut to the end of the steel rod, using pliers if needed. Twist on one steamer basket, followed by another nut. Repeat with the other two steamers and nuts, spacing the baskets 3 to 4 inches apart. Use the remaining nuts to attach the washer to the top of the rod.

HOT SAUCE

Ten years ago, if you went to your local megamart for hot sauce, there were about three choices. There'd be some stuff from Texas, some stuff from Louisiana, and some stuff with chiles floating around inside of it. But today, there are dozens of different sauces readily available from all over the planet. How did this happen? Well, some say it's just a result of the influx of various ethnic cuisines into the mainstream, but there's another theory gaining momentum. This theory suggests that it's the Baby Boomers. You see, those of us born during the great postwar spawn between 1946 and 1964 are getting older, and as we move beyond forty, we lose taste buds at an accelerated rate. It may be that this influx of heat is nothing more than a market reaction to the fact that we require increased stimulation—and we're willing to pay for it. Then again, some anthropologists believe that the consumption of hot foods is closely tied to mating rituals.

// **SOFTWARE** ///

12	whole	chicken wings	
6	tablespoons	unsalted butter	
1	clove	garlic	
¼	cup	hot sauce	
½	teaspoon	kosher salt	

// **PROCEDURE** ///

1. Load a **6-quart saucepan** with a **steamer basket** and 1 inch of water in the bottom, place over high heat, cover, and bring to a boil.

2. Remove the tips of the wings and discard or save for making stock. Using **kitchen shears or a knife**, separate the wings at the joint. Put the wings in the steamer basket, cover, reduce the heat to medium, and steam for 10 minutes. Remove the wings from the basket and carefully pat dry. Lay the wings out on a **cooling rack** set in a **half sheet pan** lined with **paper towels** and refrigerate for 1 hour.

3. Heat the oven to 425°F.

4. Replace the paper towels (under the cooling rack) with **parchment paper**. Transfer the wings from the cooling rack to the pan and roast on the middle rack of the oven for 20 minutes. Turn the wings over and cook for another 20 minutes, or until the meat is cooked through and the skin is golden brown.

5. While the chicken is roasting, melt the butter in a **small bowl** along with the garlic. Pour this, along with the hot sauce and salt, into a **bowl large enough** to hold all of the chicken and stir to combine.

6. Remove the wings from the oven, transfer them to the bowl, and toss with the sauce. Serve warm.

NOTE: You're wondering where the celery and blue cheese dressing are. Well, they're in the refrigerator! I know there are those who would argue that the celery and dressing were put with the wings because Mrs. Bellissimo knew that the heat of the wings would need some cooling balance. I don't think it diminishes her genius one bit to suggest that it was probably a happy accident, but not one I'm inclined to perpetuate. When I want to get my wings on, I don't want to stop for a salad. That's a different show. Believe it or not, I like to eat these wings with cottage cheese: tasty, believe you me.

ORANGE-GLAZED CHICKEN WINGS

4 APPETIZER SERVINGS

I realize that the Buffalo-style hot-sauce-and-butter approach may not be for everyone, which is why I offer the following succulent variation.

ONE DAY, JUST MAYBE WE'LL BREED A CHICKEN WITH WINGS LIKE THIS.

// SOFTWARE //

12	whole	chicken wings
1	6-ounce can	frozen orange juice concentrate
3	tablespoons	hoisin sauce
1	tablespoon	soy sauce
2	teaspoons	honey
1	teaspoon	rice vinegar
½	teaspoon	red pepper flakes

// PROCEDURE //

1. Load a **6-quart saucepan** with a **steamer basket** and 1 inch of water in the bottom, place over high heat, cover, and bring to a boil.

2. Remove the tips of the wings and discard or save for making stock. Using **kitchen shears or a knife**, separate the wings at the joint. Put the wings in the steamer basket, cover, reduce the heat to medium, and steam for 10 minutes. Remove the wings from the basket and carefully pat dry. Lay the wings out on a **cooling rack** set in a **half sheet pan** lined with **paper towels** and refrigerate for 1 hour.

3. Heat the oven to 425°F.

4. Replace the paper towels (under the cooling rack) with **parchment paper**. Transfer the wings from the cooling rack to the pan and roast on the middle rack of the oven for 20 minutes. Turn the wings over and cook for another 20 minutes, or until the meat is cooked through and the skin is golden brown.[1]

5. During the last 20 minutes of cooking the chicken, combine the orange juice concentrate, hoisin sauce, honey, soy sauce, vinegar, and red pepper flakes in a **small saucepan** and bring to a simmer over medium-high heat. Cook until the mixture is reduced to about ½ cup, 5 to 10 minutes. Remove the glaze from the heat and cool for at least 5 minutes.

6. Remove the wings from the oven, transfer to a **large bowl** along with the glaze, and toss to coat. Serve warm.

[1] I know that forty minutes at 425°F seems extreme for items this small, but keep in mind, there was still a fair amount of fat left inside those little jewels and some tough connective tissue that needed to soften. As for the skin, it will be very crisp, which is perhaps the most important characteristic of the Buffalo wing. And again, the smoke? There's none, not a bit.

AMERICAN CLASSICS II: APPLE OF MY PIE

EPISODE 186 | SEASON 11 | GOOD EATS

I would argue that apple pie is more than our national dessert. It is, in fact, the edible embodiment of the American spirit. And yet, very few among us ever bother to make one, and that's a shame, because not only is it our duty, like voting, paying taxes, and trying to get out of jury duty—apple pie is absolutely good eats.

If you're a loyal fan of this program, you know perfectly well that we've dabbled about with apples in the past. Who among us can forget the bourbon-laced microwave applesauce from episode 17? And, on at least two occasions, piecrust has been the focus of our efforts. But in this case I feel that if we're to set things right with our national dessert we need to investigate both of these subjects anew, with the manufacture of an honest and true apple pie as our singular goal.

KNOWLEDGE CONCENTRATE

Constructing a good piecrust is a balancing act. On one side of the equation, we have the structural members, the strengtheners such as protein and starch, and water, which help those elements come together into a kind of, well, culinary concrete. On the other side of the equation, we have the weakeners, the tenderizers, such as fats—butter, lard, and shortening—and sugar. How we play one side of the equation against the other will determine the kind of crust we create. For something like a cream pie, we might prefer a more tender crust, but for apple pie, we require a bit more structure.

If apple pie is the most American of desserts, then applejack is the most American of alcoholic beverages. You can keep your French Calvados. This apple brandy distilled from a hard cider is what America drank before there was a bourbon industry. George Washington turned his apples into the stuff, and Abraham Lincoln served it at the tavern that he used to run in New Salem, Illinois. Although applejack used to run anywhere from 50 to a whopping 120 proof, these days it's kept to 70 percent alcohol by law, and it's aged in wood for at least one year, and yes, I'm putting it in the piecrust, and not just for flavor. That's because like all spirits, applejack contains ethyl alcohol, which won't combine with wheat proteins to make gluten the way that water does. So using a spirit in the crust will hydrate the flour without promoting toughness in the final pie.

Technically speaking, the only apple native to the Americas is the crabapple, a small, bitter distant relative of the fruit that now dominates grocery store produce aisles, which most botanical historians agree came to being in one of the 'stans, most likely Kazakhstan. So how is it, then, that the American landscape from Washington State to New York, Pennsylvania to Georgia, is so strewn with different types of apples? John Chapman, a.k.a. Johnny Appleseed, of course. Yes, he really did exist and he really planted an awful lot of apple trees around Ohio, Illinois, and Indiana. And yes, he really did wear a pot on his head. Anyway, the reason there are so many different types of apples around this great nation is that immigrants from the Old World came here with apple seeds in their pockets, and they planted those seeds, and each and every one of them created a different variety of apple. Apples are kind of like humans that way.

Unfortunately, there's no such thing (to my mind) as a perfect apple-pie apple, which is why I use several kinds of *pomme* in every pie I bake. If apples are grown locally where you live, I strongly suggest you seek out and try as many combinations of those apples as you realistically can. Otherwise, you may use this list, which I feel does as good a job as can be done with nationally available varieties. Here's what I go with:

For tang, the GRANNY SMITH

For sweetness, the HONEYCRISP

For its texture, the GOLDEN DELICIOUS

For being different, the BRAEBURN

You're going to need three and a half pounds of apples, evenly divided among these varieties, for one pie. If you're not going to make pie right away, store your apples in a plastic bag in the fridge. As long as you keep them cold, they'll stay fresh for weeks. Back in the days before refrigeration, apples would be placed in barrels and sunk in rivers or lakes for the winter, and in the spring they were fresh as daisies.

Now, about spices. Right up front, let me say that cinnamon, cloves, allspice, and nutmeg are all fine spices, but they've got absolutely nothing to do with apples. If you want your apple pie to taste like pumpkin pie, go ahead and add them; it's your food. Me, I'm keeping it clean with sugar, salt, and grains of paradise, freshly ground. You may remember *Aframomum melegueta* from our okra episode. It's also called alligator pepper, although it doesn't taste like pepper or alligators, now that I think about it. You can easily find this through Internet spice purveyors. If you don't want to bother, consider the traditional Scandinavian spice for apples, caraway, in the same amount.

Although we could use a wide variety of starches to successfully bind our pie, I prefer a flour ground from cassava called tapioca flour. I like it because it dissolves more easily than cornstarch, it doesn't gum up like flour, it gels at a wide range of temperatures, even in the freezer, and it gives everything it touches a nice sparkling shine.

THE MYSTERIOUS PIE BIRD

Check out your grandmother's tchotchke shelf, and I guarantee you will find at least a couple of pie birds, developed in England during the pie-crazed nineteenth century. The bird is basically a ceramic steam stack designed to vent a pie's internal pressure. The blackbird is standard, a play on "four and twenty blackbirds baked in a pie." If you can't find one in a kitchen store or online, you can make one out of aluminum foil, or you can do what I did and just, well, take one when your grandmother's asleep.

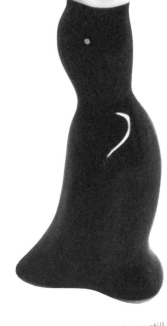

TIDBIT In England, pie birds are still considered major collectibles.

AMERICAN CLASSICS II

115

SUPER APPLE PIE

1 (9½- TO 10-INCH) PIE; 10 SERVINGS

// SOFTWARE

FOR THE CRUST

6	ounces	unsalted butter	cut into ½-inch pieces
2	ounces	vegetable shortening	cut into ½-inch pieces
5 to 7	tablespoons	applejack	
12	ounces	all-purpose flour	plus extra for dusting
1	teaspoon	table salt	
1	tablespoon	sugar	

FOR THE FILLING

3½	pounds	apples	about 6 large, a mixture of Granny Smith, Honeycrisp, Braeburn, and Golden Delicious
½	cup	sugar	
3	tablespoons	tapioca flour	
2	tablespoons	apple jelly	
1	tablespoon	apple cider	
2	teaspoons	lime juice	freshly squeezed
¼	teaspoon	kosher salt	
¼	teaspoon	grains of paradise	freshly ground

MOM

// PROCEDURE

MAKE THE CRUST:

(1) Refrigerate the butter, shortening, and applejack for 1 hour.

(2) In a **food processor**, combine the flour, salt, and sugar by pulsing 3 or 4 times. Add the butter and pulse 5 or 6 times, until the texture looks mealy. Add the shortening and pulse another 3 or 4 times, until incorporated.

(3) Remove the lid of the food processor and sprinkle in 5 tablespoons of the applejack. Replace the lid and pulse 5 times. Add more applejack as needed, and pulse again until the mixture holds together when squeezed. **Weigh** the dough and divide it in half. Shape each half into a disk, wrap in **plastic wrap**, and refrigerate for at least 1 hour and up to overnight.

MAKE THE FILLING:

4. Peel and core the apples. Slice into ½-inch-thick wedges. Toss all of the apples with ¼ cup of the sugar, place in a **colander** set over a **large bowl**, and drain for 1½ hours.

5. Transfer the drained liquid to a **small saucepan**, place over medium heat, and cook until it is reduced to 2 tablespoons. Set aside to cool. Toss the apples with the remaining sugar, the tapioca flour, jelly, cider, lime juice, salt, and grains of paradise.

6. Heat the oven to 425°F.

7. Remove one disk of dough from the refrigerator. Place the dough on a lightly floured piece of **waxed paper or parchment paper**. Lightly sprinkle the top of the dough with flour and **roll** out into a 12-inch circle. Place in a **9½- to 10-inch tart pan that is 2 inches deep**. Gently press the dough into the sides of the pan, crimping and trimming the edges as necessary. Set a **pie bird** in the center of the bottom of the pan.

8. Arrange the apples in the unbaked pie shell in concentric circles starting around the edges, working toward the center and forming a slight mound in the center of the pie. Pour any liquid that remains in the bowl over the apples.

9. Roll out the second disk of dough as the first. Place this dough over the apples, pressing the pie bird through the top crust. Press together the edges of the dough around the rim of the pie. **Brush** the top crust with the reduced juice everywhere except around the rim of the pie. Trim off any excess dough. Place the pie on a **half sheet pan** lined with **parchment paper** and bake on the floor of the oven for 30 minutes. Transfer to the lower rack of the oven and continue to bake for another 20 minutes, or until the apples are cooked through but not mushy. Remove to a rack and cool at least 4 hours, or until almost room temperature, before serving.

WHY SUGAR THE APPLES AHEAD OF TIME?

Let's say that this fabulous seaside abode is a slice of apple and that the lovely ladies inside are water molecules. Then, let's say we add sugar to the party. Being seriously hydroscopic, sugar's silent song calls to the aqua girls, eventually coaxing them out to mingle with him to form a sweet syrup that we will then drain away. If enough water vacates the premises, the apple will collapse. And that's a good thing, because if the apples don't collapse before they go into the pie, they will collapse during the baking process, and that could leave you with a phenomenon called the "pie dome," a big hollow crust with a little pile of apples in the bottom: not good eats.

AMAZING HOW USEFUL THRIFT-SHOP TOYS CAN BE.

1 - cut
2 - purge
3 - build
4 - top
5 - bake

TIDBIT | The world's largest apple pie, measuring eighteen feet in diameter and eighteen inches deep, was made at the 1982 Hilton Apple Fest.

PIE BIRD!

IF IT AIN'T BROCCOLI, DON'T FIX IT

Falsely accused of being bitter, limp, bland, and boring, the flowering body known as *Brassica oleracea*, a.k.a. broccoli, has garnered the ire of presidents and pubescents alike. I think part of the problem stems (ha) from the fact that broccoli entered this country rather late in the immigration game, at a time when the country's collective heart was hardening against newcomers. And without powerful PR to adjust the cant of culinary popular opinion, broccoli remains unjustly accused of . . . whatever. Truth is, broccoli is my favorite green vegetable (after collard greens) and is, therefore, automatically . . .

TIDBIT | A study in the *Journal of the Science of Food and Agriculture* found that microwaving broccoli reduced its antioxidant compounds by 74 to 97 percent.

KNOWLEDGE CONCENTRATE

▷ The word *broccoli* means "little arms" in Italian. It is that characteristic that makes it possible for you and me to separate broccoli from its kin, such as cauliflower, Brussels sprouts, kale, and regular old cabbage, which are all so closely related, genetically speaking, that they are little more than different sides of the same botanical coin.

▷ It is believed that broccoli was developed more than two thousand years ago, first by Etruscan gardeners and then by Romans, who became big broccoli fans. In fact, Drusus, the son of Tiberius, ate nothing but broccoli for a month until it changed his "water" green. Broccoli's big break in this country came when a couple of Italian brothers began growing it in California in the early twentieth century. Today, roughly 90 percent of the U.S. crop comes from the Golden State.

Most varieties of broccoli are flowering bodies, although there are some heading varieties, which are more closely related to cauliflower. Popular varieties include:

A CAULIFLOWER, ACTUALLY

Rapini (a.k.a. broccoli rabe), a bitter yet strangely delicious version closer to the turnip side of the family tree.

Broccolini, a hybrid cross between broccoli and Chinese kale.

Broccoli romanesco, which with its fractal arrangement of two-tone cones looks more mineral than vegetable.

When shopping for regular broccoli, look for buds that are firmly closed, florets that are tightly grouped, and a bright green color, no splotches anywhere. Also, check the base of the stem, which should be moist. If it's white and crusty some of the sugar has converted to lignin, a key ingredient in wood.

Due to its floral nature, broccoli has a tendency to spoil more quickly than other vegetables, but a few days in your chill chest's crisper drawer will do no harm. I don't even leave it in the bag, because bags can trap condensation, which can lead to accelerated decomposition of the flower buds that make up the crown.

Although I'm sure there's more than one way to trim a broccoli crown, I flip it upside down and use a paring knife to make quick diagonal cuts, which will give you a nice harvest of the florets. If the stalk (which is my favorite part) seems dry or tough, you can peel it before slicing or quartering and, of course, trimming the end if necessary.

Staying true to American culinary tradition, most home cooks boil broccoli to death, which hasn't done much to polish the great crown's reputation. Unlike cauliflower, which prefers a long cooking, broccoli responds best to quick application of high heat. Inside broccoli, nice bright green chlorophylls are kept separate from acidic elements by cell walls. If you overcook the broccoli, the cell walls collapse and the acids attack, turning our nice bright green chlorophylls into a sad, dingy gray. To add insult to injury, water-soluble vitamins and vito-chemicals rush out into the water, never to be returned. Even careful blanching tends to do more damage than good. Steaming, on the other hand, gives us more control, because although it's technically hotter than boiling water, steam is far less dense, and it can't wash nutrients away. Problem is that steaming still leaves us in the lurch when it comes to doneness, as the florets cook so much faster than the stalks. Since most of the nutrients are in the florets, I suggest a hybrid cooking method wherein we use the stalks to create a platform for the florets.

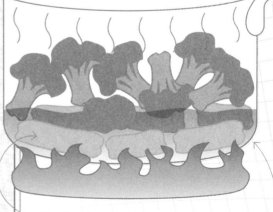

Stems simmer while crowns steam

Peeled broccoli stems

Salted H_2O

· PAN-STEAMED BROCCOLI

4 SERVINGS

MORE REASONS TO EAT YOUR BROCCOLI

Broccoli contains almost as much calcium as milk and delivers more vitamin C than an orange. It also contains vitamins K and A and is an excellent source of dietary fiber, folate, riboflavin, iron, potassium, manganese, and phosphorus. But wait, there's more! Some very special antioxidants are also on tap that can jump-start what's called phase-2 detoxification enzymes, which have the power to flush potentially harmful free radicals from your body, and that qualifies broccoli as a bona-fide super food.

FREE RADICALS!

// SOFTWARE

1 to 1½	pounds	broccoli with stalks	rinsed and trimmed
⅓	cup	H_2O	
	pinch	kosher salt	
2	tablespoons	unsalted butter	

// PROCEDURE

1. **Peel** the stalks of the broccoli. Remove the florets and cut them into 1-inch pieces. Cut the stalks in half crosswise and then slice each half into ⅛-inch-thick slices lengthwise.

2. Lay the stalk pieces in the bottom of a **2½- to 3-quart saucepan**. Add the water and salt. Lay the florets on top of the stalks.

3. Cover, place over high heat, and cook for 3 minutes. Decrease the heat to low and cook for an additional 3 minutes.

4. Remove from the heat, add the butter, and stir to combine. Serve immediately.

OVEN-ROASTED BROCCOLI

4 SERVINGS

// SOFTWARE //

1	pound	broccoli with stalks	rinsed and trimmed
2	tablespoons	olive oil	
2	cloves	garlic	minced
½	teaspoon	kosher salt	
¼	teaspoon	black pepper	freshly ground
⅓	cup	Japanese bread crumbs	a.k.a. panko
¼	cup	Parmesan or sharp Cheddar cheese	finely grated

// PROCEDURE //

1. Heat the oven to 425°F.

2. **Peel** the stalks of the broccoli. Remove the florets and cut them into bite-size pieces. Cut the stalks into ⅛-inch-thick round slices.

3. Toss the broccoli with the oil, garlic, salt, and pepper in a **large bowl** and set aside.

4. Spread the bread crumbs in a **9-by-13-inch metal pan** and bake for 2 minutes, or until lightly toasted.

5. Remove the bread crumbs from the oven and add to the bowl with the broccoli mixture. Toss to combine.

6. Return the mixture to the pan and roast just until the broccoli is tender, 8 to 10 minutes. Remove from the oven, toss in the cheese, and serve immediately.

DON'T BE BITTER

Broccoli and its kin contain compounds that are closely related to those in mustard gas, the original chemical weapon. Most of us with an average number of taste buds find this pleasant. However, about 25 percent of the U.S. population are considered "supertasters," people whose tongues house considerably more buds per square inch. Supertasters detect flavors more intensely than the rest of us and are often more sensitive to the bitter notes in broccoli. For such folks (and anyone else who complains about broccoli being bitter), I suggest roasting. Dry heat has the ability to trigger chemical changes that intensify the natural sugars in broccoli, which can balance any possible bitterness.

PEOPLE BEHIND THE PUPPETS!

NOT WHAT ACTUAL TASTE BUDS LOOK LIKE

IF IT AIN'T BROCCOLI, DON'T FIX IT

FRESH BROCCOLI SALAD

4 TO 6 SERVINGS

Wherever more than seven suburbanites are gathered, there's going to be a crudité platter featuring raw broccoli, which is not something that I, a devout broccoli lover, am ever going to eat. Sure, it's armed with a full complement of vitamins and minerals, but what good is that if you can't choke it down without a tablespoon of high-fat dressing? If you ask me, the best way to make raw broccoli palatable is to think "coleslaw."

// SOFTWARE ///

1	tablespoon	white wine vinegar	
1		lemon	zested
1	tablespoon	lemon juice	freshly squeezed
2	teaspoons	Dijon mustard	
1	teaspoon	kosher salt	
	pinch	black pepper	freshly ground
¼	cup	olive oil	
1	pound	broccoli with stalks	rinsed, trimmed, and thinly sliced on a mandoline
6	ounces	cherry or grape tomatoes	halved
3	ounces	pecans or hazelnuts	toasted and coarsely chopped
2	tablespoons	fresh basil	cut into chiffonade

// PROCEDURE //

1. **Whisk** together the vinegar, lemon zest, lemon juice, mustard, salt, and pepper in a **medium bowl**. While whisking constantly, gradually add the oil. Add the broccoli and toss to coat.

2. Cover and refrigerate for 1 hour.

3. Stir in the tomatoes, nuts, and basil. Cover and let the flavors mingle for another 15 minutes before serving.

TIDBIT | The first clear description of broccoli, or "Italian asparagus," occurred in the 1724 English gardener's dictionary.

TIDBIT | Thomas Jefferson is credited with bringing the first broccoli seeds to America from Italy (personally, I ain't buying it).

IF IT AIN'T BROCCOLI,
DON'T FIX IT

THE ALTON CROWN AFFAIR

EPISODE 188 | SEASON 11 | GOOD EATS

TRIVIA The episode title comes from *The Thomas Crown Affair*, of course, one of my personal favorites—both versions, in fact.

We usually keep things pretty simple on *Good Eats,* but every now and then we like to sup the meal fantastic, as it were, and I can't think of any meal more fantastical than a crown roast of lamb. Featuring not one but two sumptuous racks of *Ovis aries* folded into a sixteen-spire king hat, this is a dish to shock, awe, intimidate, and inspire. It's the kind of costly construct that instills fear in the hearts of cooks—but not you or me. We are undaunted, because we know that with some sound science, quality ingredients, and a few cunning contraptions, even a highbrow showstopper can become . . .

KITCHEN TWINE

Most chefs go with either a polyester or a poly-blend, but I don't care for it because it's floppy, which makes it hard to handle, and it tends to unravel. Cotton twine is much more user-friendly, but if you can find it, linen is even more so—and it stands up to higher levels of heat.

TIDBIT If knots aren't your thing, try leaning the racks together, interlocking the rib bones. This is called "guard of honor."

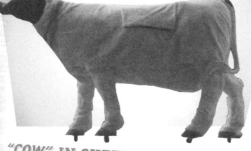

SO GLAD I PICKED UP THAT X-RAY MACHINE ON CRAIGSLIST.

"COW" IN SHEEP'S CLOTHING

KNOWLEDGE CONCENTRATE

▷○ **The sheep were probably the very first food animal to be domesticated some six thousand years ago in Persia. The fact that sheep, especially lambs (meaning any sheep under one year of age), were so important in religious sacrifices is a testimony to their value in human society. Once people figured out how to spin wool into yarn, that value greatly increased.**

The reason Americans still eat very little in the way of lamb (or the adult version, mutton) stems from a PR problem dating back to the Wool Act of 1699, when the English crown tried to control American wool producers by making it impossible for them to export any of their products. And the range wars in the late nineteenth and early twentieth century didn't help. There's nothing like being called "four-legged locusts" (cattleman slang) to ruin an animal's image.

▷○ **New Zealand lamb, which is range-raised on nice yummy grass, has become the lamb standard for the world, with Australian lamb a close second. Americans tend to prefer this meat because it is mild and tender. Personally, I prefer American lamb, not just because it isn't frozen and shipped from the other side of the planet, but because the lamb usually comes to market a little bit older, which translates to more flavor and bigger racks (stop giggling).**

Speaking of American lamb, the USDA inspects all lamb sold in retail stores, or oversees state inspection agencies with equal or higher standards. Grading of the meat is a voluntary process, paid for by the packer or processor; grades range from prime to choice, good, utility, and call, the last of which are used primarily for processed meats and pet food.

▷○ **Just like the rib roast on a steer, the lamb rack is a primal, or a major cut, located along the back between the shoulders and the loin, containing the rib-eye muscle and its ribs, numbers five through twelve. For this application, we will require two racks that are as closely matched as possible—cut from the very same animal would be best, if it's an option. (When both sides of the rack are connected by the backbone, the cut is referred to as a "hotel rack" and is tough to deal with unless you have a band saw handy.)**

TIDBIT | Unlike beef and pork, no culture or religion bans the consumption of lamb.

If you look at an X-ray of a rack, you'll see little bones sticking out on the ends. Those are the chine, and if they're not cut off, they can make carving the rack a little complicated. More on that later. If I'm just roasting or grilling a single rack, I prefer to leave the chine on because it gives the meat more structural support, but when it comes to building a crown roast, chine off is definitely the way to go.

Regardless of their final intended culinary destination, when dealing with whole racks of lamb they'll need to be frenched—that is, the narrow fingers of meat running up between the ribs will need to be trimmed out. It is not as hard as it looks, and with just a little bit of practice you'll be able to do it in three minutes per rack. Here's the recommended procedure.

1. Work your thumb into the connective tissue and peel it back. There is a good bit of meat left on the piece you're tossing, so you may want to wrap it up and refrigerate for later tinkering (stew?).

2. Next, remove the crescent of cartilage that attaches to the shoulder bone, as it has no culinary use whatsoever.

3. Flip the rack and make a sideways cut all the way across the rack about two and a half inches down from the ends of the ribs and carefully poke the blade of your boning knife all the way through in between each of the ribs.

4. Use the point of your knife to split the membrane on the backside of the ribs.

5. Continue your horizontal cut on the other side, then flip again.

6. Cut out the little fingers of meat in between the ribs. If you made your cuts right on both sides, this will be easy going. These are also pieces you might want to save for that stew we were talking about.

7. Next we need to clean up these ribs. I have a handle pole that I got at a hardware store and a loop of heavy cotton string, and I just put the loop over the bone, push it down to the end of the cut, twist a couple times, then pull all that nasty stuff right off the bones. (This is the actual frenching part.) Make sure you do this with the ribs curving upward so that the force of the pull won't be working against you.

Why is it imperative that you "rest" roasted red meats? A steak or any piece of meat is kind of like a kettle, and when you're cooking it you've got heat pushing on the tissues, forcing juice into the steak. If you were to poke into it or cut it at this point, the heat would just push the juices out onto the plate, and you'd be left with, well, a nasty little dried piece of meat sitting in a pool of juice, which isn't so nice. Resting the meat is like taking a kettle off the heat, although not as fast. You take it away from the heat and give the pressure time to recede, and the juices redistribute through the meat. What could have been a piece of leather is now a juicy steak.

THE FINAL PRODUCT!

THE ALTON CROWN AFFAIR

CROWN ROAST OF LAMB

6 TO 8 SERVINGS; 2 CHOPS PER PERSON

// SOFTWARE

2	1- to 1½-pound	racks of lamb	6 to 8 ribs each, frenched
1	tablespoon	olive oil	
1	teaspoon	kosher salt	
½	teaspoon	black pepper	freshly ground
6	cloves	garlic	minced
4	teaspoons	fresh thyme	chopped
1½	teaspoons	ground coriander	
1 to 1½	tablespoons	sherry vinegar	
½ to 1	teaspoon	Dijon mustard	
½ to 1	teaspoon	fresh rosemary	chopped
4	cups	cooked stuffing of your choice	see note, below

// PROCEDURE

1. Heat the oven to 375° F.

2. Bend each rack into a semicircle (meat side in, fat side out) and conjoin by tying together the ends with **kitchen twine**. The rib ends should be pushed outward to create the look of a crown.

3. Rub the lamb with the oil. Combine the salt, pepper, garlic, thyme, and coriander and press the mixture all over the lamb. Place the roast in a **Bundt pan** with the center of the pan coming up through the middle of the roast.

4. Roast on the middle rack of the oven for 30 to 35 minutes, until the meat reaches an internal temperature of 130°F,[1] 8 to 12 minutes per pound. Remove from the oven, transfer the roast to a **cooling rack**, cover with **aluminum foil**, and rest the meat for 20 minutes.

5. While the meat is resting, add the vinegar, mustard, and rosemary to the juices that accumulated in the pan while cooking. Stir to combine. Taste and adjust the seasoning as needed. Cut the string away from the roast and place cooked stuffing, rice, or barley in the center, if desired. Serve the warm sauce with the roast.

[1] The United States Department of Agriculture Food, Safety, and Inspection Service recommends that whole lamb cuts, such as loin, shoulders, legs, and racks, be cooked to a minimum internal temperature of 145°F to ensure that any possible food-borne pathogens have been eliminated. Those of you who do everything your government says, go ahead. Toast your roast. Me? I'm pullin' it at 130.

NOTE: Although I do believe it is a bad idea to cook a crown roast with stuffing inside, it is a good idea to bring it to the table with stuffing inside. I usually go with a simple rice pilaf, but you could also stuff this with roasted vegetables.

Cupcakes are supposed to make people happy, not only by giving them a few delicious bites but by transporting them back to childhood. But these days the *petit gateau* has gone all gourmet and people stand in line for hours just to lock lips with fussy, heavy, cloyingly clever, and all too often sickeningly sweet fistfuls of condescension. That said, today's upwardly mobile cupcakes do actually have snobbery in their shortening, seeing as how their ancestor is the queen cake, a small individual pound cake with fruit baked in paper cups and popular with upper-crusty eighteenth-century Brits. Heritage aside, I still say the cupcake should be of the people, by the people, and for the people. In other words . . .

I'VE TOLD LUCKY A DOZEN TIMES NOT TO STARE AT THE LIGHTS.

CUPS FOR YOUR CAKE

In many eighteenth-century kitchens, the use of cups for baking gave way to the iron gem pan, which was the precursor of the nonstick muffin tin we will employ in the following application. Of course, we could line the pan with paper cups. (A lot of people don't think it's a cupcake unless they get the Christmastime effect of unwrapping it.) You can use either paper or foil, but I will say this: The ones that come in the little tubes seem to fit better than the ones that come in the bags.

The pastry as we know it is strictly American fare, but that doesn't mean its history is simple to trace. For instance, in American baking, there is the "cupcake" and then the "cup cake." The cup cake evolved out of an almost complete lack of standard weights and measures in colonial America. When it came to volumetric measure, about all we really had was the Queen Ann gallon, which weighed ten pounds. Anything less and you were pretty much on your own. Seeking convenience and consistency, American bakers reached into their cupboards and found, ironically, a cup—a teacup, to be exact. Although it might not deliver the eight fluid ounces we're used to today, it was something that colonial housewives could relate to. The use of the cup as a referential measure heralded in a whole new age of cake recipes, which came to be known as cup cakes. What does this have to do with cupcakes? That depends.

Back in the days before the enclosed iron oven, most cooking and baking was done hearthside. Stews, beans, and whatnot simmered in a Dutch oven, meats roasted on spits, and a lot of baking got done too, but it was tedious, and large cakes were especially hard to pull off, so folks got into the habit of baking lots of little bitty cakes in things like, that's right, cups—heatproof ones, of course. Batter would go in, and they would just set them right at the edge of the fire and bingo: a cup cake, which would also be a cupcake. Get it?

Most cakes spring from a handful of humble ingredients. The differences among the many final forms come in part from the exact amounts, but more often than not it's the mixing technique that matters. Most American cakes are born of the creaming method, in which sugar and/or butter or shortening are beaten until the sugar punches zillions of little holes into the fat, which are then blown up by the chemical leavening during the baking process. Such high-fat batters are tasty, to be sure, but I find them too heavy for cupcakes. Thanks to a Los Angeles insurance salesman, we have another option. Let me tell you a story.

Once upon a time, in the 1920s, there was a Los Angeles insurance salesman named Harry Baker. Now, Harry wanted nothing more in life than to become a famous cake baker. After years of experimenting with different recipes, he finally came up with a light and delicate cake. It took Hollywood by storm. It was called the "chiffon cake." What was the secret? Harry wouldn't tell. For twenty years, his cakes were the stuff of legend, until finally, in 1947, he shared his secret with the most popular—albeit nonexistent—baker in the land, Betty Crocker. A year later, Betty shared it with the rest of the world. The secret ingredient was . . . oil. Rather than butter or shortening, Harry just skipped the solid fat altogether and used cooking oil to create a fluffy, golden cake. Of course, you can't beat bubbles into liquid oil, so Harry designed his chiffon to get its lift from the same source as an angel food cake or a soufflé: an egg-white foam.

Egg whites are pretty much born to foam due to their unique mixture of protein and water. All we have to do is bust up the surface tension a little so they can start blowing bubbles. And we have to avoid getting yolks in them because yolks contain fat, and fat lubricates proteins, thus limiting the ability of a foam to, well, foam.

Harry Baker on a Cake Quest

THE CAKE MASTER

APPLICATION — CHIFFON CUPCAKES

APPROXIMATELY 24 CUPCAKES

// SOFTWARE

5¼	ounces	cake flour	
1½	teaspoons	baking powder	
1	teaspoon	kosher salt	
5	large	eggs	separated
6	ounces	sugar	divided
¼	cup	H₂O	
¼	cup	vegetable oil	
1	teaspoon	vanilla extract	
⅝	teaspoon	cream of tartar	

// PROCEDURE

1. Heat the oven to 325°F.

2. Line **2 (12-cup) muffin tins** with **paper or foil liners** and set aside. (If you prefer, set 12 ovenproof coffee mugs on a half sheet pan and set aside.)

3. **Whisk** together the flour, baking powder, and salt in a **medium bowl**. Set aside.

4. Combine the egg yolks and 5 ounces of the sugar in the bowl of a **stand mixer fitted with the whisk attachment** on high speed for 2 minutes, or until the mixture becomes pale yellow and forms ribbons when the whisk is lifted. Add the water, oil, and vanilla and whisk to combine. Add the dry ingredients and whisk just to combine. Transfer the batter to a **large bowl** and set aside.

5. Combine the egg whites and cream of tartar in a clean stand-mixer bowl and whisk on high speed until the mixture becomes foamy. Decrease the speed to low and gradually add the remaining 1 ounce sugar. Increase the speed to high and continue whisking until stiff peaks form, approximately 2 minutes.

6. Add one-third of the egg whites to the batter and whisk until well combined. Add the remaining egg whites and fold in gently.

7. Scoop the batter into the prepared muffin tins or coffee mugs, evenly dividing the batter among the cups. Place both muffin tins on the middle rack of the oven or, if using mugs, place them on the **half sheet pan** on the bottom rack of the oven. Bake for 30 minutes, or until a **toothpick** inserted in the center of one comes out clean or the cupcakes reach an internal temperature of 205° to 210°F. Remove to a **cooling rack** and cool completely before frosting.

ON EGG-REGATION

When it comes to separating eggs, I use the quarantine approach, which ensures that if one of my egg whites becomes contaminated with a foam-destroying broken egg yolk, it won't spread to the rest of the egg-white pool. The method requires three bowls:

▶ Bowl 1: Yolks

▶ Bowl 2: Whites

▶ Bowl 3: Quarantine: Egg whites are broken into this bowl and inspected before being moved to bowl 2.

WHY CREAM OF TARTAR?

Cream of tartar is an acid, potassium bitartrate, and is a by-product of the winemaking process. Since it is acidic it can lower the pH of a mixture by bringing extra hydrogen ions to the party. Add enough of these to the protein, and they'll reach what's called the isoelectric point, and they will relax and unfurl. By adding more cream of tartar at the get-go, you start the protein party earlier in the process, and that means smaller bubbles, ergo a finer texture, and that translates to a lighter and more tender cupcake for you.

TIDBIT | For optimum leavening minus the chemical flavor, use aluminum-free baking powder.

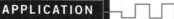

CHOCOLATE CHIFFON CUPCAKES

APPROXIMATELY 24 CUPCAKES

// **SOFTWARE** ///

4	ounces	cake flour	
1½	teaspoons	baking powder	
1	teaspoon	kosher salt	
¼	cup	hot H$_2$O	
1¼	ounces	cocoa powder	Dutch process
5	large	egg yolks	
6	ounces	sugar	
¼	cup	vegetable oil	
1	teaspoon	vanilla extract	
4	large	egg whites	
½	teaspoon	cream of tartar	

// **PROCEDURE** ///

(1) Heat the oven to 325°F.

(2) Line **2 (12-cup) muffin tins** with **paper or foil liners** and set aside. (If you prefer, set 12 ovenproof coffee mugs on a half sheet pan and set aside.)

(3) **Whisk** together the flour, baking powder, and salt in a **medium bowl**. Set aside.

(4) Combine the hot water and the cocoa powder in a **small bowl** and whisk until smooth. Set aside.

(5) Combine the egg yolks and 5 ounces of the sugar in the bowl of a **stand mixer fitted with the whisk attachment** and whisk on high speed for 2 minutes or until the mixture becomes pale yellow and forms ribbons when the whisk is lifted. Add the cocoa mixture, oil, and vanilla and whisk to combine. Add the dry ingredients and whisk just to combine. Transfer the batter to a **large bowl** and set aside.

(6) Combine the egg whites and cream of tartar in a clean stand-mixer bowl and whisk on high speed until the mixture becomes foamy. Decrease the speed to low and gradually add the remaining 1 ounce sugar. Increase the speed to high and continue whisking until stiff peaks form, approximately 2 minutes.

(7) Transfer one-third of the egg whites to the batter and whisk until well combined. Add the remaining egg whites and fold in gently. Transfer the batter to the prepared muffin tins or coffee mugs, evenly dividing the batter among the cups. Place both muffin tins on the middle rack of the oven or, if using mugs, place all of them on the half sheet pan on the bottom rack of the oven. Bake for 30 minutes, or until a **toothpick** inserted in the center of one comes out clean or the cupcakes reach an internal temperature of 205° to 210°F. Remove to a **cooling rack** and cool completely before frosting.

HONEY, I SHRUNK
THE CAKE

SIMPLE VANILLA BUTTERCREAM FROSTING

APPROXIMATELY 2 CUPS

TIP | Looking for chocolate frosting? See page 388.

Although I do not agree with those who insist that a cupcake is simply a delivery device for frosting, I will agree that without a good frosting a cupcake is a little too much like a muffin. Given the texture and flavor of our chiffon cupcakes, a nice buttercream would be in order.

// SOFTWARE ///

6	ounces	unsalted butter	at room temperature
2	ounces	vegetable shortening	
1	large	egg	at room temperature
1	pound	confectioners' sugar	
1	teaspoon	vanilla extract	

// PROCEDURE ///

(1) Cream the butter and shortening in a **stand mixer fitted with the paddle attachment** on high speed until light and fluffy, 3 to 4 minutes. Add the egg and beat until well combined, approximately 1 minute.

(2) Turn off the mixer and add ½ cup of the confectioners' sugar. Mix on low speed until combined. Stop to scrape down the side of the bowl. Repeat until all of the sugar has been incorporated. Add the vanilla and beat until the frosting is smooth and light, 2 to 3 minutes. Use immediately, or store in an **airtight container** at room temperature for up to 4 hours or refrigerated for up to 1 week. Bring to room temperature before using.

TIP | The raw egg can be replaced with 1 ounce of mayo. Really.

TIDBIT | Ovenproof cups or mugs make perfect baking vessels. The cupcakes that come out of these will be twice as big as your average paper-bound cupcakes, and that means they'll be twice as delicious.

Notice the perched bowl upper left. One twist of the speed rail and it's sprinkle time!

HONEY, I SHRUNK THE CAKE

I have a deep, abiding love for my Dutch oven.

It's old. It's iron. It's coal black, with a cure that I lovingly maintain. I take it for walks in the park and to the movies, but sometimes we just kick back and cook by firelight—or in it, actually. I am very into the hearth-cookery experience and often simmer stews and such right down in the coals. And sometimes when we really get crazy and we invite my Dutch oven's cousin the camp stove, we bake, right down in the coals and ashes. And believe you me, once you master a few basic techniques, whether you do it in the fireplace or outside with charcoal, the rustic results will be . . .

TIDBIT | Even if your new cast iron was cured at the factory, you'll probably need to cure it again once a year.

TAKING THE CURE

1. Wash the target vessel in hot soapy water and rinse. If your pan is used, this will serve to clean it (duh). If it's new, this operation will remove the food-grade wax that iron pieces are coated with in order to prevent rusting during shipping and storage. Dry thoroughly.

2. Smear on a thin but even layer of fat. I find that shortening is easier than liquid oils to deal with in this regard. Use your fingers to massage it all over the vessel, inside and out, top, bottom, lid top, lid bottom—everything. The only thing you don't have to worry about is the wire bail, if you have one,

because that's made out of a different kind of steel.

3. Crank your oven to 350°F and place the piece on a middle rack upside down so that melted fat won't pool inside the vessel. (Pooling fat can cook into a plasticlike polymer that is very sticky and almost impossible to remove from cast iron without removing the cure. So be sure to run the oven's self-clean cycle, after removing the vessel, to eliminate any drips.

4. Cook the piece for 1 hour, then deactivate the oven and leave the piece inside until it's cool enough to touch.

To clean a cured pan: Add a tablespoon of oil and a couple tablespoons of kosher salt to the hot pan and carefully scrub with a wad of paper towels until the salt is dark gray. Dump the salt (careful, it's hot), wipe out the pan, cool, and store. I only use soap and water if things get really grody, or before re-curing, which I do once a year. If something goes seriously wrong (burnt caramel, for instance), you may have to completely remove the cure and start over. Simply park the piece in the oven and run the self-clean cycle. Wash, dry, and re-cure immediately.

A Dutch oven is a heavy cast-metal vessel with a tight-fitting lid, two loop handles, and sometimes a wire bail for suspending on a jack, crane, or chain. A camp stove features three stubby legs for perching in coals and a lip around the edge of the flat lid for corralling coals. Although aluminum models are light and efficient heat conductors, they react to a lot of different foods and can actually melt if they hit 900°F, a temperature easily attained in a fireplace or a pit. Iron is extremely dense, so it holds heat well and, if properly cured, will not react with food—and it won't melt until it hits about 2000°F.

The problem with iron is that it reacts with water and oxygen to create a brand-new substance called iron oxide, a.k.a. rust. To prevent rust we must keep air away by applying a thin protective surface. New raw-iron pieces are always coated with food-grade wax to protect them during shipping and storage, but since wax melts at very low temperatures, it's a temporary fix at best. Carbon, however, is an excellent choice, as it's nontoxic and easily applied in the home kitchen environment. Now, before you go checking your cabinets for a can of carbon, let's consider the structure of fat—or, rather, a fatty acid.

ANOTHER DAY, ANOTHER MODEL

A fatty acid is essentially a chain of carbons with little bonding points capable of attaching to hydrogen atoms. If we apply enough heat, this structure decomposes, many of the hydrogen and associated molecules are driven off, and we're left with carbon. If lubed properly from time to time, the carbon will provide the hydrophobic protection our cast iron craves.

Although I typically cook in the fireplace, it takes quite a bit of experimentation to get the hang of it, which is why I usually tell people to start with charcoal briquettes, which are easily quantifiable. Problem is, since charcoal gives off carbon monoxide, my attorneys will simply not allow me to present fireplace instructions using charcoal unless said fireplace is outdoors. If you don't have an outdoor fireplace, these applications have been developed for use with a Dutch oven cooking table, available via the Internet or at many army-navy supply stores. Designed to have charcoal placed directly on it, it's a handy item even if you have a charcoal grill, and can also be used in lieu of a fireplace.

As for fuel, your average megamart-brand charcoal briquette contains some pretty nasty stuff like borax, nitrates, even petroleum. "All-natural" briquettes, on the other hand, contain nothing but semicarbonized wood and a touch of starch to hold it together. Such briquettes burn smoothly, cleanly, and evenly.

TIDBIT | The teeth on the underside of Dutch oven lids are designed to drip condensation evenly back onto the food.

The miners and prospectors of the Old West, who never went far without their trusty Dutch ovens, were known for baking up a specific style of bread that was leavened by wild "starters" kept in leather pouches around their necks. Each time they made dough they added some of the starter and then returned some of the dough to the pouch. Due to their tangy flavor these breads became known as "sourdoughs." Luckily, with a Dutch oven we can re-create much of the rustic appeal of these loaves using modern yeast.

APPLICATION — KNEAD NOT SOURDOUGH

1 LOAF

Wheat breads get their chewy tooth from gluten, that elastic and plastic mesh that forms whenever we mix wheat-flour proteins with water. Typically we give birth to this structure by kneading and kneading and kneading and kneading. However, agitation is not the only way to conjure gluten forth. Time alone can do the trick and has the distinct advantage of creating considerable flavor as well.

SOFTWARE

17½	ounces	bread flour	plus extra for shaping
¼	teaspoon	active dry yeast	
2½	teaspoons	kosher salt	
12	ounces	H$_2$O	filtered would be best
2	tablespoons	cornmeal	

PROCEDURE

1. **Whisk** together the flour, yeast, and salt in a **large bowl**. Add the water and stir until combined. Cover the bowl with **plastic wrap** and leave at room temperature for 19 hours.

2. Turn the dough out onto a lightly floured work surface. Punch down the dough and turn it over onto itself a couple of times. Cover with a **tea towel** and rest for 15 minutes. After 15 minutes, shape the dough into a ball, dusting your hands with flour if needed to prevent sticking. Sprinkle the tea towel with half of the cornmeal and lay the dough on top of it, with the seam side down. Sprinkle the top of the dough with the other half of the cornmeal and cover with the towel. Set aside to rise for 2 to 3 hours or until the dough has doubled in size.

FOR OVEN BAKING:

3. While the dough is rising the second time, heat the oven to 450°F. Place a **5-quart Dutch oven** in the oven while it preheats. When the dough is ready, carefully transfer it to the heated Dutch oven. Cover and bake for 30 minutes. Remove the lid and bake for another 15 minutes or until the bread reaches an internal temperature of 210° to 212°F. Transfer the bread to a **cooling rack** and cool for at least 15 minutes before slicing.

FOR BAKING WITH COALS OUTDOORS:

3. Heat charcoal in a **chimney starter** until ash covers all of the coals. Place 20 to 24 coals on a Dutch oven table. Place a **cooling rack or other wire rack** that is at least 2 inches high directly over the coals. Set a **5-quart Dutch oven** on top of this rack and preheat it during the last 30 minutes of the second rise. Carefully transfer the dough to the Dutch oven and cover with the lid. Place 20 coals on top. Bake for 45 minutes or until the bread reaches an internal temperature of 210° to 212°F. Transfer the bread to a **cooling rack** and cool for at least 15 minutes before slicing.

WHY "DUTCH"?

The story goes that Abraham Darby was an English Quaker who studied the Dutch processes for casting iron and molds made of compressed sand. Back in England, he perfected these methods and started mass producing cast-iron pieces that were needed by England's various colonial interests, especially ours. Since he was inspired by the Dutch, he *may* have called these vessels Dutch ovens, but I wonder why he didn't instead call them English ovens or maybe Darby cookers.

I think it's far more likely that when it came to supplying the thirteen colonies with Dutch ovens, the Dutch East India Company undercut the English manufacturers through their colony, New Amsterdam, which later became New York. However they got their name, one thing is for sure: The settling of America would never have been possible without the Dutch oven. And as far as I'm concerned, a properly cured five-quart Dutch oven is one of the most powerful multi-taskers in the culinary cadre.

TRUE DUTCH OVENS ARE STILL CAST IN SAND MOLDS.

DUTCH OVEN CHERRY CLAFOUTIS*

8 SERVINGS

In the Mousson region of France, the abundant cherry crop is celebrated with clafoutis, a dish that's a cross between a pie, a custard, and a pancake. Most Americans won't go near it, because it sounds like something you'd have to get a shot for, but once you make your first clafoutis, many more will follow.

TIDBIT *Clafoutis* comes from an old Occitan word meaning "to fill up."

// SOFTWARE

		unsalted butter	for the Dutch oven
12	ounces	cherries	fresh or frozen, stemmed and pitted
2	large	eggs	
¼	cup	sugar	
½	cup	whole milk	
1	teaspoon	vanilla extract	
½	cup	all-purpose flour	

// PROCEDURE

1. Heat the oven to 400°F or prepare a charcoal fire for cooking outdoors by heating coals in a **chimney starter** until hot and ashy.

2. Butter the bottom and sides of a **5-quart Dutch oven**. If using frozen cherries, put them in a **colander** to thaw (and drain) completely before using; discard the juice. Spread the fresh or thawed cherries evenly in the bottom of the Dutch oven.

3. In a **large bowl**, **whisk** together the eggs and sugar until frothy and lightened in color. Add the milk, vanilla, and flour and whisk to combine. Pour the batter over the cherries.

FOR OVEN BAKING:

4. Bake on the middle rack of the oven, uncovered, for 30 minutes, or until golden on top and a knife comes out clean when inserted in the middle.

FOR BAKING WITH COALS OUTDOORS:

4. Place 18 or 19 coals on a **Dutch oven table**. Set a **cooling rack or other wire rack** that is at least 2 inches high directly over the coals. Place the Dutch oven on the rack directly over the coals. Cover with the lid and place 22 or 23 coals on top. Cook with the lid on for 25 minutes. Remove the lid and cook for another 5 minutes, or until golden on top and a knife comes out clean when inserted in the middle.

5. Cool for 30 minutes before removing from the Dutch oven, slicing, and serving.

DUTCH OVEN HOECAKES

8 TO 10 (3- TO 4-INCH) ROUND CAKES

Benjamin Franklin once wrote that nokehicks, or hoecakes, were finer than any English Yorkshire pudding, and I tend to agree. When you add a little maple syrup they are, absolutely, late-night good eats.

// SOFTWARE ///

1	cup	cornmeal	
2	teaspoons	baking powder	
¾	teaspoon	kosher salt	
1	large	egg	
¾	cup	H$_2$O	
½	cup	corn	fresh or thawed frozen
		vegetable oil	

// PROCEDURE ///

(1) Put the cornmeal, baking powder, salt, egg, and water in a **bowl** and **stir** to combine. Stir in the corn. The mixture should be the consistency of pancake batter.

— FOR STOVETOP COOKING:

(2) Place a **cast-iron skillet or griddle** over medium heat. **Brush** with oil and heat until shimmering. Pour enough batter onto the skillet or griddle to form a 4-inch round, approximately 2 tablespoons. Depending on the size of your griddle or skillet, you can cook more than one cake at a time. Cook until brown on both sides, 2 to 3 minutes per side. Serve immediately or transfer to a warm (200°F) oven until all of the cakes are done.

— FOR BAKING WITH COALS OUTDOORS:

(2) Prepare charcoal for cooking outdoors by heating coals in a **chimney starter** until hot and ashy.

(3) Using a **Dutch oven with feet**, turn the oven upside down. Place 22 hot, ashy coals on the bottom of the inverted oven. Lay the lid upside down on top of the Dutch oven feet and over the coals and heat for 10 minutes.

(4) **Brush** the lid with oil and heat until shimmering. Pour enough batter onto the lid to form a 4-inch round, approximately 2 tablespoons. Depending on the size of your lid, you can cook more than one cake at a time. Cook until brown on both sides, 2 to 3 minutes per side. Serve immediately.

TIDBIT | The hoecake also goes by the names Johnnycake, Shawnee cake, Journey cake, and no cake.

POPOVER SOMETIME

EPISODE 191 | SEASON 12 | GOOD EATS

Each year, I suspect some 100,000 recipes are presented worldwide via books, periodicals, the Internet, and, of course, television. Add to that the billions of cookbooks written since the first English-language cookbook, titled *This Is the Book of Cookery Where Beginneth a Noble Book of Feasts Royal, a Book for Princes Households or Any Other Estates*, was first published in A.D. 1500, and I figure that the planetary recipe collection is something like 6 kagillion, give or take a quadrillion. If you tried, say, a million recipes, and liked a hundred thousand of them, you'd still need a hundred big three-ring notebooks to hold them all and a staff of a dozen to manage the data input. I know; I've tried. The best way to combat this onslaught without going insane is to maintain a core cuisine to call your own, a small repertoire of applications that you have committed to memory so that you can pull them out at a moment's notice with neither thought nor hesitation.

2 LARGE EGGS
1 C WHOLE MILK
4¾ OZ. AP FLOUR
1 Tbs. BUTTER (MELTED)
1½ tsp. KOSHER SALT

KNOWLEDGE CONCENTRATE

One of the cards in my recipe collection reads:

Now, pretend that you don't know what this episode is about and just try to figure out what this formula might produce. As you can no doubt deduce by the high liquid-to-dry ratio, this is a batter, a wet one, which means it will be capable of generating a large amount of steam. Because it expands so dramatically and carries so much energy with it, steam is ideally suited to performing work.

We also know that the batter contains two structural elements, what we call "strengtheners": proteins in the egg whites and starch in the flour. Different types of flour contain different amounts of proteins, so which flour we use matters. This formula requires AP flour, which is stronger than low-protein flours like pastry flour and not as tough as high-protein flours like bread flour, so we know that most of the structure of the finished product will have to come from the eggs and steam.

Let's see what we get when we put it all in a blender or food processor and spin it for 30 seconds. Just as you suspected: a batter. But for what? A cake, you say? No, there's nowhere near enough fat in there for that. Besides, cake batters typically contain more flour than moisture. Pancakes? Come on, you're just guessing. Pancakes would include leavening. Let's take a look at the batter with a microscope. Bubbles. Lots of tiny bubbles.

Think about this: If one were to apply high, fast heat to this, all that water might just turn to steam and quickly expand inside the batter, and if the egg proteins were to coagulate, and the starches in the flour were to gelatinize, and the milk sugars were to caramelize at just the right time . . .

Well, what do you think? Say we just poured it in a hot pan? We'd quickly ascertain that our mystery batter is too stiff to make a crêpe but not thick enough to really be anything else. And there's way too much surface area for those bubbles to do any real lifting, as their effort lacks focus. What we need is a pan that encloses the batter, like the barrel of a mortar, capable of steering whatever vertical velocity may be generated in the oven. Said pan would also need to absorb heat very quickly so that the energy can be transferred into the batter. Something like this:

Of course, that wouldn't hold a lot, so we'd need to replicate the form, like this:

Now, if we lube the "barrels" with a little butter, crank the oven to 400°F, then mix the batter only when the oven is hot, fill the barrels halfway, and bake right in the middle of a hot oven for 40 minutes without opening the door, which would only impede inflation, what might happen?

I think it is safe to say that the high heat of the oven would rapidly penetrate the metal cups, causing the batter at the sides and bottom to rapidly set, a process aided by the fact that we started with room-temperature rather than cold ingredients. The batter bubbles are trapped and begin to expand in the only direction available to them: up. Here's the cool part: The ratio of liquid to starch and protein is balanced, so that as the top of the rising batter sets and splits and sets and splits, just enough internal pressure is produced to force the bubbles inside to fuse together into one or two über bubbles, which will continue to push up and out, stretching what is essentially a hollow blister until equilibrium is reached between the expansion of the steam and the elasticity of the batter, which then sets in the final expanded position. We call the resulting food a "popover."

The outside is crunchy, golden brown, and delicious, because the proteins and starches were cooked by the dry heat of the oven. Inside, however, is a different story. The inner walls of this big bubble are soft and moist because steam did the cooking, but this can also become a problem. If this moisture remains inside, it will eventually condense and turn gooey. So, as soon as they're cool enough to handle, find a little crag in the top and stab it (just a little) with a paring knife or skewer. Thus vented and cooled, popovers can remain viable for a couple of days, sealed in a plastic bag.

Those of you unfamiliar with popovers may be wondering, what's so great about a big hollow crusty ball? For one thing, popovers are delicious, and since they are fast, they are a fantastic replacement for dinner rolls, which are usually heavy to eat, not to mention time-consuming to make. But since popovers are hollow they can house a wide variety of fillings. You could, for instance, butter one up and fill it with a luscious broth, or perhaps chicken salad or chocolate pudding or lemon curd. In other words, a popover is a bread and a serving vessel.

This amazingly convenient device, not too surprisingly, is an American invention, but it was born of English ancestry. Once upon a time in England, *pudding* referred to just about any dough that was either boiled or baked that wasn't considered out-and-out bread. In his 1577 blockbuster, *A Description of England*, William Harrison wrote, "Each part of the country has its own puddings: Devonshire, white cloud; Gloucester, bad pudding; Hampshire, hasty pudding; Worcester, black pudding; and Yorkshire, Yorkshire pudding." Yorkshire, of course, is a region on the northeastern coast just below Northumbria. Now back in the Middle Ages, up in these parts, meat, fresh meat at least, was actually pretty hard to find. When large critter hunks or joints were available, they were generally cooked on a spit—not over the fire, but just in front of it. Flavorful drippings and rendered fat were captured in a pan here on the hearth. Somewhere along the line, a thrifty cook figured that a little meat would seem to go a lot further if it was served with something else that was kinda meaty. So the pan with the fat was placed on the fire, and when the fat sizzled, a batter was poured directly onto it and baked.

APPLICATION ⎍⎍⎍ BASIC POPOVERS

6 LARGE POPOVERS

// SOFTWARE //

1	tablespoon	unsalted butter	melted and cooled, plus 1 teaspoon for the pan
4¾	ounces	all-purpose flour	
1½	teaspoons	kosher salt	
2	large	eggs	at room temperature
1	cup	whole milk	at room temperature

// PROCEDURE //

1. Heat the oven to 400°F.

2. Grease a **6-cup popover pan** with the 1 teaspoon of butter.

3. Combine the 1 tablespoon of butter, the flour, salt, eggs, and milk in a **food processor or blender** and process for 30 seconds.

4. Divide the batter evenly among the cups of the popover pan, filling each one-third to one-half full. Bake on the middle rack of the oven for 40 minutes, taking care not to open the oven door. Remove the popovers to a **cooling rack** and pierce each one in the top with a **knife** to allow steam to escape. Serve warm.

This is a classic eighteenth-century Yorkshire pudding, and you'll notice that the ingredients list is almost exactly the same as that for our popovers, at left. The only real difference is the use of drippings instead of butter. (We could use butter here instead of drippings, but then we wouldn't be making Yorkshire pudding, now, would we?) Any roast meat fatty enough to give you a few tablespoons of drippings will do, but beef, lamb, or mutton (if you can get it) are preferred. A three-bone standing rib roast cooked in a 9-by-13-inch roasting pan will give you enough drippings for the pudding. Prepare the pudding while the roast is resting.

// SOFTWARE //

¼	cup	beef drippings	
9	ounces	all-purpose flour	
1½	teaspoons	kosher salt	
4	large	eggs	at room temperature
2	cup	whole milk	at room temperature

// PROCEDURE ///

1. Heat the oven to 400°F.

2. Leave 2 tablespoons of drippings in the **9-by-13-inch roasting pan** and place it in the oven.

3. Combine the flour, salt, eggs, milk, and remaining 2 tablespoons of drippings in a **food processor or blender** and process for 30 seconds. Pour the batter into the hot roasting pan and bake for 35 to 40 minutes, until puffed and golden brown. While the pudding is cooking, carve the roast. Serve the pudding with the roast.

TIDBIT Yorkshire pudding was called "dripping pudding" in the 1737 book *The Whole Duty of a Woman*.

TIP To reheat the next day, place directly on the middle rack of a 400°F oven for 3 minutes.

Popovers make a great luncheon item, Yorkshire pudding a classic supper dish, but what of breakfast? Well, have you ever munched down on a Dutch baby? Supposedly the term *Dutch baby* was coined by Original Pancake House owner Lester Hyatt, who was trying to think up a new name for a dish based on German pancakes. The parts list for our version, as you can see, is just a little bit different from that for our popovers.

// SOFTWARE

3	tablespoons	unsalted butter	melted
2⅜	ounces	all-purpose flour	
3	tablespoons	vanilla sugar	plus extra for serving
½	teaspoon	kosher salt	
2	large	eggs	at room temperature
½	cup	whole milk	at room temperature
		lemon wedges	for serving

// PROCEDURE

1. Heat the oven to 375°F.

2. Pour 2 tablespoons of the melted butter into a **10-inch cast-iron skillet** and place it in the oven. Set the remaining 1 tablespoon butter aside to cool slightly. Wait 10 minutes before assembling the other ingredients.

3. Combine the flour, vanilla sugar, salt, eggs, milk, and remaining 1 tablespoon butter in a **food processor or blender** and process for 30 seconds. Carefully pour the batter into the heated skillet. Bake on the middle rack of the oven for 30 to 35 minutes, without opening the oven, until the edges are puffed and brown. Sprinkle with additional vanilla sugar and serve with lemon wedges for squeezing.

NO DUTCH BABIES WERE HARMED IN MAKING THIS DISH

CELERYMAN

Apium graveolens, a.k.a. celery, is a member of the parsley family and certainly one of the most versatile bits of vegetation in existence, seeing as how it serves as a vegetable, a starch, an herb, and a spice. Think about it: celery stalks, celery root, celery greens, and celery seeds. Even if there were nothing better in the world than the aroma of cooking celery, those credentials would be enough to qualify celery as . . .

SCENES FROM A
LOCAL GROCERY STORE

Thousands of years ago, around the Mediterranean and in China, celery was a bitter herb with skinny little ribs. Its use was strictly medicinal, and supposedly it was issued as an aphrodisiac. The Greeks used celery much as the Romans used laurel leaves, as garlands for their athletes, who were also refreshed with celery wine, which was supposedly fairly invigorating stuff.

By the sixteenth century, the original wild form of celery had developed into three distinct varieties:

a leafy variety still available today in China and parts of Europe but rarely in America;

good old-fashioned rib celery, which it should be noted was planted by Dutch farmers who settled in and around Kalamazoo, Michigan, in 1874; and

celeriac, or celery root, developed specifically for its enlarged, starchy root ball that is so ugly that very few Americans eat it, which is a shame.

Storing celery root is easy. Just twist it up in a couple layers of plastic wrap and refrigerate for up to a month. As for rib celery, moist means fresh, so I like to give it the flower-vase treatment with a little water in a halved soda bottle. A plastic shower cap makes a very nice topper. When prepping stalks for storage, skip the water. Washing will only make peeling harder, as a slick and slimy exterior will result.

When working with celery roots, I typically quarter them with a serrated knife, then peel them with a serrated vegetable peeler. It takes time to get down in the cracks and crevices, but it's worth the work. As the peeling is done, stash the pieces in some water laced with a little lemon juice or vinegar to prevent browning.

TA DA! CELERY ROOT MATCHSTICKS!

Celeriac remoulade is one of my favorite raw-vegetable applications. A celebrated French bistro standard, remoulade is essentially a highly flavored slaw. It's typically served with roasted poultry or steak, but if you really want to put the *mon dieu* into your French friends, put it on a hot dog. This application requires matchstick cuts, and although this can certainly be tackled with a knife, a mandoline or slicer with a matchstick blade makes the job much easier; do be sure to use the hand guard.

// SOFTWARE

1½	tablespoons	lemon juice	freshly squeezed
1½	tablespoons	Dijon mustard	
¾	cup	crème fraîche	
1	1-pound	celery root	
¼	teaspoon	kosher salt	
	pinch	black pepper	freshly ground

// PROCEDURE

1. **Whisk** together the lemon juice, mustard, and crème fraîche in a **medium bowl**. Set the dressing aside.

2. **Brush** any excess dirt off of the celery root. Cut off the bottom and top of the root. Cut the root into quarters and peel with a **serrated peeler**. Rinse in cool water if there is any remaining dirt or debris. Slice each quarter on a **mandoline** into 1-inch-long matchstick pieces and transfer directly to the dressing. Add the salt and pepper and stir well to combine. Cover and refrigerate for at least 1 hour and up to 3 hours before serving.

CELERYMAN

APPLICATION ——⊓⊔⊓⊔— CELERY SODA

2¼ CUPS SYRUP; ENOUGH
FOR ABOUT 18 SERVINGS

Celery tonics have been around for at least a century, and have at various times been touted as diuretics, digestive aids, anti-lactogens, carminatives, general tonics (whatever that means), and of course aphrodisiacs. Eventually the FDA forced manufacturers to downgrade the word "tonic" to "soda," because no one was actually able to prove all those unproven medical claims. I don't know if celery possesses any curative properties whatsoever, but I do know that there is plenty of flavor in the celery's tiny seeds.

// **SOFTWARE** ///

2	cups	sugar	
1	cup	H_2O	
2	tablespoons	celery seed	freshly ground
		soda water	to serve

// **PROCEDURE** //

1. Combine the sugar and water in a **medium saucepan** over medium-high heat. Continue to stir frequently until all of the sugar has dissolved. Remove from the heat, add the celery seed, cover, and steep for 1 hour.

2. Strain through a **fine-mesh strainer** into a **heatproof container** and place in the refrigerator, uncovered, until completely cool. Store in an **airtight container** for up to 6 months.

   TO USE:

3. Add 2 tablespoons syrup to 1 cup soda water and stir to combine.[1]

TRIVIA This scene was shot in the same motor home used in *Feasting on Asphalt*, a.k.a. The Brown Flame.

[1] Although 2 tablespoons syrup to 1 cup soda water is tasty, 3 ounces will grow your hair back.

CURES WHAT AILS YA!

TIDBIT In Iran, celery seeds are boiled down to extract the essential oil, apiol, the fumes of which are inhaled to relieve headaches.

BRAISED CELERY

4 SERVINGS

Lest you think I forgot the good ole celery stalk, here's an application that softens the stalk to a buttery smooth texture while amplifying its flavor. Consider serving this with roast turkey instead of stuffing.

// SOFTWARE ///

8	stalks	celery	rinsed and trimmed, leaves chopped and reserved
1	tablespoon	unsalted butter	
	pinch	kosher salt	
	pinch	black pepper	freshly ground
½	cup	beef stock or broth	

// PROCEDURE ///

1. Peel any fibrous outer stalks of celery with a **vegetable peeler**. **Slice** the celery into 1-inch pieces on the bias.

2. Heat the butter in a **10-inch sauté pan** over medium heat until melted. Add the celery, salt, and pepper and cook for 5 minutes, or until just beginning to soften. Add the broth and stir to combine. Cover and reduce the heat to low. Cook until the celery is tender but not mushy, approximately 5 minutes.

3. Uncover, increase the heat to high, and continue to cook for 5 minutes, or until the liquid has been reduced to a glaze. Transfer to a **serving dish**, and garnish with the reserved leaves.

I'm a firm believer in the pantry principle, which states that when armed with a well-stocked cupboard, the cook never runs dry of edible options. But I have to admit that sometimes even a packed cupboard can look oddly barren. It's not the pantry's fault, of course, it's mine. Like so many other cooks, I've become too set in my ways.

An oddly familiar big blue fish, Alvin the Albacore, descends into the frame on a giant hook.

ALVIN: Trying to pump out another one of those pantry raid shows, huh?

AB: It's Alvin the Albacore!

ALVIN: (sarcastic) Well, how nice. You remember.

AB: His picture was on every can of tuna that I ate when I was a kid, and I ate a lot of canned tuna.

ALVIN: Yeah, I haven't seen much of you since.

AB: Well, I grew up.

ALVIN: Yeah, I know. You became this big-shot TV cook. Don't need Alvin anymore. Don't need my flaky goodness.

AB: It's just——as the taste matures...

ALVIN: What is it now? Hand-massaged, sake-fed, bluefin tuna at a Benjamin a bite?

AB: It's not like that. It's just——

ALVIN: Don't worry about it. I've come to accept the fact that all I'm good for is old-lady casseroles and lunchbox sandwiches. There's not much future in being Alvin the Albacore, that's for sure. You know, I doubt there's anyone in the world brave enough, clever enough, skilled enough in the ways of the kitchen to ever turn old can-bound Alvin into...

Although other varieties sneak in from time to time, if the words "light" and "chunk" are on the can, the pieces interred therein are probably skipjack tuna, which looks a little like this:

It should be noted that this fish only has a three-year lifespan and an average catch weight of three to seven pounds, so it's a relatively small fish. Now, many different types of tuna can be referred to as "fancy" or "solid" tunas, but by law only albacore can be sold as "white" tuna.

The albacore is much larger than the skipjack, with an average market weight of between twenty and forty pounds (although some can grow much fatter) and a lifespan of up to five years. Albacore "solid" tuna is just that. The fish is steamed to ease de-boning and then a can-size section of loin muscle is punched out of the carcass and entombed. The result: a solid piece of meat. These days most fancy white tuna is packed in salt water.

In order for tuna to be properly preserved during canning, it has to be cooked, then sealed in the can, and then cooked again in a process called "retort" to kill any lurking microorganisms. The results are massively overcooked by any standard. Oil can be added to soften the texture and mouthfeel, but I don't know anyone who isn't a cat who actually likes eating water-packed canned tuna. Tuna sealed in airtight pouches is different because pouches offer more surface area so the retort can be accomplished very quickly. The result is a pleasing texture and flavor that's almost like fresh—and of course pouches are a lot easier to manipulate than cans. The fresher flavor of pouched tuna comes through in hot applications such as my tuna croquettes.

Some other points to remember:

Remember, canned "light" tuna more often than not means skipjack, a relatively small variety that doesn't grow big enough or live long enough to accumulate much mercury.

Albacore or white tuna can contain more mercury than canned light tuna. So when you're choosing your two meals of fish and shellfish for the week, we recommend you consume no more than six ounces of albacore tuna per week.

Yellowfin and bluefin tuna can harbor even higher levels of the mercury than smaller varieties.

Tuna is a treasure trove of nutrition, including vitamin D, selenium, protein, and omega-3 fatty acids, which are critical to the development of sound minds and strong bodies.

The Cadillac of canned fish is *ventresca*. The word comes from the Italian word for "belly," and you can recognize canned tuna by looking at the grain structure that shows the loose, leaflike structure of the abdomen. Although *ventresca* was once canned all along the Mediterranean coast, today the best examples come from Spain. To be honest, I would rather eat this tuna than any other kind save sushi. This is pricey stuff compared to other canned tuna, but it is becoming easier to obtain in the United States thanks to the good old Internet.

TIDBIT | The first commercial canning factory opened in England in 1813.

TIDBIT | Vacuum-packed tuna in pouches hit the market in 2000.

TUNA NIÇOISE UNDONE

2 SERVINGS

The most famous tuna salad in the world, Tuna Niçoise, hails from Nice and is a composed or layered salad that includes the small, black niçoise olives, green beans, sometimes potatoes, and tuna—canned tuna. I've never really been a fan of the traditional application, so I've made a few small adjustments.

// SOFTWARE

6 to 8	ounces	*ventresca* tuna	canned, packed in olive oil
4	leaves	butter lettuce	rinsed and patted dry
2	tablespoons	shallots	finely chopped
2	tablespoons	red or orange bell pepper	finely chopped
2	tablespoons	Hard-Cooked Eggs (page 42)	finely chopped
1	tablespoon	nonpareil capers	
1	tablespoon	micro greens	
¼	teaspoon	black lava sea salt[1]	
½		lemon	
		toast points	

// PROCEDURE

1. Carefully remove the tuna from the can, leaving the pieces intact. Reserve the oil. Put the tuna in the refrigerator while you prepare the remaining ingredients.

2. Divide the lettuce between **2 plates** and carefully lay the tuna atop the leaves. Top with the shallot, bell pepper, capers, egg, and micro greens. Sprinkle with the sea salt. Drizzle with the reserved oil and a squeeze of lemon juice. Serve with toast points.

[1] Looks nice, but really, any coarse salt will do.

Nice, France

GOOD

BETTER

If you're into classical Italian cuisine, you may have heard of the peculiar yet delicious *vitello tonnato*, or cold veal with tuna sauce. Now, I'm not a big fan of veal, but I am a big fan of tuna sauce, which with the proper acidic additives can become one of the healthiest and creamiest dip/salad dressing/breakfast spread/car waxes around.

// SOFTWARE ///

1	7-ounce pouch	albacore tuna	
¼	cup	mayonnaise	
2	tablespoons	red wine vinegar	
1	tablespoon	lemon juice	freshly squeezed
1	tablespoon	olive oil	
1	tablespoon	capers	with their juices
	pinch	black pepper	freshly ground

// PROCEDURE ///

Combine all of the ingredients in a **small food processor** and process until creamy, 1½ minutes. Serve as a dressing, dip, or on a sandwich. Store in an **airtight container** in the refrigerator for up to 4 days.

HEAVY METAL FISH

The curious metal mercury (Hg) naturally occurs in many rocks, like coal. Burn the coal at, say, a power plant and the mercury goes skyward out the smokestacks. Precipitation carries it back to the ground, and streams and rivers then move it into the sea. There it is set upon by bacteria, which turn it into the far more dangerous methyl mercury. Microscopic amounts end up in small fish, which are consumed by medium fish, which are then consumed by large predators, including big tuna, which, due to their long life spans, tend to store up more mercury in their bodies than other fish. When we eat them, some small portion of the mercury becomes ours for a long time.

So here we have this powerful pantry pal, chock full of culinary possibilities and nutritional goodness, which most of us grew up munching, and now we're told it could, maybe, possibly be dangerous to . . . whom, exactly?

Here's what our government says: High levels of mercury in the blood stream of fetuses and young children may harm the developing nervous system. With this in mind, the FDA and the EPA have designed an advisory for children, pregnant women, nursing mothers, and women considering becoming pregnant in the near future:

▶ Avoid consuming shark, swordfish, king mackerel, or tile fish, which can contain high levels of mercury.

▶ Consume up to twelve ounces a week (approximately two meals' worth) of a variety of fish and shellfish that are lower in mercury, such as canned *light* tuna.

TUNA CROQUETTES

// SOFTWARE

1	7-ounce pouch	albacore tuna	drained well and shredded
2		scallions	finely chopped
2	teaspoons	Dijon mustard	
2	large	eggs	beaten
1	teaspoon	lemon juice	freshly squeezed
½	teaspoon	kosher salt	
¼	teaspoon	black pepper	freshly ground
¾	cup	Japanese bread crumbs	a.k.a. panko
		olive oil	for sautéing

// PROCEDURE

1. Combine the tuna, scallions, mustard, eggs, lemon juice, salt, pepper, and ¼ cup of the bread crumbs in a **medium bowl**. Divide the mixture into 8 rounds and set aside on a **half sheet pan** lined with **parchment paper** for 15 minutes.

2. Put the remaining bread crumbs in a **pie plate**. One at a time, coat each round with the bread crumbs on all sides.

3. Heat enough oil to cover the bottom of a **12-inch sauté pan** over medium heat until shimmering. Add the croquettes and cook for 2 to 3 minutes on each side, or until golden brown. Remove to a **cooling rack** set over a **half sheet pan** lined with **paper towels**. Cool for 2 to 3 minutes before serving.

TIDBIT | The patron saint of American gastronomes, James Beard, was heard to say that tuna was the only ingredient that was better canned than fresh.

Oil. If there's a more potent symbol of wealth, I don't know what it is. Sure, gold and diamonds are pretty, but oil means power, because oil means energy and energy means work. Oil is also valuable as a lubricant and as a heat-transfer medium, and of course certain oils taste darned good. Today's global grocery offers oils from fruits, like olives and avocados; seeds, like sunflower, sesame, mustard, and grape; nuts, as in walnut, palm kernel, and hazelnut; and legumes, like soybeans and peanuts. If all these choices leave you in a daze, you are not alone. Most of us don't have a notion of how to sort out our lipidinous options, in part because we don't know much about oils to begin with. Let's see if we can do something about that.

HIGHLY SKILLED
BALLOON
PROFESSIONAL

OIL SMOKE POINTS

EXTRA VIRGIN OLIVE OIL 350
CANOLA (RAPE SEED) OIL 400
SESAME OIL 435
GRAPESEED OIL 430
HAZELNUT OIL 450
PEANUT OIL 390
SUNFLOWER OIL 450
VEGETABLE (SOY BEAN) OIL 450
SAFFLOWER OIL 450
AVOCADO OIL 520
PALM OIL 450
WALNUT OIL 325

KNOWLEDGE CONCENTRATE

▷○ **Whether we're talking olive oil or light crude, oils are hydrocarbons, which, simply put, are chemical energy stored as carbon and hydrogen atoms arranged thusly:**

This is a hydrocarbon chain, and depending on its length it could be found in diesel fuel. If you tinker with it just a wee bit and hook it up to a glycerol molecule along with two more similar chains, you'd have a triglyceride, which is the form all culinary oils take, which is not to say all culinary fats are the same. If every carbon bonding point has a hydrogen attached, the fatty acid is referred to as "saturated." If one position happens to be open, the resulting structure is "monounsaturated"; if more than one position's open, it's "polyunsaturated." Unsaturated fatty acids also have kinks in their chains, which explains why they are liquid at room temperature (as opposed to saturated fats, which are usually solid at room temp). Some oils are higher in polyunsaturates while others are higher in monos, but regardless of composition, all culinary oils carry around nine calories per gram, which is twice what you would find in a gram of either protein or carbohydrate.

▷○ **An oil's smoke point is the temperature at which it begins to deteriorate rapidly and give off smoke. It is not a good thing to have happen, because it creates a lot of flavors, all of them bad. And if the temperature continues to climb, you could reach the flash point, which is a very dangerous point. Many charts and tables attempt to quantify smoke points, and I'm here to tell you they're all complete hooey. The truth is there are just too many factors going into a smoke point to make concrete claims. I will say this, though: High heat will destroy the fruity goodness of an extra virgin olive oil or the nutty goodness of a walnut oil, but you can sauté with just about any oil as long as you work fast.**

▷○ **One of the most powerful culinary operations that oil can play a role in is the sauté. Although the term often refers to a particular step in the preparation of a dish, it can also signify any dish prepared by sautéing. Heck, it's even got a pan named after it. The method is hot, and it is fast, which might lead you to immediately reach for an oil with a high smoke point. My favorite sauté oils contain a relatively high ratio of monounsaturated to saturated fats. Canola, peanut, and avocado all fit the bill, but so do sesame oils—toasted sesame oil is nice because it can bring a distinct Asian flavor and aroma to the party. When the sauté train pulls out of the station, there's no stopping, so proper prep is key. Have everything sliced and diced in the size and shape that will guarantee that when it all comes out of the pan, it will be perfectly done.**

Ever wonder how oil keeps things from sticking to a pan? The same way motor oil keeps your engine parts chugging along at several thousand RPMs. A pan, like an engine part, looks smooth. But on a microscopic level, your pan and the average piston are covered with pits, nooks, crannies, and fissures; these cause friction in moving parts in an engine and plenty of sticking in a hot pan. Now, oils—be they motor or cooking—tend to cling to metal because of a slight negativity, and since their long molecules slip and slide on one another, friction and sticking are reduced.

Oils are also efficient heat absorbers, which means they can move heat away from hot engine parts or toward cold foods. That's why food browns so nicely and cooks so quickly when oil is invited to the party.

Besides triglycerides, food oils contain a host of other organic compounds, which can contribute to flavor and aroma, as well as alter the cooking characteristics. This is a factor of the source ingredient, of course, but it's also a factor of how the oil is extracted.

Oils that are extracted simply by pressure alone are referred to as cold-pressed oils; these oils are capable of delivering considerable flavor and aroma. A good example would be extra virgin olive oil.

If heat is applied, more oil can be removed from the source, but the resulting product cannot be referred to as cold press.

Expeller extraction employs a worm screw capable of applying twenty thousand kilopascals (i.e., a lot) of pressure to squeeze oils from less fatty seeds and grains. The extreme pressure produces temperatures near 400°F, which destroys most flavor compounds. Unless the words "crude" or "unrefined" appear on the container, you can assume an expeller oil has been refined with corrosive alkali or steam.

Some seeds like grape seeds and legumes such as soy beans contain so little oil that they have to be ground, scalded, and doused with caustic solvents to get anything at all useful out of them. The resulting oil is then filtered, bleached, and deodorized, resulting in a crystal-clear elixir free of any and all impurities.

What's important to extract from this is that cold-pressed oils are full of a lot of flavor and aroma, but they can't take much heat. Refined filtered oils are squeaky clean with almost no flavor or aroma, but they can take the heat. As you might expect, both deserve places in the kitchen.

Oils, especially those high in polyunsaturated fatty acids, tend to break down and go rancid if they're exposed to oxygen, and the process is accelerated by exposure to light and heat. So consider storing cold-pressed oils in a cool, dark place or even the refrigerator. Just remember that cold oils tend to cloud, a condition that reverses once they return to room temperature. The one common exception is safflower oil, which stays clear regardless of temperature, which is why it's so popular in salad dressings.

Although most experts frown on it, I've become a big fan of frying with plain old refined olive oil, which, despite being 14 percent saturated fat, leads the pack in heart-healthy monounsaturated fats at 76 percent.

TIDBIT | The engine Rudolf Diesel cranked up at the 1900 Paris World Exposition ran on peanut oil.

TIDBIT | Refined and filtered oils are the best for frying because they withstand heat for prolonged periods of time.

THE ORIGINAL IS FULL OF HOT AIR TOO.

// SOFTWARE

4	teaspoons	toasted sesame oil	
1	clove	garlic	minced
1	tablespoon	fresh ginger	minced
8	ounces	carrots	cut ¼ inch thick on the bias
½	teaspoon	kosher salt	
	pinch	black pepper	freshly ground
4	ounces	sugar snap peas	
4	ounces	Savoy cabbage	shredded
¾	ounce	chopped scallion	
1	tablespoon	rice vinegar	
2	teaspoons	fresh cilantro or mint	chopped

TIDBIT In ancient China, sesame oil was used not only for cooking but also for lighting.

// PROCEDURE

1. Heat the oil in a straight-sided **10-inch sauté pan** over medium heat. When the oil begins to shimmer, add the garlic, ginger, carrots, salt, and pepper and sauté for 4 minutes.

2. Add the sugar snap peas and sauté for 1 minute. Add the cabbage and scallion and sauté for 1 minute. Remove from the heat, add the vinegar, and stir to combine, scraping any bits off the bottom of the pan. Sprinkle with the cilantro and toss to combine. Serve immediately.

POTATO CHIPS

4 SERVINGS

As in many simple applications, potato chips are all about details. For instance, the pieces need to hit the oil one at a time. That's the only way to make sure that they don't stick. If they're stuck together when they hit the oil, odds are you'll never be able to pry them apart. This also means that you need to keep them moving gently throughout the entire cooking cycle (but don't worry, it's only going to take a few minutes). Also, as water boils out of the potatoes, it's going to move into the oil before evaporating. This will cool the oil by as much as twenty degrees in just the first couple of minutes, so you've got to keep one hand on the spider and the other hand on the throttle to keep that oil as close to three hundred as possible.

// **SOFTWARE** ///

1	pound	russet potatoes	4 medium, scrubbed and rinsed
2	quarts	olive oil	not extra virgin
	to taste	kosher salt	

// **PROCEDURE** //

1. Heat the oil in a **5-quart cast-iron Dutch oven** over medium-high heat to 300°F.

2. While the oil heats, line a **large bowl** with **paper towels**.

3. On a **mandoline or with a sharp knife**, cut 8 to 10 slices of the potatoes, widthwise, to about the thickness of a dime. Carefully add the slices one at a time to the hot oil. Using a **spider**, constantly move the slices in the hot oil for 3 to 4 minutes, or until golden brown and crisp. Remove the chips with the spider and hold over the oil to drain off as much excess oil as possible.

4. Move the finished chips to the lined bowl and shake to remove additional oil. Adjust the heat as necessary to maintain 300°F and continue slicing and frying the potatoes in small batches. When the final batch has finished frying, sprinkle the chips with salt and shake the bowl to distribute the salt evenly. Remove the paper towels and serve.

 TIDBIT | Potato chips were invented by Chef George Crum at the Moon's Lake Lodge in Saratoga, New York, in 1853.

FRUITY OIL ICE CREAM

APPROXIMATELY 1½ QUARTS

The marketplace is saturated these days with fairly flavorful and even exotic fruit and nut oils that deliver both flavor and heady aroma. Although useful in sauces and vinaigrettes, many of these oils are especially delicious when served cold. Very cold.

// **SOFTWARE** ///

3	cups	whole milk	
1	cup	heavy cream	
6	large	egg yolks	
9	ounces	sugar	
½	cup	cold-pressed fruit or nut oil	such as walnut, pistachio, or extra virgin olive

// **PROCEDURE** ///

1. Combine the milk and cream in a **medium saucepan** over medium heat. Bring the mixture just to a simmer, stirring occasionally, then remove from the heat.

2. **Whisk** the egg yolks until they lighten in color in a **medium bowl**. Gradually add the sugar and whisk to combine. Add the oil and whisk to thoroughly combine.

3. Temper the egg mixture by adding small amounts of the hot cream mixture, approximately a tablespoon at a time, stirring constantly, until about one-third of the cream mixture has been added. Pour in the remaining cream mixture and stir to combine.

4. Return the mixture to the saucepan and place over medium-low heat. Cook, stirring frequently, until the mixture thickens slightly and reaches 170° to 175°F, 5 to 7 minutes. Strain the mixture through a **fine-mesh strainer** into a **container** and refrigerate, uncovered, until it is cool enough not to form condensation on the lid. Cover and refrigerate for 4 hours or up to overnight, until the temperature reaches 40°F or below.

5. Pour into an **ice cream maker** and process according to the manufacturer's directions, 25 to 35 minutes. Serve as is for soft-serve or freeze for another 3 to 4 hours, until the ice cream is firm.

Welcome to your freezer. Bet you've never seen it from quite this perspective. If it looks a little ramshackle, it may be because millions of Americans treat it more like a trash compactor than a time machine, tossing in bits and pieces of leftover this and surplus that, which then disappear into the darkness to be as forgotten as the ark at the end of *Raiders*. Shame, too, because this is probably the most potent food preservation device ever devised, and the items placed herein can, with proper prep and packaging, rank with the very best . . .

TIDBIT | One of the challenges of freezing food is that water molecules, which are normally clumped together, spread out in a regular formation just at the freezing point. This explains why ice takes up more room than the same amount (by weight) of liquid water.

Man has been actively preserving food by freezing for at least three thousand years. In ancient China, fresh foods were stashed in ice caves. The Greeks and the Romans stored snow in straw-lined holes in the ground, though in those climates it probably couldn't keep things frozen, just refrigerated. Both the early Egyptians and Indians dabbled with cooling systems based on evaporation, but it wasn't until Frenchman Ferdinand Carre patented an ammonia compression freezer in 1864 that mechanical deep chilling became a reality. A truly practical method of industrial freezing wouldn't come around for another sixty-five years, when a fur trader and biologist named Clarence Birdseye started using brine-chilled metal plates to freeze blocks of cooked vegetables. The freezing industry got a huge shot in the frosty arm during World War II, when Japanese forces took over much of the world's tin supply, sending the price of cans through the roof and the U.S. armed forces on a food-freezing frenzy. Pretty soon, frozen foods were being designed for consumption on airplanes, tanks, even submarines. When the war ended, the industries that had made so many advancements set their sights on an equally difficult target: the American housewife. Some would argue it was all downhill from there.

Producing quality frozen foods in the home environment means grappling with several physical foes. The first is found in the food itself: the universal ingredient, water. Water's tricky stuff because when it gets cold enough its molecules line up to form crystals, which take up more room than did the original liquid form. This expansion can wreak havoc on food cells.

Consider this beef strip steak, which has spent the last eight hours in the freezer. Deep inside, a great deal of the moisture is bound up in crystals, and that means that any present bacteria are going to have a devil of a time finding the moisture they require to survive. Since bacteria also contain H_2O, freezing halts bacterial activity altogether, though some of the little beasties can survive to decompose another day. While it is in this frozen state, the meat will remain unspoiled for years, but there's a hitch: Home freezers work very slowly, which means that as those little H_2Os start to line up inside, they'll create huge, sharp, jagged crystals that will rise up, slicing and dicing their way through cell walls, muscle fiber, and pretty much anything else that gets in the way. While the meat is frozen, you won't notice this damage, but when it comes time to thaw, all of those perforated cells will start to leak out moisture. This is called "drip loss," and it's a sign of bad eats.

One way to prevent drip loss is to freeze the target food very quickly so that instead of huge, nasty, jagged ice crystals, very tiny ice crystals result. Big commercial freezing operations use massive blast chillers to move heat away from the food with frigid winds. There are other ways of doing it, however. If the food in question is small and relatively uniform—say, like a pea—they float the food in liquid nitrogen, which just happens to boil at 320.5 degrees below zero and can freeze a pea so fast that the resulting ice crystals don't have time to grow to a consequential size.

Most of us don't have blast chillers or liquid nitrogen on hand, but that doesn't mean we can't effectively freeze foods in our relatively warm home freezers. We just need a strategy. Let's say that your butcher went insane and decided to sell you an entire beef strip loin sub-primal at two dollars a pound. You would be a fool not to take it, but you can't eat it all at one time. The goal: Freeze it quickly by increasing the surface-to-mass ratio. Strategy: Cut it into steaks first. I find the best results come from slicing inch- to inch-and-a-half-thick pieces. I even use a ruler to ensure uniformity.

Once your steaks are cut, chill them in the refrigerator on a rack, over a pan, unwrapped, for 1 hour: The colder the meat is when it enters the freezing phase, the faster the freeze and the smaller the ice crystals. Using a rack will enhance air circulation, thus slightly drying the meat's surface. Reducing surface moisture reduces surface ice, which can downgrade the quality in the final product. When they're thoroughly chilled, wrap the steaks tightly in two layers of plastic wrap and place them on an aluminum pan right on the floor of the freezer. The more contact the steaks have with the pan the better. Flip them after a couple of hours and when they're rock hard, stack them up and move them to a heavy-duty zip-top bag that also contains an index card on which you've written down two dates, a "best by" date three months in the future, and a "maximum" date six months in the future. So, if I'm freezing the steaks on April 1, the card says July 1 and October 1.

Fruits and vegetables are a challenge as well. Not because of ice crystals but because of what won't go into an ice crystal. Only the water inside the food will technically freeze, and as the water molecules start joining up and forming crystals, all the other stuff gets pushed out until it forms a syrup that is so concentrated it can never actually freeze. This is one of the reasons a sweet sorbet never freezes rock hard; there's always a liquid phase. This can be a problem with cut fruits and vegetables because these foods contain chemical agents called enzymes, which set various natural changes into action, such as decomposition and ripening, and, unlike bacteria, enzymes are impervious to cold. Enzymes can also go into overdrive in a concentrated environment, which is why fruits and vegetables turn brown and mushy in the freezer. Luckily, enzymes can be neutralized.

High temperatures, such as those delivered by boiling water, can shut down the enzymatic engines of destruction. Of course, high heat can also turn target foods to mush. So for home freezing we employ the blanch-and-shock method, wherein small pieces of the food are quickly boiled, then chilled in ice water before being dried and frozen. Blanching and shocking does not work quite as well for fruits, especially soft fruits that brown quickly from oxidation. Dealing with those enzymes requires a powerful chemical such as ascorbic acid, a.k.a. vitamin C, which can be delivered via maceration in a sugar syrup. Since it's hygroscopic, sugar holds on to water, helping to prevent drying in the freezer. By combining sugar and ascorbic acid, you can maintain sliced, ripe fruit in a state of suspended animation for years.

THE ART OF THE THAW

How you choose to bring your frozen cache back to culinary life greatly affects its quality. A slow thaw in the fridge is best, because it allows time for the food to reabsorb some of the moisture that might be lost due to internal ice crystallization. Of course, the cold environment will help prevent any reawakening surface bacteria from running rampant. Since condensation usually leads to drippage, always thaw in clean, watertight containers. The downside to this method, of course, is time. It could take twelve to twenty-four hours for a couple of steaks to thoroughly thaw. Luckily, there is a shortcut.

If you've seen our award-winning duck episode, you'll no doubt recall that cold water is a very efficient thawing medium, especially if it's moving a little and thus gaining convective action. So for a quick thaw, simply sink sealed bags of frozen food in a pot, bowl, or other container and place it under barely trickling water until thawed. With meat, a weight of some type may be required to keep said item sunken.

PARTS OF A FREEZER

A freezer's nothing but a big insulated box with a heavy door and some bins and shelves hooked up to a souped-up air-conditioning system.

▶ The first part of this system is an electronic thermostat, which monitors the temperature inside your freezer, usually the refrigerator, too.

▶ The thermostat is connected, via wiring, to a device called a compressor, which is either on the bottom or the top of the unit. The compressor resembles a tank, and it compresses what is called a refrigerant, usually Tetrafluoroethane (R134A) or something like it. The refrigerant is compressed until it becomes extremely hot and condenses into a liquid form.

▶ This heat needs to be dissipated, so it's fed through a big set of cooling coils on the back of your unit, slowly giving off its heat, while still being held in a liquid state under pressure.

▶ This coil basically punches through to your freezer, and the refrigerant goes through something called an expansion valve, which releases all of the pressure and allows the refrigerant to immediately evaporate back into a vapor form in the evaporator coil. The process of re-evaporation, called a "phase change," absorbs a huge amount of heat, making the coil extremely cold and therefore capable of sucking the heat out of your food. Regardless of make and model and the various sophistications built into the system, that's really all it comes down to.

Most refrigerator freezers are essentially the same, which means we can generalize our frozen storage approach.

▶ Since the door bins spend a good bit of time swinging out into your nice, warm kitchen, only store items up there that you'll use quickly or that are less likely to sustain damage from partial thawing and refreezing. Examples would include nuts, coffee beans, butter, and bread.

▶ Now, about the main compartment. I want you to promise me that you will always keep a freezer thermometer inside here so that you will know that your box is sticking to zero or colder.

▶ Proper packaging of frozen foods is critical, because freezer air is so dry that it can literally rip water molecules off of frozen food in a process called "sublimation." The unfortunate result: freezer burn, which manifests itself on meat in the form of leathery, dry, whitish spots.

▶ Unlike refrigerators, freezers work best when they are full, but if you just shove stuff in here, you'll never really be able to utilize the space, and you'll never be able to find a darned thing. I use organizational tools that I get at hardware and office supply stores, such as wired shelving and whatnot, so that I can place things in different parts of the freezer and maneuver. I also stash two or three water bottles in there to take up space and act as heat sinks in the event of a power outage. If I need more room, I just move these down to the fridge.

"MISTER, YOU GOTTA STOP CUTTING THE BACKS OUT OF THE APPLIANCES!"

APPLICATION ◰ FROZEN STONE FRUIT

1 POUND FROZEN FRUIT

TIP | Scoop cookie dough onto a sheet pan and freeze, then transfer to a zip-top bag for long-term freezer storage.

// SOFTWARE //

4	ounces	sugar	
1	teaspoon	ground children's vitamin C tablets	
½	teaspoon	smoked paprika	
1	pound	peeled fresh peaches	sliced ½ inch thick

// PROCEDURE //

Combine the sugar, vitamin C, and paprika in a **1-gallon zip-top bag**, seal, and shake to combine. Add the peaches and toss to coat well. Lay the bag flat on a counter and, using a **straw**, suck out any remaining air in the bag. Seal and freeze for up to 6 months.

USE IN PIES, COBBLERS, SMOOTHIES, OR ANY OTHER PLACE YOU WOULD USE FRESH PEACHES.

APPLICATION ◰ FROZEN GREEN PEAS

1 POUND PEAS

// SOFTWARE //

1	gallon	H_2O	plus 2 quarts
1	teaspoon	kosher salt	
1½	pounds	ice	
1	pound	fresh green peas	

// PROCEDURE //

1. Combine the 1 gallon of water and the salt in an **8-quart pot** and place over high heat. Just before the water boils, combine the remaining 2 quarts of water and the ice in a **large bowl**. Set aside.

2. When the water boils, add the peas and cook for 1 minute. Immediately drain in a **colander**, then transfer to the ice water for 1 minute. Pour the peas back into the colander and transfer to a **half sheet pan** lined with **three layers of paper towels**. Pat dry with additional paper towels. Place the pan in the refrigerator for 1 hour.

3. Remove the paper towels and place the sheet pan on the floor of the freezer. Leave the peas on the sheet pan for 2 hours. When frozen, transfer them to a **1-gallon zip-top bag**. Lay the bag flat on a counter and, using a **straw**, suck out any remaining air in the bag. Seal and store in the freezer for up to 3 months.

OH MY, MEAT PIE

EPISODE 196 | SEASON 12 | GOOD EATS

Every now and then a viable *Good Eats* subject stays on the table for a few years, just sorta waiting for a story line to come to it. Such was the case with meat pies. I've always been a fan of shepherd's pie in particular, but I just couldn't come up with the story that would make it watchable for the general public. After all, it's not that flashy, and to tell you the honest truth there's just not that much science involved.

Then Tim Burton's *Sweeney Todd* film came out and I realized all I had to do was get our show inside Mrs. Lovett's London Pie Shop and wind the clock back a hundred or so years. So we painted the set, cast longtime *Good Eatsers* Widdi Turner and Daniel Petrow as Mrs. Lovett and the demon barber, and rented some Victorian clothing. All I had to do at that point was hold on for 21½ minutes, sprinkling a bit of actual food knowledge throughout.

I'VE BEEN WANTING TO GOOF ON THIS MUSICAL FOR YEARS.

Know your pies:

A POT PIE is composed of chopped meat—poultry, typically—with cooked vegetables and a thickened sauce enclosed in either a short dough, puff pastry, or biscuit crust and baked. (Thickening can come from either a béchamel sauce or potatoes.)

A MINCEMEAT PIE does not actually contain any meat, mincemeat being a sticky combination of dried fruit, spices, nuts, and occasionally spirits, bound with a bit of beef suet and baked in a crust.

A CAPE BRETON PORK PIE is a lot like a mincemeat pie, but its fruit mixture is composed primarily of dates. Although pork may have been used at one point (perhaps in the form of lard in the crust), modern recipes generally are void of porcine matter. The pie gets its name, oddly enough, from Cape Breton Island, Nova Scotia, which was originally settled by Scots. Not that that has anything to do with pork.

A COTTAGE PIE is simply a thick meat-and-vegetable stew baked inside a crust of mashed potatoes.

A SHEPHERD'S PIE is a cottage pie containing ground shepherd. In the event that a shepherd is not available, mutton or lamb may be used.

POT PIE

MINCEMEAT PIE

CAPE BRETON PORK PIE

COTTAGE PIE

Mrs. Lovett: Mr. Todd's a barber. His shop's right over our heads.

Mr. Todd: My chair is now open, Mr. Brown.

Mr. Brown: Oh, a bit of a shave would be lovely. Tell me, Mrs. Lovett, exactly what kind of animal is this?

Mrs. Lovett: Um, you're the cook, you tell me.

Mr. Brown: (Picks up some meat and inspects it.) Well, is it mutton?

Mrs. Lovett: Well, of course it's mutton! You're a bit obsessed about the cleanliness, aren't you?

Mr. Brown: Actually, I like to call it sanitation.

Mr. Todd: What have we here, Mrs. Lovett?

Mrs. Lovett: Oh, it's a shepherd's pie, Mr. Todd.

Mr. Todd: I wasn't aware we had any shepherd.

OH MY, MEAT PIE

SHEPHERD'S PIE

8 SERVINGS

// SOFTWARE

FOR THE POTATOES

1½	pounds	russet potatoes	
¼	cup	half-and-half	
2	ounces	unsalted butter	
¾	teaspoon	kosher salt	
¼	teaspoon	black pepper	freshly ground
1	large	egg yolk	

TIP | For boiling, russet potatoes or other "mealy" varieties like Yukon gold are preferred over Red Bliss because a smooth consistency is critical. And please, don't beat them to death unless you want your pie topped with wallpaper paste.

FOR THE MEAT FILLING

2	tablespoons	canola oil	
1	cup	chopped onion	
2		carrots	peeled and finely diced
2	cloves	garlic	minced
1½	pounds	ground shepherd	in a pinch, substitute mutton or lamb stew meat
1	teaspoon	kosher salt	
½	teaspoon	black pepper	freshly ground
2	tablespoons	all-purpose flour	
2	teaspoons	tomato paste	
1	cup	chicken broth	
1	teaspoon	Worcestershire sauce	
2	teaspoons	fresh rosemary	chopped
1	teaspoon	fresh thyme	chopped
½	cup	corn kernels	fresh or frozen
½	cup	English peas	fresh or frozen

// PROCEDURE

1. Heat the oven to 400°F.

2. **Peel** the potatoes and cut them into ½-inch dice. Put them in a **medium saucepan** and cover with cold water. Set said pan over high heat, cover, and bring to a boil. Uncover, drop the heat to maintain a simmer, and cook until tender, 10 to 15 minutes.

3. Heat the oil in a **12-inch sauté pan** over medium-high heat until shimmering. Add the onion and carrots and sauté just until they begin to take on color, 3 to 4 minutes. Add the garlic and stir to combine. Add the meat, salt, and pepper and cook until browned and cooked through, approximately 3 minutes.

4. Sprinkle the meat with the flour, toss to coat, and continue to cook for another minute. Add the tomato paste, broth, Worcestershire sauce, rosemary, and thyme and stir to combine. Bring to a boil, then decrease the heat to low, cover, and simmer slowly for 10 to 12 minutes, until the sauce is thickened slightly.

5. Meanwhile, combine the half-and-half and butter in a microwave-safe container and nuke till warmed through, about 35 seconds.

6. Drain the potatoes and return them to the saucepan. Mash the potatoes (a **masher** is an excellent tool for this, though a hand mixer will also do), then add the hot half-and-half mixture, as well as the salt and pepper. Mash to smoothness, then stir in the egg yolk.

7. Add the corn and peas to the meat mixture and spread evenly in a **7-by-11-inch glass baking dish**. Top with the mashed potatoes, starting around the edges to create a seal to prevent the mixture from bubbling over, and smooth the top with a **rubber spatula**. Place on a **half sheet pan lined with parchment paper** on the middle rack of the oven and bake for 25 minutes, or just until the potatoes begin to brown. Remove to a **cooling rack** and let rest for at least 15 minutes before serving.

ZOEY'S ADVISING ME ON HOW TO BLOCK HER SCENE.

4 SMALL PIES OR 1 LARGE
PIE; 10 TO 12 SERVINGS

Don't be daunted by the number of steps here. They're really quite small and all the components can be prepped ahead of time.

// SOFTWARE ///

FOR THE MINCEMEAT

2		Granny Smith apples	peeled, cored, and quartered
8	ounces	golden raisins	
6	ounces	dark brown sugar	
4	ounces	dried figs	coarsely chopped
2	ounces	dried cherries	
2	ounces	beef suet	coarsely chopped
1	ounce	Crystallized Ginger (page 194)	coarsely chopped
½	cup	brandy	
1		orange	zested and juiced
1		lemon	zested and juiced
½	teaspoon	nutmeg	freshly grated
¼	teaspoon	allspice	freshly ground
¼	teaspoon	cloves	freshly ground

FOR THE CORNMEAL CRUST

12	ounces	all-purpose flour	plus additional for dusting
2½	ounces	stone-ground cornmeal	
1½	ounces	sugar	plus extra for sprinkling
1	teaspoon	table salt	
8	ounces	unsalted butter	chilled
2	ounces	apple cider or juice	
2	ounces	cold H_2O	
1	large	egg	beaten with 1 teaspoon H_2O

SWEET SUET

Suet is often called for in meat pie recipes—and, of course, in the fruit-based mincemeat. Suet is fat that is taken from around the loin and kidneys of a beef or sheep carcass. Its flavor and melt consistency (and mouth-feel) are unique and not, in my opinion, replaceable. That said, I've used fatback as a stand-in with acceptable results.

Mincemeat pie, of course,
contains no meat at all.

MAKE THE MINCEMEAT:

(1) Combine all the ingredients in a **food processor** and pulse 8 to 10 times. Alternatively, if you prefer a finer texture, put the apples, dried fruit, and suet in a **meat grinder with a large die** and grind them together. Transfer to a **bowl** and stir in the remaining ingredients. You may also finely chop the apples, dried fruit, and suet by hand. Transfer to an **airtight container** and store in the refrigerator for at least 3 days or up to 6 months before using.

MAKE THE CRUST:

(2) **Whisk** together the flour, cornmeal, the 1½ ounces sugar, and the salt in a **large bowl**.

(3) Grate the butter on the large side of a **box grater** directly into the dry ingredients. Work together with your hands until the mixture is crumbly.

(4) Add the cider and water and stir with a **spatula** to combine. Knead the dough 5 or 6 times and spritz with additional water if the dough is dry. Shape into a disk, wrap in **plastic wrap**, and chill in the refrigerator for 20 minutes.

(5) Heat the oven to 400°F.

(6) Unwrap the dough and divide it into 4 pieces. Put 2 pieces of the dough on a piece of **parchment paper** and roll each out into an ⅛-inch-thick round that is 6 to 8 inches in diameter.

(7) Spoon about ½ cup of the mincemeat into the center of each round and fold up the edges of the dough to form a wall all the way around.

(8) **Brush** the edges of the crust with the egg mixture and sprinkle lightly with sugar. Transfer the pies on the parchment to a **half sheet pan**. Bake on the middle rack of the oven for 30 minutes, or until the crust is golden brown. Remove from the oven and cool for 30 to 45 minutes before serving. Repeat with the remaining dough and filling.

NOTE: If you prefer one large pie, roll out the dough on a piece of parchment into a 15- to 16-inch round, ¼ to ⅛ inch thick. Trim the edges with a pizza cutter. Carefully slide the rolled-out dough, still on the parchment paper, onto an upside-down half sheet pan. Spoon about 1½ pounds of the mincemeat onto the center of the dough, leaving a 2- to 3-inch margin around the edge of the crust. Fold up the edges of the dough. Bake for 35 minutes, or until the crust is golden.

SAMPLING THE WARES

MRS. LOVETT AND MR. TODD
IN THE 21ST CENTURY

OH MY, MEAT PIE

169

The soybean (*Glycine max*) is a culinary chameleon that,

due to its unique chemical attributes, has managed to work its way into our daily lives in innumerable guises, many of which are delightfully edible. Tofu, soy sauce, miso paste, soybean oil, soy crackers, and even dry-roasted versions of the beans themselves. In addition, the curious and complex chemical composition of *Glycine max* makes it a welcome player in a vast array of nonfood items—from candles to crayons, fuel additives to flooring, hair-care products to pens, even shirts. And then there is the vegetable side of *Glysine max*. If picked young and green, the beans are referred to as edamame, and just a decade ago most Americans had never heard of them, despite the fact that for the last four hundred years or so the Japanese have been calling them . . .

TIDBIT | If you want to grow your own edamame, some popular varieties include Butterbaby, Green Pearls, and Envy.

TIDBIT | Japan Airlines began serving edamame on flights from San Francisco to Japan in 1991.

EDAMAME, THE WONDER FOOD

Whether a protein is considered "complete" depends upon whether it contains the essential amino acids that the human body must acquire from the outside world, including: histidine, leucine, isoleucine, lysine, phenylalanine, threonine, tryptophan, and valine. If we don't get our daily fix of these amino acids we can't make the replacement parts that the body constantly needs, and our existence on this planet could be . . . compromised.

Animal proteins are considered complete proteins, but consuming them usually means dosing up on saturated fats and cholesterol. Soybeans, edamame included, are the only plant food capable of delivering these complete proteins. In other words, you could live off them, which, given their tremendous versatility, doesn't sound like such a bad thing.

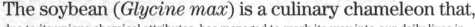

GETTING YOUR AMINOS STRAIGHT

Although the first written record of edamame in Asia comes from a letter written by a Buddhist priest in 1275, the pod's American experience is relatively recent. An entrepreneur name of Samuel Bowen introduced soybeans (which were called "Chinese vetch" in those days) to the Georgia colony in 1765, but those beans were traditional "row" or "commodity" soybeans, which were and still are used primarily as animal fodder.

The first big break for edamame awareness came out of the USDA-sponsored Dorsett-Morse Agricultural Expedition that ventured through Asia in the early 1930s. Expedition leader William J. Morse became America's leading proponent of soybean cultivation. In 1935, Dr. John Kellogg of Battle Creek, Michigan, fame attempted (unsuccessfully) to can them. Soybeans didn't get a real leg up on the American palate until the sushi boom started in California. Sushi was usually served with Japanese beer, but Americans can't sit at a bar with a beer without having something to snack on, so instead of the more standard peanuts and pretzels, the sushi bar owners started to put out a more traditional Japanese accompaniment: edamame, quick boiled, drained, and tossed in coarse sea salt.

Many Asian supermarkets and farmers' markets stock fresh edamame during the summer growing season, and so do a few quality megamarts. If you find them, look for firm, deep-green pods that show no signs of bruising or any other damage and contain at least two if not three beans per pod. If you are unable to find fresh pods, look to edamame that have been blanched and frozen, either shelled or in the pod (the latter being my personal favorite). IQF (individual quick frozen) beans are nearly bulletproof as long as they remain frozen, but fresh edamame just don't improve with age and should be cooked and consumed as quickly as possible.

Edamame conveniently only require water for cooking. All we have to do is excite that water a bit, and for that we need a magnetron. A magnetron emits radio waves in the range of 2.5 gigahertz, a frequency of waves possessing a curious characteristic in that they can be absorbed by water and certain other asymmetrical molecules. Of course, $E = MC^2$ so something has to happen to that energy, and in this case that translates to heat. By focusing the radio output of the magnetron onto the beans, we can cook them without actually applying heat. You could build such a device yourself if you have a few thousand dollars to spare and wicked soldering skills. Or you could just use the microwave.

TRIVIA Okay, so this isn't really an early magnetron or a Sputnik. It's a Weber kettle grill hanging from a rope. . . . We're on a budget, ya know.

Woodson

BASIC EDAMAME

4 SERVINGS IN THE SHELL,
APPROXIMATELY 12 OUNCES SHELLED

// SOFTWARE ///

1	pound	edamame	fresh or frozen, in or out of shell
¼	cup	H$_2$O	
	kosher salt		

// PROCEDURE //

Combine the edamame and water in a **large microwave-safe bowl**. Microwave on high power for 4 to 6 minutes. Drain any excess water, toss with salt to taste, and serve.

ON SHELLING

A whole new world of culinary possibilities opens up when you take a bunch of edamame out of their shells. Some markets do carry shelled beans, but most don't. Which means we're going to need a reliable method for shelling, preferably one aided by mechanical means. I use a regular old counter-mount manual pasta roller for the job.

Just bolt down per the directions and fashion a catch tray out of a clean polystyrene meat tray or some heavy-duty aluminum foil or the like. Then simply set the machine to wide, insert a cooked edamame pod into the rollers from below, and crank so that the pod feeds upward. As the pod passes through the rollers the beans will pop right out and fall into the tray. No muss, no fuss, and gosh darn it, it's kind of fun.

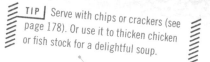

TIP Serve with chips or crackers (see page 178). Or use it to thicken chicken or fish stock for a delightful soup.

ET TU, MAME?

APPLICATION

EDAMAME DIP

APPROXIMATELY 2 CUPS

// SOFTWARE ///

12	ounces	shelled edamame (above)	cooked and cooled
¼	cup	diced onion	
½	cup	fresh cilantro or parsley	
1	clove	garlic	
¼	cup	lemon or lime juice	freshly squeezed
1	tablespoon	brown miso paste	
1	teaspoon	kosher salt	plus additional if desired
1	teaspoon	red chile paste	
¼	teaspoon	black pepper	freshly ground
5	tablespoons	olive oil	

// PROCEDURE //

1. Combine the edamame, onion, cilantro, garlic, lemon juice, miso paste, salt, chile paste, and pepper in a **food processor** and process for 15 seconds. Stop to scrape down the sides of the bowl, then process for another 15 to 20 seconds. With the processor running, slowly drizzle in the oil. Once it's fully integrated, stop and scrape down the bowl, then process for another 5 to 10 seconds. Taste and adjust the salt, if desired.

2. The dip can be refrigerated in an **airtight container** for up to 5 days.

APPLICATION — DRY-ROASTED EDAMAME BRITTLE

1½ POUNDS

TIDBIT Edamame can be used instead of chickpeas in hummus recipes.

TIDBIT During the Civil War, soldiers used roasted soybeans as a substitute for coffee beans.

TIDBIT The cast-iron skillet helps distribute heat evenly across the saucier and prevent scorching.

Just as with its cousin legume, the peanut, our edamame is often dry roasted and turned into a tasty treat commonly available at health food stores and Asian markets. Even though the processing reduces the nutritive value somewhat, these are still a darn fine substitute for a bag of Goobers, especially when you consider the fact that they contain 70 percent less fat and 40 percent more protein, and are a lot less likely to cause allergic reactions. Consult with your doctor.

// SOFTWARE

7	ounces	dry-roasted edamame	
1	tablespoon	soy sauce	
½	teaspoon	cayenne pepper	
½	teaspoon	kosher salt	
22	ounces	sugar	
12	ounces	H_2O	

// PROCEDURE

1. Combine the edamame, soy sauce, cayenne pepper, and salt in a **small bowl**.

2. Line a **half sheet pan** with a **silicone baking mat**.

3. Place a **3-quart saucier** inside a **large cast-iron skillet**. Add the sugar and water to the saucier and cook over high heat, stirring occasionally with a **wooden spoon**, until it comes to a boil. Stop stirring, cover, and cook for 3 minutes.

4. Uncover, lower the heat to medium, and cook until the sugar is a light amber color, approximately 25 minutes.

5. Remove from the heat and stir in the edamame mixture. Working quickly, pour the mixture onto the prepared half sheet pan and spread it thin with an **oiled spatula**. Cool completely, approximately 30 minutes, then break into pieces. Store in an **airtight container** for up to 2 weeks.

FLAT IS BEAUTIFUL IV: GOING CRACKERS

EPISODE 198 | SEASON 12 | GOOD EATS

It's a crying shame so many Americans don't know where basic foods come from. Take crackers. Few edibles have as rich a history or are as easy to make or as satisfying to munch, and yet the average Joe still thinks crackers are baked up by elves with pointy little hats that live in a tree. Too bad, too, because homemade crackers are . . .

TREE ELVES IN TECH-SUPPORT MODE

REHEARSING THE FOREST SCENE

A few hundred years ago, a hard crackerlike bread called hardtack was the standard kibble for sailors and fighting men worldwide. Hardtack was baked twice, a process the French called *bis-cuit*, which is where the English later got the word *biscuit*.[1] The drying made hardtack impervious to spoilage and nearly impossible to eat without breaking a few teeth. Then, in 1801 a ship's cook named Josiah Bent concocted a thinner, more delicate version of hardtack called water crackers. Before long, barrelfuls of these crackers were being shipped to general stores all over the country.

Later, in 1898, the first modern American food company was born. Nabisco not only invented national distribution and marketing, the company also figured out a way to package crackers in freshness-friendly waxed paper, which helped to keep pesky rodents at bay.

No show on crackers would be complete without that manna of the kindergarten crowd, the graham cracker, which is named for a Presbyterian preacher–cum–nutritional reformer by the name of Sylvester W. Graham. Graham preached the virtues of a diet centered on whole grains, fruits, and vegetables back in the mid-nineteenth century, long before science could back up his beliefs. But then, his beliefs were a little . . . strange. To Graham, the problem wasn't cholesterol or fat or calories, it was lust. And he firmly held that lust was fired by irritations in the body caused by an overstimulating diet. Blandness was literally next to godliness. Graham was also firmly convinced that spices could cause insanity.

Clearly a man with some issues.

And yet, in New Jersey in 1822 Graham developed a special flour formula: white flour blended with coarsely ground bran and germ.[2] Theoretically, you could whip up your own graham flour by sifting together two-thirds of a cup of all-purpose flour, a third of a cup of coarsely ground bran, and one and a half teaspoons of wheat germ. But graham flour is relatively easy to find, certainly at health food stores, so I'm not sure I'd go to the trouble.

[1] American biscuits are not cooked twice, though Italian biscotti are.

[2] It is this proportional blending that differentiates graham flour from whole-wheat flour which, in its purest form, is simply ground whole-grain wheat.

TIDBIT | "Polly wants a cracker" was the original slogan for Premium Saltines.

LUST!

SOFTWARE

5	ounces	whole-wheat flour	
4¾	ounces	all-purpose flour	plus extra for rolling
⅓	cup	poppy seeds	
⅓	cup	sesame seeds	
1½	teaspoons	table salt	
1½	teaspoons	baking powder	
3	tablespoons	olive oil	
6½	ounces	H_2O	

PROCEDURE

(1) Heat the oven to 450°F. Line a **half sheet pan** with **parchment paper**.

(2) **Whisk** together both flours, the seeds, salt, and baking powder in a **medium bowl**. Add the oil and stir until combined. Stir in the water until the dough comes together.

(3) Turn the dough out onto a floured surface and knead 4 or 5 times. Divide the dough into 8 equal pieces, cover with a **tea towel**, and rest for 15 minutes.

FOR A THIN SNACKING CRACKER:

(4) On a lightly floured surface, **roll** out one piece of dough to ⅟₁₆ inch thick and place it on the prepared pan. If there is room on the pan, repeat with a second piece of dough. Bake on the middle rack of the oven for 4 minutes, then flip the crackers over and bake for an additional 2 to 3 minutes, or until golden brown. Remove from the oven and place on a **cooling rack**. When cool, break into desired size pieces. Repeat with the remaining dough.

(5) Store in an **airtight container** for up to 2 weeks.

FOR A THICKER DIPPING CRACKER:

(4) On a lightly floured surface, **roll** out the dough as above but to ⅛ inch thick. Bake for 6 minutes, then flip and bake for another 4 to 6 minutes. Remove from the oven and place on a **cooling rack**. When cool, break into desired size pieces. Repeat with the remaining dough.

(5) Store in an **airtight container** for up to 2 weeks.

N O T E : You can use a regular rolling pin as described above, but for an even thickness and easier rolling, use a lightly floured pasta roller. Flatten the dough until it will pass through the first setting and keep rolling until you've gotten to the highest number that your pasta roller will allow without tearing the dough. Bake according to the thin cracker instructions above. Be sure to watch the crackers carefully as they bake; cooking times will vary depending on the thickness of the dough.

TIDBIT | Not only will the seeds in these crackers add subtle nutty flavors, they'll bring a fair amount of nutrition to the party. Sesame seeds, for instance, are a great source of manganese, copper, calcium, magnesium, iron, phosphorus, vitamin B₁, zinc, and dietary fiber. And poppy seeds . . . well, they taste great, and they have calcium in them—and you don't have to worry, because despite what you've read online they will not cause you to fail a workplace drug test.

GRAHAM CRACKERS

25 TO 30 (2-INCH) CRACKERS

Making your own graham crackers is well worth the time. And, unfortunately for the bland memory of Mr. Graham, they are anything but bland.

// **SOFTWARE** ///

8⅜	ounces	graham flour	
1⅞	ounces	all-purpose flour	
3	ounces	dark brown sugar	
¾	teaspoon	aluminum-free baking powder	
½	teaspoon	baking soda	
½	teaspoon	kosher salt	
⅛	teaspoon	ground cinnamon	
3	ounces	unsalted butter	cut into ¼-inch cubes and chilled
2¼	ounces	molasses	
1½	ounces	whole milk	
½	teaspoon	vanilla extract	

// **PROCEDURE** ///

(1) Combine the flours, brown sugar, baking powder, baking soda, salt, and cinnamon in a **food processor** and pulse several times. Add the butter and pulse until the mixture resembles cornmeal. Add the molasses, milk, and vanilla and process until the dough forms a ball, approximately 1 minute. Press the ball into a ½-inch-thick disk, wrap in **plastic wrap**, and refrigerate for 30 minutes.

(2) Heat the oven to 350°F.

(3) Unwrap the chilled dough. **Roll** the dough out to ⅛ inch thick between two large pieces of **parchment paper**. Slide the rolled dough and parchment paper onto a **half sheet pan**. Remove the top sheet of parchment paper and, using a **rolling pizza cutter**, cut the dough into 2-inch squares. Trim off any rough edges. Using a **fork**, poke holes all over the top of the dough.

(4) Leave the crackers on the pan and bake on the middle rack of the oven for 25 minutes, or until the edges just start to darken. Remove from the oven, set the sheet pan with the crackers on a **cooling rack**, and cool completely. Break into individual crackers and store in an **airtight container** for up to 2 weeks.

CONCERNING BAKING POWDERS

Basic or "single-acting" baking powders are simply a mixture of one part baking soda and two parts cream of tartar, an acidic crystal harvested from inside red wine barrels. When dissolved in water, the acid and base react, releasing carbon dioxide, which provides the leavening. The addition of aluminum—sodium aluminum sulfate, to be exact—slows the reaction so that much of the gas is released only when the dough or batter is good and hot. Problem is, aluminum is quite bitter, a fact that may not cause problems when strong flavors like chocolate are in the spotlight, but in the subtle flavor landscape of the cracker, aluminum stands out in a big, bad way. Although they don't puff out as much CO_2, "double-acting" baking powders utilizing neutrally flavored calcium acid phosphate are the way to go when neutrality is desired.

10 TO 12 SERVINGS

Although Americans can certainly take pride in their cracker heritage, ours is not the only cracker-happy region in the world. One of the oldest crackers, lavash, is a traditional Middle Eastern flatbread, which was originally made with just flour, water, and salt and baked in a clay or brick oven. Don't have a clay or brick oven? No problem; we can adapt.

// SOFTWARE

14½	ounces	all-purpose flour	plus extra for rolling
1	tablespoon	table salt	
½	teaspoon	sugar	
⅔	cup	H_2O	plus additional if needed
1	large	egg	
5	tablespoons	butter	melted and cooled

// PROCEDURE

1. **Whisk** together the flour, salt, and sugar in a **medium bowl**. In a separate **small bowl**, whisk together the water, egg, and 2 tablespoons of the butter. Add the egg mixture to the dry ingredients and stir until the dough comes together, adding additional water if the dough is dry. Knead the dough in the bowl 5 or 6 times. Turn the dough out onto the counter, divide into thirds, cover with a **tea towel**, and rest for 30 minutes.

2. Heat the oven to 375°F.

3. Place a **half sheet pan** upside down on a surface that will prevent sliding. Lightly butter the back of the half sheet pan using some of the remaining butter. Working with one ball at a time, place the dough on the back of the sheet pan and roll the dough out to an even ⅛-inch thickness. Gently stretch the edges of the dough so they fall slightly below the edge of the pan and hold the dough in place.

4. Lightly **brush** the dough with butter and bake on the middle rack of the oven for 10 to 15 minutes, until golden brown. Remove the lavash to a **cooling rack**. Repeat with the remaining dough, on a cooled half sheet pan. Break each sheet into shapes and sizes as desired. When completely cooled, store in an **airtight container** for up to 5 days.

No dish represents Creole cuisine like beans and rice, and by Creole, we mean the cuisine of New Orleans, right? Well, not so fast. Truth is, New Orleans is the great northern capital of a Creole empire encompassing Cuba, Puerto Rico, and most of the West Indies. It is here that the Old World and the New, the light and the dark, the imperial and the indigenous, first converged. So, when making "authentic" red beans and rice we must divide our grocery list along cultural lines. (Yes, I realize that placing any such label on a single recipe is dangerous, but hey, you have to take a stand somewhere.)

A BOWL OF FIBER AND VITAMINS

In red beans and rice, we have ourselves a nice, big, delicious bowl of fiber, vitamins, minerals, and some protein. But mostly we've got a big, delicious bowl of carbohydrates. I hesitate to point this out because folks tend to freak at the mere mention of the word. Truth is, just as different proteins and fats affect the body in myriad ways, so do different carbohydrates.

At their most basic, carbs are composed of oxygen, carbon, and hydrogen and come in three basic models:

▶ MONOSACCHARIDES, or single sugars, like glucose blood sugar;

▶ DISACCHARIDES, or double sugars, like sucrose (regular table sugar); and

▶ POLYSACCHARIDES, or complex carbs, which are constructed from at least three sugars and often many, many more.

What's important to keep in mind is that simple carbs are the only form our bodies can actually absorb. So what really matters here is how the carbs are broken down. Carbs are fuel, but they can't be used by our cells until the pancreas secretes the hormone insulin, which essentially grants our cells chemical permission to suck in the fuel. A large intake of simple carbs—like, say, a candy bar—triggers a massive outflow of insulin, which can be a problem because once the sugar has been

socked away in the cells there is usually a surplus of insulin in the blood. And like all hormones, that insulin demands activity, so it tells the brain, "Send more sugar." Thus the consumption of mass quantities of simple carbs tend to beget the continued mass consumption, and, sure as shootin', that leads to Sansabelt slacks. (Too young to remember Sansabelt? Go look it up.)

A bowl of beans may be all carbs, but most of those molecules are "complex" in nature and therefore break down very slowly in the system. Insulin is produced and released but at a slower, more controlled rate that doesn't result in a spike of blood sugar. And that helps to prevent Cujo-like candy rampages.

THE BEANS: By the seventeenth century, West Africans, kidnapped and put to hard labor on sugar plantations, had become the majority population in the islands of the Caribbean. Fortunately, they brought their wisdom regarding the nutritiousness of beans with them. Although "pigeon" peas ruled in the Lesser Antilles and black beans in Cuba and Central America, in Puerto Rico, Jamaica, and New Orleans, the red kidney was the once and future bean. New Orleans cooks tend to prefer smaller varieties, but I say that if it's red and kidney shaped, it's welcome in my pot. Canned beans may be a temptation, but one you should resist. The slow exchange of starch and flavored broth that takes place in the pot is critical to a successful pot of beans.

THE RICE: Slavery was abolished in the British West Indies in 1833, leaving the plantations there woefully understaffed. This vacuum was filled with indentured servants from China and India, which just so happen to be the two most rice-centric cultures on earth. Long-grain rices are the standard for most bean-and-rice dishes, but I prefer to stick with locally grown product whenever possible, and some mighty fine American basmati rices are grown in Texas, Louisiana, and Arkansas. Whatever you do, avoid parboiled, converted, and boil-in-the-bag rices.

THE TRINITY: Next stop: the European continent. In the sultry Caribbean climate, mirepoix, the ubiquitous chorus of onion, carrot, and celery upon which so much French cuisine is constructed, and *sofrito*, the tomato, garlic, and pepper foundation so critical to Spanish plates, intermarried and gave birth to the "trinity": one onion, two green peppers, and three ribs of celery. Most red-bean-and-rice applications also call for two dry herbs from Europe, bay and thyme. As for the New World, well, we can never forget cayenne pepper, a nod to the fiery foods of Jamaica, mon.

THE PORK: The final ingredient is lesser known, but one hundred percent New Orleans. In the days before refrigeration, most of the pork that was slaughtered in or around hot and humid New Orleans was preserved not by smoking, but by pickling. True red beans and rice is indeed seasoned with the tangy goodness of pickled pork, and once you taste it, you'll know why. It's pretty tough stuff to find outside of Louisiana, but you can make your own from a bit of plain old pork butt.

TIDBIT | In 1926, a plate of red beans and rice in New Orleans would set you back about 26 cents.

TIDBIT | The man for whom the New Orleans International Airport is named used to sign autographs, "Red Beans and Ricely Yours, Louis Armstrong."

APPLICATION · PICKLED PORK

APPROXIMATELY 1½ POUNDS

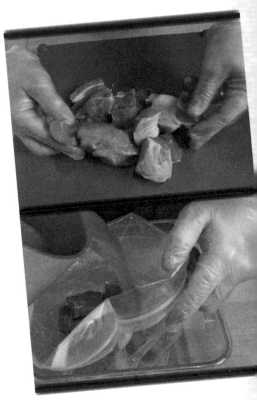

// SOFTWARE

2	cups	H$_2$O	
1	cup	apple cider vinegar	
¼	cup	kosher salt	
6	cloves	garlic	peeled and crushed
2	tablespoons	sugar	
2	tablespoons	yellow mustard seeds	
2	tablespoons	hot sauce	
1	tablespoon	celery seeds	
1		bay leaf	
¼	teaspoon	whole black peppercorns	
8	ounces	ice	
1½	pounds	boneless pork butt	cut into 2-inch cubes

// PROCEDURE

1. Combine all of the ingredients except the ice and pork in a **2-quart nonreactive saucepan** set over high heat, and bring to a boil. Lower the heat and maintain a simmer for 3 minutes. Remove from the heat, add the ice, and stir.

2. Put the pork in a **1-gallon zip-top bag** and add the cooled pickling liquid. Remove as much air as possible; seal the bag and refrigerate for at least 3 days, turning the bag occasionally. Use within 2 weeks or remove the pork from the brine and freeze.

DESPERATELY TRYING TO REMEMBER MY LINES...

RED BEANS AND RICE

8 SERVINGS

The method I use for cooking the rice is a rather unorthodox one. It's speedy, and I find it results in a better, more consistent product than plain steaming. Because the rice is sautéed over high heat, more of the grains' nutty flavors are released.

// SOFTWARE

FOR THE BEANS

2	tablespoons	vegetable oil	
1	medium	onion	chopped
2	medium	green bell peppers	chopped
3	stalks	celery	chopped
2	teaspoons	kosher salt	
1	teaspoon	black pepper	freshly ground
5	cloves	garlic	minced
12	ounces	Pickled Pork (page 181)	cut into 1-inch pieces; see note
3		bay leaves	
1	teaspoon	dried thyme	
1	teaspoon	hot sauce	
½	teaspoon	cayenne pepper	
2	quarts	H_2O	
1	pound	red kidney beans	rinsed and picked of debris

FOR THE RICE

3	cups	H_2O	
1½	tablespoons	unsalted butter	
2	cups	long-grain rice	
½ to 1	teaspoon	kosher salt	

// PROCEDURE

MAKE THE BEANS:

1. Heat the oil in a **7-quart Dutch oven** over medium-high heat. Add the onion, bell pepper, celery, salt, and black pepper. Cook, stirring frequently, until the onion and celery are semi-translucent and the bell peppers are tender, 6 to 8 minutes. Add the garlic and cook for 1 to 2 minutes, stirring constantly. Add the pickled pork, bay leaves, thyme, hot sauce, cayenne pepper, water, and beans and increase the heat to high. Cook, stirring frequently, until the mixture comes to a boil, 6 to 8 minutes.

TIDBIT The United States grows only about 1 percent of the world's rice.

TIDBIT Archeological evidence indicates that beans were cultivated as far back as 7000 B.C.

(2) Lower the heat to maintain a simmer, cover, and cook for 1½ hours, stirring every 30 minutes. Uncover, increase the heat slightly to maintain a steady simmer, and continue to cook for another 30 to 40 minutes, until the beans are tender and the sauce is thickened to your liking. If you prefer an even creamier texture, mash some of the beans with a **potato masher**.

WHILE THE BEANS ARE COOKING, MAKE THE RICE:

(3) In a kettle or saucepan, bring the water to a boil.[1]

(4) Meanwhile, put the butter in a **3-quart saucepan** over medium heat. When the butter begins to bubble, add the rice and stir to combine. Add the salt and cook for 2 to 3 minutes, stirring frequently.

(5) Carefully pour the boiling water over the rice. (There will be a lot of sputtering and spitting.) Slap on the lid and decrease the heat to the lowest setting. Cook for 15 minutes, kill the heat, and rest, uncovered, for 5 minutes.

(6) Turn the rice out into a large bowl and toss with a large fork. This will help to set the starch coat on each grain and prevent sticking.

(7) Spoon the rice onto plates, top with the beans, and don't forget to say the blessing.

NOTE: If you don't have time to pickle your pork, use unsmoked slab bacon cut into chunks.

[1] An electric kettle is my preferred tool for the job, as it will bring the H_2O to 212°F in the time it takes to sauté the rice.

HARVESTING THE KIDNEY BEANS IS A TRICKY BUSINESS.

SWITCHED ON
BAKLAVA

EPISODE 200 | SEASON 12 | GOOD EATS

Hello, and welcome to the ever-swelling menagerie

of maleficent comestibles known as the Food Gallery. Today, we stroll a peculiar hall that houses foods much feared, not for their flavors, but for the struggles required to put them to plate. Consider the confoundingly contradictory baked Alaska, the tempestuously temperamental *tarte tatin*, and, of course, the famously delicious and infamously cantankerous baklava, an antagonistic amalgamation of nuts, syrup, and phyllo dough, a substance that many modern cooks won't allow in the house for fear of finding in its unfurling pages of crackling, crinkling horror a foe insurmountable and inedible. I would argue that phyllo's nasty reputation has been falsely generated by manufacturers intent upon selling you their *spanakopita*, their *burek*, and, yes, their baklava. Furthermore, the cook who fights this fear with solid science, righteous technique, and a handful of decent ingredients will surely be rewarded, not just with dessert, but with . . .

KNOWLEDGE CONCENTRATE

▷○ **Phyllo is bread, plain and simple. You're not afraid of bread, are you? Sure, it's as thin as a page from the family Bible, but it's still just bread. Look, if phyllo's gotten a bad rap, it's because people want to fuss over it all the time, and we're not going to do any fussing. But we do have to do some shopping.**

Luckily for all, nearly every megamart freezer case in the country offers up frozen boxes of phyllo, and personally I wouldn't buy it any other way. Just remember, the stuff is very sensitive to time and temperature abuses, which can leave it dry, crusty, and clumped together. So I suggest you either grab from the very back of the stash or shop at a market where a high turnover is guaranteed, such as a Middle Eastern or a Greek market. And bring a cooler and pack it in between other frozen goods, like ice cream and, well, more ice cream, and get it home ASAP.

▷○ **Although *phyllo* means "leaf" in Greek, and many Greek restaurants feature dishes wrapped in its delicate crunch, baklava was actually born far to the north, where once upon a time nomadic Turks dined on unleavened griddle breads called *yufka*, while the Persians next door snacked on nut-and-honey concoctions. Somehow the two delicacies collided, and gooey goodness and leafy crispness came together.**

Why pistachios? This drupe was probably born in northeastern Iran or Afghanistan, and was such a favorite with Nebuchadnezzar that the Babylonian king planted pistachio trees in his legendary hanging gardens. Legend also holds that the queen of Sheba passed a law declaring pistachios to be a royal food, forbidden to common folk. Fast-forward to Rome, A.D. 30, when the emperor Vitellius introduced pistachios to the city states, and from what they say, he loved them so much he finished every single meal with a big ol' handful.

Why walnuts? Walnuts were also featured in the hanging gardens of Babylon, but there is also a strong Greek connection. Once upon a time the god Dionysus (who really got around) fell in love with a mysterious woman named Karya. When she died, he turned her into a tree. (Wacky lovers, those Greeks.) The Romans also dug walnuts, as the name itself stems from *Jovis glans*, which loosely translates to "the royal nut of Jove," who was of course the Roman version of Zeus. Although any walnuts will serve adequately, I prefer the Persian varieties, which are meatier and more authentic to the dish. They're also just about the only commercial type available.

Baklava was born along the old Middle Eastern trade routes, which explains why most classic recipes for the dish call on both cinnamon and allspice—very precious commodities in those days. We would never, ever reach for preground megamart spices for a dish like this, and this is especially true of allspice. The little berries of *Pimento officinalis* are very regular in shape and size and are therefore easy to dose out and grind. Cinnamon's a little trickier, because most of what is sold as cinnamon in this country is actually *Cinnamomum cassia*, which has a rather harsh flavor and aroma. What we need for this dish is true cinnamon, *Cinnamomum zylanicum*, which is available from any good Internet spice shop. Its quills are lighter in color than those of cassia, and the best stuff comes from the base of the tree and can be rather loglike.

Basic phyllo handling and layering tips:

— When ready to work, move a one-pound package straight from the freezer to the microwave oven and nuke on high for sixty seconds.

— Phyllo is easier to work with if it's the right size. So just lay your target pan across the stack and use it as a guide, trimming with a sharp knife or, even better, a sharp pizza cutter.

— Traditionally, a moist towel is laid across the phyllo stack to keep it from drying out. Hogwash, I say. Just work fast and skip futzing with the towel.

— Always brush the target pan with butter and don't skimp on the corners.

— When laying on the sheets, move your hands so that the side of the sheet farthest from you goes down first. Imagine you're putting a top sheet on a bed, fluffing it outward and laying down the side you're holding last.

— Sprinkle some butter all over the sheet, then smooth it with the brush, moving from the inside out in all directions. This way, the sheets stay smooth and any air captured between them is worked out.

THE CREW LOVES TO PLAY DRESS-UP.

CLARIFIED BUTTER

Melt a pound of butter in a heavy saucepan over low heat and slowly cook until the bubbling ceases and the liquid turns clear, 30 to 40 minutes depending on the water content. Strain and cool, being sure to leave any solids in the bottom of the pan. Or, once the butter is clear, remove the pan from the heat and quickly add two inches of hot tap water. Since it is less dense than water, the now clarified butter will float to the top, and in a few hours in the refrigerator it will solidify into a big yellow Frisbee that you can lift out and use. Use it immediately or wrap in wax paper and refrigerate, or add aluminum foil and freeze it for up to two months.

// SOFTWARE ///

FOR THE PASTRY

1	5-inch	cinnamon stick	broken into 2 or 3 pieces
15 to 20	whole	allspice berries	
6	ounces	blanched almonds	
6	ounces	raw or roasted walnuts	
6	ounces	shelled raw or roasted pistachios	
⅔	cup	sugar	
¼	cup	H_2O	
1	teaspoon	rosewater	
1	pound	phyllo dough	thawed
8	ounces	clarified unsalted butter	melted (see sidebar, left)

FOR THE SYRUP

1¼	cups	honey	
1¼	cups	H_2O	
1¼	cups	sugar	
1	5-inch	cinnamon stick	
1	2-inch piece	fresh orange peel	

// PROCEDURE //

MAKE THE PASTRY:

1. Heat the oven to 350°F.

2. Grind the cinnamon stick and whole allspice in a **spice grinder** until fine.

3. Pulse the almonds, walnuts, pistachios, sugar, and freshly ground spices in a **food processor** until finely chopped, but not pasty or powdery, about 15 quick pulses. Set aside.

4. Combine the water and rosewater in a **small spritz bottle** and set aside.

5. Trim the sheets of phyllo to fit the bottom of a **9-by-13-by-2-inch metal baking pan**. **Brush** the bottom and sides of the pan with butter, lay down a sheet of phyllo and brush with butter. Repeat this step 9 more times, for a total of 10 sheets of phyllo. Top with one-third of the nut mixture and spread thinly. Spritz thoroughly with the rosewater. Layer 6 more sheets of phyllo with butter in between all of them, followed by another third of the nuts, and spritz with rosewater. Repeat with another 6 sheets of phyllo, butter, the remaining nuts, and rosewater. Top with 8 sheets of phyllo, brushing with butter in between sheets. Brush the top generously with butter.

6. Bake for 30 minutes. Remove from the oven and cut into 28 squares. Return the pan to the oven and bake for another 30 minutes. Remove from the oven, place on a **cooling rack**, and cool the pastry for 2 hours before adding the syrup.

MAKE THE SYRUP:

7. During the last 30 minutes of cooling, combine the honey, water, sugar, cinnamon, and orange peel in a **4-quart saucepan** over high heat. Stir occasionally until the sugar is dissolved. Bring to a boil and boil for 10 minutes, stirring occasionally. Remove from the heat and discard the orange peel and cinnamon stick.

8. After the baklava has cooled for 2 hours, re-cut the entire pan following the same lines as before. Pour the hot syrup evenly over the top of the baklava, allowing it to run into the cuts and around the edges of the pan. Set aside, uncovered, until completely cool. Cover and store at room temp for at least 8 hours and up to overnight before serving. Store, covered, at room temperature for up to 5 days.

TIDBIT | Sugar from cane really didn't make it to the Middle East until the tenth or eleventh century, which is why most of the classic desserts of the region are sweetened exclusively with honey.

Butter and oil hide here

CONCERNING BASTING BRUSHES

Most cooks don't think too much about basting or basting brushes despite the effect that they can have on the final appearance, flavor, and texture of many foods. Let us consider the options, beginning with shapes.

▶ Round brushes are ideal for distributing shortening into nooks and crannies of pans—say, a Bundt pan or an intricate kugelhopf. It's a blunt tool meant to be jabbed and poked rather than brushed.

▶ For actual brushing, we have the classic flat paintbrush style, which comes in varying widths and lengths, and like the hardware-store models they resemble, they smoothly apply low- to medium-viscosity liquids such as melted butter and oil.

▶ A "mop" brush is meant to slop and plop barbecue sauce and the like onto big ol' hunks of hog and other critters. Not exactly a precision tool.

Let's talk materials.

▶ Natural bristles or hog's-hair brushes load well, which means that they soak up a lot of material, and they neatly apply a wide range of viscosities. But they tend to be hard to wash and they can pick up and hold strange flavors. What's worse is that as they age, they start dropping bristles into your food, which is never good eats.

▶ Nylon bristles don't load up very well, they're vulnerable to heat damage, and they're a pain to clean. Nylon brushes are cheap, but you get what you pay for—and I, for one, am not willing to send one more to the landfill.

▶ If you hang out in a cooking emporium or have over the last few years, you have no doubt noticed that silicone basting brushes, with their goofy shapes and bright candy colors, have come to monopolize the racks. Silicone is easy to clean, it's dishwasher safe, it can tolerate temperatures in excess of 600°F, and the brushes are perfect for tickling things, which may or may not matter, depending on . . . never mind. Problem is, silicone loads lousily, and that means making a lot of drippy trips back and forth from the reservoir to the target. I would pooh-pooh these things altogether were it not for one small advance. Certain models now sport little flat flaps, right in the middle of the bristles, which are full of liquid-holding holes, and they are very efficient indeed. I still keep a few other brushes around for specialty tasks, but for butter there can be only one and this is it.

I don't know about you, but I can remember being a kid and sitting at the dinner table and having my mom screech, "Eat your vegetables!" When I asked why, she'd say, "Because they're good for you." I would parry with the always-irritating-when-heard-in-rapid-repetition "Why?" And then Mom would have to fall back on the one line that gives every kid a feeling of smug satisfaction: "Because I say so."

Truth is, Mom didn't have an answer, and I knew it. Sure, she might have been able to play the vitamin card, but she knew I would counter with the classic chewable Flintstone's maneuver, and she'd be right back where she started, only with a bad case of the rage shakes. These days, kids have a tougher time, because research is piling high about the nutritional power of food. Some edibles are so packed with complex chemical goodness that they're now being looked upon as bona-fide superfoods, which, now that we know what they're actually capable of, we'd be silly not to consume in mass quantities. The problem is, many of these foods aren't really everyday fare.

Consider the cranberry. Although consumption of cranberry juice cocktail and dried cranberries is up, most of us down a dose of fresh berries maybe once a year, usually just after a mouthful of turkey and right before a football game. And that's a shame, because not only are cranberries good medicine, they're most definitely . . .

PECTINS

Like other connecting tissues—say, gelatin or starch—pectins are long-chain carbohydrates whose primary function is to help hold fruit cell walls together while the fruit itself ripens. In that way, they function a lot like rebar, which is used to reinforce concrete buildings and keep them from crumbling. In most fruit, pectins dissolve during the final stages of ripening, but in cranberries these soluble fibers just hang around, which is a good thing if you like cranberry sauce, which will solidify in almost any shape you pour it into.

TIDBIT | It takes about 4,400 cranberries to produce 1 gallon of juice.

TIDBIT | The cranberry is one of the only fruits that becomes less sweet as it ripens.

There is no written reference to tell us whether or not cranberries were actually served during that mythic first Thanksgiving, the three-day feast held between the settlers and the natives in 1621, but we do know that the local natives had been eating cranberries out of hand for centuries, and grinding them with dried meat and fat to create the power provision known as pemmican, which they consumed during the winter months. Not only did the acidic berries act as a preservative for the meat, but the vitamin C also helped to prevent scurvy. We can also assume that the English settlers recognized these New World cranberries as a larger version of a similar fruit found all over England called thin wortel or marsh wortel. Over the next hundred and fifty years, wild cranberries worked their way into many a settler's supper, in everything from breads and puddings to meat courses, in which the acidity of the berries helped to cut the fattiness of New World game.

Cranberries are technically epigynous or "false" berries that grow on long, low vines over soft marshy ground referred to as bogs. They're harvested via one of two methods.

GETTING BOGGED DOWN IN MY WORK

In DRY HARVESTING, berries are picked right off their pesky little vines. Typically, dry berries are packaged and sold as either fresh or frozen whole berries. This is a very small percentage of the crop. A great majority go into sauces or juice or other applications where physical condition isn't as critical as tonnage, which is why most cranberries are harvested via the WET METHOD. Inside each and every little ruby-red cranberry is a little air bubble. Ergo, cranberries float. So, to easily separate them from the vine, all you have to do is flood the bog in twelve to eighteen inches of water. Then you drive through the bog with a strange-looking contraption called a "beater," which essentially flogs the berries right off the vine so they can be corralled together and sucked up via vacuum into tanks for transport.

Once they're delivered to the plant, the truck dumps the wet berries back into water, which moves them into the processing area. Dry-harvest berries go through additional handling. The field bins are dumped into a giant vibrating sorter that separates out the sticks and stones and vines and pretty much anything that isn't a berry. A conveyor then whisks what's left into giant separators that utilize the cranberries' bounce-ability to sort out the perfect from the not so perfect, as well as the downright malformed, soft, and soggy.[1]

CONVENTIONAL
MASSACHUSETTS
Loose Cranberries
$1.99 LB

From bog to bag, very little happens to cranberries to alter their natural state. They're not even washed, because that would seriously shorten the impressive shelf life of bagged *Vaccinium macrocarpon*, which can be as long as two months in the refrigerator or six months in the freezer.

Since World War II, most of the cranberry crop in this country has gone into quivering columns of canned goo labeled "cranberry sauce." It's a great concept for two reasons:

1. Cranberries are kind of tough to take on their own, and the sauce approach helps allied flavors come into play.

2. Although several fruits possess the mysterious ability to form jellies without the addition of gelatin or pectin, no fruit is better at it than cranberries, and best of all, this power can be easily harnessed at home.

[1] Some of the best sorting devices in use today are old wooden models that have been around since the 1920s. One of the nicest things about visiting a cranberry plant is seeing these crazy old devices still working away.

I'm something of a purist and prefer to keep my cranberry sauce on the simple side, but feel free to spice things up at will. You could add nutmeg to the mix, or cloves, or ginger. If something tropical suits, you could stir in some finely minced chiles or some chopped vanilla bean, or perhaps cardamom. Heck, as far as flavorings go, the sky's the limit. Just don't tinker around in the engine room: The amount of fruit, water, acid, sweetness, and time need to remain constant.

// SOFTWARE

¼	cup	orange juice	freshly squeezed
¼	cup	100% cranberry juice	not cocktail
1	cup	honey	
1	pound	fresh cranberries	washed and sorted

// PROCEDURE

1. Combine the orange juice, cranberry juice, and honey in a **2-quart saucepan** over medium-high heat. Bring to a boil, then lower the heat to medium-low and simmer for 5 minutes.

2. Add the cranberries and cook for 15 minutes, stirring occasionally, until the cranberries burst and the mixture thickens. Do not cook for more than 15 minutes, as the pectin will start to break down and the sauce will not set as well. Remove from the heat and cool for 5 minutes.

3. Carefully spoon the cranberry sauce into a **3-cup mold**. Refrigerate for at least 6 hours and up to overnight.

4. Once the cranberry sauce has cooled, overturn the mold and slide out the sauce. Slice and serve.

NOTE: Just to impress my friends and intimidate my enemies, I make my own mold by joining two clean 16-ounce cans together. The resulting tube of jiggling goodness is an awesome sight to behold.

CRANBERRIES AND UTI

An impressive pile of research has shown that vitochemicals in cranberries called proanthocyanidins, or PACs for short, can prevent bacterial infections in various parts of the body, especially the mouth, stomach, and urinary tract, where bacteria can adhere to healthy tissue and colonize, making you sick. Of course, antibiotics seek to kill these same bugs but often just make bacteria mad and grant them an opportunity to develop a resistance to the drug. PACs, on the other hand, stick to the bonding structures on the bacteria, preventing them from sticking to your insides. If they can't stick, they can't make you sick. Of course, this is a preventative measure, but if you ask me it's one worth taking.

2 empty cans (soup, beans, etc.)

Duct tape over aluminum foil

The cranberry goop

BOB'S BE

BEANS

CRAN OPENING

THE CRANBERRY TUBE OF DOOM!

APPLICATION — CRANBERRY GRANITA

6 TO 8 DESSERT SERVINGS

// **SOFTWARE** //

2	cups	H_2O	
5½	ounces	cranberries	washed and sorted
¾	cup	sugar	
½	teaspoon	lime zest	finely grated

// **PROCEDURE** //

1. Simmer the water, cranberries, and sugar in a **small saucepan** over medium-high heat until the berries begin to pop, approximately 7 minutes.

2. Remove from the heat. Puree with an **immersion blender** for 1 minute. Pass the mixture through a **fine-mesh strainer** directly into a **9-by-13-inch metal pan**. Do not press on the skins. Simply allow the juice to drip through the strainer. Add the lime zest and stir to combine.

3. Freeze until set, at least 6 hours and up to overnight. Scrape the mixture with a **fork** to create a shaved ice texture. Serve immediately.

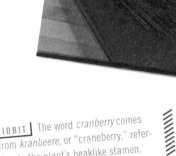

TIDBIT The word *cranberry* comes from *kranbeere*, or "craneberry," referring to the plant's beaklike stamen.

TIDBIT In 1810, Henry Hall, a Revolutionary War veteran, made the first attempt to cultivate the wild cranberry.

APPLICATION — FRESH CRANBERRY COSMO

1 COCKTAIL

With its not-too-sweet flavor and crimson hue, cranberries have long been popular with mixologists, but until recently it was only bottled juice full of sugar that barkeeps reached for. I'm happy to say that now the whole berry is making its way back to the bar, due in part to the popularity of drinks such as the cosmopolitan, an unabashedly girly descendant of the martini.

// **SOFTWARE** //

1	ounce	vodka	
2½	ounces	Cranberry Granita (above)	
½	ounce	lime juice	freshly squeezed

// **PROCEDURE** //

Shake all the ingredients in a **cocktail shaker** until the granita melts completely. Pour into a **martini glass** and serve immediately.

CRAN OPENING

191

TIDBIT | Ginger comes from a Sanskrit word meaning "horn root."

TIDBIT | Gingerbread men were created for the court of Queen Elizabeth I.

Scene opens with AB sitting in a chair with a pad of paper. On the couch before him lies the Gingerbread Man.

```
AB: I want to make sure I understand this. You ran away from
your elderly parents, then narrowly escaped being consumed by,
let me see, it was a chicken, a dog, a cow, and a horse, before
you were attacked and injured by a wily fox. Is that right?

The Gingerbread Man displays his bandaged arm.

AB: Oh, that is nasty, and yet what you find really upsetting
is that after just a nibble, this fox let you go, saying that
you didn't taste very good. Is that right?

The Gingerbread Man nods.

AB: That's not surprising, really. You are, after all, an
American gingerbread man, and unfortunately, unlike the
French or Germans or even the English, American cooks are,
well, stingy with the ginger, and what's worse is that they
typically only use store-bought, pre-ground powders that lack
verve, potency, pep. As the Brits say, you need gingering
up, my friend, and that's just fine with me, because although
you may be fairly flavorless, ginger is nothing if not...
```

LADIES AND GENTLEMEN,
THE GINGERBREAD MAN.

▷○ Unlike flashy, red ornamental ginger, which you often see in flower shops, culinary ginger, *Zingiber officinale*, is lackluster to look at. But the reediness above ground belies the spice that lies below. Although it's often referred to as ginger root, it is neither root nor tuber. It is, in fact, a self-replicating horizontal stem called a rhizome. Each one of its little fingers (the whole structure is called a "hand") is capable of producing a new plant genetically identical to the mother plant. Very young ginger from Hawaii or Pacific countries can often be found in Asian markets from spring to summer, and is typified by a translucent, sometimes flaky skin, which does not have to be peeled before use. Since the skin is fairly thin, you should always wrap fresh ginger in plastic and stash it in the fridge.

▷○ Mature hands are familiar to most American cooks, though a skilled eye is needed to differentiate between the small, almost delicate hands of Hawaii from, say, the big clunky baseball mitts grown in Costa Rica.

▷○ Mature rhizomes have far more fibrous flesh than young varieties, and the flavor is a bit more fiery. Since the skin is fairly thick, it can be refrigerated without any additional covering, which would in fact speed rotting.

▷○ In Chinese culture, foods are considered to be either cooling (*yin*) or warming (*yang*), and no food is more *yang* than ginger, which is often used to balance the lesser attributes of certain foods—say, the gaminess of duck or the fishiness of seafood. Of course, in that part of the world, the line between meal and medicine is often blurred, and Confucius himself recommended taking ginger every single day to ensure health and longevity. It's still widely believed that the chemical compounds responsible for ginger's unique flavor and aroma—namely, phellandrene, citral, linalool, and gingerol—are thought to calm heads, heal hearts, and cure athlete's foot and even cancer. Above all, ginger is thought to cure, or at least prevent, motion sickness.

THE VOMITRON

To test the theory that ginger can prevent motion sickness, we constructed the Vomitron, an optokinetic drum, souped up with strobe lights. It's designed to create an environment wherein visual information from the eyes, vestibular data from the inner ear, and kinetic information from the body clash in the brain, resulting in lots of barfing.

Many claim that ginger does repress motion sickness, but researchers have yet to discover exactly how it might work. The nausea of motion sickness is caused by an interruption of normal stomach cycles, which are set in motion by something called the cephalic vagal reflex. Certain chemicals in ginger, like gingerol, can boost those reflexes, keeping the cycles in check, but I'm here to tell you that it didn't make any darned difference to me. I got out of the Vomitron before I hurled—but just barely.

Production designer Todd Bailey enjoys some private time in the Vomitron.

CANDIED GINGER (GINGER SUGAR, TOO)

APPROXIMATELY 1 POUND

One of my favorite forms of ginger is crystallized ginger, which has been candied or cured in sugar. And it's almost as easy to make as it is to buy. Now that you will soon have plenty of candied or crystallized ginger, what might you do with it? Well, it is ideal in baked goods, but it's also darned tasty on ice cream, breakfast cereal, believe it or not, salads, and just for out-of-hand eating.

// SOFTWARE

1	pound	fresh ginger	
5	cups	H_2O	
1	pound	sugar	

// PROCEDURE

1. Spray a **cooling rack** with **nonstick spray** and set it in a **half sheet pan lined with parchment paper**.

2. **Peel** the ginger and slice into ⅛-inch-thick slices using a **mandoline**. Put the slices in a **4-quart saucepan** with the water and set over medium-high heat. Cover and cook for 35 minutes, or until the ginger is tender.

3. Drain the ginger in a **colander**, reserving ¼ cup of the cooking liquid. Weigh the ginger and measure out an equal amount of sugar. Return the ginger and the reserved cooking liquid to the pan and add the sugar. Set over medium-high heat and bring to a boil, stirring frequently. Lower the heat to medium and cook, stirring frequently, until the sugar syrup looks dry, has almost evaporated, and begins to recrystallize, approximately 20 minutes.

4. Transfer the ginger immediately to the cooling rack and spread to separate the individual pieces. When completely cool, store in an **airtight container** for up to 2 weeks. Save the sugar that drops beneath the cooling rack and use it to top Gingersnaps (opposite), sprinkle over ice cream, or sweeten coffee.

TIDBIT | In medieval Europe, a popular confection called *gingerbras* was composed of ginger boiled with honey and bread crumbs.

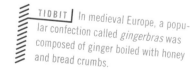

APPROXIMATELY 4 DOZEN COOKIES

In the early days of commercial aviation, ginger cookies or "snaps" were often served during turbulence. I don't know if they work, but they sure taste good.

// SOFTWARE

9½	ounces	all-purpose flour	
1½	teaspoons	baking soda	
1	tablespoon	ground ginger	
½	teaspoon	ground cardamom	
½	teaspoon	ground cloves	
½	teaspoon	kosher salt	
7	ounces	dark brown sugar	
5	ounces	unsalted butter	at room temperature
3	ounces	molasses	by weight
1	large	egg	at room temperature
2	teaspoons	fresh ginger	finely grated
4	ounces	Candied Ginger (left)	finely chopped

// PROCEDURE

1. Heat the oven to 350°F.

2. **Whisk** together the flour, baking soda, ground ginger, cardamom, cloves, and salt in a **medium mixing bowl**.

3. Cream the brown sugar and butter in a **stand mixer fitted with the paddle attachment** and beat on low speed until light and fluffy, 1 to 2 minutes. Add the molasses, egg, and fresh ginger and beat on medium speed for 1 minute. Add the candied ginger and, using a **rubber spatula**, stir to combine. Add the dry ingredients to the wet and stir until well combined.

4. Using a **2-teaspoon-sized scoop**, drop the dough onto a **half sheet pan lined with parchment paper**, approximately 2 inches apart. Bake on the middle rack of the oven for 12 minutes for slightly chewy cookies or 15 minutes for crisper cookies, rotating the pan halfway through baking.

5. Remove from the oven and leave the cookies on the sheet pan for 30 seconds before transferring to a **cooling rack** to cool completely. Repeat with all of the dough. Store in an **airtight container** for up to 10 days. If desired, you may scoop and freeze the cookie dough on a sheet pan and, once frozen, transfer to a **zip-top bag** to store. Bake directly from the freezer.

GROUND GINGER

I suspect that most American cooks, bakers at least, are familiar with ground dried ginger. Although some quality examples are available from specialty purveyors, the magical molecules that grant ginger its zing are fleeting, so I would rather buy chunks or slices, which remain viable for months if not years, and grind them myself. But then, of course, I have a laboratory-grade pulverizer and I'm thinking maybe you don't. So buy the powdered stuff in small batches from a reputable Internet source and skip the grocery-store stuff, which at best will deliver half the power.

APPROXIMATELY 2 QUARTS

Until the mid-nineteenth century, beer was the everyday drink of Britain, but besides grain-based beers, special low-alcohol, or "small," beers were brewed with aromatics such as spruce and ginger, which by the eighteenth century was being imported from Jamaica. Originally, ginger beers contained around 11 percent alcohol, but the Excise Act of 1855 slapped a tax on brewed beverages containing more than 2 percent, so manufacturers started diluting ginger beer with a variety of substances—including more ginger—and thus the age of the soft drink was born. Due to the presence of gingerol, ginger ale is both warming and refreshing, characteristics most appreciated by denizens of the British Isles.

TIDBIT Traditional ginger beers are cloudy, while ginger ales are clear.

// SOFTWARE ///

1½	ounces	fresh ginger	finely grated
6	ounces	sugar	
7½	cups	filtered H_2O	
⅛	teaspoon	active dry yeast	
2	tablespoons	lemon juice	freshly squeezed

// PROCEDURE ///

1. Combine the ginger, sugar, and ½ cup of the water in a **2-quart saucepan** and set over medium-high heat. Stir until the sugar has dissolved. Remove from the heat, cover, and steep for 1 hour.

2. Pour the syrup through a **fine-mesh strainer** set over a **bowl**, pressing down to get all of the juice out of the mixture. Chill quickly by placing the bowl in an **ice bath** and stirring, or place in the refrigerator, uncovered, until at least room temperature, 68° to 72°F.

3. Using a **funnel**, pour the syrup into a clean **2-liter plastic bottle** and add the yeast, lemon juice, and remaining 7 cups of water. Put the cap on the bottle, gently shake to combine, and leave the bottle at room temperature for 48 hours. Open and check for desired amount of carbonation. It is important that once you achieve your desired amount of carbonation that you refrigerate the ginger ale. Store in the refrigerator for up to 2 weeks, opening the bottle at least once a day to let out excess carbonation.

4. Serve chilled but not ice cold, lest you crush the compounds that make this ale so ridiculously delicious.

A ceramic ginger grater is a multifaceted multitasker, especially when topped with a layer of plastic wrap.

A CABBAGE SPROUTS IN BRUSSELS

EPISODE 203 | SEASON 12 | GOOD EATS

When I told my daughter that I wanted to make a show about Brussels sprouts she coolly replied, "So you actually don't want anyone to watch, huh?" That undeserved lack of respect may typify the attitude of the average American, but if I can convince even a handful of naysayers to accept my favorite green vegetable—that's right, my absolute favorite green vegetable—then I've done my duty to this tiny gem that with its flavor, nutrition, and versatility more than qualifies as . . .

Brussels International Airport is actually our reception desk.

197

KNOWLEDGE CONCENTRATE

Ladies and gentlemen, behold: the brassicas, a botanical family so tightly knit, genetically speaking, you'd expect at least one of them to be playing a banjo. The original, ancestral plant, basic *oleracea*, was a short, loose-leaf variety that grew wild along coastal areas in Europe. As farmers took these plants and began to manipulate them, isolating mutations and then crossbreeding them, the family slowly but surely diversified into what is today a vegetal dynasty, some four hundred members strong, but they do all fit, roughly, into five broad categories: 1. curly-leaf brassicas such as kale and collards; 2. brassicas composed of masses of flowering buds, such as broccoli and cauliflower; 3. pointy cabbages, like Chinese cabbage; 4. round cabbages, including white, green, and red; and 5. Brussels sprouts.

Brussels sprouts are what they look like: baby cabbages. They came onto the scene relatively late, in the first few years of the eighteenth century. As for the name, it probably came from France, where nineteenth-century botanical nomenclaturists were crazy about adding place names to each and every moniker, whether the place had anything to do with the plant or not. Although it might be possible to grow Brussels sprouts in Brussels, I know of no one currently engaged in that endeavor.

Brussels sprouts are available year round, but they are at their fresh peak from fall to early spring, when cold weather concentrates their natural sugars, which is very important to the cook. When purchasing, look for firm, compact heads with bright, dark-green leaves, as you would with any cabbage. Avoid soft or pudgy sprouts or anything with yellow leaves. Yellow is a sure sign of age, because it means that the more time-sensitive green chlorophyll has given up the ghost, leaving the long-lasting yellow behind. If you find good-looking sprouts still on the stalk, you'll definitely want to buy them. Not only are the stalks really cool looking, they are also life-support units. In fact, if you trim the ends and park your stalks in clean water in a cool place, your sprouts could remain viable for upwards of a week, during which time you can simply cut off what you need with a sharp paring knife.

If you can land only off-stalk sprouts, put them in an open bag, and put it inside your crisper drawer, set for maximum humidity. In here, you'll get three to four days max, but only if you do not wash them or peel off the outer leaves.

When Brussels sprouts are cooked just right, they're not hard, they're not mushy, they're just slightly chewy. The problem is that the breaking down of the cell walls releases some unfriendly chemical compounds such as cynarin, which is a type of glucose cyanade, a class of organic compound that also contains sulfur and nitrogen. As the sprouts cook, the cynarin begins to degrade into allyl isothiocyanate, or mustard oil, which explains the nasty-tasting compounds and the less-than-appealing aroma, somewhere between rotten eggs and sweaty army socks. You could dilute these by cooking the sprouts in a large amount of water, but a lot of the nasty-tasting compounds are powerful nutrients—cancer fighters, in fact—and they're mostly water soluble. So the more water you use, the more you wash away. Your best bet is to cook sprouts as quickly as possible in as little water as possible.

<table>
<tr><td>APPLICATION</td><td></td><td>BASIC BRUSSELS SPROUTS</td></tr>
</table>

4 SERVINGS

// SOFTWARE

1	pound	Brussels sprouts	rinsed
½	cup	H$_2$O	
¼	teaspoon	kosher salt	

// PROCEDURE

Cut off the stem end of each Brussels sprout and remove any yellowing outer leaves. Cut each Brussels sprout in half from top to bottom. Put the Brussels sprouts, water, and salt in a **3- to 4-quart saucier** and cover. Place over high heat and cook for 5 minutes, or until tender. Remove and serve immediately.

If you don't have a food processor, you can slice the sprouts thinly with a knife or a mandoline.

<table>
<tr><td>APPLICATION</td><td></td><td>BRUSSELS SPROUTS WITH PECANS AND CRANBERRIES</td></tr>
</table>

6 TO 8 SERVINGS

// SOFTWARE

1	pound	Brussels sprouts	rinsed and trimmed
3	ounces	pecans	coarsely chopped
3	tablespoons	unsalted butter	
¼	teaspoon	kosher salt	
¼	teaspoon	black pepper	freshly ground
4	ounces	dried cranberries	coarsely chopped

// PROCEDURE

(1) Slice the Brussels sprouts using the **thinnest slicing disc of a food processor**.

(2) Set a **10-inch straight-sided sauté pan** over medium-high heat and add the pecans. Cook, stirring continually, until the pecans darken and begin to give off a toasted aroma, approximately 2 minutes. Add the butter to the pan and stir to combine. When the butter has melted, add the Brussels sprouts, salt, and pepper and cook, stirring continually, until the color brightens and the sprouts are just tender, approximately 6 minutes. Remove the pan from the heat, add the cranberries, toss, and serve.

A CABBAGE SPROUTS
IN BRUSSELS

199

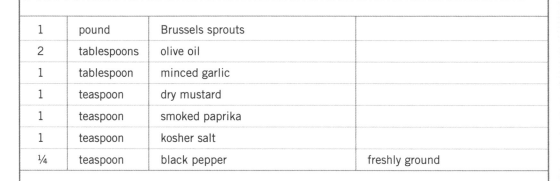

APPLICATION	GRILLED BRUSSELS SPROUTS

4 SERVINGS

And now, my favorite application for my favorite green vegetable of all time. Yes, grilling—and believe you me, the flavors released by the high heat of the grill are sublime. Use Brussels sprouts that are as uniform in shape and size as possible to facilitate even cooking.

// SOFTWARE ///

1	pound	Brussels sprouts	
2	tablespoons	olive oil	
1	tablespoon	minced garlic	
1	teaspoon	dry mustard	
1	teaspoon	smoked paprika	
1	teaspoon	kosher salt	
¼	teaspoon	black pepper	freshly ground

// PROCEDURE ///

1. Heat a charcoal grill to medium.

2. Cut off the stem end of each Brussels sprout and remove any yellowing outer leaves. Put the Brussels sprouts in a **large, microwave-safe bowl** and heat in a **microwave oven** on high power for 3 minutes.

3. Add the oil, garlic, mustard, paprika, and salt and toss to combine. Cool the sprouts until you can handle them.

4. Skewer the sprouts onto **metal skewers**, 4 or 5 per skewer, with the stem ends facing in the same direction, leaving at least ½ inch between them. Place the skewers on the grill with the stem ends closest to the flame. Cover and cook for 5 minutes. Turn the skewers over and cook for another 5 minutes.

5. Serve as is or, for additional flavor, remove the sprouts from the skewers, return them to the bowl, and toss with any of the remaining oil-and-garlic mixture before serving.

TIDBIT | In Belgium, Brussels sprouts are traditionally cooked with chestnuts.

TIDBIT | California grows 98 percent of America's Brussels sprouts.

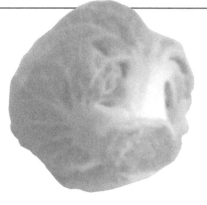

ORANGE AID

EPISODE 204 | SEASON 12 | GOOD EATS

It's rather ironic that in this day and age if you want to experience the multifaceted personality of the orange, you're actually better off going to your local paint store than the megamart. Why? I don't think it's because designers respect the fruit, per se; I think it's because sometime in the '50s and '60s we boiled the flavor of the orange into this bright, concentrated power chord that we really appreciate in our morning OJ. We're happy to use it in kids' treats, but otherwise we've kind of let it fall by the wayside. And that has just got to change, because although orange in its many forms is a fine color (Sinatra's favorite, in fact), it also happens to be one of my favorite . . .

FINDING THE RIGHT SQUEEZE

Most of us who buy citrus in this country buy it to juice it. Since juicing is an activity best aided by technology, this begs the question: Which juicer?

First thing I want to do is rule out high-speed electric juicers, which—by masticating, centrifuging, or triturating—glean juice from things like grass, wood, and, for all I know, small rocks. Oddly, pulp renders them almost completely useless, so they're pretty lousy with citrus.

A reamer is a ribbed device that is twisted into the fruit to rupture the juice sacks. I do keep an inexpensive wood hand reamer around for small jobs, but the large electric reamers that are meant for harvesting large volumes of juice I find do a bad job, rendering too much pulp—and they're a considerable pain in the hand.

The third type of juicer relies simply on pressure, lots of pressure, delivered by a lever—not just one lever, but a compound lever. Such juicers can deliver up to a ton of pressure per square inch. My favorite model utilizes a lever connected to a rack-and-pinion system to convert rotational energy into linear energy.

▷○ **The orange is one of the most widely propagated fruits in the world and yet it does not exist in the wild. It probably evolved in China or India and made its way west in the hands of the French, Italians, Portuguese, and Spaniards who were responsible for introducing the ubiquitous orb to North America. Although hundreds of actual varieties are grown today, all oranges fall into one of two varieties: sour and sweet.**

▷○ **There are hundreds of different sweet oranges. Some are raised for juice, others for out-of-hand eating. Here are some greatest hits.**

— NAVEL oranges are typically large with something that looks like a belly button at the blossom end—there's actually a miniature second orange lodged in there. Just halve a navel pole to pole, and you'll see it clearly displayed. Navel oranges have thicker skins and relatively dry, easy-to-separate segments. Most of these are grown in California.

— HAMLIN oranges are one of the most popular juice oranges of Florida. The seedling was developed in a Florida grove and propagated because of its cold resistance and high juice content.

— The MORO TARROCO is Italy's finest orange and considered by many to be the best in the world. It features dark red flesh and zip pips.

— The VALENCIA orange is the most popular orange variety in the world due to its thin skin and extremely high juice yield. Originally from China, the Valencia was taken west by Portuguese merchants, then to the Azores, and finally to modern-day Florida in 1870.

▷○ **Sour oranges are easily recognized by their thick, bumpy rind and juice that's, well, sour—sometimes *really* sour. Although often used in marinades in southeast Asian and Latin cuisines, a great majority of the world's sour oranges go into marmalade and liqueur. (A classic Cuban *mojo* consists of sour orange juice, olive oil, onion, and garlic.) The Seville orange, brought to Spain by the Moors, is not only sour but distinctly bitter, which makes its tender flesh and zest especially prized by the marmalade industry. If you can find them during their brief season (December to February), snatch them up and get to canning.**

▷○ **The inside of a mature orange contains a number of segments, anywhere from ten to fifteen, each of which is filled with small juice sacks, or vesicles. Each of these segments is wrapped in a protective and indigestible layer called the albedo. To cut wedges that are free and clear of the albedo, try this: Start by cutting a little piece off of each end of the orange so you can stand the little guy up. Then slice off the peel, including the white pith, from top to bottom. Then you can get the knife down in between the albedo and the flesh to remove a perfect wedge. The pristine wedges that result from successfully mastering this maneuver are called *suprêmes*.**

Suprême

Membrane

Cut each segment on the inside of the membrane to produce a *suprême*.

With all the *suprêmes* removed, nothing but nasty membrane remains.

ORANGE DELICIOUS

2 SERVINGS

In 1926, a Mr. Julius Freed opened an orange juice stand in Los Angeles, California, only to find that, though his product was excellent, business was not. One of Freed's associates, a chemist by trade, decided to experiment with juice augmentation formulas, and through his finagling he managed to create a concoction that is with us to this day.[1]

// SOFTWARE //

8½	ounces	orange juice	freshly squeezed
2	teaspoons	orange zest	
½	cup	whole milk	
1	tablespoon	confectioners' sugar	
½	teaspoon	vanilla extract	

// PROCEDURE //

1. Pour 6½ ounces of the orange juice into an **ice-cube tray** and freeze until solid, approximately 2 hours. Store the remaining 2 ounces juice and the zest in an **airtight container** in the refrigerator until ready to use.

2. Combine the frozen juice cubes, reserved orange juice and zest, milk, confectioners' sugar, and vanilla in a **blender** and blend until smooth and slushy, 30 to 45 seconds. Serve immediately.

TIP If finely grated zest is desired, try a micro rasp. Simply strum the orange across the zester, not the other way around.

If a larger piece of zest is desired, first use a vegetable peeler and carve off a strip. Next get yourself a paring knife or even a sharp pocket knife and simply scrape the pith off the strip. Don't try to cut it off; scrape it off. Once you've removed all the white you can, julienne or mince the zest, or use it as is.

[1] Trademark and copyright laws prevent me from actually naming this beverage, but if you take the name of the fruit and follow it with the first name of the guy who owned the stand, you should be able to work it out for yourself.

TRIVIA Props man Paul Merchant installing another one of his title boards.

ORANGE SHERBET

APPROXIMATELY 1 QUART

Sorbet/Sherbet/Sherbert: In its earliest form, sherbet was called *sherab*, an old Arab word meaning "sweetened drink." The word later evolved into *sherbot*, specifically a nonalcoholic fruit drink. In the sixteenth century, *sherbot* became a *sorbetto* in the hands of the Italians, and then morphed to *sorbet* in French and Spanish. Only in England did the word maintain the original "h," as in *sherbet*. Now, here in America, sherbet contains milk and has a specific definition.

// SOFTWARE //

7	ounces	sugar	
1½	tablespoons	orange zest	finely grated
¼	teaspoon	kosher salt	
2	cups	orange juice	freshly squeezed
1	tablespoon	lemon juice	freshly squeezed
1	teaspoon	vanilla extract	
1½	cups	whole milk	well chilled

// PROCEDURE //

1. Combine all the ingredients except the milk in a **food processor** and process until the sugar is dissolved, approximately 1 minute. Transfer to a **large bowl** and **whisk** in the milk. Cover the bowl and put it in the refrigerator until the mixture reaches 40°F or below, approximately 1 hour.

2. Pour the mixture into an **ice-cream maker** and process until it is the consistency of soft-serve ice cream. You may serve now or transfer to an **airtight container** and place in the freezer until firm, approximately 3 hours.

TRIVIA The "Agents" and I at a wedding: Key grip Marshall Millard on one side, culinary operative Meghan Foley on the other.

TIDBIT An orange is technically a hesperidium, a specialized berry with a leathery exterior.

// SOFTWARE

1¾	pounds	oranges	4 to 5 medium
1		lemon	zested and juiced
6	cups	H$_2$O	
60	ounces	sugar	

// SPECIAL HARDWARE

10 (8-ounce) canning jars with rings and lids, wide-mouth funnel, ladle, jar lifter, and 12-quart pot with a jar rack in the bottom (or place a round cake rack or metal mesh basket on the pot bottom).

// PROCEDURE

1) Wash the oranges and lemon thoroughly. Cut the oranges into ⅛-inch slices using a **mandoline**, removing the seeds as you go. Stack the orange slices and cut them into quarters with a **knife**.

2) Put the oranges in an **8-quart stainless-steel pot**. Add the lemon zest and juice and the water, set over high heat, and bring to a boil. Lower the heat to maintain a rapid simmer and cook, stirring frequently, for 40 minutes, or until the oranges are very soft.

3) Meanwhile, fill a **large pot (at least 12 quarts) with a rack in the bottom** three-quarters full with water, set over high heat, and bring to a boil. Place **10 (8-ounce) canning jars and rings**, **wide-mouth funnel**, **ladle**, and **jar lifter** in the boiling water and make sure the water covers the jars by at least 1 inch. Boil for 10 minutes. Turn off the heat, add the **lids**, and leave everything in the pot until the marmalade is ready.

4) Put a **small plate** in the freezer. Increase the heat under the orange mixture to return to a full boil. Add the sugar and cook, stirring continually, until the mixture reaches 220° to 223°F and darkens in color, 15 to 20 minutes. You may need to adjust the heat in order to prevent boilover. Test the readiness of the marmalade by placing a teaspoon of the mixture onto the chilled plate for 30 seconds. Tilt the plate. The mixture should be a soft gel that moves slightly. If it is thin and runs easily, it is not ready.

5) Fish the jar lifter out of the water and use it to remove the jars and set them on a **clean towel**. Put the funnel on the top of one of the jars and ladle in the marmalade to just below the bottom of the threads of the jar. Repeat until all of the jars have been filled. The yield may vary by 1 to 2 jars. Wipe the rims and threads of the jars with a moist **paper towel** and top each with a lid. Put a ring on each jar and tighten finger tight.

6) Return the jars to the pot with the water, being certain that they don't touch the bottom of the pot or each other. Add water, if necessary, to cover the jars by at least 1 inch. Boil for 10 minutes. Using the jar lifter, remove the jars from the water, place in a cool, dry spot, and leave at room temperature for at least 24 hours before moving or opening them. Once open, store in the refrigerator. Unopened marmalade will last for 6 months.

IT'S SCOTTISH!

Orange marmalade is a curiously tart preserve containing not only bits of orange, but also actual peel. Strange stuff, and with an interesting history. Quince jelly, or marmalade, came to England on Portuguese ships back in 1495. Back then it was sold as a solid in a box and was served as an after-dinner digestive, but in 1797 a Scottish importer named James Keeler took delivery of a shipment of Spanish oranges in the port of Dundee. Turned out they were too bitter to eat, but, not wishing to waste them, Keeler's wife cooked the oranges with water and sugar and boom: an overnight breakfast sensation in Scotland. The English didn't get hip to marmalade until the nineteenth century, which just affirms the old saying, "If it's not Scottish, it's . . ." well, you know.

Once upon a time, molasses was the sweetener of choice for Americans who couldn't afford the high prices of refined sugar. Historical precedent notwithstanding, molasses is far more vital stuff than you might think. Sure, it's a little slow on the pour and, I don't know, opinionated on the palate; it may be a little old-fashioned, but believe you me, molasses is deep, dark, and daring . . .

CASEY'S BLACKSTRAP Unsulphured MOLASSES NET 15 FL OZ

NEED TO SHOOT AN AMISH SCENE?

THE FIRST THING YOU NEED: BEARDS . . . LOTS OF BEARDS.

Molasses is a by-product of sugar making, and most American sugar is born in the rich muck of southern Florida, where sugarcane stretches as far as the eye can see and the helicopter is the preferred mode of travel. When the tropical grass matures in winter, the green leaves are burned away so that the harvesters can reap the sugar-bearing stalks, a process that just a generation ago was accomplished exclusively by hand and machete. The chopped cane is loaded into trailers and then trucked to a mill and dumped onto conveyers, which feed the "tandems," massive engines of destruction that repeatedly chop, grind, mangle, squash, and then squeeze the plant fibers until they surrender every possible molecule of sucrose. (And just so that nothing goes to waste, most mills take the spent cane, or bagasse, and burn it to generate electricity.) The resulting cane juice, or mother liquor, as it's called, must be clarified to remove impurities like dirt and bug parts before it can continue the refining process.

The squeaky-clean cane syrup is then boiled in machines called vacuum pans to initiate the formation of sugar crystals. The mixture that comes out of these machines is then spun in a centrifuge, which works like the spin cycle of a home washing machine to separate those raw sugar crystals from the first strike, or what's called fancy molasses. Some of this is shipped to a grateful world. The rest is boiled and spun several more times until finally every scrap of crystal-worthy sucrose has been gleaned and all that's left is the harsh, smoky, edgy molasses known as blackstrap, a product good for feeding to cows and, once upon a time, distilling into rum.

Although we typically think of molasses as an ingredient in cooking, its primary use in colonial America was distilling. You see, long before there was a sugar industry in Florida, there were massive cane plantations in the Caribbean, where African slaves toiled under the whips of greedy colonials who, like modern-day drug lords, grew fat selling Europe its fix of the white powder, sugar. There was no Old World market for the leftover molasses, so it was hauled up to New England, where it became kill devil, a.k.a. rum bullion, or rum, which Americans consumed at a per-capita rate of three gallons a year—the little kiddies, too. Rum was so cheap that even the budget-strangled Continental Congress quaffed a steady river of the stuff while debating Richard Henry Lee's resolution for independency. Ironically, molasses use also led to freedom. British tariffs on sugar and molasses fired up colonists far more than any taxes on tea. Even John Adams himself was later quoted as saying, "I know not why we should blush to confess that molasses was such an essential ingredient in American independence. Many great events were preceded by small causes."

Of course, not all of the molasses that came into the docks of New England ended up in rum barrels. In Boston, for instance, two classic dishes get their be-all, end-all essence from molasses and its spicy goodness—Boston brown bread and baked beans. The very attributes that enable molasses to hold on to moisture in baked goods can also be employed in marinades for meat. Not only does a soak in a molasses-ade help with moisture retention and up the flavor quotient, but the liquid can also be boiled down into a sauce as the meat cooks.

TAKING A LOOK AT SUGAR PRODUCTION IN SOUTH FLORIDA

TIDBIT | The Molasses Act of 1733 placed such high taxes on molasses that maple syrup became the sweetener of choice.

TIDBIT | One cup of molasses weighs about twelve ounces—heavy stuff!

BOSTON BROWN BREAD

2 (4-INCH) LOAVES

Originally, Boston brown bread was cooked on the hearth by steaming it in a cylindrical mold, in the tradition of an English pudding. These molds are pretty tough to find these days, but an empty coffee can will suffice. Besides the molasses, Boston brown bread is defined by a trio of grains: wheat, rye, and corn. This arrangement may have resulted from ever thrifty New Englanders needing a bread that worked with their limited and ever shifting resources. The fact that all three grains are used in the manufacturing of spirits is probably coincidental. Probably. Serve this hearty bread with baked beans or slice, toast, and serve it with cream cheese.

// SOFTWARE

2½	ounces	whole-wheat flour	
2½	ounces	rye flour	
2½	ounces	cornmeal	
½	teaspoon	baking soda	
½	teaspoon	baking powder	
½	teaspoon	kosher salt	
½	teaspoon	ground allspice	
6	ounces	molasses	by weight
8½	ounces	buttermilk	
1	teaspoon	vanilla extract	
½	teaspoon	orange zest	finely grated

// SPECIAL HARDWARE

2 empty (26.5-ounce) metal cans

// PROCEDURE

1. Move a rack to the bottom third of the oven and heat the oven to 325°F.

2. Spray the insides of the **cans** with **nonstick cooking spray** and place them in a **deep 3-quart oven-safe pot**. Begin heating enough **boiling water** to come halfway up the sides of the cans when poured into the pot.

3. **Whisk** together the flours, cornmeal, baking soda, baking powder, salt, and allspice in a **medium bowl**. Add the molasses, buttermilk, vanilla, and orange zest and whisk to combine. Divide the mixture evenly between the prepared cans. Cover the tops with a double thickness of **aluminum foil** and tie securely with **string**. Pour the boiling water into the pot. Carefully place in the oven and bake for about 1 hour and 15 minutes, or until the edges of the bread begin to pull away from the sides of the cans. Remove the cans from the pot of water, uncover, place on a **cooling rack**, and cool for 1 hour before removing the bread from the cans.

MOLASSES-AND-COFFEE-MARINATED PORK CHOPS

4 SERVINGS

// SOFTWARE ///

1	cup	strong coffee	cooled
6	ounces	molasses	by weight
2	tablespoons	apple cider vinegar	
1	tablespoon	Dijon mustard	
2	cloves	garlic	minced
1	teaspoon	kosher salt	
½	teaspoon	ground ginger	
6 to 8	sprigs	fresh thyme	
½	teaspoon	black pepper	freshly ground
4	1-inch-thick	bone-in pork chops	6 to 8 ounces each

// PROCEDURE ///

1. Combine all the ingredients in a **1-gallon zip-top bag**, seal, and shake to combine. Put in the refrigerator to marinate for at least 2 hours or up to overnight.

2. Heat a **charcoal grill** to medium-high.

3. Remove the pork chops from the marinade. Transfer the marinade to a **small saucepan** and place it over high heat. Bring to a boil, lower the heat to medium-high, and boil gently, stirring often, until reduced to about ½ cup, 12 to 15 minutes. Remove and discard the thyme sprigs after the glaze has reduced.

4. Meanwhile, grill the pork chops for 3 to 4 minutes per side, until they reach an internal temperature of 145°F. Rest the pork chops for 4 to 5 minutes before serving with the glaze.

"I brake for shoofly pie" is the official state bumper sticker of Pennsylvania, and for that, we've got the Pennsylvania Dutch to thank. We have the Pennsylvania Dutch to thank for a lot of things, but especially this gooey, wet-bottom pie, which is said to be so sweet and delicious that you just can't keep the flies off it. It is especially alluring to me because unlike most modern American desserts, which are sweet but little else, shoofly has character, depth—molasses.

TRIVIA To all those who emailed me about this bumper sticker: Yes, I mean "break," not "brake."

// SOFTWARE

FOR THE CRUST

6	ounces	all-purpose flour	
½	teaspoon	kosher salt	
3	ounces	unsalted butter	chilled
1	ounce	lard	chilled
4	tablespoons	ice H_2O	in a spritz bottle

FOR THE CRUMBS

5½	ounces	all-purpose flour	
4	ounces	dark brown sugar	
2	tablespoons	unsalted butter	chilled
¼	teaspoon	kosher salt	

FOR THE FILLING

¾	teaspoon	baking soda	
¾	cup	boiling H_2O	
8	ounces	molasses	by weight
1	large	egg	beaten
1	teaspoon	vanilla extract	

// PROCEDURE

MAKE THE CRUST:

1. Combine the flour and salt by pulsing 3 or 4 times in a **food processor**. Add the butter and pulse 5 or 6 times, or until the texture is mealy. Add the lard and pulse another 3 or 4 times. Remove the lid of the food processor and **spritz** the surface of the mixture thoroughly with ice water. Pulse 5 times. Add more water and pulse again until mixture holds together when squeezed. Put the mixture in a large **zip-top bag**, squeeze together until it forms a ball, then press into a rounded disk and refrigerate for 30 minutes.

2. Heat the oven to 425°F.

3. Put **2 (9-inch) metal pie pans** in the refrigerator to chill.

4. Remove the dough from the refrigerator and **roll** it out in the bag until it reaches the edges of the bag and is 10 to 11 inches in diameter. **Cut** along two sides of the bag, open the bag to expose the dough on one side, and turn it into one of the pie pans, plastic side up. Gently pull the remaining side of the plastic bag off of the dough. Press the dough into the edges around the pan, using the second pan to press it firmly, and trim off any excess dough. Press the edges of the dough over the lip of the pan. Refrigerate for 15 minutes.

5. Using a **fork**, poke holes in the sides and bottom of the dough. Fit a large piece of **parchment paper** into the crust and fill it with about **32 ounces dried beans**. Press the beans into the edges of the crust, set the pan on a **half sheet pan**, and bake for 10 minutes. Remove the parchment and beans and bake until light golden, approximately 7 minutes. Set on a **cooling rack** and cool completely while preparing the filling.

6. Decrease the oven temperature to 350°F.

MAKE THE CRUMBS:

7. Put the flour, brown sugar, butter, and salt in a food processor and process until it forms crumbs. Reserve ¼ cup and set both portions aside.

MAKE THE FILLING:

8. Put the baking soda in a **medium heatproof bowl** and pour the boiling water over it. Add the molasses, egg, and vanilla and **whisk** to combine. (See sidebar.) Add the larger portion of crumbs and whisk just to combine. Pour this mixture into the prepared crust. Sprinkle the remaining ¼ cup of the crumb mixture evenly over the top of the filling. Bake on the middle rack of the oven for 40 to 45 minutes, until the filling puffs, begins to look dry, and starts to crack slightly. Transfer to a cooling rack and cool completely before cutting.

STRANGE MIXING

In all the baking we've done on this show, we've never used the technique of mixing baking soda with boiling water before combining it with the rest of the batter ingredients. Why do we do it in the pie filling? Well, what we want here is a batter that bakes up dark, rich, and moist, and to accomplish that the batter should be alkaline. Molasses is acidic, so we need to add baking soda to create a slightly alkaline mixture. Why not just dump the soda into the batter the way we've done before? Because when baking soda and acid come together, carbon dioxide is released, which provides leavening. This is what we want in most batters, but in this case we don't want any leavening. By dissolving the soda before the acid ingredient is added to it, we create an alkaline acquiesce solution. The CO_2 will be released quickly, leaving us with a higher pH but no real lift.

APPLICATION	HOMEMADE DARK BROWN SUGAR

APPROXIMATELY 1 POUND

// **SOFTWARE** //

1	pound	sugar	
3	ounces	molasses	by weight

// **PROCEDURE** //

Combine the sugar and molasses in a **food processor** and process until the molasses is completely incorporated into the sugar, approximately 1 minute. If necessary, stop and scrape down the sides of the bowl. Store in an **airtight container** for up to 1 month.

TIDBIT | Lancaster, Pennsylvania, is home to the "World's Greatest Shoofly Pie Bake-Off."

Salmon is one of the most popular hunks of seafood in America today. Once upon a time, this big, tasty, pelagic, anadromous critter was a special treat, a "celebration" meal. But over the last twenty years efficient (notice I didn't say "improved") aquaculture methods have made it possible for Atlantic salmon to come to the American table for around $9 a pound, which is pretty darned cheap in the fish world. The problem is, farmed salmon are neither sustainable nor (*in my opinion*) as flavorful or even as healthful as wild fish, which are, as you might expect, more expensive. When we do eat wild-caught salmon, then, it seems we ought to have processes, techniques—rules, even—for how to handle them properly so that instead of just big, beautiful, expensive fish they're most definitely . . .

KNOWLEDGE CONCENTRATE

Wild salmon versus farmed salmon, expensive versus cheap, nature versus nurture. Let's compare the two by first examining the life cycle of a wild salmon.

1. Our hero is born way up some cold freshwater stream where his family has been hatching for countless generations.

2. When he's just a small fry, he heads down into the big ocean, where he swims far and wide for two to seven years, depending on his species, feasting all the while on Poseidon's rich buffet.

3. One day, he gets a funny itch, an urge, an inkling to get back home, and if he can maneuver upstream past the hydroelectric dams and bears and whatnot, he'll make it, thanks to a mysterious type of biophysical GPS.

4. Once there, he hooks up with a mate, spawns, and then promptly goes belly up.

Since our hero lived his life to the fullest and his body wanted to prepare for that long upstream swim, by the time he reached the mouth of the river, where the fishermen were waiting for him, of course, his body was at its succulent, flavorful, and fatty best.[1]

Let us now consider the contrasting existence of the farm-raised fish.

1. This fish is born into a nice, safe hatchery tank far away from any predators or discomfort.

2. Eventually he's chucked into an offshore pen with a few thousand of his other friends. Unchallenged and bored, he grows fat on fish chow, which is chockfull of ground-up other fish that he would never eat in nature and astaxanthin, which adds color to his otherwise gray flesh.

3. When he hits market weight, he meets his end, typically by electrical shock or a blow to the head.

I'm not going to tell you not to buy farmed salmon, because I'd rather you eat farmed salmon than no salmon at all, but trust me when I tell you that when it is available, wild salmon is well worth the investment.

There are six major varieties of salmon available to the American market. The first is ATLANTIC salmon, which exists in the wild only in parts of Europe, specifically Scotland and Ireland. There are no wild Atlantic salmon left in U.S. waters. There are, however, lots and lots of farm-raised Atlantic salmon, most of which come to market in the 4- to 12-pound range. Farmed Atlantics are easily recognized by the large dark spots that appear on the upper part of their bodies and by their stubby, underdeveloped fins, a product of pen living.

In the spring, the Pacific brings big old KING or CHINOOK salmon. Then in summer, the SILVER or COHO come to answer the call of the wild. The SOCKEYE, whose deep red flesh is my personal favorite, run all the way from spring to fall. Two other varieties are common: the CHUMS, a.k.a. KETA, and the smaller PINKS. They're often available as late as October, though more often than not they end up in cans. Point is, by the end of fall, most of the wild salmon are gone. I say *most*, because Kings sometimes arrive out of season in California, Oregon, and Washington, but those fish rarely, if ever, leave the local markets.

Ideally, fish should be cooked the day of purchase, but this is the real world, so finding the best method of storage is key. To my mind that means ice, but as the ice melts you risk waterlogging the fish. Make a bed of ice in a perforated plastic container and cover it with aluminum foil. Put the fish on top of the foil. Because the box is full of holes, the water drains away as the ice melts. A second container below captures the water. On ice, you can expect to hold your investment for three days, tops.

My motto when it comes to fish cookery: *Primum non nocere*, "First do no harm." What follows are three cooking methods that will not let you down. They look simple, and they are, but the details are important, so don't gloss over them. We'll start with the simplest and graduate to more refined techniques.

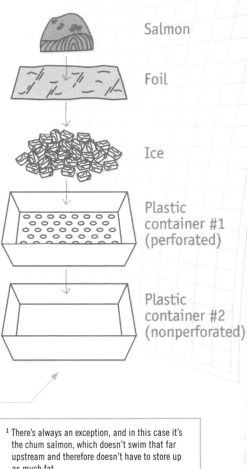

Salmon

Foil

Ice

Plastic container #1 (perforated)

Plastic container #2 (nonperforated)

[1] There's always an exception, and in this case it's the chum salmon, which doesn't swim that far upstream and therefore doesn't have to store up as much fat.

In this sauté scenario, the blitzkrieg-like march of heat into the meat creates a tasty sear on the outside and creamy, moist goodness within. But when first off the fire, there's still a lot of heat wandering around in there. If you go slicing into the goodness right away, that heat will come rushing out, bringing lots of juice with it. Allowing the fish to rest for a while will give the heat time to naturally abate, and the juice will stay where it belongs: in the food.

// SOFTWARE //

2	6-ounce	salmon fillets	1⅛ to 1¼ inches thick, pinbones removed
2	teaspoons	vegetable oil	
¼	teaspoon	kosher salt	
		black pepper	freshly ground

// PROCEDURE //

1. Set a **10-inch nonstick sauté pan** over medium heat. Brush the fillets with the oil and sprinkle with salt and pepper.

2. Put the fillets in the pan flesh side down. Cook for 2 minutes.

3. Turn over and cook for another 2 minutes.

4. Transfer the fillets to a plate, cover loosely with **aluminum foil**, and rest for 5 minutes before serving.

SALMON AND HEALTH

Salmon, especially wild salmon, is undeniably good for you, as it's packed with protein and those omega-3 fatty acids your doctor has been nagging you about. Well, what exactly is omega-3? Well, let's take a microscopic look at, well, the very end of a fatty-acid molecule. We know that this is an unsaturated fatty acid, because it's got at least one double bond between those carbons, and that puts kind of a kink in the molecule. Now, if the last double bond occurs three atoms from the end, or omega, of the molecule, then you've got yourself an omega-3 fatty acid; there are a lot of different examples of those, but not too many places to get them. Nothing's better than wild salmon. So eat up, and keep the old pill-pushing man at bay.

BUILDING YOUR OWN FATTY ACID MODEL IS FUN AND AFFORDABLE.

TIDBIT Salmon is loaded with nutrients like niacin, vitamins B₆ and B₁₂, selenium, magnesium, protein, and phosphorus.

BILEVEL KING SALMON FILLET

2 SERVINGS

Here we're dealing with a thicker piece of fish, which means that if you desire a perfectly seared exterior and creamy center, you must perfect the dual-heat method.[2]

//**SOFTWARE**//

1	12-ounce	skinless king salmon fillet	1½ to 1¾ inches thick, pinbones removed
2	teaspoons	vegetable oil	
	to taste	kosher salt	
	to taste	black pepper	freshly ground

//**PROCEDURE**///

1) Heat the oven to 475°F.

2) Set a **10-inch ovenproof sauté pan** over medium heat for 2 minutes. Brush the fillet with the oil and sprinkle with salt and pepper. Place the fillets in the pan flesh side down and cook for 3 minutes.

3) Turn the fillet over and put the pan in the oven. Cook for 5 minutes. Transfer the fillet to a plate, cover loosely with **aluminum foil**, and rest for 5 minutes before serving.

[2] You may remember this method from episode 1, Steak Your Claim, where it was used to great effect on a rib-eye steak.

YOUR OVEN LIES

If you think that flashing light on the front of your oven or the number on the little knob is a truthful representation of what's going on inside that box, I've got news for you. Ovens lie, or at the very least they tell you what they think you want to hear. There are just too many factors—the size and shape of the oven, the placement of the heating elements, where the food actually is in the space, and how much food's involved—that can make a profound difference in oven performance. And, of course, ovens cycle on and off, which means their heat output isn't a straight line but more like a daily tides graph.

What's a cook to do? Get yourself an oven thermometer—or two. Here are two different types of thermometers designed to reside in the hot box 24/7. Some have round dials, and they are always armed with a little coil in the back, and that coil is made out of two different kinds of metal laminated together; the metals expand and contract at different rates, and that means that as the oven gets hotter or cooler, the coil opens up or closes. That moves the dial. They're easy to read, they're cheap, and almost completely unreliable.

What I depend on instead are old-fashioned bulb-style thermometers. Some still actually have mercury in them, and others have dyed alcohol that's a little easier to read than the mercury. This model, made to hang on a rack, is very convenient. Whatever you do, go for something that's very, very easy to read and position it halfway between the wall and the center of the oven.

BROILED SOCKEYE SALMON WITH CITRUS GLAZE

4 TO 6 SERVINGS

CONCERNING "FRESHNESS"

You have to stop thinking that fresh and raw are the same thing. If we define fresh as the closest condition to live, then in many cases frozen wins. In fact, fish that are flash frozen (immediately after capture and kept at a proper frozen temperature) are considered by many—including us—as being much better than fresh or raw. That said, we don't want any refrozen or rethawed product. That would mean ice damage, and ice damage is never good eats.

// SOFTWARE ///

1	1½- to 2-pound	side of sockeye salmon	skin on, pinbones removed
⅓	cup	dark brown sugar	firmly packed
2	tablespoons	lemon zest	finely grated
1½	teaspoons	kosher salt	
½	teaspoon	black pepper	freshly ground

// PROCEDURE ///

(1) Position a rack in the oven 3 inches from the broiler. Line a **half sheet pan** with **aluminum foil** and place the salmon on the pan.

(2) Combine the brown sugar, lemon zest, salt, and pepper in a **small food processor** and process for 1 minute, or until well combined. Evenly spread the mixture onto the salmon and set aside for 45 minutes at room temperature.

(3) Preheat the broiler to high for 2 minutes. After 2 minutes, put the salmon in the oven and broil for 6 to 8 minutes, until the thickest part of the fish reaches an internal temperature of 131°F.

(4) Remove from the oven and rest, uncovered, for 8 to 10 minutes. Serve immediately.

**THE COLDEST FREAKING
WATER IN THE WORLD**

These are tough days for seafood lovers. We have supped freely at Poseidon's buffet for far too long and I fear we will soon be left standing, plates in hand, waiting on the trident-man to restock the steam table. Problem is, when he's out . . . he's out, and he's nearly out of several of the more popular items on the menu as it is.

The problem is that Americans have very limited seafood portfolios. If we want our kids' kids to be able to enjoy bluefin tuna, wild salmon, or oysters, that portfolio must be diversified. Take lobster, for instance. Why not turn to its diminutive freshwater cousin the crawfish, which bite-for-bite is just as sweet and is pleasantly sustainable? (At least here in America, which grows not only the best crawfish but the only crawfish I'll eat.) I know what you're thinking: Crawfish—a.k.a. crawdads, crawdaddies, crayfish, lollies, mudbugs, yannies, ditchbugs—are strictly blue-collar Cajun fare. Well, I say, not only are these delicious decapods an answer to one of the seafood lover's nagging questions, they're absolutely . . .

TRIVIA | My first plane, a Cessna 206T—perfect for hauling mudbugs.

Natchitoches
Regional Airport
Natchitoches, LA-3:25pm

CRAWFISH SPA

Odds are good that your crawfishes' GI tracts are going to contain some . . . stuff. Personally, I don't find this offensive as long as they are thoroughly cooked. But if the idea of squeaky-clean insides appeals to you, consider soaking them in clean, fresh water (not saltwater) for at least twenty-four hours. Because crawfish are heavy breathers and as little as one pound of them could suck all the O$_2$ out of five gallons of water in no time, here's what you need to do:

Get a cooler in the fifty-four-quart range with a drain plug. (Yes, this can be the same cooler you transported them in.) Fill it half full of water, and then install a $30 aquarium pump rated for eighty gallons. Don a pair of heavy gloves and gently scoop the bugs into their spa. Close the lid, but not so tightly that you pinch the air hoses. Let the pump gurgle away for twelve hours, then kill the pump, open the plug, and drain. Refill with fresh water to the original level, then percolate for another twelve hours and drain. There you have purged crawfish, fresh as daisies.

KNOWLEDGE CONCENTRATE

▷○ The word *crayfish* comes from the French word *esquavese*, meaning "to crawl," but in this country crayfish are just plain crawfish. Thomas Say, the first American zoologist to make serious study of them, in 1817, called them crawfish, and that's good enough for me. Crawfish are freshwater decapods (ten legs) and they are indeed related to lobsters. North and Central America are home to 340 species, including *Cambarus unestami*, which I used to stalk in the chilly streams of Georgia back in my youth. But when it comes to culinary service, there is but one species to consider, the Red Swamp Crawfish, which is native to Louisiana.

▷○ The Tale of the Traveling Lobster: Once upon a time, the lands now known as the Canadian Maritimes were called Acadia, and they were home to a large population of French colonists, who called themselves Acadians. In 1713, the French crown ceded most of the lands to England. King George ordered the Acadians to take an oath of allegiance to him or get out. Afraid that taking such an oath would one day force them to take up arms against their fellow countrymen or the Indian tribes that they had lived alongside for so many years, the Acadians refused the hospitality. England rewarded them by kicking fourteen thousand people out of their homes in what became known as *La Grand Dérangement*, the Great Expulsion. After years of wandering, the remainder of the Acadian people settled in what is now Louisiana, where the word Acadian eventually morphed into Cajun. According to legend, however, another lesser-known exodus took place soon thereafter.

During their years in Canada, the Acadians formed a tight bond with lobsters, who so missed their human friends after the expulsion that they hauled up out of the surf to follow them. The journey took them years and years, but the lobsters finally caught up. The endeavor was so grueling it shrunk the majestic crusties to a fraction of their original size. That's how we came to have the crawfish.

▷○ Although tail meats are sold separately, as far as I'm concerned crawfish should only be purchased whole and alive, to get the most flavor out of them. That makes transport home something of a challenge. Place the mesh bag, which usually contains thirty-five to forty pounds, into a cooler and cover it completely with frozen gel-style cold packs—five or six should do the trick. Slap on the lid, and do not open again. If they're fresh from the water, you just bought yourself forty-eight hours—though I strongly suggest you cook them the day you buy them if at all possible.

Legend of the Crawfish Exodus

CRAWFISH ROLL

2 SANDWICHES

I realize that there are probably a few flannel-clad down-easters up in Maine moaning right now that our boil was nothing but a pigmy lobster bake, and you know what? You'd be right, only our boil's a whole lot easier to pull off and not nearly as expensive for those of us who are not lucky enough to actually live in Maine. Of course, if you have visited Maine, especially in summertime, you have probably experienced the mythic marriage of lobster and bun known as a lobster roll. Well, guess what? Crawfish can dance to that tune too.

// SOFTWARE

3	tablespoons	mayonnaise	
2	teaspoons	lemon juice	freshly squeezed
	pinch	cayenne pepper	
	pinch	kosher salt	
	pinch	black pepper	freshly ground
8	ounces	cooked crawfish tail meat	(from Crawfish Boil, page 220)
2		New England–style hot dog buns	toasted

// PROCEDURE

Whisk together the mayonnaise, lemon juice, cayenne, salt, and black pepper in a **small bowl**. Add the crawfish meat and stir to combine. Divide the mixture evenly between the buns and serve immediately.

TIDBIT | Native American tribes in Louisiana introduced the crawfish, as dinner, to the Acadians.

TIDBIT | Although any old hot dog buns are just fine for this application, I actually prefer the New England version, which have cut sides, and because of that they brown a lot better. So, just a couple minutes in a toaster oven or under a broiler, then load up and serve.

CRAWFISH BOIL

10 TO 12 SERVINGS

If you prepare crawfish only one way it should be as a "boil," an out-of-doors culinary community event that I believe in performing at least twice a year.

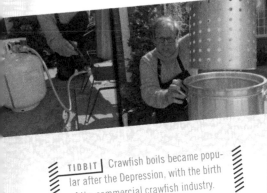

// SOFTWARE

2	tablespoons	whole cloves	
1	tablespoon	whole black peppercorns	
1	tablespoon	whole coriander seeds	
1½	tablespoons	whole allspice	
5	gallons	H_2O	
1	pound	kosher salt	
4	tablespoons	cayenne pepper	
2	tablespoons	garlic powder	
2	tablespoons	paprika	
1	tablespoon	onion powder	
1	tablespoon	dried thyme	
1	tablespoon	dried oregano	
1	tablespoon	dried dill	
1	tablespoon	dry mustard	
6		bay leaves	crumbled
10	pounds	live crawfish	
3	pounds	small red potatoes	cut in half if larger than 2 inches in diameter
8	ears	corn	halved
2	heads	garlic	unpeeled, but cloves separated
1	pound	andouille sausage	cut into 1-inch pieces

// PROCEDURE

1. Combine the cloves, peppercorns, coriander, and allspice in a **spice grinder** and grind for 10 to 15 seconds.

2. Fill a **40-quart pot** with the water and add the freshly ground spices, salt, cayenne, garlic powder, paprika, onion powder, thyme, oregano, dill, dry mustard, and bay leaves. Cover and bring to a boil over high heat (this will take approximately 40 minutes).

3. Rinse the crawfish thoroughly in the bag in which they were packed to remove excess dirt, mud, poop, and so on, then move the crawfish to a **large container** (a 5-gallon bucket works well; so does a kitchen sink) and rinse thoroughly with cool water. Use tongs or heavily gloved hands to pick out any dead guys. Drain the water and repeat the rinsing process until the water looks clean.

4. Once the seasoned water comes to a boil, add the potatoes, corn, garlic, and sausage. Cover and cook for 10 minutes.

5. Add the crawfish, cover, and cook for 3 minutes. Turn off the heat and allow the pot to sit, covered, for 10 minutes. Drain well (reserve the cooking liquid for another use) and serve immediately.

NOTE: If you are serious about your boils, you may want to double, triple, or even quadruple the spice mixture. Tightly sealed in glass, it will maintain full potency for up to three months.

TRIVIA It was after seeing field footage from this show that I decided I needed to divorce myself from fifty pounds of ugly fat, a process that took the better part of a year.

SUSTAINABILITY

The Red Swamp Crawfish is a North American native. It's from here and is used to living here and more importantly the rest of the ecosystem is used to them too. As a result, modern crawfish aquafarming has relatively little negative impact on landscape. They are raised in clean water on quality feed and shipped relatively short distances. A great majority of the crawfish that come to market do so because of the efforts of small family operations run by people who live on the land they farm. Let's compare this with, say, crawfish raised in China, which—despite the distance they're shipped—are typically cheaper than the American product. They are raised under conditions that could only be described as sanitarily challenged, they wreak havoc on the environment because they escape into and decimate rice paddies, and they push other native species out of their natural habitats. It's a bad deal, folks, and I most certainly would not feed them to my family. Remember, please, that cheaper is not always better—especially when it comes to frozen food shipped from the other side of the planet.

SHOOTING THE "MONSTER" CRAWFISH SEQUENCE

Ladies and gentlemen, allow me to present the tamale: cooked corn dough formed around a spicy filling, all wrapped up in a corn husk and steamed. Tamales are pure simplicity. They've fueled Americans on the go for centuries, from the halls of Montezuma to the Mississippi Delta, but like all simple things they are very easy to mess up. American strip malls are packed to the piñatas with Tex-Mex mess halls serving up tamales so gnarly you need a goblet of green margarita goo just to wash one down. But it doesn't have to be that way. If you're willing to obtain a few basic ingredients, conquer a few simple techniques, and apply some sound science, there's no reason your own tamales can't be nutritious, delicious . . .

TIDBIT | In a tamale, the masa can be either sweet or savory, and the fillings can be meat, vegetables, beans, or fruit.

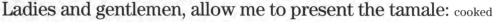

Ancient ruins in the jungle? Nah—rental plants and lots of styrofoam.

222

Flavorful fillings may form the heart of a tamale, but the soul is all corn. Meso-Americans derived a huge percentage of their daily calorie intake from maize, which wasn't anything like what we slather butter on in summertime. Maize was tough stuff, very starchy and quite hard. Early culinarians figured out how to soften the kernels by cooking them in an alkaline solution made with calcium oxide and wood ashes. What they didn't realize at the time is that they were altering the nutritional content of the kernels, thus freeing niacin and other essential amino acids, a process known as nixtamalization, without which we wouldn't have tamales—or tortillas, for that matter—because the civilizations that invented them would have died out from malnutrition before they made their mark on the world. Once nixtamalization is complete, the maize can be ground into a dough, called masa, which we made in our tortilla show a while back, but iconic though tortillas are in this culture, they had nothing on tamales, which were not only everyday food but highly portable meals suitable for feeding working folk like soldiers and builders, which are pretty important if you're looking to assemble an empire.

Tamales implement masa harina, a corn-based flour that is available in just about every megamart in America these days. Avoid bags that say "instant" on them, though, because they can contain leaveners, and we want no part of that.

A lot of folks these days tend to reach for parchment paper as a wrapping, but I find that tamales born of silicone are usually dense and often downright greasy. Cooks in some Central American countries, like Colombia, lean toward banana leaves, but they're highly perishable, and that kind of derails the whole convenience angle. I stick with good, old-fashioned, dirt-cheap, and one-hundred-percent-natural corn husks, dried versions of which are available year round. They're usually right next to the masa harina at the old megamart.

Tamale fabrication is less cooking than factory work, and the more you think like Henry Ford the more consistent your tamales are going to be. The key is to have your work area all laid out with software and hardware within easy reach. I rarely make tamales alone. Have a few friends over, get them to rollin', and in a couple of hours everyone will be able to take a couple dozen home. Remember: Food's a social thing. It likes company.

Although steaming is the standard for Mexican and Latin American tamales, down in the Delta hot tamales are simmered long and low in the filling's cooking broth.

TIDBIT In Nicaragua, the tamale is called *nacatamal*; in Guatemala, *paches*; in Venezuela, *hallaca*; in Columbia, *bollo*.

TIDBIT *Zacahuil* is a legendary meter-long tamale that can supposedly feed an entire village.

SWEATSHOP? ME?

DON'T BE RIDICULOUS. THEY'RE WORKING ON A MERIT BADGE.

Although vegetarian and even sweet fillings are commonplace, for me, tamales mean meat. Although the big three—pork, chicken, and beef—are certainly common tamale elements, if we're to strive for any historic accuracy here, and I see no reason why we shouldn't, we must consider the meat selection available to pre-Columbian Central American cooks. There were no pigs, nor cows, nor chickens. What they did have was plenty of rabbit, and they had turkey, which is certainly ubiquitous today.[1]

// SOFTWARE

FOR THE MEAT FILLING

2	teaspoons	chili powder	
1½	teaspoons	cumin seeds	toasted and ground
1	teaspoon	cayenne pepper	
1	teaspoon	dried oregano	
1	teaspoon	kosher salt	
1	teaspoon	black pepper	freshly ground
2		turkey legs	2¼ pounds
¼	cup	vegetable oil	
1	small	onion	finely chopped
3	cloves	garlic	minced
1		serrano chile	seeded and minced

FOR THE WRAPPERS

| 2 | dozen | dried corn husks | |

FOR THE DOUGH

15	ounces	masa harina	about 3½ cups
1	tablespoon	kosher salt	
2¼	teaspoons	baking powder	
4	ounces	lard	
2 to 4	cups	reserved meat cooking liquid	

CONCERNING LARD

Sure, you could use shortening in your tamales; the texture would be nice and light, but the flavor would be flat. Lard, or rendered pig fat, gives you texture and flavor. Lard is lower in saturated fat than butter, and it contains about the same percentage of monounsaturated fats as sunflower oil. What's more, many of the lards on the market are free of the trans fats that so often lurk inside shortening. Or, you can make your own simply by . . . oh, that's another show.

LARD

[1] It should be noted they also had dogs—and, yes, there is evidence that they ate them. We, however, shall not.

// PROCEDURE

MAKE THE MEAT FILLING:

1. Combine the chili powder, cumin, cayenne, oregano, salt, black pepper, and turkey legs in a **6-quart pot** and add enough **water** to completely cover the meat, approximately 2½ quarts. Cover, place over high heat, and bring to a boil. Decrease the heat to low and

simmer until the meat is very tender and falling apart, 1½ to 2 hours. Remove the meat from the cooking liquid and set aside to cool. Leave the cooking liquid in its pot.

2. When the turkey legs are cool enough to handle, remove the meat from the bones and shred, discarding any skin or cartilage.

3. Place a **4-quart saucepan** over medium heat and add the oil. When it is shimmering, add the onion and cook, stirring occasionally, until semi-translucent, approximately 2 minutes. Add the garlic and chile and cook for another minute. Add the meat and ½ cup of the reserved cooking liquid and cook until it is heated through and the liquid has evaporated, 2 to 3 minutes. Set aside until ready to assemble.

PREPARE THE WRAPPERS:

4. While the meat is cooking, put the corn husks in a **large bowl** or container and cover completely with hot water. Soak the husks until they are soft and pliable, at least 45 minutes and up to 2 hours. (If you have an electric kettle, put the husks in the kettle, fill with water, and turn on. When the kettle turns off, let the husks soak for 1 hour in the hot water.)

MAKE THE DOUGH:

5. Combine the masa, salt, and baking powder in a **large bowl**. Add the lard and, using your hands, knead together until the lard is well incorporated into the dry mixture. Gradually add enough of the reserved cooking liquid to create a dough that is the consistency of thick mashed potatoes. The dough should be moist but not wet. Cover the bowl with a damp towel until ready to use.

ASSEMBLE AND STEAM THE TAMALES:

6. Remove a corn husk from the water and pat to remove excess water. Working in batches of 6, lay the husks on a **towel** and spread about 2 tablespoons of the dough in an even layer across the wide end of the husk to within ½ inch of the edges. Spoon about 2 teaspoons of the meat mixture in a line down the center of the dough. Roll the husk so the dough surrounds the meat and fold the bottom under to finish creating the tamale. Repeat until all the dough and filling are used. Tie the tamales around the center, individually or in groups of 3, with **kitchen twine**.

7. Place a **steamer basket** in the bottom of an **11-quart pot** and add enough water to come to the bottom of the basket. Stand the tamales close together on their folded ends and lean them in toward the center, away from the sides of the pot. Bring the water to a boil, then cover and lower the heat to maintain a simmer. Check the water level every 15 to 20 minutes, and add boiling water, if necessary, by pouring it down the side of the pot. Steam until the dough is firm and pulls away from the husk easily, 1 to 1½ hours.

8. Serve warm. Store leftover tamales, tightly wrapped in **plastic wrap**, in the freezer, for up to a month. To reheat, remove the plastic wrap and steam until heated through.

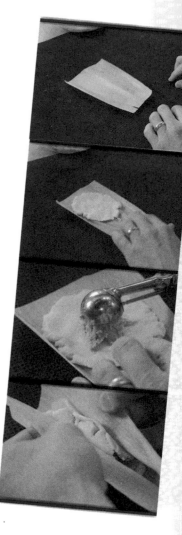

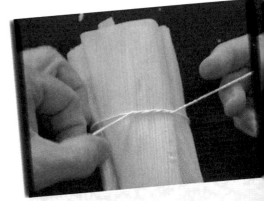

LUCKY YATES—
DEVIL MAN

DOWN IN THE DELTA

Down in the Mississippi Delta, that mysterious ellipse of land that runs west of Highway 55 from Vicksburg to Memphis, the "hot tamale" is king, the result of the cultural and culinary influence of migrant Mexican workers who, around the turn of the last century, taught their African-American field-mates the wonders of this highly nutritious, cheap, comforting, and communicable dish. They remain to this day as much a part of the Delta as the blues.

// SOFTWARE ///

FOR THE MEAT FILLING

¼	cup	chili powder	
2	tablespoons	kosher salt	
1	tablespoon	paprika	
1	tablespoon	smoked paprika	
1	tablespoon	garlic powder	
1	tablespoon	onion powder	
2½	teaspoons	cayenne pepper	
2	teaspoons	black pepper	freshly ground
1	teaspoon	cumin seed	toasted and ground
2	pounds	boneless pork butt	untrimmed
½	cup	vegetable oil	
1	large	onion	finely chopped
4	cloves	garlic	minced
1		jalapeño	seeded and minced

FOR THE WRAPPERS

4 to 5	dozen	dried corn husks	

FOR THE DOUGH

2	pounds	yellow cornmeal	about 6 cups
1½	tablespoons	kosher salt	
1	tablespoon	baking powder	
7½	ounces	lard	
3 to 4	cups	reserved meat cooking liquid	

// PROCEDURE ///

MAKE THE MEAT FILLING:

1. Combine the chili powder, salt, paprika, smoked paprika, garlic powder, onion powder, cayenne, black pepper, and cumin in a **small bowl**. Divide the mixture in half and reserve one half for later use.

(2) Cut the pork butt into 6 equal pieces and put them in a **6- to 8-quart saucepan**. Add half of the spice mixture and enough **water**, 3 to 3½ quarts, to completely cover the meat. Set over high heat, cover, and bring to a boil. Decrease the heat to low and simmer until the meat is very tender and falling apart, 2 to 2½ hours. Remove the meat from the cooking liquid and set aside, then remove the cooking liquid from the pot and reserve.

(3) Let the meat and liquid cool slightly. Remove any large pieces of fat and shred the meat into small pieces, pulling it apart with your hands or **two forks**.

(4) Place a **4-quart saucepan** over medium heat and add the oil. When it is shimmering, add the onion and cook, stirring occasionally, until semi-translucent, approximately 3 minutes. Add the garlic, jalapeño, and remaining spice mixture and cook for another minute. Add the meat and cook until it is heated through, 2 to 3 minutes. Remove from the heat.

PREPARE THE WRAPPERS:

(5) While the meat is cooking, put the corn husks in a **large bowl** or container and cover completely with hot water. Soak the husks until they are soft and pliable, at least 45 minutes and up to 2 hours.

MAKE THE DOUGH:

(6) Combine the cornmeal, salt, and baking powder in a **large bowl**. Add the lard and, using your hands, knead together until the lard is well incorporated into the dry mixture. Gradually add enough of the reserved cooking liquid to create a dough that is the consistency of thick mashed potatoes. The dough should be moist but not wet. Cover the bowl with a damp towel until ready to use.

ASSEMBLE AND SIMMER THE TAMALES:

(7) Remove a corn husk from the water and pat to remove excess water. Working in batches of 6, lay the husks on a **towel** and spread about 2 tablespoons of the dough in an even layer across the wide end of the husk to within ½ inch of the edges. Spoon about 1 tablespoon of the meat mixture in a line down the center of the dough. Roll the husk so the dough surrounds the meat and fold the bottom under to finish creating the tamale. Repeat until all the dough and filling are used. Tie the tamales around the center, individually or in groups of 3, with **kitchen twine**.

(8) Stand the tamales upright on their folded ends, tightly packed together, in the same pot that the meat was cooked in. Add the reserved meat cooking liquid and additional water so the liquid comes to 1 inch below the tops of the tamales. Try not to pour the broth directly into the tops of the tamales. Cover, place over high heat, and bring to a boil. Remove the lid, lower the heat to maintain a low simmer, and cook until the dough is firm and pulls away from the husk easily, 1 to 1½ hours.

(9) Serve the tamales warm. For a "wet" hot tamale, serve with additional simmering liquid. Store leftover tamales, tightly wrapped in **plastic wrap**, in the freezer, for up to a month. To reheat, remove the plastic wrap and steam until heated through.

Southern hot tamales always simmer in liquid.

AMERICAN CLASSICS IV: SPAGHETTI & MEAT SAUCE

EPISODE 209 | SEASON 13 | GOOD EATS

Say "spaghetti and meat sauce" and most folks

think of candles stuck in Chianti bottles and checkerboard tablecloths and Pan Am "See Naples" posters. Well, I've got a little surprise for you: spag and meat sauce is just about as American as it can get. Still, to unlock its secrets we must first journey to a city famous for its own meat sauce, Bologna, in the Emilia-Romagna region of Italy, a country that knows from . . .

```
Waiter: Eh, pronto di ordinare, Signore?
(Will you be ordering today, sir?)

AB: Ahh, si, excuse. Vorrei il ragu alla
Bolognese con gli spaghetti, per favore.
(Ahh, yes, pardon me. I'll have the ragu
alla Bolognese with spaghetti, please.)

Waiter: Spaghetti. Ma, é sicuro?
(Spaghetti? Are you sure?)

AB: Certamente sono sicuro. Sono Americano.
(Of course I'm sure. I'm an American.)

AB: No matter what comes out through that
door, I guarantee you it won't look like
what you and I think it ought to look like.
```

```
The waiter returns and places two dishes
on the table before AB; one contains ragu,
the other spaghetti.

Waiter: Ecco, spaghetti é ragu alla Bolognese.
(Spaghetti and ragu alla Bolognese.)

AB: Li voglio misto insieme.
(I want them together.)

Waiter: Allora la mescoli le. Buon giorno.
(Then put them together yourself. Good day.)

AB: Buon giorno.
(Good day.)

The waiter leaves, disgusted.
```

Now, in America, *ragu* might not sound very special, but the word is actually derived from the French *ragouter*, meaning "to revive the taste," and it is very special indeed. In the case of Bologna, it is a meaty stew based on long-simmered aromatics: carrots, onions, celery, minced meat, a bit of tomato product, and, oddly enough, milk. Although most Americans would not recognize it as a "meat sauce," *ragu alla Bolognese* is no doubt the rich uncle of our meat sauce.

▷○ **Here's the deal:** Spaghetti, long strands of durum wheat pasta, extruded, dried, then boiled, and *ragu alla Bolognese*, a chunky, heavy meat stew, are physically incompatible. In Italy, spaghetti is tossed with oil, cheese, and herbs, while heavy sauces are married to big, tube shapes, or fresh ribbons like tagliatelle. So how did a dish that's unheard of in Italy become the poster dish for Italian cuisine in the United States? The answer can be found on a small island, and I don't mean Capri.

From 1892 to 1954, some 12 million immigrants began their American experience on Ellis Island. Some were rich, others poor beyond imagining. Many had their identities changed, while some lost them altogether. Culturally, Ellis was an engine of homogenization. You might walk in Tuscan, Sicilian, or Venetian, but you walked out Italian, and the American came later on. Bound by little more than a common language, many of these strangers in a strange land settled in tight-knit communities inside larger urban landscapes. No longer forced to dine on black bread and beans, the cooks of such Little Italys began to innovate, giving birth to many of the dishes that Americans consider to be Italian today. What's more, many of these new dishes quickly moved onto the plates of mainstream America, compliments of an active, motivated, and highly organized Italian-American manufacturing community.

▷○ **A good example:** the powerful National Macaroni Manufacturer's Association, which was like an extruded-pasta cartel in the old days. During the 1920s, they published and distributed WASP-friendly recipes, including a wildly popular one for something called Italian spaghetti and meatballs, which was basically meat sauce. What was interesting is that it was cooked and served as a casserole. Fascinating! The association also offered up fanciful food mythologies in their magazine, *Macaroni Journal*. In fact, an association writer may have actually invented the whole "Marco Polo bringing pasta to Venice from China" legend. Nice piece of viral marketing, that. But the full Americanization of Italian-American cuisine would actually have to wait until 1953, when a U.S. Army hospital cook named Garibaldi Lapolla wrote *Italian Cooking for the American Kitchen*, which, despite vast popularity, was about as Italian as Florence Henderson.

TIDBIT Spaghetti houses of the 1920s boiled cauldrons of pasta in their windows. A plate with sauce sold for around thirty-five cents.

TRIVIA It took me about a week to learn my Italian lines for the restaurant scene.

DRIED PORCINI

Behold, the porcini mushroom: unique in the fungal world, not only for its size but for its high concentration of meaty flavors, which are due in large part to amino acids, including glutamic acid, the active ingredient in MSG. Porcinis, which are quite rare in this country (in fresh form, at least), also contain high amounts of sulfur compounds capable of creating meaty aromas. Luckily, the meaty attributes of most mushrooms, and porcinis in particular, are preserved by drying. A mere ounce of dried porcini, finely chopped, will add an earthy depth to all that meaty goodness, but odds are, no one will ever know it's there.

Don't freak out looking at the long software list below. This meat sauce is really just a simple stew. When in Bologna, you will no doubt enjoy meat sauces tossed with wide noodles, but this is America, and we want our spaghetti. But at least make it a nice Italian spaghetti, which tends to be a little thicker than our domestic product and so will hold the sauce better.

// SOFTWARE ///

FOR THE MEAT SAUCE

6	ounces	thick-sliced bacon	cut into 1-inch pieces
2	large	onions	finely chopped
1½	teaspoons	kosher salt	
½	teaspoon	black pepper	freshly ground
3	whole	cloves	
1	pod	star anise	
3	ribs	celery	
5	cloves	garlic	3 minced and 2 sliced
3	tablespoons	olive oil	divided
8	ounces	coarsely ground beef chuck	
8	ounces	coarsely ground pork butt	
1¼	cups	white wine[1]	
¾	cup	evaporated milk	
3	cups	beef broth	
1	ounce	dried porcini mushrooms	finely chopped
2	28-ounce cans	diced tomatoes	
1	tablespoon	dried oregano	
2	teaspoons	dried basil	
2	teaspoons	dried marjoram	
2	tablespoons	tomato paste	
1	tablespoon	ketchup	
1	tablespoon	sherry vinegar	
1	teaspoon	Worcestershire sauce	
⅓	cup	finely grated Parmesan cheese	

FOR THE PASTA

2	tablespoons	kosher salt	
8	ounces	dried spaghetti	

[1] You may have been expecting red wine here, but what we really need in this case is some sweetness, some kind of woody flavor, and some bright acidity. Red's full of bossy stuff, like tannins, that tend toward astringency when cooked. We don't need that.

// PROCEDURE //

MAKE THE MEAT SAUCE:

(1) Place an **8-quart Dutch oven** over low heat and add the bacon. Cook slowly until the bacon is crisp and has rendered its fat, 25 to 30 minutes. Remove the bacon from the pot and reserve for another use. Add the onions, salt, and pepper to the fat in the pot and stir to combine. Put the cloves and star anise in a **small spice bag**, add to the pot, and stir to combine. Cook, uncovered, over low heat, stirring occasionally, until the onions caramelize, 45 to 60 minutes. Add the celery and minced garlic to the pan and cook over low heat until the celery is semi-translucent, approximately 30 minutes. Remove the spice bag from the pot.

(2) Meanwhile, place a wide, **4-quart sauté pan** over high heat. Add 1 tablespoon of the oil and, when it is shimmering, add the beef and pork and cook, stirring frequently, until the meat is well browned, 4 to 5 minutes. Transfer the meat to a **colander** to drain. Return the pan to high heat, add ½ cup of the wine, and deglaze the pan, scraping up any browned bits from the bottom of the pan. Transfer these bits and any remaining wine to the Dutch oven, along with the meat.

(3) Add another ½ cup of the wine, the evaporated milk, broth, and mushrooms to the Dutch oven and stir to combine. Cover and cook over low heat, stirring occasionally, for 3 hours.

(4) After the meat has cooked for 1½ hours, return the sauté pan to medium heat and add 1 tablespoon of the oil. When it is shimmering, add the sliced garlic and cook for 30 to 45 seconds, until fragrant. Do not allow the garlic to brown. Add the tomatoes, oregano, basil, and marjoram and cook until most of the liquid has evaporated, approximately 30 minutes. Add the remaining ¼ cup wine, the tomato paste, ketchup, vinegar, and Worcestershire sauce and stir to combine. Decrease the heat to low and simmer for 30 minutes. Increase the heat to medium-high; add the remaining 1 tablespoon oil and fry, stirring constantly, for 2 to 3 minutes.

(5) Transfer the tomato mixture to the meat mixture and stir to combine. Simmer the sauce, uncovered, over low heat, stirring occasionally, while cooking the pasta.

MAKE THE PASTA:

(6) Bring **1 gallon water** and the salt to a boil in a **large pot** over high heat. Carefully add the pasta, stirring quickly to separate. Cover and return to a boil, being careful that the water does not boil over. Uncover and cook until slightly less than al dente, 5 to 6 minutes. Drain in a colander.

(7) Add the pasta to the sauce and cook over low heat for 2 to 3 minutes, until the pasta is al dente. Add the cheese, toss to combine, and serve.

TIDBIT The Maillard reaction is the browning of proteins and carbohydrates (as in meats or baked goods), resulting in pleasingly complex flavors.

TIP Tightly sealed, meat sauce will keep in the freezer for up to six months.

TENDER IS THE PORK

EPISODE 210 | SEASON 13 | GOOD EATS

Over the last few decades, our culture, fixated on fast, cheap, low-fat convenient protein, has come to rely more and more on *Gallus domesticus*. It's like the movie *Soylent Green*, only with chickens instead of . . . you know. We need to find an alternative, an antidote, if you will, before it's too late.

But before I make my nomination, let us consider the most popular cut of our feathered friend: the breast. It contains a high percentage of fast-twitch musculature, which is primarily anaerobic, so it lacks hemoglobin and therefore is light in color. Since these muscles don't work very often, there isn't much connective tissue, hence it is tender. And since poultry scientists, geneticists, and feed engineers have whittled away at its fat content until it's on a par with an underfed Russian supermodel, it's—well, it's about as lean as lean gets.

So what can replace this super-lean, super-white meat? Let's consider the beef critter. It's tasty, but with an average feed conversion ratio of 5.5 to 1, an average fat content of about 20 percent, and an average cook time of well over two hours for, say, a four- to five-pound roast, this is not exactly a replacement for chicken, is it? Now let us consider the pig. Although many of the cuts found therein require either long cooking times or mechanical tenderization, there's one particular muscle, or rather two per pig, that rivals the chicken breast for convenience, flavor, and fat content. It is the tenderloin, and what I like most about it is that it doesn't taste a bit like chicken, which certainly qualifies it as . . .

TIDBIT | According to the USDA, a three-ounce portion of pork tenderloin contains only 2.98 grams of fat compared to an equal portion of skinless chicken breast, which contains 3.03 grams of fat. Plus, pork is packed with B vitamins and plenty of iron.

TIDBIT | Hernando de Soto introduced the first pigs to America when he landed in Tampa, Florida, in 1539.

TIDBIT | Most pigs in the United States are a cross between the Duroc, Hampshire, and Yorkshire breeds.

TIDBIT | Cincinnati earned the nickname Porkopolis in the 1860s.

WHEN SCIENCE TYPES FIGHT

The particular pieces that we hope to harvest from Wilbur are buried deep within his almost entirely edible chassis, but that doesn't mean they're hard to get to. In fact, you'll notice lodged right along the inside of the rib cage, next to the spine, two beautiful little tubes of meat, one on either side. These are the tenderloins, and their convenient placement is, as far as I'm concerned, proof positive that we were meant to eat them.

A great many tenderloins come in heavy, plastic cryo bags, which always contain two whole tenderloins along with a fair amount of liquid. They are hermetically sealed and have a very long shelf life. (I've kept one of these viable in the chill chest for well over two weeks.) But beware! Many such sacks contain "enhanced" pork, meaning that the liquid in question is heavily laced with the likes of potassium, lactate, sodium diacetate, and sodium phosphates. Because tenderloins cook quickly, and since they contain zip for fat, the meat can dry out. Liquid enhancers are injected into the meat to make up for that. In other words, we breed most of the juicy flavor goodness out of the pig and then re-inject it with a salt brine. Well, if I want my pork brined I'm going to do the brining myself.

But, before we get into home pork enhancement, we need to do a wee bit of butchery. The tenderloin contains neither bones nor gristle, but a small strip of undigestible reticulum, or "silverskin," sheathes part of the muscle, and that has got to go. Insert the end of a narrow boning knife or paring knife under the skin, pointing away from you, and slide it enough to get your finger in and then pull the silverskin off, sliding the knife along it as you go. Try not to saw back and forth too much. Turn the loin around, hold the skin, and remove the other end. Repeat until all the white stuff (or most of it) is gone.

When it comes to meat flavor enhancement, there are three scenarios to consider:

1. DRY RUBS are super-charged surface seasonings either dredged, sprinkled, or rubbed onto the surface of the meat mere moments before the heat is introduced. This creates a nice tasty crust.

2. BRINES are simple or complex salt solutions capable of initiating changes in the structure of the meat, the osmotic action. We often employ brines to prevent bigger hunks of critter from drying out during long periods in the oven.

3. MARINADES are also flavorful solutions, but, unlike brines, they always contain a fair amount of acid.

Due to its size, shape, and general lack of connective tissue, pork tenderloin cooks curiously quickly. It also has the annoying habit of drying out very quickly. This makes it a perfect candidate for marinating and high-heat grilling.

// GRILLED PORK TENDERLOIN

4 SERVINGS

THE TRUTH ABOUT MARINADES

What does a marinade actually do? Well, let me tell you what it *doesn't* do. It doesn't tenderize. Even if marinades could penetrate big hunks of meat enough to reach tough inner fibers, and they can't, it would take days or maybe weeks for the work to be done. However, the salt in a marinade affects the proteins at the surface of the meat, a process called solubilization, so that the space between the meat fibers opens up, thus allowing for better absorption—what the meat industry calls "pickup." The acid weakens the proteins so they can better bind with the liquid, thus increasing the meat's water-holding capacity, or WHC. Then, in the *coup de grâce*, the salt swells outer fibers, eventually sealing them, so the moisture is locked inside. The result: a flavor-loaded piece of meat that's less likely to dry out during cooking.

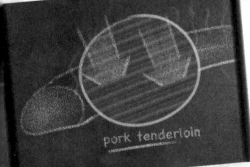

pork tenderloin

// SOFTWARE ///

1	1-pound	whole pork tenderloin	
1		lime	zested
½	cup	lime juice	freshly squeezed
¼	cup	honey	
1½	teaspoons	kosher salt	
½	teaspoon	garlic powder	
1		chipotle chile in adobo sauce	chopped
1	teaspoon	vegetable oil	
1	tablespoon	chopped fresh cilantro	

// PROCEDURE ///

1. Trim the tenderloin of any excess fat and silverskin.

2. Put the lime zest, lime juice, honey, salt, and garlic powder in a **small, lidded jar** and shake to combine. Pour half of this marinade into a **1-gallon zip-top bag**, add the chipotle, and slosh around to combine. Add the tenderloin to the bag and seal, removing as much air as possible. Set the bag in **leakproof containment** and refrigerate for 6 to 24 hours, flipping the bag halfway through. Cover and put the remaining marinade in the refrigerator.

3. Remove the tenderloin from the bag and let it sit at room temperature while preparing the grill. Remove the reserved marinade from the refrigerator.

4. Fill a **large chimney starter** with natural-lump charcoal and light it. When the charcoal is ashy and white, after approximately 30 minutes, dump the hot charcoal onto the lowest grate of the grill and spread it into an even layer using extra-long tongs. Put the cooking grate back on the grill and cover with the lid; heat the grate for 2 to 3 minutes.

5. **Brush** the grate with the oil. Remove the tenderloin from the bag and place it in the center of the grate. Cover and cook for 12 to 15 minutes, turning every 1½ to 2 minutes, until the tenderloin reaches an internal temperature of 140°F.

6. Remove the tenderloin from the grill and put it on a large piece of **heavy-duty aluminum foil** folded up at the edges to create a basket, and pour on the reserved marinade. Wrap tightly and let rest for 10 minutes. Garnish with cilantro, slice, and serve.

PORK WELLINGTON

4 SERVINGS

// SOFTWARE //

1	large	egg	
1	tablespoon	H_2O	
1	ounce	dried apple rings	
1	1-pound	whole pork tenderloin	
4½	ounces	thinly sliced prosciutto	
¼	teaspoon	kosher salt	
¼	teaspoon	black pepper	freshly ground
1	teaspoon	fresh thyme	chopped
1	teaspoon	all-purpose flour	
1	sheet	puff pastry	thawed
1	tablespoon	whole-grain mustard	

// PROCEDURE //

1. Put a rack in the upper third of the oven and heat to 400°F.

2. **Whisk** the egg and water in a **small bowl** and set aside. Process the apple rings in a **mini food processor** for 30 to 45 seconds, until they are medium diced. Set aside.

3. Trim the tenderloin of any excess fat and silverskin. Split the tenderloin down the middle lengthwise, creating two separate pieces. Position the tenderloin pieces next to each other head to tail, to make the bundle the same thickness at each end.

4. Arrange the prosciutto slices in the center of a 12-by-16-inch piece of **parchment paper** so that they overlap, creating an uninterrupted layer as long as the tenderloin. Top with a second sheet of parchment, and roll over it with a **rolling pin** so that the prosciutto slices will kind of meld together.

5. Remove the top parchment paper and sprinkle the prosciutto with the salt, pepper, and thyme. Set the tenderloin bundle down the middle of the prosciutto. Sandwich the dried apples between the two pieces of tenderloin, then, using the parchment to assist, wrap the prosciutto around the tenderloin to completely enclose it in a package.

6. Sprinkle a work surface with the flour and roll out the pastry to a 12-by-14-inch rectangle. Spread the mustard thinly in the center of the pastry and set the prosciutto-wrapped tenderloin in the center, on the mustard. Fold the puff pastry up and over the top of the tenderloin, then roll to enclose, brushing the edges of the pastry with the egg wash to seal. Turn the tenderloin over so the side with the double thickness of pastry is on the bottom. Pinch the ends to seal, then brush the entire parcel with the egg wash.

7. Place the tenderloin on a **half sheet pan lined with parchment paper** and bake for 25 to 30 minutes, until the pork reaches an internal temperature of at least 140°F. Transfer to a **cooling rack** and rest for 10 minutes before slicing and serving.

THE TASTE OF VICTORY

Beef Wellington was named after an Irishman named Arthur Wellesley, the first duke of Wellington. On June 18, 1815, in a muddy little hole called Waterloo, Wellington led the English army (in concert with the Prussian army) to a devastating defeat of French forces under the command of one Napoleon Bonaparte. As was the habit back in those days, a dish—in this case a raw tenderloin of beef wrapped in a pastry crust and cooked—was devised and named for the victory. The dish went in and out of fashion, and by the 1960s it had accumulated things like truffles, foie gras, cooked mushrooms, and whatnot. It then languished in obscurity for thirty-something years. Well, I say it's time for a triumphant return, only with pork tenderloin.

TENDER IS THE PORK

UNDERCOVER VEGGIES

EPISODE 211 | SEASON 13 | GOOD EATS

Kids, by and large, do not care for vegetables. There is a logical reason for this. Unlike sweet foods, which almost always contain plenty of energy in the form of carbon-rich sugars, bitter foods often contain alkalis, which are often found in poison, prescription drugs, industrial cleaners, petroleum products, and the like. All of which are potentially deadly. Our palates have evolved in such a way that they send messages to the brain that say "yuck" when they encounter bitterness, and in doing so have saved many a life. As we mature, we come to appreciate bitterness, which is a good thing because if we didn't we wouldn't enjoy dark chocolate, spinach, black coffee, or Scotch—and that would be a shame.

Many parents attempt to coax their kids into eating their veggies the Mary Poppins way, by smothering them in fat or sugar, either of which tends to void the reason for cajoling them into eating them in the first place. I prefer the stealth method, by which we choose vegetables that already contain a fair amount of sugar and that lend themselves to a wide range of cooking possibilities. Consider parsnips. If ever there were a vegetable capable of flying in stealth mode, it is this pale cousin of parsley, brought to the British Isles in the fifteenth century by Flemish weavers escaping religious persecution in Spain. Parsnips are versatile, flavorful, nutritious, and capable of almost disappearing into the background of a wide range of dishes. And that is certainly enough to qualify them as . . .

TIDBIT | Parsnips are an excellent source of the B vitamin folate, as well as vitamin C and dietary fiber.

TIDBIT | Due to their increasing popularity, parsnips are now available year-round.

LADIES AND GENTLEMEN, THE PARSNIP.

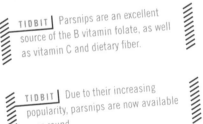

▷○ Parsnips are on the comeback trail these days and have returned to many a megamart produce department, where they're often placed next to celery root. At its best from fall through spring, the parsnip looks like a beige carrot. Look for an evenly colored skin and avoid anything that looks shriveled or dry. Parsnips keep very well as long as they're cool and dry, so wrap them in paper towels before stashing them in plastic and interring in the fridge.

▷○ Parsnips can deliver an amazing amount of sweetness, but only if they spend the winter in the ground. The reason is a phenomenon called "cold sweetening," and to a certain degree it happens to all vegetables that have storage organs—potatoes and carrots are other examples. These structures are essentially starch packs whose payload is converted to simpler sugars via respiration. However, when the ground temperature drops below 50 degrees, respiration slows and the sugars accumulate. Eventually the moisture inside the parsnip becomes so saturated with sugar that the freezing point of that liquid drops (due to the dissolved solids) until the resulting liquid functions like botanical antifreeze protecting the root from cold damage.

▷○ Parsnips have a very distinct flavor. They are nutty and savory; sweet, yet a tad musky, with a hint of celery. The flavor is so cagey that parsnips are rather difficult to pin down, which just may explain why they work so well in so many "un-vegetal" foods, foods in which veggie haters would never expect nutrition to be so cunningly concealed.

TRIVIA | The parsnip cutaway set was one of the hardest we've ever built. Dirt has a mind of its own.

UNDERCOVER VEGGIES

237

12 MUFFINS

// SOFTWARE

1	ounce	sliced almonds	
8½	ounces	all-purpose flour	
1	teaspoon	baking powder	
¾	teaspoon	baking soda	
½	teaspoon	nutmeg	freshly grated
½	teaspoon	kosher salt	
3	large	eggs	
¾	cup	plain full-fat yogurt	
¼	cup	vegetable oil	
8	ounces	sugar	
10	ounces	grated parsnips	

// PROCEDURE

1. Put the almonds in a single layer in a **pie pan** and put them in the oven. Heat the oven to 375°F. Bake until lightly toasted, approximately 20 minutes while the oven heats. Meanwhile, spray a standard **12-cup muffin tin** with **nonstick cooking spray** and set aside.

2. Combine the flour, baking powder, baking soda, nutmeg, and salt in the **bowl of a food processor** and process for 5 seconds.

3. **Whisk** the eggs, yogurt, oil, and sugar in a **large mixing bowl** until combined. Add the flour mixture and parsnips and fold with a **spatula** until all the flour is moistened. Don't overmix the batter; there will be some lumps.

4. Divide the batter evenly among the muffin cups using a level **2½-ounce disher or ⅓-cup measure**, then sprinkle the top of each muffin with the toasted almonds.

5. Bake for 20 to 25 minutes, rotating the pan halfway through, until the muffins reach an internal temperature of 210°F and are golden brown.

6. Use a **small knife or offset spatula** to loosen the muffins and immediately move them from the tin to a **cooling rack**, where they should rest peacefully for 15 minutes prior to service. Completely cooled muffins may be stashed in an **airtight container** for up to 3 days, or frozen in a **zip-top bag** for up to 3 months.

TIDBIT | Be sure to weigh the parsnips after grating, as the roots come in a wide variety of sizes.

TIDBIT | Italian pigs destined for prosciutto are often fattened on parsnips.

"PEARSNIP" SAUCE

ABOUT 1 QUART

// SOFTWARE

1	pound	parsnips	peeled and cut into 1-inch pieces
1	pound	pears	peeled, cored, and cut into 1-inch pieces
3	tablespoons	maple syrup	
1	teaspoon	orange zest	
1½	cups	orange juice	freshly squeezed
¼	teaspoon	ground cardamom	
	pinch	kosher salt	
	pinch	freshly ground cloves	
1	tablespoon	lemon juice	freshly squeezed

// PROCEDURE

1. Put the parsnips, pears, syrup, orange zest, orange juice, cardamom, salt, and cloves in a **sealable 3- to 4-quart microwave-safe container**. Cover with a lid, leaving one corner open to allow steam to escape, and microwave on high power for 10 to 15 minutes, until the parsnips and pears are fork tender.

2. Add the lemon juice and puree using an **immersion blender or potato masher**. Serve warm or chilled. Store in an **airtight container** for up to 3 days.

ROASTED PARSNIPS

Heat the oven to 375°F, then bring 2 quarts of water and 1 teaspoon of kosher salt to a boil over high heat. Scrub 1½ pounds of parsnips to remove excess dirt, and slice off their tops and tips. Cut each parsnip into 2-inch pieces, then cut each piece in half lengthwise. Cook the parsnips in the boiling water for 3 minutes, then drain.

Transfer to a 13-by-9-inch pan, toss with 1 teaspoon of kosher salt, 2 tablespoons of olive oil, and ½ teaspoon of freshly ground black pepper, and spread in an even layer. Roast for 20 minutes. Gently toss and return to the oven for another 20 to 25 minutes, until golden brown. Serve hot.

TIDBIT "Fair words butter no parsnips" was a popular proverb back in 1639.

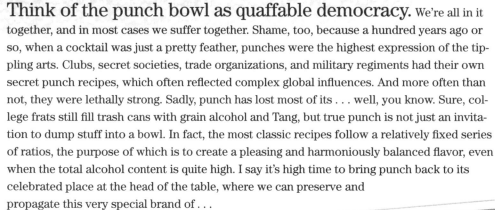

Think of the punch bowl as quaffable democracy. We're all in it together, and in most cases we suffer together. Shame, too, because a hundred years ago or so, when a cocktail was just a pretty feather, punches were the highest expression of the tippling arts. Clubs, secret societies, trade organizations, and military regiments had their own secret punch recipes, which often reflected complex global influences. And more often than not, they were lethally strong. Sadly, punch has lost most of its . . . well, you know. Sure, college frats still fill trash cans with grain alcohol and Tang, but true punch is not just an invitation to dump stuff into a bowl. In fact, the most classic recipes follow a relatively fixed series of ratios, the purpose of which is to create a pleasing and harmoniously balanced flavor, even when the total alcohol content is quite high. I say it's high time to bring punch back to its celebrated place at the head of the table, where we can preserve and propagate this very special brand of . . .

TIDBIT | A punch low in alcohol is technically called a "cup."

I DON'T KNOW THESE PEOPLE!

On the final day of the year 1600, a royal charter was issued to a commercial venture officially named "The Governor and Company of Merchants of London Trading into the East Indies." The express mission of this organization was to import spices and goods directly to England from the Indian subcontinent and the surrounding lands, thus sidestepping the markups levied by the middlemen who lined the old spice land route. Over the next century, the British East India Company, or "the Company," became so powerful that it commanded its own armed forces. Its influence grew so considerable on the subcontinent that by the time the crown dissolved its charter in 1873 it got complete control of India in the bargain. When Company men made return trips to England, they brought with them the exotic makings of punch.

The word *punch* comes from *panch*, the Hindi word for "five," a significant sum, because the beverage is built upon five categories of flavors that are assembled by what is called the "rule of fives":

— One part sour,

— Two parts sweet,

— Three of strong,

— And four of weak;

— Spice makes five.

Old punch recipes (or "receipts") often call for mixing the stronger alcoholic components together days, weeks, sometimes even months ahead of punch time. Back then, spirits were often sold young and unblended—in other words, harsh. Premixing and aging the punch base at home helped to curb the curse. Although this step isn't the necessity it was a hundred years ago, I still like to build my strong team ahead of time in a gallon vessel, because having it on hand will make it easier for me to quickly reinforce the punch as the party progresses.

Many classic punch recipes call for "champagne," but I'm not going to dump a $40-plus bottle of French bubbles in a punch bowl. I usually reach for an American sparkling wine or an Italian Prosecco in the $12 range. If you have an option, reach for the extra-dry version.

MAKING YOUR OWN ICEBERG

A single block of ice is far superior to ice cubes because blocks melt much more slowly. If you don't have access to block ice, fill a medium-size balloon half full with water, set it in a bowl, and freeze it solid. Break the balloon and peel it away to reveal a perfect orb of ice. Rinse it off, then float it in the punch. If you don't want the punch diluted, just leave the balloon in place (after making sure none of your party suffers from a latex allergy).

BRING FORTH THE WRITING SLATE!

GOOD EATS COMPANY PUNCH

APPROXIMATELY 30 (4-OUNCE) SERVINGS

According to British East India Company records, the original incarnation of punch looked something like this. I know what you're probably thinking: ships, high seas, rum! Wrong. Rum, or *rumbullion*, was primarily a Caribbean beverage, found on the other side of the planet from where punch was first concocted. No, the strong drink of choice back then was Batavia Arrack, a potent potable from Java distilled from fermented sugarcane and red rice.

// SOFTWARE ///

16	ounces	lime juice	freshly squeezed, hulls reserved; about 20 limes
32	ounces	demerara sugar	
64	ounces	warm black tea	
48	ounces	Batavia Arrack	
		ice block	
		nutmeg	freshly grated

TIDBIT | Batavia Arrack has been produced on Java since the seventeenth century and is available today on the Internet.

// PROCEDURE ///

1. Combine the lime juice, lime hulls, and sugar in a 5-quart container. Add the tea and stir until the sugar dissolves completely, 2 to 3 minutes. Add the Batavia Arrack and stir to combine. Chill in the refrigerator to at least 40°F, approximately 1 hour.

2. Strain the punch into a punch bowl over a large ice block and serve with nutmeg.

LOOKS INNOCENT...

BUT THERE'S ALWAYS SOME OLD LADY READY AND WILLING TO SPIKE THE PUNCH.

CAPE FEAR PUNCH

APPROXIMATELY 40 (4-OUNCE) SERVINGS

My favorite regional punch is Cape Fear Punch, a secret recipe of one Cape Fear club, supposedly the oldest gentlemen's club in the South. Various versions have been leaked over the years, but the real McCoy always contains an ingredient critical to many a classic punch: Cognac.

// SOFTWARE

FOR THE BASE

750	milliliters	rye whiskey	
750	milliliters	H_2O	
½	cup	demerara sugar	
3	bags	green tea	
375	milliliters	rum	
375	milliliters	cognac	
4		lemons	

FOR THE PUNCH

2	small	oranges	thinly sliced
4	small	lemons	thinly sliced
2	750 ml bottles	sparkling wine or champagne	
1	liter	seltzer or sparkling water	
		ice block	
		nutmeg	freshly grated

// PROCEDURE

MAKE THE BASE:

(1) Pour the whiskey into a **4-quart container**. Fill the now empty whiskey bottle with water, pour it into an **electric kettle**, and bring to a boil. Turn off the kettle, add the sugar, and stir until the temperature drops to 190°F. Put the tea bags in the kettle and steep for 3 minutes.

(2) Add the tea, rum, and cognac to the whiskey. Peel the zest from the lemons, being careful to remove the white pith. Wrap the lemon bodies in **plastic wrap** and reserve in the refrigerator. Add the lemon zest to the liquor mixture and stir to combine. Cover and refrigerate overnight.

MAKE THE PUNCH:

(3) Strain the base into a **large punch bowl**. Juice the reserved lemon bodies and add the juice to the punch bowl. When ready to serve, add the oranges, sliced lemons, sparkling wine, and seltzer; stir to combine. Add the ice block and serve with nutmeg.

APPROXIMATELY 13 (4-OUNCE) SERVINGS

In the days before central heat, anything that added warmth to winter was a good thing, including punch. Landlords in Edwardian England were in fact expected to prepare hot punches from time to time in order to prevent Jack Frost from nipping their tenants' noses clean off.

Remember our one of sour, two of sweet, three of strong, and four of weak, plus spice equation? Words to live by, to be sure, but this drink is going to be served hot, and heat amplifies aromatic elements as well as the sweetness of sugar, so I'm going to adjust the proportions. The sour's going to go down to just a few slices of lemon. We'll cut down on the sugar as well, so that our final formula is going to look more like some of sour, one of sweet, five of strong, and eight of weak, plus spice.

// SOFTWARE ///

1		lemon	thinly sliced
½	cup	demerara sugar	
1	quart	H_2O	
2½	cups	Scotch whiskey[1]	
		nutmeg	freshly grated

[1] Because a hot toddy requires its base liquor to have a fair amount of body, use a single-malt Scotch rather than a blended one. Single malts are generally distilled in pot stills, which create spirits with a heavier body than column stills.

// PROCEDURE //

1. Combine the lemon, sugar, and water in a **2- to 3-quart slow cooker** set to high. Cover and heat, stirring occasionally, until the sugar dissolves completely, 20 to 30 minutes.

2. Add the Scotch and stir to combine. Set the slow cooker to low and serve warm with lemon slices and nutmeg.

THE CURE FOR A COLD NIGHT...
OR ANY OTHER KIND OF NIGHT

GOOD EATS TURNS 10

No one was more surprised

than I was that *Good Eats* made it to ten years. But when it became clear that the line would indeed be crossed, we knew we had to do something big, and that even bigness wouldn't be enough. It needed to be big and scary, at least for us. Someone (no one can actually remember who) came up with the idea of doing a live show. Perhaps we could rent out a "small theater" somewhere, we thought, and have a kind of birthday party. Well, a "small theater" turned into the 2,750-seat Cobb Energy Centre, and the "party" became a two-hour variety show featuring everything from witty conversation (I still owe Ted Allen big time), a twelve-foot-tall glowing birthday cake, a game show, a food demo using a fire extinguisher to freeze fruit for a smoothie, and, of course, puppets. In the end it took a crew of over a hundred, including every single member of my faithful core *Good Eats* crew, my musical director Patrick Belden, and several players from my other job, on *Iron Chef America*, including my good friend Eytan Keller, who came in to direct (multicamera scares me), and Seth Melman, who stage-managed us out of the valley of darkness.

I don't know how the shows actually came out on tape, as live shows like this rarely (if ever) capture the mojo of being there, but for those of us who *were* there, it was a special day. For me, the best moment was just before the afternoon show. After the band closed the preshow set with a righteous cover of Joe Walsh's "Rocky Mountain Way," we sent out my attorneys Itchy and Twitchy to read the required legal disclaimer regarding cameras, recording devices, and so on. As usual, the lawyers were played by our production coordinator, Jim Pace, and assistant editor, Brett Sol, who had put on the suits of justice at least a dozen times over the last few years. I was standing at this special door, way down stage left, waiting for my cue, when the guys went out, and the second they hit the stage the audience went wild. It was a beautiful moment and the show hadn't even started yet.

If you're reading this and were in either of the audiences that night (especially if you were in the poncho zone), thank you. It was one of the top ten days of my life.

Here now, some images from that fateful day . . . and night.

PATRICK BELDEN AND THE BAND

Back in the video truck

The AB puppet,
made by Lucky Yates

WORKING ON THE "BERRY BLASTER"

GOOD EATS LIVE

The crew shirts . . .
hot items on eBay

ULTRAVIOLET FROSTING!

HAPPY BIRTHDAY!!

THE "BLASTER" BLASTS.

Sister Marsha managing pancakes

REHEARSING THE GIANT CAKE

I GOT SILLY-STRUNG.

These aren't so much happy smiles as gone-insane smiles.

BEWARE THE PONCHO ZONE!

Setting up the *Good Eats* trivia death match

MY TRAINER, ROGER SCOTT, AS CLARENCE

By and large, American men can't feed themselves. I know this because I've talked to thousands of men over the last decade about their eating habits and this is the one, simple, unifying truth that permeates the male experience. Personally I blame the fact that boys do not become Boy Scouts in the droves they once did. When you learn to cook your breakfast over fire, you become a man . . . or at least take a significant step toward becoming one.

But I digress.

Back in episode 101, we goofed the now-defunct TV series *The Man Show* by doing a show about guy-centric food—corn dogs, sliders, stuff guys like to eat. And the show struck a power chord, so much so that guys would stop me in hardware stores, gun shops, motorcycle rallies, and bars (not in that order) and ask me for more. Breakfast seemed like a good place to start. Always on the lookout for a gimmick, we decided to shoot this one from the perspective of a client whose mother has hired me to get her grown son off her culinary back. Such work requires an enforcer, and so we have the white-jacketed Clarence, who in real life is my trainer, Roger, making his show-biz debut. But enough talk. Men, let's get to the . . .

CONCERNING AN EGG PAN

Eggs contain a great deal of protein. You could, in fact, think of them as liquid meat. So what happens to proteins when they cook? They coagulate. And that's why they stick to pan surfaces. Pans aren't really smooth, after all, at least not on the microscopic level. So when it comes to eggs, you want a nonstick surface. (Although such surfaces come by many names, in the end we're talking about polytetrafluoroethylene, otherwise known as Teflon.) For one or two eggs, something in the eight-inch range will do, and don't you ever, ever scrub it with an abrasive or I will hunt you down and . . . well, let's leave it at that.

Coffee is a "brew"—that is, a solution resulting from soaking a soluble solid in a solvent, in this case ground coffee beans and hot water. Processing said brew requires a piece of equipment that can actually place the coffee grounds in contact with water. Now, a bunch of different tools will do the job—a percolator, an auto-drip machine, a vacuum pot—but I usually tell beginners to start with a French press, a fabulous multitasker.

Coffee is a spice. Think about it: The beans are dried seed, full of volatile compounds that we want to preserve until we're ready to get them out. I store coffee beans as I would store spices, in airtight containment away from heat and light. Freezing is okay, but only for long-term storage, as repeated thawing and refreezing will cause condensation, which will degrade the beans.

The number one thing you can do to improve the coffee in your cup is to grind the beans yourself immediately prior to brewing. Blade grinders are inexpensive, and can certainly get the job done, but the blades never create a really uniform grind, which is why I prefer a burr grinder, which utilizes a big-toothed, conical grinding wheel that nests down into a stationary-toothed receiver. The beans are fed in from the hopper and ground to the same size, and the grind can be adjusted.

Slower brewing methods, like percolating, take longer, so you want to use a larger grind; espresso and Turkish coffee, on the other hand, need an almost talcumlike, fine-powder grind. French press is a medium-slow method, so I go with a grind that is right slap-dab in the middle of the setting range.

Quality American megamarts can feature up to ten different kinds of bacon in a wide array of styles, at a vast range of prices. Artisanal producers take fresh pork bellies and rub them down with salt and herbs, then allow them to cure for days or even weeks before smoking them long and low over smoldering hardwood.[1] Budget-minded national brands often just pump previously frozen bellies full of all kinds of chemicals—sodium, eyrthorbate, sodium nitrate, phosphates, and the like—and then spray them down with liquid smoke. The results are . . . well, you get what you pay for. Another way of sorting bacon is by flavor: hickory, mesquite, apple wood, maple, brown sugar, and, my favorite, black pepper.

When navigating the bacon universe, It's best to start at the full-service counter. If there is slab (unsliced) bacon, get that—and ask the butcher to slice it thickly. Pre-sliced rashers at the service counter are almost certainly better than prepackaged stuff, so go with that if slab isn't available.

Not all markets, however, offer such a porcine bounty, so let's peruse the average megamart display. Steer clear of the bottom rack, which is usually stocked with budget bacon, flabby stuff, full of chemicals and water. Don't reach for the top shelf either, as it's usually home to bacon at the opposite extreme. Stick to the middle rack and look for packaging that gives you a relatively clear view of the meat inside. Make sure you look for the words "center cut" on the package, as rashers cut from the middle of the belly tend to be meatier than fringe cuts. "Thick" is good, not only because you get more bacon per slice but because thick pieces tend to tear less than thin ones when they're peeled off the slab.

FRENCH PRESS

Coffee grounds

[1] Some of my favorite bacons are cured but not smoked, but they are the exception, not the rule.

4 (6-OUNCE) CUPS OF COFFEE

If you find this brew too weak for your taste, try decreasing the grind size. But do not extend the brew period or you will overextract, and that will lead to bitterness.

// SOFTWARE ///

24	fluid ounces	filtered H_2O	
½	cup	freshly ground coffee beans	
	pinch	kosher salt[2]	

// PROCEDURE //

Bring the water to a boil in an **electric kettle or microwave**. Meanwhile, put the ground coffee and salt in a **French press carafe**. Pour the water over the grounds. Place the plunger in the carafe, but do not press down. Brew for 4 minutes, then slowly push the plunger down. Drink immediately or hold in a **Thermos** for up to 3 hours.

[2] Just a pinch of kosher salt, which is actually more effective at blocking bitterness than sugar (sorry, Ms. Poppins), will take the edge off.

APPLICATION ⊐⊏⊐⊏ **MAN BACON**

1 SERVING

Cooking bacon can be as treacherous as buying bacon. That's because as the moisture cooks out of the slices, the internal temperature can elevate quite suddenly, leading to burning; in addition, the fat and lean contract at different rates, and that leads to wrinkles, which only makes things worse. The oven is an attractive option, as roasted bacon remains flat; and because the fat can drain away, it crisps evenly. Alas, it is a slow method, and so we turn to one of my favorite everyday multitaskers, the waffle iron.

// SOFTWARE ///

3	rashers	thick-sliced bacon	halved crosswise

// PROCEDURE //

Heat a **waffle iron or panini press** to medium. Lay the bacon on the **waffle iron** and close the lid. Cook for 2½ minutes. Move the bacon pieces so the unseared areas come in direct contact with the metal. Close the lid and cook for another 2½ to 5 minutes, depending on desired crispness. Transfer the bacon to a **plate lined with paper towels**. Reserve rendered fat for another use (such as the Man Hash Browns, opposite).

APPLICATION — MAN HASH BROWNS

1 SERVING

The best hash browns in town will always be found at the local diner, but there are some hash-brown tips to be gleaned from this environment. Consider the proper potato, the russet. It is the standard baking potato, and it was the model for Mr. Potato Head.

// SOFTWARE

4	ounces	Idaho or russet potatoes	scrubbed and rinsed, but not peeled
1	tablespoon	bacon fat	
	pinch	kosher salt	

// PROCEDURE

(1) Place a **10-inch cast-iron skillet** over medium-low heat for 5 minutes.

(2) While the pan is heating, grate the potato on the largest holes of a **box grater**. Squeeze the grated potatoes in a **tea towel** to remove excess moisture.

(3) Add the fat to the pan and scatter the potatoes evenly in the pan. Sprinkle with salt and cook for 5 minutes without disturbing. Lower the heat to low, flip the potatoes, and cook for another 5 minutes. Serve immediately.

GRATER MODIFICATION

A box grater is a robust piece of practical technology, but even the largest holes on most models produce strips so thin that they bond when cooked. We don't want that. We want strips that remain separate. After all, they're hash *browns* not hash *brown*. What's a clever short-order cook to do? He or she takes some needle-nose pliers and inserts the closed prongs into each hole and kind of pries it open. It'll take you about ten minutes to carefully enlarge each hole. When you're finished you'll be in possession of one mean piece of potato ordinance.

TIDBIT The word *hash* comes from the French *hacher*, meaning "to hack or chop."

APPLICATION — MAN EGGS

1 SERVING

// SOFTWARE

2	large	eggs	
1	teaspoon	unsalted butter	
	pinch	kosher salt	
	pinch	black pepper	freshly ground

// PROCEDURE

Place an **8-inch nonstick skillet** over low heat for 2 minutes. Crack the eggs into a **custard cup**. Melt the butter in the pan and when it foams, gently add the eggs. Sprinkle with the salt and pepper. Cover and cook for 3 minutes for slightly runny yolks or 5 to 6 minutes for set yolks. Serve immediately on a **warm plate**.

MAN FOOD II

251

For centuries, cookbook authors,

recipe hawkers, showbiz chefs, and, of course, the French have touted the virtues of cooking with various forms of alcohol. Sometimes the libation in question is a high-proof spirit, but those are going to have to wait for their very own show, because I want to spend some time with the low-alcohol players, wine and beer. Can they do everything their proponents claim? Can they intensify flavors, tenderize meats, liberate aromas? Or are these claims simply excuses to . . . tenderize the cook, if you get my meaning?

KNOWLEDGE CONCENTRATE

When deciding on whether or not to cook a food in or with wine or beer, I pose a crude but effective query, which is simply this: Would the food I'm targeting taste better with black currant jam, a sort of exaggerated version of many of wine's coarser attributes, or bread, the edible embodiment of beer? Let's turn the question around and say you had some black currant jam. Would you pair it with chocolate, potatoes, or lamb shoulder?

Well, chocolate does have some fruity friends—raspberries, for instance—but all too often the pairing only serves to underline the bitterness of chocolate, not its sweetness or other complexities, especially when heat is involved. Potatoes? Here's the problem: The blandness of potatoes can be so overwhelmed by heavy fruit flavors that, well, they just disappear entirely. As for the lamb shoulders . . . interesting. Lamb is a little bit gamey and earthy, and so are many wines, Pinot Noir for one. Lamb is also well suited to spices like pepper and cinnamon, which are common flavors in many wines. Lamb shoulders also contain a considerable amount of connective tissue, and are therefore best prepared braised; that is, cooked at a relatively low temperature in liquid. The main component in wine is water. This would all seem to be a nearly perfect marriage of ingredients, but we must choose our wine wisely.

The first rule of cooking with wine is: Never cook with cooking wine. Second rule of cooking with wine is: Never cook with cooking wine. The stuff is absolutely abominable: crummy quality, high acidity, and astronomic levels of salt—which, by the way, is added to prevent people from getting bombed off the stuff.

Since they're a little trickier to handle, and are called for in more recipes, we will focus on red wines rather than whites here. Your best bet is to stick with a blended red in the ten- to twelve-dollar range. My favorites include the varietals Mourvèdre, Grenache, and Shiraz. You might also keep your eyes peeled for: *Meritage*, which is by definition a blend, and can be had for a really good price, and *Côtes du Rhône*, which indicates a classic French blend, surprisingly affordable despite the fact that it's French. Both are quite tasty, and that's important because one of the great pleasures of cooking with wine is drinking the wine you're cooking with while you're doing the cooking. To quote the immortal Julia Child, "I enjoy cooking with wine. Sometimes I even put it in the food I'm cooking."

Marinades, acidic or otherwise, really cannot penetrate meat, unless it's left there so long that the meat basically decomposes. So why bother? Wine contains tricky little chemicals called polyphenols, and recent research has shown that water and phenols can react with protein at the surface of the meat, hardening it, so that the moisture inside the meat is less likely to get out during cooking. So, while marinating in wine doesn't necessarily tenderize meat, it may very well preserve the tenderness that is already there. Reactions also take place with the browning agents created during the searing, and that intensifies the overall flavor. So a short marinade in wine, just two to three hours, does serve a purpose. Going all night or several days, however, is just crazy chef talk.

Quick . . . to the beer! Let's conduct the same questionnaire we performed with the wine except with bread standing in for beer. I understand some folks would say that bread goes with everything, but let's just play this out. Let us say that we had some bread. Would we pair it with a beautiful piece of cod, a pile of kale, or a lovely Cheddar cheese?

The cod is a very mild fish, and is often cooked in a beer-based batter, but alas, that's another show. As for kale and other dark leafies, they contain a fair number of bitter compounds, which tend to clash with the roasty, toasty goodness of bread. I would argue that the best match here is definitely the Cheddar cheese. After all, what could possibly be more satisfying than a grilled cheese sandwich? It would be tough to actually replace the bread in this equation with beer, but they are both grain-based, which is why beer is so darned wonderful to bake with.

Ah, but which beer? I am an unabashed beer lover, and at any given time my garage beer fridge is stocked with suds of myriad styles and provenances. When it comes to baking, three specific models come to mind. For soups, fondues, and fish batters, I reach for a plain old lager, whose bottom-fermenting yeast ensures a clean, crisp beer flavor. Dark, spicy porters are quite good in chocolate cakes and brownies, which I occasionally serve to visiting children on Christmas Eve (nighty night), but for a particularly cheesy bread I think that a pale ale with hoppy bitterness is the best way to go.

RESIDUAL ALCOHOL

When alcohol is added to a boiling liquid and simply removed from the heat, 85 percent of the alcohol remains in the final dish. If the alcohol is flamed, then 75 percent remains. Fifteen minutes brings the alcohol down to 40 percent of the original dosage. By two and a half hours, only 5 percent remains, but rest assured that no matter how long you cook it, some alcohol will remain.

LAMB SHOULDER CHOPS WITH RED WINE

4 SERVINGS

// SOFTWARE

4	8- to 12-ounce	lamb shoulder blade chops	
2	teaspoons	vegetable oil	
16	ounces plus 1 tablespoon	red wine	such as Shiraz, Grenache, or Mourvèdre
4	large sprigs	fresh rosemary	plus 1 teaspoon finely chopped
3	ounces	dried plums	finely chopped
3	ounces	dried apricots	finely chopped
2	tablespoons	unsalted butter	chilled and cut into 4 small pieces
	to taste	kosher salt	
	to taste	black pepper	freshly ground

// PROCEDURE

1. Place a **10-inch straight-sided sauté pan** over medium heat for 5 minutes. Toss the lamb with the oil in a **medium bowl**. Sear the lamb for 1 minute on each side. Remove to a plate and cool for 3 to 4 minutes. Put the meat in a **1-gallon zip-top bag** and add the 16 ounces wine and 4 rosemary sprigs. Remove as much air as possible so that the wine is completely surrounding the meat. Put the bag in a **container** to prevent leaks and refrigerate for 3 hours.

2. Heat the oven to 250°F.

3. Transfer the contents of the bag back to the sauté pan and cover. Braise on the middle rack of the oven for 3½ hours, or until the meat is tender and falling away from the bone.

4. Remove the meat to a **platter**, discard the rosemary, and cover with **aluminum foil** to keep warm while finishing the sauce.

5. Pour the pan juices into a **gravy separator** and allow it to separate before pouring 2 cups of the liquid back into the pan. Place over medium-low heat and add the dried plums and apricots. Cook, **whisking** frequently, for 10 minutes, or until the sauce has reduced and thickened slightly. Whisk in the butter one piece at a time, adding another piece only after the previous piece has melted. Whisk in the 1 tablespoon wine and 1 teaspoon chopped rosemary and cook for another minute. Taste and adjust the seasoning by adding salt and pepper if desired. Serve immediately.

TIDBIT To save leftover red wine for cooking, freeze it in ice cube trays or muffin tins, then move to freezer bags for long-term storage.

APPLICATION ▭▭▭ BEER BREAD

10 TO 12 SERVINGS

// SOFTWARE

8	ounces	all-purpose flour	
4	ounces	whole-wheat flour	
1	tablespoon	baking powder	
1½	teaspoons	kosher salt	
1	teaspoon	sugar	
1	teaspoon	fresh dill	chopped
4½	ounces	sharp Cheddar cheese	grated
12	ounces	cold beer	ale or stout
1 to 2	tablespoons	sunflower seeds	optional

// PROCEDURE

1. Heat the oven to 375°F. Coat the inside of a **9-by-5-inch loaf pan** with **nonstick cooking spray** and set aside.

2. **Whisk** together the flours, baking powder, salt, sugar, and dill in a **large bowl**. Stir in the cheese. Stir in the beer just to combine. Spread the batter evenly in the prepared pan. Sprinkle with the sunflower seeds, if using.

3. Bake on the middle rack of the oven for 45 to 55 minutes, or until the bread reaches an internal temperature of 210°F.

4. Cool the bread in the pan for 10 minutes. Transfer the loaf to a **cooling rack** for 10 to 15 minutes before slicing and serving.

TIDBIT In the third century B.C., Egyptians were malting barley and wheat to make beer.

TIDBIT Hildegard, a twelfth-century Benedictine nun, was the first to mention the use of hops in brewing beer.

GUESS WHO WE'RE GOOFING ON AND WIN A PRIZE.

FOOD UNDER THE INFLUENCE

255

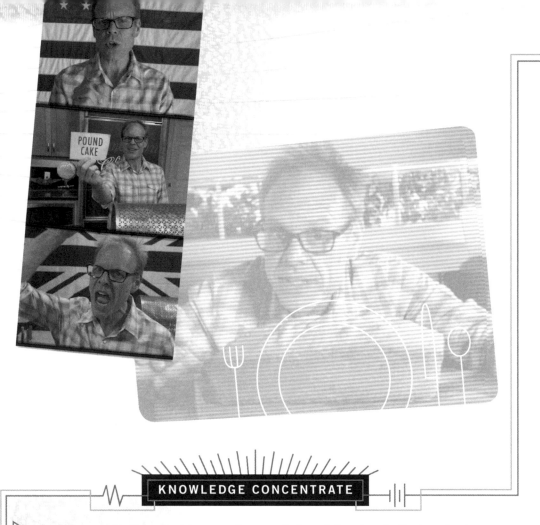

What in the world happened to cake?

Oh, I don't mean fussy French gateaux with their mushy middles, or Austrian tortes with all their sugar-dusted almond-flour-pastry-ness. Nor do I refer to those fudgy doorstops American pastry chefs keep fostering under the false moniker of flourless chocolate cake. No, I mean cake, as in the stuff you get at birthday parties and, for better or worse, weddings. When, dear viewer, was the last time you baked a cake that didn't come from a box?

Well, America, it's high time we got our cake groove back, and if you ask me that means going back to the beginning, to the ubiquitous albeit often ignored and shamelessly put-upon pound cake, the cornerstone of the American bakery pantheon upon which the entirety of our national cakedom rests. Of course, like a great many American traditions, the pound cake was born upon foreign shores, but that doesn't mean it's not red, white, blue, and . . .

KNOWLEDGE CONCENTRATE

▷○ Historians and anthropologists generally agree that most American butter-based cakes, from birthday to wedding and everywhere in between, descend from one great mother cake, the pound cake. They also agree that the pound cake was born in jolly old England, a country that, thanks to climate, geography, Roman invasion, and returning crusaders, found itself by the Middle Ages in possession of butter, eggs, sugar, and wheat flour, as well as oven technology. It was simply a matter of time before some enterprising baker figured out that equal portions of those four ingredients would bake up very nicely indeed. The fact that a "pound" cake recipe didn't make it into print until 1847 is no big surprise, seeing how everyone short of the village idiot could easily memorize the recipe.

▷○ Modern recipes writers claiming the classic is heavy or not sweet enough like to tinker around with the pound cake parts list, but I think that the proportions are just fine. Although the balanced scale hints at a symbiotic symmetry, to really understand the inner workings of a pound cake, one must look through the ingredients to the molecular mysteries within.

SUGAR is 100 percent sucrose, the most common of kitchen disaccharides.

FLOUR is composed mostly of starch and protein.

EGGS contain fat, protein, water, and phospholipids (which are natural emulsifiers).

BUTTER contains 80 to 85 percent fat, the rest being water and milk solids, including lactose, or milk sugar. The fat in butter actually comes in three forms. There is the continuous phase, the phase in which all the other stuff including the water is floating; the globules from the original cream that survive the churning process; and the fat crystals, which are especially important in batter formation.

That means that the primary molecular players in pound cake are:

PROTEIN: Toughener

SUGAR: Tenderizer

FATS: Tenderizers

STARCHES: Driers

WATER: Moisteners

Each of these culinary characters assumes a specific role in the baked-good drama. Proteins play tougheners. If you like chewy, crusty French baguettes and the like, thank proteins. Sugar and fats, on the other hand, are tenderizers, which break down or lubricate tougheners so that they aren't so tough anymore. Starches and powdered goods, flours, cornstarch, and cocoa powder are all driers because they absorb moisteners, which are always played by water and water-type liquids. Although tough and tender, moist and dry are in fact opposites on the quadraphonic Zen wheel of kitchen life, they can and should balance each other out if our formulations are correct and our technique precise. This is what pound cake is all about: moist, dry, tough, and tender, all working together.

Although the parts list for classic pound cake is simple, the procedures can be anything but. Early permutations were especially labor-intensive, with batters requiring sometimes an hour (as in sixty minutes) of beating. Why? Because when creamed together diligently, butter and sugar will produce a light, airy mixture, which will form the foundation of a cake that will rise beautifully without any chemical leavening whatsoever.

In order to cream, the fat in the butter must be warm enough to be malleable but not so warm that its structure collapses or, heaven help us, melts. Anything between 65° and 70°F is fine, and the only way to be sure is to take its temperature, which is exactly what I do with an instant-read thermometer stuck right in the butter.

When we finally cream the butter and sugar together, all the little jagged pills of sugar push into the plastic mass of the butter, opening up oodles of tiny air pockets. As the sugar granules begin to dissolve in the water phase of the butter, those air pockets will remain, supported by butterfat crystals. But here's the thing: Not all butterfat crystals are alike. Your standard grocery store–brand butter is typically churned very quickly, because time is money and the processor wants to get on with making more butter. Fast churning creates large butter crystals, and large butter crystals support the construction of large bubbles, which in turn make for a big, rough, unrefined texture inside baked goods. European butters, on the other hand, are typically slow churned, which creates small fat crystals that support small bubbles to produce a finer texture in cakes. So I suggest in this case you splurge for good European-style butter. Your cake will thank you.

Probe
Thermometer

74°

┌─────────────────────┐   ┌──────────────────────┐
│   **APPLICATION**   │──┐   ┌──│   **POUND CAKE**   │
└─────────────────────┘ └────┘ └──────────────────────┘

                              ┌──────────────────────────┐
                              │   10 TO 12 SERVINGS   │
                              └──────────────────────────┘

// SOFTWARE

16	ounces	unsalted butter	softened, plus 1 tablespoon for the pan
16	ounces	cake flour	plus 2 tablespoons for the pan
16	ounces	sugar	
9	large	eggs	at room temperature
1	teaspoon	vanilla extract	
½	teaspoon	kosher salt	

WHY CAKE FLOUR?

First, cake flour is milled from low-protein or soft wheat. When agitated with water, wheat proteins create gluten, those bungee-cord-like molecular structures that result in a great deal of chewiness. Not exactly what we want in a cake. The lower the protein, the less gluten. Second, cake flour is milled extra fine. These smaller pieces integrate into batter very easily and soak up moisture quickly, and that translates to less stirring and less gluten production. Finally, cake flour is much brighter because it's bleached. Not only does this result in a lighter product; it also changes the pH of the granules so the starches swell and gel more efficiently, and that translates to a lighter, more pleasing texture.

TIP The best way to portion batter: weigh it.

// PROCEDURE

1. Place a rack in the middle of the oven and heat to 350°F. Butter and flour a **10-inch aluminum tube pan or two 9-by-5-inch loaf pans**.

2. Combine the remaining 16 ounces butter and the sugar in the bowl of a **stand mixer fitted with the paddle attachment** and cream for 5 minutes on medium speed. Stop once to scrape down the sides of the bowl with a **spatula**. With the mixer running at the lowest speed, add the eggs one at a time, making sure each is fully incorporated before adding the next. Stop once to scrape down the sides of the bowl. This will take approximately 3 minutes, and the mixture may look curdled. Add the vanilla and salt and beat on medium speed for 30 seconds.

3. With the mixer on the lowest speed, add the flour in 3 installments, making sure each is fully incorporated before adding the next. After the final addition, scrape down the sides of the bowl, then beat for 30 seconds on medium speed until almost smooth.

4. Scoop the batter into the prepared pan(s), dividing evenly if using two pans. Bake for 1 hour, or until the internal temperature reaches 210°F and the top is golden brown and springs back when pressed; the crack around the center of the tube cake will appear moist.

5. Cool in the pan(s) on a **cooling rack** for 10 minutes. Remove from the pan(s) and cool on the rack. Store on the rack, covered with a tea towel, for up to 3 days.

BUTTERMILK POUND CAKE

10 TO 12 SERVINGS

What if you wanted the flavor and texture of pound cake but without the pounds? That would mean replacing some of the eggs and butter with another protein and tenderizing agent. The only conceivable substitution is whole buttermilk—that is, milk whose lactose or milk sugar has been converted into lactic acid by the addition of bacteria, usually a form of *Streptococcus lactis*. Batter building will be similar but with some important detours.

// **SOFTWARE** ///

12	ounces	unsalted butter	softened, plus 1 tablespoon for the pan
16	ounces	cake flour	plus 2 tablespoons for the pan
16	ounces	sugar	
4	large	eggs	at room temperature
1	teaspoon	vanilla extract	
½	teaspoon	kosher salt	
1	cup	whole buttermilk	at room temperature

// **PROCEDURE** //

1. Place a rack in the middle of the oven and heat to 375°F. Butter and flour a **10-inch aluminum tube pan or two 9-by-5-inch loaf pans**.

2. Combine the remaining 12 ounces butter and the sugar in the bowl of a **stand mixer fitted with the paddle attachment** and cream for 6 minutes on medium speed. Stop once to scrape down the sides of the bowl with a **spatula**. With the mixer running at the lowest speed, add the eggs one at a time, making sure each is fully incorporated before adding the next. Stop once to scrape down the sides of the bowl. This will take approximately 1½ minutes. Add the vanilla and salt and beat on medium speed for 30 seconds.

3. With the mixer on the lowest speed, add the flour in 3 installments, alternating with the buttermilk, beginning and ending with the flour and making sure each addition is fully incorporated before adding the next. After the final addition, beat the batter for 30 seconds on medium speed until almost smooth.

4. Scoop the batter into the prepared pan(s), dividing evenly if using two pans. Bake for 1 hour in a tube pan or 40 minutes in loaf pans, or until the internal temperature reaches 210°F and the top is golden brown and springs back when pressed; the crack around the center of the tube cake will appear moist.

5. Cool in the pan(s) on a **cooling rack** for 10 minutes. Remove from the pan(s) and cool on the rack. Store on the rack, covered with a tea towel, for up to 3 days.

TAKE ITS TEMPERATURE!

As the batter heats up in the oven, all the microscopic bubbles created by the creaming expand, forcing the batter to rise. At around 140°F, water vapor forms, expanding the bubbles further. Then at 180°F (give or take a degree or two), starches swell and undergo gelation—they form gels. Soon after, the proteins coagulate, forming a latticelike structure around the bubbles. The final step is, of course, browning, which doesn't set in until 200°F. At this point, enough moisture has been driven out or absorbed that the sugars at the surface can caramelize and the proteins can undergo the Maillard reaction. The crust turns golden brown and delicious, at which point the internal temp of the cake should be right around the boiling point of water, which is when you want to pull the cake from the oven.

But wait! The starches and proteins won't be stable until the temperature drops considerably. So think of a fresh-baked cake as a newborn, all shiny and fragrant but very vulnerable. This is why we cool it in the pan for at least ten minutes prior to removal.

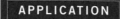

APPLICATION — CITRUS GLAZE

APPROXIMATELY ⅔ CUP GLAZE

Some folks like a finishing glaze on their pound cake, and although I'm not about to say it's a necessity, it can be a nice touch.

// SOFTWARE //

6	ounces	confectioners' sugar	
1	teaspoon	orange or lemon zest	finely grated
2½	tablespoons	freshly squeezed orange or lemon juice	you may combine juices for a well-balanced acidity
	pinch	kosher salt	

// PROCEDURE //

(1) Combine the confectioners' sugar, zest, juice, and salt in a **medium bowl** and **whisk** until smooth.

(2) Drizzle immediately over completely cooled cake or store glaze in the refrigerator in an **airtight container** for up to 2 days. Stir well before using.

TIDBIT Franklin Delano Roosevelt celebrated his 1945 inauguration with chicken salad and pound cake.

Americans have a big appetite for a short list of large fish,

like tuna, swordfish, and salmon. In fact, commercial fishing operations sweep them out of the water so quickly that the populations simply cannot sustain themselves. What's more, for every 3.7 million metric tons of fish we do want to catch, we pull in 1 million we don't want. They simply die on the decks and are shoveled back into the sea.

But wait! There's more. Because they live so long, big, top-of-the-food-chain predators can store pollutants like mercury and other harmful chemicals in their bodies that are then passed on to the eaters, like us. The answer? We need to aim our forks lower down the food chain, and dine on smaller fish that grow quickly, breed quickly, and, frankly, die quickly, all on their own. If we don't, well, take a look below at the graphic representation of our wild fisheries just a hundred years ago. In the middle you'll see what today looks like, and on the right, what we'll be looking at in 2048 if projections bear out. Get the picture?

TIDBIT | Trout were the first farmed fish in North America.

100 years ago　　Today　　2048

TUNA VS. TROUT:

Tuna are big predators that grow slowly.

Trout are small and grow pretty quickly.

Why not just farm-raise big fish? The problem is, they've got a terrible conversion rate: You have to feed them a lot in order for them to gain even a little bit of weight. Consider your average bluefin tuna.

You have to feed him twelve to thirteen pounds of food just so he'll gain a pound of weight. It's like farming lions. Imagine the number of gazelle, deer, antelope, and such—that you and I could eat—that we'd have to raise, slaughter, and grind into lion chow just to grow a few cats big enough to take to market. And then there's the living environment. You've got these animals, born to roam wide-open spaces in search of a varied diet, and you're sticking them in a pen together and feeding them manufactured food.

Which is not to say that all fish farming is bad. Aquaculture has been around for thousands of years. The Chinese were cultivating carp captured in small ponds from receding flood waters as early as 2500 B.C., while the Alekoko fishponds in Kauai were a robust source of protein for native Hawaiians a thousand years ago. Today, farmed fish and shellfish account for more than half of the seafood consumed on this planet. What effect that has on our little spinning orb depends on three factors: species, method, and location. If the fish in question requires a great deal of space, gobbles massive quantities, and leaves equally massive biological deposits, then penning up said creature with a few thousand of his fellows in cramped conditions will probably lead to disease and waste seepage into the surrounding ecosystem. Imprisoned thusly, such fish rarely grow to market dimensions without the aid of pharmaceutical agents such as antibiotics and hormones. Although large open-water-pen operations are changing things for the better, the farming of large predatory finfish does not yet qualify them for good-eats status. Other species, however, including catfish, tilapia, and trout, are very efficient at converting feed to body mass. They don't mind living in close quarters and are often cultivated well inland, where their waste and contamination can be effectively contained and managed. The real key to aquaculture success is in protective legislation, regulation, and management. Although we are far from perfect, the United States leads the world in such matters. So if you're going to buy farm-raised fish, do us all a favor and buy American.

My favorite sustainable aquacultured fish is rainbow trout, sometimes sold as "golden" trout. Trout is a sweet, sweet fish. It's got enough fat that it doesn't overcook very easily, it contains plenty of healthy omega-3 fatty acids, and the fish are small enough to handle whole at home. They're also what I call "ramp" fish: They're a good on-ramp to other smaller, even tastier sustainable fish like anchovies and sardines. Best of all, they pickle real tasty.

TIDBIT Smoking fish was originally used as a preservation technique.

Besides eating it out of hand, smoked trout is delightful in a wide range of dishes. Consider making it into a dip with sour cream and chives, or serving it with apples and cheese, on a sandwich, in a salad, on top of eggs, or, of course, instead of bananas in a banana split.

// SOFTWARE

½	cup	kosher salt	
1	quart	H_2O	
2	pounds	trout fillets	3 to 5 ounces each, skin on, pinbones removed if necessary

// SPECIAL HARDWARE

6 ounces unsoaked hardwood chips, smoker

// PROCEDURE

1. Combine the salt and water in a **4-quart container** and stir until the salt has dissolved, 1 to 2 minutes. Add the trout fillets, making sure they are submerged. Cover and refrigerate for 3 hours.

2. Remove the fillets from the brine, rinse thoroughly, and pat dry. Arrange the fillets, skin side down, on a **cooling rack set in a half sheet pan**. Dry in the refrigerator for 21 to 24 hours, until the skin becomes shiny and somewhat tacky to the touch.

3. The next day, turn a **smoker filled with unsoaked hardwood chips** on so that it maintains a temperature of 150° to 160°F. Put the fillets on **smoking racks**, skin side down, separating them by at least ¼ inch, and put them in the smoker. Adjust the heat as needed and cook for 2½ to 3 hours, until the fish is cooked through, has darkened in color, and has the desired level of smoke flavor. Refrigerate unused portions in an **airtight container** for up to 1 week or vacuum-seal and freeze for up to 1 month.

COOKING INSIDE THE BOX

If you're a fan of this show, you are no doubt familiar with my predilection for smoking and cooking in unorthodox—some might say unauthorized—contraptions: cardboard boxes, flowerpots, that sort of thing. Much like Marcel Duchamp and the Dadaists, I find high art in the repurposing of the ordinary and the mundane. Plus I really like hanging out in army surplus stores, which is where I found this super-sweet wooden box.

I have no idea what the military designed this to actually do, but I do know that if you drill a few holes in it for air and smoke and load it up with some cheap oven racks, you've got yourself a nice smoker. The exterior insignia? Optional, but highly recommended. Feel free to use a charcoal grill for smoking. Just know that you're going to have to manage the heat, keeping it very low, ideally between 150° and 160°F, and that is tough to do with charcoal.

TROUT ON A STICK   TROUT SUNDAE, ANYONE?

During the Biedermeier period, drinking establishments in and around Berlin became known for tall jars called *hungerturm* or "hunger towers," which were often filled to the brim with pickled herring rollmops. *Roll* from *rollen* or "rolled," and *mops* meaning "blockhead," of all things. (They used the same word to describe pug dogs. I don't know what to say about that.) This tasty treat was little more than a piece of fish preserved, rubbed with mustard, wrapped around a pickle, and marinated. Herring's mid-millennial popularity eventually led to overfishing and populations that are still a little shaky to this day, but that's okay, because we've got trout.

// **SOFTWARE** //

TO BRINE

½	cup	kosher salt	
1	quart	H$_2$O	
1	pound	trout fillets, ½ inch thick	from 6- to 8-ounce whole fish, scaled, skin on, pinbones removed

FOR THE PICKLE

2	cups	H$_2$O	
2	cups	cider vinegar	
1	tablespoon	sugar	
8	whole	cloves	
8	whole	allspice berries	
6	whole	black peppercorns	
4		bay leaves	
1	teaspoon	red pepper flakes	
2	tablespoons	Dijon mustard	
16 to 20		cornichons and/or pickled onions	halved as needed
1	medium	onion	julienned
12	shoots	fresh chives	

16 to 20 sturdy toothpicks

// **PROCEDURE** //

BRINE THE TROUT:

(1) Put the salt and water in a **4-quart container** and stir until the salt has dissolved, 1 to 2 minutes. Add the trout fillets, making sure they are submerged. Cover and refrigerate overnight.

MEANWHILE, MAKE THE PICKLE:

(2) Combine the water, vinegar, sugar, cloves, allspice, peppercorns, bay leaves, and red pepper flakes in a **2-quart saucepan** over medium-high heat. Cook, stirring occasionally, until the liquid comes to a boil, approximately 5 minutes. Cool to room temperature, then refrigerate overnight.

(3) Remove the trout from the brine and rinse thoroughly under cold running water for 1 minute. Submerge the fillets in clean cold water and refrigerate for 1 hour.

(4) Drain and rinse the fillets. Pat dry. Lay the fillets in a single layer, skin side down, on a work surface and **brush** each with mustard. Place a cornichon or a pickled onion on the fillet. Roll up each fillet and secure with 1 or 2 **toothpicks**. Alternate layers of rollmops and julienned onion in a **glass jar or ceramic crock**.

(5) Pour the chilled pickling mixture over the rollmops and onion, cover, and refrigerate for at least 5 hours and up to 2 days. Drain and serve chilled with crusty bread.

TIDBIT | Rainbow trout have been known to weigh as much as fifty pounds.

TRIVIA | This was a special show for my daughter and me because we're very into oceanography and marine biology. We're big supporters of Monterey Bay Aquarium and their Seafood Watch program. We decided to set this show in a familiar (food capsules, strange wigs, lots of wrinkles) but grim future. The message: Eat sustainable seafood . . . or else. Zoey dug wearing go-go boots and a huge white wig. My itchy latex wrinkles were less enjoyable.

ESCABECHE OF TROUT

4 SERVINGS

If you're looking for a darn tasty but practical procedure for a small oily fish—like, say, trout—consider escabeche, which is a Spanish dish, though the word is actually Persian for "acid food" (it's better than it sounds). Although sardines would be the authentic ingredient, trout will do just fine.

// SOFTWARE

⅓	cup	all-purpose flour	
1½	teaspoons	kosher salt	
½	teaspoon	black pepper	freshly ground
4	6- to 8-ounce	small whole trout	head on, scaled, gutted, and rinsed
⅓	cup	olive oil	
1	medium	red onion	julienned
3	cloves	garlic	sliced
6	sprigs	fresh thyme	
½	teaspoon	freshly ground coriander	
½	teaspoon	smoked paprika	
1½	cups	dry white wine	
½	cup	white wine vinegar	
3	strips	lemon zest	approximately 1 inch by 3 inches

// PROCEDURE

1. Combine the flour, 1 teaspoon of the salt, and ¼ teaspoon of the pepper in a **1-gallon zip-top bag**. Pat the trout dry and toss in the bag with the seasoned flour to coat.

2. Heat the oil in a **12-inch sauté pan** over medium-high heat until it shimmers. Carefully add the trout to the pan. Cook on each side for 1 minute.

3. Using **tongs or a fish spatula**, transfer the trout to a **9-by-13-inch glass baking dish**. Lower the heat to medium, add the onion to the pan, and cook until translucent, approximately 5 minutes. Add the garlic and cook for 1 minute. Add the remaining ½ teaspoon salt, ¼ teaspoon black pepper, the thyme, coriander, paprika, wine, vinegar, and lemon zest. Lower the heat to low and simmer, uncovered, for 10 minutes.

4. Remove from the heat and pour the marinade over the trout. Refrigerate, uncovered, for at least 1 hour before serving. Serve cool or at room temperature with the sauce and onions. Refrigerate, covered, for up to 12 hours.

GREAT WIG!

NOT BELUSHI, BUT CLOSE

Although many Americans tend to think of Japanese cuisine only in terms of fresh foods—sushi, sashimi, and such—the real workhorse ingredients of that island nation are pantry ingredients, which can be easily procured with neither a passport nor a fistful of yen. As a Japanese cuisine *otaku*, or fanatic, I've been able to find just about everything that I could want on that newfangled World Wide Web, but your local megamart most likely stocks more Japanese items than you might think. Your town may even host a small Japanese market, as does mine. And though I don't speak any Japanese past "Domo arigato Mr. Roboto," I manage to walk out every time with some strange, new . . .

I BELIEVE IN A RESPECTFUL, MATURE MANAGEMENT STYLE.

BART TOLD ME HE KNEW JAPANESE, BUT I DIDN'T UNDERSTAND A WORD HE SAID.

The first item of business here is to brew up a dashi, or cooking stock. What isn't served raw, grilled, or fried in Japan is generally simmered in dashi, and now that I think of it, dashi goes into most of the sauces that are served alongside foods that are raw, grilled, or fried, so it truly is a ubiquitous liquid. A great many things can go into a dashi, but two are absolutely required.

KOMBU looks like something you might make a wallet out of at camp, but it is actually a form of kelp, harvested from cold water, which is dried and folded and packaged like this:

Kombu is interesting stuff because it contains high levels of glutamate, which is essentially an unrefined version of monosodium glutamate, or MSG, a substance that possesses the uncanny ability to make everything it touches taste *oishii*: delicious. Kombu is also fascinating from a nutritional standpoint because although it's technically a vegetable, it contains high amounts of iodine, iron, potassium, B vitamins, and carotene, so it's delicious and unctuous, and you could live off it for a while if you had to.

KATSUOBUSHI looks like a dark, hard, miniature wooden baseball bat, only it's a piece of fish—skipjack tuna, to be exact, one of the few tuna varieties that's really considered to be sustainable or in healthy stocks worldwide. So how do you take a fish and make a tiny baseball bat?

1. The fish is caught (this is done by many fishermen on the same boat, each with his own line).

2. Once ashore, the fish are filleted into two pieces, and the big ones are halved again.

3. The fish is then simmered in water for twenty minutes to set the protein structure.

4. The bones are removed and the fish are smoked over oak or cherry wood for six hours a day for two weeks before being placed in the sun to dry.

5. The fish are moved into a cave containing a special mold.

6. After two weeks, the fish are placed back in the sun, then moved back into the cave, until the fish is as hard as a piece of oak.

Once the skipjack has been converted into katsuobushi it's not good for much until it is grated or shaved, and that's done with a device that looks like a wooden box mounted with a plane blade, which is exactly what it is, only there's a little drawer underneath to catch the shavings.

Most folks, however, buy their katsuobushi flakes conveniently preshaved, in bags. The flakes are long lasting provided you keep moisture at bay. (I've managed to keep some in my pantry for up to six months.)

DASHI

APPROXIMATELY 2 QUARTS

// SOFTWARE ///

2	4-inch square pieces	kombu	wiped with a damp cloth to remove mildew residue
2½	quarts	H_2O	
½	ounce	bonito flakes (a.k.a. katsuobushi)	about 2 cups

// PROCEDURE ///

1. Put the kombu in a **4-quart saucepan**, cover with the water, and soak for 30 minutes.

2. Set the saucepan over medium heat and cook until the water reaches 150° to 160°F and small bubbles appear around the sides of the pan, 9 to 10 minutes.

3. Remove the kombu from the pan. Increase the heat to high and bring to a boil, 5 to 6 minutes. Lower the heat to low and add the bonito flakes. Simmer gently, stirring frequently, for 10 minutes.

4. Pour the liquid through a **fine-mesh strainer** lined with **muslin or several layers of cheesecloth** into a **large container**. Reserve the bonito flakes for another use (see next page).

5. Store in an **airtight container** in the fridge. Use within 1 week or freeze for up to 1 month.

TIDBIT | Eats rich in umami flavor: Vegemite, soy sauce, mushrooms, Worcestershire sauce.

CONCERNING "UMAMI"

In 1908, a scientist named Kikunae Ikeda isolated an amino acid from seaweed called glutamate. The flavor of this substance was pleasant and unique, so Ikeda named it *umami*, which means "tasty" in Japanese. Ikeda quickly patented this formula for monosodium glutamate, and it became the big flavor success story of the early twentieth century. By the mid-'30s, MSG was being dosed out from salt shakers on Japanese tables, even the table of the emperor. Obviously MSG raked in some big old buckets of yen,

which had to make guys like Ikeda pretty happy. It even made it into the United States. Despite a bump in the road called World War II, MSG became a major ingredient in several famous American spice blends, and it really caught on with Chinese restaurants. Then, in the 1960s, word started to spread of a mysterious ailment. All across the country, fans of Chinese chow began complaining of heart palpitations, numbness of the fingers, and headaches, all eventually laid at the door of poor old monosodium glutamate

despite the fact that subsequent studies never pinpointed the problem. Of course, the MSG industry wasn't giving up. They dug back through Ikeda's old research, and rediscovered one particular word: *umami*. What followed were years of new tests and research projects, many of which were funded by the MSG industry. Some now tout *umami* as the "fifth taste." I'm not saying they're wrong, but when any research is so powerfully pushed by industry, I'm not quick to buy in.

MISO SOUP

8 SERVINGS

// SOFTWARE //

1	12-ounce block	firm silken tofu	
2	quarts	Dashi (page 269)	
6	tablespoons	dark/red miso	
2	tablespoons	light/white miso	
4		scallions	thinly sliced

// PROCEDURE //

1. Wrap the block of tofu in **two layers of paper towels** and place it on a **plate**. Invert a second **plate** atop the tofu and weight it down with a **28-ounce can**. Let drain for 20 minutes, then unwrap and cut the tofu into ¼- to ½-inch cubes.

2. Heat the dashi in a **4-quart saucepan** over medium-high heat. When the dashi reaches 100°F, **ladle** 1 cup of it into a **small bowl**, add the dark and light misos, and **whisk** until smooth.

3. Bring the remaining dashi to a bare simmer, approximately 10 minutes. Add the miso mixture and whisk to combine. Return to a slight simmer, being careful not to boil the mixture. Add the tofu and scallions and cook for another minute, or until heated through. Remove from the heat and serve immediately.

MEET THE MISOS

Miso is a paste made from soybeans that have been ground with a grain such as rice or barley that's been inoculated with a mold-based fermenting agent called a koji. Miso is often called Japanese peanut butter, not only because it looks, feels, and, to some extent, tastes like the American staple, but because it is nearly as ubiquitous.

▶ WHITE MISO gets its color from a high percentage of rice koji and fewer soybeans. It has the highest carbohydrate content of any miso, which explains its subtle sweetness. White miso is made quickly but also has a short shelf life. It's used primarily for salad dressings and fish dishes. It also finds its way into Japanese desserts.

▶ RED MISO is produced from white rice, barley, or soybeans, and fermentation takes one to three years. It contains more protein than any other miso type. It's most commonly used in stir-fries, miso soup, and meat marinades.

▶ BARLEY MISO contains soybeans but also a high percentage of barley and barley koji. It's very dark and salty, which has caused it to lose some popularity in modern times. Still, its earthiness is welcome in stews and bean dishes.

▶ SOYBEAN MISO is made exclusively from soybeans. Because the beans are relatively low in carbohydrates, fermentation takes a very long time. It's most often used in soups.

EASY TOFU DRESSING

APPROXIMATELY 3 CUPS

Serve as a dressing for a salad, a sauce for a hamburger, or a dipping sauce for vegetables.

// SOFTWARE //

12	ounces	firm silken tofu	
½	cup	buttermilk	
¼	cup	ketchup	
2	tablespoons	sweet pickle relish	
1	tablespoon	Dijon mustard	
1	tablespoon	lemon juice	freshly squeezed
1	teaspoon	kosher salt	
½	teaspoon	black pepper	freshly ground

// PROCEDURE //

Put all the ingredients in a **blender** and blend until smooth. Store in an **airtight container** in the refrigerator for up to 1 week.

APPLICATION

MISO-AND-HONEY-GLAZED FISH

4 SERVINGS

// SOFTWARE //

2	tablespoons	light/white miso	
2	tablespoons	honey	
4	6-ounce	black cod or halibut fillets	¾ to 1 inch thick

// PROCEDURE //

1. Heat the oven to 475°F.
2. **Whisk** together the miso and honey in a **small bowl**. Lay the fish fillets in a **6-by-10-inch glass baking dish** and **brush** with the glaze. Bake on the middle rack of the oven for 15 to 20 minutes, until the fish reaches an internal temperature of 135°F. Let rest in the dish for 5 minutes before serving.

THE COW OF CHINA

Tofu is born of the soybean, which has been referred to as "the cow of Asia," an apt moniker considering the fact that tofu production is nearly identical to cheese making, only instead of cow's milk you use soymilk.

To produce soymilk: 1) Take the inner beans from the pods. 2) Dry the beans. 3) Crush the beans. 4) Cook the beans in water. 5) Drain the beans to render out the soymilk. 6) Add either calcium sulfate from gypsum, or magnesium chloride, to coagulate the soymilk.

This process leaves you with something that looks a lot like a cheese curd. You can squeeze the curd to remove some of the moisture, thus producing firm tofu. Or you can leave the moisture inside, which will give you very soft, silken tofu that can be squirted into shelf-stable aseptic containers where it will keep for months at room temperature. A potent, protein-laden pantry pal if ever there was one.

GLAZED BONITO FLAKES

4 SERVINGS

Serve this flavorful mixture over short-grain rice, noodles, or fish.

// SOFTWARE

½	cup	wet leftover bonito flakes from making Dashi (page 269)	
2	tablespoons	mirin	
2	tablespoons	soy sauce	
½	teaspoon	sugar	
2	tablespoons	white sesame seeds	toasted

// PROCEDURE

1. Finely chop the bonito flakes and put them in an **8-inch nonstick skillet** over medium heat. Cook, stirring constantly, until the flakes are fragrant, dry, and toasted, approximately 4 minutes. Add the mirin, soy sauce, and sugar and cook, stirring constantly, until the mixture is dry and appears glazed, 2 to 5 minutes.

2. Remove from the heat and stir in the sesame seeds. Transfer the mixture to a **plate** and spread out to cool.

APPLICATION

TSUYU SAUCE

1½ CUPS

Serve this sauce with soba noodles.

// SOFTWARE

1	cup	Dashi (page 269)	
¼	cup	soy sauce	
¼	cup	mirin	

// PROCEDURE

Combine the dashi, soy sauce, and mirin in an **airtight container**, shake to combine, and refrigerate until cold, approximately 1 hour.

THE PROOF IS IN THE PUDDING

EPISODE 219 | SEASON 13 | GOOD EATS

More times than not, when alcohol is called for in the kitchen, we're talking

about a low-octane tipple—beer and wine and such—which
is folded in for subtle effect. Other times, however, the booze gallops in full force, in the
form of a distilled spirit—whiskey, vodka, or a fortified wine, like Marsala or brandy.
In either case, maximizing the potion's potential contribution to cuisine requires clear
understanding, careful consideration, and a conservative wrist. Join us, won't you, as we
look at alcohol, hooch, booze as an ingredient. Is it just an excuse to lube up the cook,
or is it truly . . .

INTOXICATION

The toxic elements in ethanol
work on humans by infiltrating
cell membranes and wreaking
mild to severe havoc with their
normal functions. This havoc,
of course, is manifested by
a serious downgrade of social
graces, table manners, and
the ability to operate heavy
machinery.

LAWYERS GONE WILD

273

CH₃OH (Methanol)

$$H$$
$$H-C-O-H$$
$$H$$

C₃H₈O (Isopropyl alcohol)

$$H\quad H\quad H$$
$$H-C-C-C-H$$
$$H\quad OH\quad H$$

C₂H₅OH (Ethanol)

Hydroxyl group

$$H\quad H$$
$$H-C-C-O-H$$
$$H\quad H$$

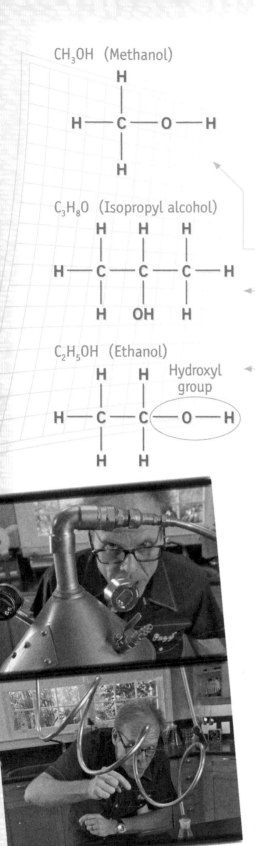

▷○ **If we are to cook with alcohol, we need to know a little bit more about this curious compound. The term** *alcohol,* **which comes from a very old Arab word for "eye shadow," refers to many members of a class of organic compounds bearing hydroxyl groups.**

That is, oxygen and hydrogen hooked up to carbon. There are a mess of these things, and each and every one of them is toxic. Now, this is methyl alcohol, or methanol. One sip of this and you could go blind or drop dead.

Here we have isopropyl or rubbing alcohol. It's a drying agent and a disinfectant, used to torture children who have suffered a scrape or cut.

This is ethyl alcohol, or ethanol. It's also toxic but not as toxic as most of the other alcohols, and relatively easy for the human machine to metabolize. Ethanol is a by-product of fermentation, the life cycle of yeast, which consumes sugar and gives off gas, carbon dioxide, and ethanol.

▷○ **If the yeast is allowed to consume the sugars in grapes or fruit juice, the resulting liquid is usually called wine. If grains provide the caloric intake, the fermented liquid would be called beer. Both wines and beers can be distilled to create beverages with higher alcohol content, such as brandy, vodka, Scotch, bourbon, and the like. Distilling has to do with our old friend ethanol, which is very volatile, evaporating at a relatively low temperature, 78° Celsius, in fact. This means we can isolate it, but for that we need a still.**

(I should probably point out that home distilling of spirits is highly illegal in the United States because it's very dangerous and it cuts into tax revenues. *So do not try this at home. This is strictly educational. I mean it.*) Anyway, liquid containing ethanol—say, wine—goes into the boiler. The liquid is brought to 176°F. At that point, the ethanol evaporates, leaving the water behind. Granted, trace amounts of other extraordinarily nasty compounds evaporate along with the ethanol, which is why real moonshiners usually dump the first run anyway. The ethyl alcohol will concentrate here, and then move up and into the condensation tube, where it will change from a vapor back into a liquid. Boom: hooch! If you did drink this and did not actually die or go blind, you would earn yourself a hangover that would make you wish you were dead, so typically this would be distilled again, maybe several times, and then filtered through charcoal to scrub out any impurities, which is generally the plan with top-drawer vodkas, which are, by definition, colorless and odorless. If, however, you were making Scotch whiskey or bourbon, you would leave some impurities, called congeners, behind so they can mingle with the chemicals in the wooden barrels that you are no doubt going to be aging your beverage in.

▷○ **Fortified wines, such as port, sherry, and Madeira, are powerful cooking liquids. When the yeast fermenting these wines aren't quite done converting sugar from the grapes, the processor kills them off by adding a big dose of distilled spirits, which ups the alcohol level to the point that the yeast cannot survive. The resulting beverage is quite strong, usually about 20 percent alcohol, and usually on the sweet side due to the residual sugars.**

FLAMING SHRIMP AND GRITS

4 SERVINGS

// SOFTWARE

FOR THE GRITS

2	cups	whole milk	
2	cups	H_2O	
1½	teaspoons	kosher salt	
1	cup	grits or coarse-ground cornmeal	
½	teaspoon	black pepper	freshly ground
¼	cup	unsalted butter	
4	ounces	sharp Cheddar cheese	grated

FOR THE SHRIMP

1	pound	shrimp (31/35 count)	peeled and deveined
2	ounces	bourbon whiskey	
¼	teaspoon	hot sauce	optional
	to taste	kosher salt	
	to taste	black pepper	freshly ground

// PROCEDURE

MAKE THE GRITS:

1. Bring the milk, water, and salt to a boil in a **4-quart saucepan** over medium-high heat.

2. While continually **whisking**, gradually add the grits. Lower the heat to low and cover. Cook for 15 to 20 minutes, or until thick and creamy, removing the lid and whisking every 3 to 4 minutes to prevent the grits from sticking or forming lumps.

3. Remove from the heat, add the pepper and butter, and whisk to combine. When the butter is melted, gradually stir in the cheese. Cover and set aside until the shrimp is ready.

MAKE THE SHRIMP:

4. Place a **10-inch nonstick sauté pan** over medium heat for 2 minutes. Add the shrimp and toss once or twice. Remove the pan from the heat. Gently pour the whiskey into the pan, carefully ignite with a **long match** or **stick lighter**, and return to the heat. Toss continually until the flame extinguishes, 1 to 2 minutes. Sauté until the shrimp are cooked through, 1 to 2 minutes more. Season with hot sauce, if desired, and salt and pepper. Serve over warm grits.

FLAME ON

Before preparing flambé dishes, always take the following precautions:

▶ Clear your airspace. There can't be anything flammable up over the pan.
▶ Make sure the heat source is turned off before the hooch goes in.
▶ Have a tight-fitting lid standing by at all times in order to smother the flames, should the need arise.

For flambés I generally use an alcohol that's 80 proof (40 percent ethanol). Anything higher makes it difficult to control the flame; anything lower won't produce a reliable burn. In terms of the heat level, you want to just maintain a boil. I turn the heat back on after ignition so that I can continue to provide gas for the burn and cook out as much of the alcohol as possible.

No one is really sure where the boozy egg foam that Italians call *zabaglione* and the French call *sabayon* came from, but most food historians point to the Medici court of Florence, which, of course, is where all Italians point when they don't know something about where their food came from. What we do know is that it's based on ancient egg-thickened drinks called *caudles*, which were originally meant to comfort the sick and infirm.

MARSALA

Marsala comes in three colors—*oro* (gold), *ambra* (amber), and *rubino* (ruby)—and at least three levels of sweetness—*secco* (dry), *semisecco* (semidry), and sweet. Due to its balanced flavor, golden glow, complex aroma, balanced acid, and alcohol, the sweet *ambra* is especially well suited to desserts, including my favorite on-the-fly dessert of all time, *zabaglione*, which is, as far as I'm concerned, reason enough to keep marsala close at hand.

TIDBIT *Zabaglione can be transformed into a savory sauce by eliminating the sugar and adding herbs.*

// SOFTWARE //

6	large	egg yolks	
½	cup	sugar	
½	cup	marsala	
	pinch	kosher salt	
		fresh berries	

// PROCEDURE //

1. Bring **1 inch of water** to a boil in a **4-quart saucepan** over high heat.

2. Put the egg yolks and sugar in a **large glass bowl**. Using an **electric hand mixer** set to the highest speed, whisk the eggs and sugar until the mixture is thick and pale yellow and the sugar is completely dissolved, 4 to 5 minutes. Decrease the mixer speed to low and add the marsala and salt.

3. Decrease the heat under the water to maintain a simmer and place the bowl atop the saucepan, making sure the bottom of the bowl is not touching the water. Using the mixer on medium speed, whisk the mixture until it is thick and frothy, holds a ribbon, and reaches 145° to 150°F, 12 to 15 minutes.

4. Spoon the warm mixture into **custard cups or serving glasses** and serve immediately or allow to cool slightly. Serve with berries, if desired.

LIMONCELLO

APPROXIMATELY 36 OUNCES

Remember our oh-so-volatile ethanol molecule? If you could closely examine it, you'd see that part of its molecular arrangement bonds easily with water, while the other end binds quite efficiently with fatty acids. This means that ethanol is a solvent, capable of extracting flavor compounds that H_2O simply cannot touch, which is why it's used to make things like vanilla extract. We can also use it to extract the oils from the microscopic glands at the surface of a very popular citrus fruit.

Those of you who have spent time around Sorrento, Italy, will no doubt recognize this as the absolute essence of lemon in beverage form, and a fine testament to the solvent powers of alcohol. The luxurious body of this drink does come in part from sugar, but also keep in mind that when alcohol and water come together, some of their molecules hook up, forming a more viscous beverage than either could form on its own. Just thought you should know.

// SOFTWARE ///

2	pounds	lemons	about 8 to 10
1	750-ml bottle	100-proof vodka	
⅔	cup	H_2O	
⅔	cup	sugar	
		fresh berries	

// PROCEDURE ///

1. Carefully remove the zest from the lemons using a **rasp grater**, being careful not to remove any of the white pith. Reserve the lemons to make lemonade or squeeze and freeze juice for later use.

2. Put the lemon zest in a **lidded glass container** that will hold at least 2 quarts. Pour the vodka over the zest, cover, and place in a cool, dark spot for 7 days.

3. Strain the liquid through a **fine-mesh strainer** lined with **muslin or several layers of cheesecloth** and return it to the container.

4. Combine the water and sugar in a **small saucepan** over high heat and cook, stirring continually, until the sugar is completely dissolved, approximately 3 minutes. Let cool completely, then add the sugar syrup to the vodka and stir to combine.

5. Cover and chill in the freezer for at least 4 hours. Limoncello can be stored in the freezer for up to 1 year.[1]

LIMONCELLO-INDUCED VISION

[1] Actually, near as I can tell it'll keep in there forever.

EPISODE 220 | SEASON 13 | GOOD EATS

This was only our third hour-long episode and it's one of my favorites. Dickens fans might just find the overall story structure somewhat . . . familiar. That's because I stole it. But at least I included the ghost of Charles Dickens, not to mention a fairy with a mean streak, and an oyster-obsessed Uncle Sam, and a crusty old Santa. The show's a Christmas pageant gone wrong, I admit, but it also produced some mighty fine good eats.

Indulgent though it may be, I include herein a few script snippets to introduce each dish, and to lend a bit of illumination on various seasonal subjects.

TIDBIT | Christmas didn't become a holiday in America until 1870.

TIDBIT | Santa Claus is based on the bishop of Myra, on the southern coast of modern-day Turkey, who was the patron saint of sailors, archers, and children. The Dutch version, Sinterklaas, was the first Santa to be accessorized with a big bag of toys.

SANTA SLUMMING

ONE OF THE CRATCHET KIDS

▷○ The original celebration that we now know as Christmas may even predate the birth of Christ. It was originally a Winter Solstice festival that evolved from Roman Saturnalia, the Persian Mithra festival, or the Babylonian Sacaea. The church tried to shut down the holiday for centuries. Cromwell and his cronies actually outlawed Christmas at one point in England, and Governor Bradford did the same thing in Plymouth in 1659. Puritans don't like fun, but the people wouldn't have it, so the church finally decided that Christ was born on December 25, thus adopting the holiday as their own.

▷○ You know, up until about 150 years ago, Christmas celebrations were really an opportunity for some wild and crazy times. So you may not recognize the following applications as holiday favorites, unless you were born in the sixteenth century.

— "Here We Come a-Wassailin'" is a scary song that was once sung as part of the caroling tradition. It's about a gang of midnight marauders demanding booze, food, and money from an innocent homeowner. And if they don't get what they want . . . well, let's just say that the original custom has more in common with trick-or-treating than anything we modern Americans might associate with Christmas. The word WASSAIL comes from the old Norse *ves heill*, which became *wes hal* in old English. It means "be in good health." It also means a drink, a strong drink. If you've ever had mulled wine around the holidays, you've enjoyed a modern version of wassail. Generally speaking, it's the same thing, only it's made with wine and ale and apples. Apples are an important symbol of the solstice. Oh, and some versions of wassail have eggs, too. You know, eggs are symbolic of fertility and creation and all that.

— Dickens may have waxed poetic about the Christmas goose (for more on that, see page 283), but since modern cooks may have a hard time securing such a bird, we opted for ROAST DUCK instead. There was a time when there were so many ducks in North America that the skies sometimes went dark with migrating flocks. Those birds, gamey and tough, were best cooked either very, very, very rare or stewed for days and days and days. Today's commercial ducks are all descendants of a mere handful of white Pekin (no "g") ducks that made it from China to New York via clipper ship in 1873, and they are far more succulent and cook-friendly. Although most megamarts do carry Long Island, or white Pekin, ducks, I strongly recommend that you buy them fresh directly from a processor via the Internet. You will pay more, to be sure, but you and your dinner guests will be glad you did.

— The earliest mention of SUGARPLUMS as a confection is from 1668. While the English defined it as a type of comfit (a sugar-crusted seed or fruit), *sugar plum* can also mean "something very pleasing or agreeable; esp. when given as a sop or bribe," a use of the term that dates back to 1608. The word *plum* in Victorian times usually suggested a raisin or dried currant, not the fruit we think of today.

PROP GUY PAUL AS "PA" CRATCHET

CULINARY OPERATIVE MEGHAN AS "MA" CRATCHET

'TWAS THE NIGHT BEFORE GOOD EATS

APPROXIMATELY 3 QUARTS

// SOFTWARE ///

6	small	apples (4 to 5 ounces each)	cored
1	cup	dark brown sugar	
1	cup	H_2O	
72	ounces	ale	
1	750 ml bottle	Madeira	
10	whole	cloves	
10	whole	allspice berries	
1	2-inch stick	cinnamon	
1	teaspoon	ground ginger	
1	teaspoon	nutmeg	freshly grated
6	large	eggs	separated

(AB peers out window at attacking wassailers.)

AB: Wait a second. What is that? What are they doing?

Santa Claus: Bonfire. Standard procedure. I'd get on that wassail if I were you.

AB: Well, how? I don't know what wassail is! What is it?

Santa Claus: It's a strong drink with wine and ale and apples. Listen to the song: "Call up the butler of this house, put on his golden ring. Let him bring us a glass of beer, and the better we shall sing. Bring us out a table and spread it with a cloth. Bring us out a moldy cheese, and some of your Christmas loaf . . ."

AB: Moldy cheese. That's impossible. I've never had moldy cheese in this house.

Santa Claus: Here's the kicker. "We have a little purse made of ratching leather skin. Give us some of your small change to line it well within . . ."

// PROCEDURE ///

1. Heat the oven to 350°F. Put the apples in a **small glass baking dish**. Spoon the brown sugar into the center of each apple, dividing the sugar evenly among them. Pour the water into the bottom of the dish and bake for 45 minutes, or until tender.

2. Meanwhile, put the ale and Madeira in a **large slow cooker**. Put the cloves, allspice, and cinnamon in a **small muslin bag or cheesecloth tied with kitchen twine** and place in the slow cooker along with the ginger and nutmeg. Set the cooker to medium and bring the mixture to at least 120°F. Do not boil.

3. Using a **hand mixer**, beat the egg whites in a **medium bowl** until stiff peaks form. In a separate **bowl**, beat the egg yolks until lightened in color and frothy, approximately 2 minutes. Add the egg whites and yolks to the slow cooker and **whisk** to combine.

4. Add the apples and the liquid from the baking dish to the slow cooker and stir to incorporate any undissolved brown sugar. Ladle into cups and serve.

TIDBIT | Wassail was also known as Lamb's Wool, describing the foam from heated ale, egg, and apple pulp.

PREPARING THE WASSAIL

SUGARPLUMS

APPROXIMATELY 80 (¼-OUNCE) BALLS

// SOFTWARE ///

6	ounces	slivered almonds	toasted
4	ounces	dried plums	
4	ounces	dried apricots	
4	ounces	dried figs	
¼	cup	confectioners' sugar	
½	teaspoon	anise seeds	
¼	teaspoon	caraway seeds	
¼	teaspoon	ground cardamom	
	pinch	kosher salt	
¼	cup	honey	
1	cup	coarse sugar	

// PROCEDURE //

1. Put the almonds, plums, apricots, and figs in the bowl of a **food processor** and pulse 20 to 25 times, until the fruit and nuts are chopped into small pieces but before the mixture becomes a ball.

2. Combine the confectioners' sugar, anise, caraway, cardamom, and salt in a **medium mixing bowl**. Add the nut-and-fruit mixture and the honey and, using gloved hands, combine well.

3. Scoop the mixture into ¼-ounce portions and roll into balls. If serving immediately, roll in coarse sugar and serve. If not serving immediately, put the balls on a cooling rack and leave uncovered until ready to serve. Roll in sugar just prior to serving. Sugarplums may be stored on the cooling rack for up to 1 week. After a week, store in an airtight container for up to 1 month or freeze.

Fairy: Were you going to go and deprive the little children of this house their rightful Yuletide sweets? Were you? Huh?

AB: No, no!

Fairy: Well, I should hope not. That would make me a very angry little fairy.

AB: No, no. I was . . . I was going to make them some . . .

Fairy: Sugarplums? Sugarplums? Weren't you?

AB: Absolutely.

Fairy: Oh, I just adore sugarplums. I'm the Sugarplum Fairy, you know. Now, tell me what goes in them.

AB: Uh, plums.

Fairy: Wrong, wrong, wrong, wrong. Sugarplums are English, and over there a plum used to mean a date or a fig or an apricot or even a raisin—any dried fruit, really, and of course there's sugar and spice.

AB: And everything nice.

Fairy: No, just sugar and spice. But they're nice enough, don't you think? Oh, let's make some. I want some right now.

YES, VIRGINIA, THERE IS SUCH A THING AS SUGARPLUMS AND THEY REALLY ARE GOOD EATS.

THE SUGARPLUM FAIRY PACKS A PUNCH!

'TWAS THE NIGHT BEFORE GOOD EATS

ROAST DUCK WITH OYSTER DRESSING[1]

4 TO 6 SERVINGS

OYSTERS AND CHRISTMAS

When Europeans first arrived in the New World, they found estuaries, tributaries, and bays teeming with *Crassostrea virginica* the size of slippers. All you had to do was reach overboard with a shovel or a rake and pull in as many as you wanted. The natives around Manhattan had binged on these for millennia, but then the Dutch and English arrived and all but wiped out the wild stocks, which are rebounding nicely today—due largely to sustainable harvesting practices. Since oysters are filter feeders, where they grow greatly affects the size, flavor, and texture of the final critter. That is why Malpeques taste like Malpeque, Chesapeakes taste like Chesapeake, and Apalachicolas taste like Apalachicola even though they're all technically the same species.

[1] When dressing is cooked inside the bird it's called "stuffing," and it is, for various reasons, evil.

// SOFTWARE

1	5- to 6½-pound	duck	neck and giblets removed and neck reserved
3	teaspoons	kosher salt per pound of duck	about ⅓ cup
¼	cup	duck fat	reserved after cooking the duck
1	pound	stale cornbread	crumbled
1½	cups	chopped onions	
1	cup	chopped celery	
½	teaspoon	kosher salt	
¼	teaspoon	black pepper	freshly ground
5	ounces	oyster crackers	crumbled
1½	teaspoons	dried thyme	
1	teaspoon	dried sage	
2	large	eggs	lightly beaten
1	pint	small oysters	with liquor

// PROCEDURE

1. Put the duck, breast side down, on a **cutting board**. Using **kitchen shears**, cut up one side of the spine, starting at the tail (or pope's nose), and moving all the way to the top. Turn the bird around and cut back down the other side of the spine, being careful not to cut into the thigh. Press down on the bird to flatten and make a shallow cut through the breastbone to further flatten it. Remove the neck flap and any extra pockets of fat. Turn the duck over, breast side up, and make a long slash in the skin and fat of each breast, making sure not to puncture the meat.

2. Line the bottom of a **broiler pan** with **paper towels**. Sprinkle both sides of the duck with the kosher salt and lay the duck, breast side up, on the top of the pan. Put the pan with the duck, uncovered, on the bottom shelf of the refrigerator for 3 to 4 days, or until the skin is dry and reaches a near parchment consistency.

3. Heat the oven to 350°F.

4. Remove the duck from the refrigerator. If there is still salt visible, brush it off. Remove the paper towels from the bottom of the pan, put the pan on the middle rack of the oven, and roast the duck for 30 minutes. Rotate the pan 180 degrees and continue to cook until the thigh reaches an internal temperature of 180°F on an instant-read thermometer, about 30 more minutes.

5. Remove the duck from the oven and increase the heat to 450°F. Once the oven has come to temperature, return the duck to the oven and roast until the skin is golden brown and crispy, about 10 minutes.

6. Remove the top of the broiler pan, with the duck still on it, and put it on a **sheet pan** to rest. Pour off the duck fat from the bottom of the pan, measure ¼ cup, and reserve the rest for another use. Decrease the oven heat to 350°F.

7. Put the broiler pan on the stove over medium heat and add the ¼ cup of fat. Add the onions, celery, salt, and pepper. Cook, stirring frequently, until the onions and celery are translucent, about 10 minutes.

8. Meanwhile, combine the cornbread, oyster crackers, thyme, sage, eggs, oysters, and their liquor in a **large mixing bowl** and use your hands to mix well, breaking up the oysters as you go. Add the onion-and-celery mixture to the bowl and stir to combine. Transfer the dressing back into the broiler pan and spread evenly. Put the dressing on the middle rack of the oven and bake for 30 to 35 minutes, until golden brown and crisp around the edges. Transfer the duck to a serving platter and serve with the dressing.

TIDBIT | Due to their thick layer of subcutaneous fat, ducks are conveniently self-basting.

SPATCHCOCKED DUCK

See page 21 for more on spatchcocking a bird.

(AB confronts a ghost, who's perusing his cookbook collection.)

Ghost: Consider me the ghost of Christmas fowl, as in birds, and I must say I'm sorely vexed at your suggestion that the groaning board would be better served sans goose.

AB: Groaning board. You've been reading too much Dickens.

Ghost: Ah, you know my work.

AB: I...I...I'm sorry. Uh, you're Charles Dickens?

Dickens: Indeed. Now out with it, sir. What have you against a good goose? Besides being wholly delicious, the goose is a symbolic continuation of Celtic Samhain and German Yule ceremonies, among others. Ritually devoured, the goose was thought to magically ensure the regeneration of winter into spring, and on a practical note, the goose with its size is perfectly suited to the family table. Now, I want you to protect my legacy by bringing it back.

(Cut to meat market)

Dickens: We'd like to see your Christmas fowl. Where are the geese?

Butcher: This is America, buddy. We've got duck.

AB: Look, Dickens, ducks are a lot like geese. They're just smaller, and they don't have long necks, but they float. They fly. It's the same thing.

Dickens: I'm afraid it's just not the same thing. This is very depressing. You'll have to carry on without me, my good man.

(Dickens disappears.)

HANGIN' WITH DICKENS

Gaze, if you will, upon this behemothic form.

At first viewing you might mistake this as a candid shot of Marlon Brando waddling onto the set of *Apocalypse Now* circa 1978. The truth is, it's me, waddling around a Louisiana crawfish farm circa 2009. (The horror . . . the horror.) The day after I viewed this hideous image I stepped on a scale for the first time in several years and was shocked to find the number 213.5 staring back at me.

I decided there and then that, starting that day, things would be different—that I would shed fifty pounds of ugly me. It took me nine months, but I did it, and I'm happy to say that a year and a half later I've kept the blubber at bay and have even added ten pounds of muscle, which means that at forty-eight years old I'm as close to buff as I've ever been in my life. Although I wouldn't normally consider this *Good Eats* material, fans showed interest in impressive numbers so I decided to share a few of my methods in this episode.

NOTE: Please be advised that I am neither a physician nor a dietician, and that the information herein is experiential, experimental, and exploratory in nature. That said, in the first year since the episode aired I have met many (as in lots) of folks who after viewing it went on to lose considerable amounts of useless, ugly blubber.

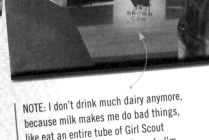

NOTE: I don't drink much dairy anymore, because milk makes me do bad things, like eat an entire tube of Girl Scout cookies, or a box of Cap'n Crunch. I'm not saying milk is bad, but we all have our triggers, and milk's it for me.

My story is neither rare nor unique. My girth was the direct result of consuming foods high in calories and low in noncaloric nutrients—that is, vitamins, minerals, antioxidants, heart-healthy fats, fiber, and complex carbohydrates, which break down slowly in the system. Sitting on my butt a lot was also a problem, but that's another show. In order to make sure my food input was nutrient positive, I sought to come up with a system that concentrated on the foods I needed to get in as much as those I was better off avoiding. This led me to . . . the Plan of the Four Lists.

List 1: Foods I must consume daily[1]

Fruits[2]	Nuts
Whole grains	Carrots
Dark leafy greens	Green tea

List 2: Foods I must consume at least three times a week:

Oily fish[3]	Sweet potato
Yogurt	Avocado
Broccoli	

List 3: Foods I can consume only one time a week—max. (This is where discipline comes into play.)

Red meat	Dessert
White starch (white rice, pasta, potato)	Alcohol

List 4: Foods I can consume zero times a week—as in never.

Fast food	Canned soups
Soda	"Diet" anything
Processed meals	

The last item there may require some explanation. I truly believe that the human brain can become addicted to sweetness, and that has negative repercussions even if that sweetness is noncaloric. Furthermore, if you drink, say, three diet sodas a day, when you do get hold of real sweetness like, say, a pile of chocolate chip cookies, you're a lot more likely to eat the whole pile because you have such a high sweetness threshold.[4]

[1] Notice that I've set myself up to succeed by choosing foods that are easy to get, prepare, and consume. Whole grains could be nothing but oatmeal, and leafy greens could be anything from chard to collards to spinach. Lettuce doesn't count.

[2] Specifically, red and purple fruits, which are much higher in antioxidants than, say, pineapple or even the revered banana.

[3] Excluding farm-raised Atlantic salmon, which never passes my lips.

[4] I have zero scientific backup for this other than my own buffitude and the fact that I never see fit people drink diet soda.

One more rule that isn't actually on the list: never, ever, ever skip breakfast. Breakfast is the most important meal of the day, and several studies have found that people who maintain significant amounts of weight loss routinely eat their breakfast. Speaking of breakfast, I like mine purple, because purple is the color of anthocyanins, which possess antioxidant powers that sweep damaged matter from the body.

// SOFTWARE

4	ounces	low-fat soy milk	for protein
4	ounces	acai, grape, or pomegrante juice	for antioxidants
4	ounces	frozen bananas	for texture, potassium
4	ounces	frozen strawberries	for texture, flavor
4	ounces	frozen blueberries	for antioxidants
4	ounces	frozen peaches	because I like them

// PROCEDURE

1. Combine the soy milk, juice, bananas, strawberries, blueberries, and peaches in the **carafe of a blender**, cover, and set in the refrigerator overnight or up to 8 hours.

2. In the morning, or when the fruit is partially thawed, place the carafe on the base of the **blender**, start at the lowest speed, and slowly accelerate to medium, until you achieve a vortex. Blend on medium for 1 minute. Increase the speed to high and blend for an additional minute. Serve immediately for big fat doses of beta carotene, fiber, foliate, iron, manganese, omega-3s, potassium, protein, and vitamins B and C.

BLENDER-CAM

SHERRIED SARDINE TOAST

4 SERVINGS

// SOFTWARE

2	3¾-ounce	cans two-layer brisling sardines in olive oil	
2	tablespoons	finely chopped fresh parsley	
1	tablespoon	sherry vinegar	
¼	teaspoon	grated lemon zest	reserve the lemon and cut into wedges
4	½-inch-thick	slices crusty bread	such as sourdough, country loaf, or rye[5]
1	ripe	Hass avocado[6]	
	to taste	coarse sea salt	
	to taste	black pepper	freshly ground

// PROCEDURE

1. Drain the oil from one can of sardines into a **small bowl** and set aside. Drain the oil from the other can into **another small bowl** and **whisk** in 1 tablespoon of the parsley, the vinegar, lemon zest, and pepper. Add the sardines, stir to combine, and set aside for up to 1 hour.

2. After 45 minutes, place a rack 3 inches from the broiler and heat the broiler to high. **Brush** each slice of bread on one side with the reserved oil. Put the bread, oil side up, on a **cooling rack** set inside a **half sheet pan** and broil for 2 to 3 minutes, until golden brown and crisp.

3. Halve the avocado and remove the pit. Smash the flesh in each half with a **fork**, then scoop out and spread on the toasted bread. Top with the sardines. Pour any remaining dressing on top and garnish with the remaining parsley. Season lightly with sea salt and serve with lemon wedges.

[5] I also enjoy using a packaged, store-bought crispbread called Wasa, and no, they don't pay me to say that.

[6] Avocados are packed with heart-healthy unsaturated fats, proteins, and nearly twenty different vitamins and minerals.

BRISLINGS

If you're not familiar with brislings, these fish are European sprat, or small herring-like shoaling fish found around the North Atlantic. Although they are rarely available in fresh form, canned versions are favorites of seafoodies everywhere because of their clean flavor, delicate texture, and pleasantly oceanic aroma. Best of all, brislings are packed with omega-3 fatty acids, which are very good for the heart, and since you consume their tiny bones they're also a formidable source of calcium, perhaps the most crucial mineral for weight loss because it seems to prevent the body from stacking on fat—and may even help you to get rid of it. And of course, being fish, brislings are protein rich. And yes, brislings are also referred to as sardines. That's right, sardines are good eats.

GINGER ALMONDS

1 POUND, APPROXIMATELY 16 SERVINGS

Snacking is not evil. It is in fact the secret to weight loss and maintenance. Between meals, grazing helps to keep the metabolism going, thus preventing you from launching on ravenous rampages every time you sit down to a meal. Of course, one must snack wisely, and I wanted something hand-friendly and crunchy and satisfying, as well as healthy. After a bit of research I settled on the only nut named on the famed Mayo Clinic's list of ten superfoods.

// SOFTWARE

1	tablespoon	ground ginger	
1	teaspoon	kosher salt	
2	teaspoons	olive oil	
1	teaspoon	dark sesame oil	
1		dried arbol chile	stemmed and cut into small pieces
1	pound	whole natural almonds	
1	tablespoon	low-sodium soy sauce	
1	tablespoon	Worcestershire sauce	

// PROCEDURE

1. Heat the oven to 250°F.

2. Combine the ginger and salt in a **large bowl** and set aside.

3. Heat the olive oil and sesame oil in a **12-inch sauté pan** over medium-low heat. Add the chile and cook, stirring frequently, until the chile begins to give off an aroma, 30 to 45 seconds. Add the almonds and cook, stirring frequently, until lightly toasted, about 5 minutes. Add the soy sauce and Worcestershire sauce and cook until they are reduced slightly and the pan looks dry, about 1 minute. Immediately remove the nuts to the bowl with the ginger mixture and toss to coat.

4. Spread the coated nuts in a single layer on a **half sheet pan** lined with **parchment paper** and bake for 20 minutes. Remove the pan to a **cooling rack** and let cool for at least 30 minutes, or until completely cool. Store in an airtight container for up to 1 week.

OF COURSE, NO DIET PLAN CAN PRODUCE RESULTS WITHOUT EXERCISE!

Consider the twin grandes dames of the American bar:

the Bloody Mary and the Margarita. Both have classic pedigrees, fascinating histories, and throngs of fans. And both have been reduced to parodies of their former selves, the first devolving into a septic salad bar and the latter to a sickeningly sweet slushy. Who did this? We did. Time to make amends.

TIDBIT | The first published recipe for the Bloody Mary appeared in the *Stork Club Bar Book*, by Lucius Beebe, in 1944.

CONCERNING VODKA

Like any other spirit, vodka is born of a carbohydrate-rich mash that is fermented by yeast. What's particularly interesting about vodka is that it doesn't really matter where the carbohydrates come from: Fruit, roots, corn, potatoes, and various grains can all be used to produce the mash or "beer" that after fermentation is distilled (meaning the alcohol is boiled out) and thoroughly filtered to produce a beverage that according to U.S. law must be colorless, odorless, and all but flavorless. Crappy vodkas may only be distilled twice and then filtered through something cheap—cardboard, for instance. Top-drawer vodka is distilled three or four times and filtered through a wide array of charcoals to remove impurities. That said, if you're wondering what the difference is between most $25 bottles and most $80 bottles, all I'll say is that the key word is *bottle*.

KNOWLEDGE CONCENTRATE

▷○ **To better understand the Bloody Mary, we must venture to Paris in the 1920s—specifically Harry's New York Bar, Harry's for short, which had become a home away from home for a gaggle of American ex-pats and Jazz Age refugees from Fitzgerald to Gershwin, who is said to have written most of *An American in Paris* at the downstairs piano. A historic setting and supporting cast, to be sure, but the real star of this particular drama was a bartender named Pete, who came to work the plank at Harry's in 1921.**

Ferdinand Pete Petiot was friendly with some Russian families who had fled the Bolsheviks back in 1917, and one of these families, the Smirnoffs, had supplied a curious spirit called vodka, or "little water," to the czar himself. Inspired by the association, the young mixologist began to experiment with the chameleonic quaff. Nobody knows exactly when Pete had his big monkey-touch-the-monolith moment, but I like to think that on one fateful morning a young reporter came in with nerves and jangle, head throbbing from a late night of drinking and fighting with his first wife. Now, good old Pete knew that what Hemingway really needed was a little hair of the dog.

In my fantasy, Pete decides to hide a shot of vodka inside the tomato juice he knew the writer liked.[1] Pete also figured he would round off the flavor of this new concoction with a few drops of something salty and spicy, so he reached for Worcestershire and Tabasco, both of which had become standards in the bar. Hemingway drank. Hemingway liked. As for the name . . . nobody knows.[2]

▷○ **Alcohol anthropologists credit Harry's Bar with creating yet another cocktail a decade later built upon brandy, orange liqueur, and lemon juice, dubbed the Sidecar, which became the poster drink for an entire class of citrus-based drinks referred to as sours. And it just so happens that the Sidecar is first cousin to the Margarita.**

Although they are both classic fruit-based cocktails, the Bloody Mary and the Margarita could not be more different. The vodka in a Bloody Mary is more phantom than spirit, ever the silent partner to the crimson nightshade, but everything in a Margarita (a good one, that is) serves the tequila. And whereas vodka can be made anywhere from anything, as long as it's thoroughly distilled and filtered, tequila is one of the most jealously guarded and regulated varietal products on the planet. It is also one of the most misunderstood. Although I could wax rhapsodic for pages concerning this mysterious spirit, this book is heavy enough as it is so we'll focus on the top four things you simply must know about tequila.

1. Tequila is made not from a cactus but from the blue agave plant, which looks like this:

When the agave is about a dozen years old it is dug out by hand, and the spikes are removed to reveal the heart, which looks so much like a pineapple they actually call it a *piña*.

2. Like Champagne and Vidalia onions, tequila can only legally be called "tequila" if it is produced in very specific areas of Mexico, including the states of Jalisco and limited regions of Guanajuato, Michoacán, Nayarit, and Tamaulipas.

Any agave-based spirit made outside these areas is called mescal.[3]

3. There are two different categories of tequila: 100 percent agave tequilas and *mixto* tequilas, which are only required to contain 51 percent agave; the other 49 percent can be . . . well, they don't call it headache in a bottle for nothing. It's worth noting that the number-one-selling tequila in the United States is in fact a *mixto*, which is mistaken for the good stuff because it usually has the word *gold* associated with it. The hue is due to the inclusion of caramel coloring.

4. Within the 100 percent agave territory, there are several classifications:

BLANCO, or white tequila, is often called silver. It's crystal clear, like vodka, and straight from the still. The flavor is pure agave, which is floral, spicy, even a little fruity.

REPOSADO tequila is stored in oak barrels for at least two months, but not more than eleven months and thirty days. The pale gold of this "rested" tequila comes from being stored in wood, which also lends a subtle smokiness.

AÑEJO tequila has been aged from one year to one day short of three years. The woodiness and smoky flavor of *añejos* resemble those of other spirits that are similarly aged, such as Scotch whisky.

EXTRA-AÑEJO tequilas are very dark due to sojourning more than three years in the barrel. These are typically expensive tequilas meant for sipping, not mixing, a role better played by 100 percent agave silver or white tequila.

THE BLUE AGAVE
HOME OF TEQUILA

Piña
in here

[1] Canned tomato juice was becoming very popular in Paris at the time as an eye opener—that is, something that one drinks when drinking is what one has been doing too much of the night before.

[2] Fantasy aside, I seriously doubt Hemingway had much contact with the Bloody Mary. If he had, I suspect he would have included it in his memoir *A Moveable Feast*, but he makes no mention of the drink.

[3] Many of which are as delicious as the finest tequilas.

TOMATO VODKA

1 (750 ML) BOTTLE

// **SOFTWARE** //

1	pound	ripe tomatoes	
1	750 ml bottle	80 proof vodka	

// **PROCEDURE** //

1. Cut each tomato into eight pieces and place in a **large glass jar**. Add the vodka, stir to combine, and cover. Place in a cool, dark place for at least 5 and up to 7 days, stirring every day. After 7 days, strain through a **fine-mesh sieve**. Discard the solids.

2. To store, pour the tomato vodka into its original bottle and keep in a cool, dark place.

GOING THE EXTRA BERRY

Tomatoes, botanically speaking, are berries and, as such, contain both water- and alcohol-soluble flavors. Vodka, being alcohol and water, is an ideal solvent for extracting those tomato flavors, but to do so thoroughly takes time, a lot longer than it would to make and drink a Bloody Mary. The answer, of course, is to make tomato vodka.

BLOODY MARY

4 COCKTAILS

// **SOFTWARE** //

1¾	pounds	cherry or grape tomatoes	rinsed and dried
2	teaspoons	hot sauce	
2	tablespoons	Worcestershire sauce	
1 to 3	tablespoons	lemon juice	freshly squeezed
½	teaspoon	kosher salt	
6	ounces	Tomato Vodka (above)	

// **PROCEDURE** //

1. Remove the stems from the tomatoes. Put the tomatoes, hot sauce, Worcestershire sauce, lemon juice, and salt in a **blender**, cover, and blend on high speed for 1½ minutes.

2. Fill an **ice cube tray** with about 2 cups of the juice and place in the freezer overnight. Pour the remaining juice into a **lidded container** and set aside at room temperature overnight.

3. Just before serving, place 3 frozen cubes in each of **4 Collins glasses** and add 1½ ounces vodka to each glass. Stir the reserved juice, pour 4 ounces into each glass, and serve immediately.

⎍⎍⎍⎍ **MARGARITA**

1 COCKTAIL

// SOFTWARE //

2	ounces	100 percent agave silver/blanco tequila	
1	tablespoon	kosher salt	
4		limes	
½	small	Hamlin or Valencia orange	(see page 202)
2	tablespoons	light agave nectar	
3 to 4		ice cubes	

// PROCEDURE ///

1. Pour ½ ounce of the tequila into a **small saucer**. Spread the salt in a separate **small saucer**. Dip the rim of a **martini or other wide-rimmed glass** into the tequila. Lift it out of the tequila and hold it upside down for 10 seconds to allow for slight evaporation. Next, dip the glass into the salt to coat the rim. Set aside.

2. Halve 2 of the limes, cut a thin slice for garnish from one, and set aside. Juice the halved limes into the bottom of a **Boston-style cocktail shaker**. Cut the remaining 2 limes and the orange into quarters and add to the juice. Add the agave nectar to the cocktail shaker and **muddle** for 2 minutes until the juices release. Strain the juice mixture through a **cocktail strainer** into the top of the shaker and discard the spent fruit bodies.

3. Return the juice to the bottom of the shaker, add the remaining 1½ ounces tequila and any remaining on the saucer. Add the ice to the shaker, cover, and shake for 30 seconds. Strain the mixture through a cocktail strainer into the prepared glass, garnish with the reserved lime slice, and serve immediately.

HISTORICAL CONCERNS

Many have laid claim to the creation of the first Margarita, but whoever did the making, I'm willing to bet five to one it went down just like this: One night in the mid-'30s, a couple of spiffy gringo swells are whooping it up in a hot night club, maybe in Tijuana or Juarez or Monterrey, and one of them turns to the barkeep and says, "We'll have two Sidecars."

The barkeep grabs for the orange liqueur but sees that he's out of brandy. Figuring his customers will never know the difference, he subs tequila. Then maybe instead of reaching for lemons (not exactly common in Mexico back then), he reaches for limes. He shakes it up, and he pours it out, and the customers drink them down without ever noticing that they were actually consuming the first Margaritas on earth. And that's how I just know it happened. How? Because if the Margarita had been built from scratch, I'm betting the orange liqueur would never have made it into the glass in the first place. And so I say, unless you really like drinking orange liqueur or Sidecars, just skip it altogether and spend the money on better tequila and a little bit of agave nectar, a natural sweetener produced by extracting the sap from the *piña*, or core, of a mature agave—just like tequila.

THE BALLAD OF SALTY AND SWEET

EPISODE 223 | SEASON 13 | GOOD EATS

In the history of the kitchen, there are many love stories, but none quite as poignant or powerful as that of salty and sweet. Consider the peanut butter and jelly sandwich, or prosciutto-wrapped melon, or chocolate-covered pretzels, or feta cheese and fruit, or honey-roasted peanuts. As is true of human relationships, however, this particular culinary compatibility reflects a deeper, more complex chemistry, a genuine gustatory gestalt, if you will. Salt actually possesses the ability to alter the way our sensory apparatus perceives flavor, heightening and intensifying the sweetness of whatever sweetness is there while chemically framing the other subtle flavors that might be surrounding it. And, as we shall soon see, salt also has the ability to squelch bitterness, far better than even sugar (sorry, Mary Poppins).

HOW THE BRAIN RECEIVES TASTES

A closer look at the tongue's surface

reveals thousands of tiny receptors,

each designed to accept one basic taste.

Bitter foods

enter bitter receptors

Don't believe me? Consider the curious case of grapefruit, whose fruity flavors are typically overpowered by naringin, a powerful antioxidant, which can be good medicine if you can get past its intense bitterness. But first let's talk tongue.

Sweetness and bitterness are both sensed by the same type of apparatus, namely membrane-embedded protein receptors located on taste cells. Sweetness goes through one of these chemical doors while bitterness goes through another. If they both pass through their respective doors at the same time, your brain senses them both. You could, perhaps, overwhelm the bitterness of that grapefruit with sugar, but it would take a lot more than a spoonful, that's for sure.

When salt hits your saliva, which, of course, is technically a salt solution, the sodium and the chloride break apart. Sodium is an ion, meaning that it either has one extra electron or is lacking one electron. Ions can cross into taste receptor cells directly through amazing protein structures called ion channels, which are present on all the taste receptors regardless of whether they are designed to bond with sweet, bitter, or umami, if you believe that even exists. It's pretty complicated neurobiological stuff. Let it suffice to say that when it comes to getting into your taste buds, sodium does not have to wait in line. But wait, there's more. For reasons that still have the lab coat set scratching their noggins, sodium actually blocks bitterness, preventing it from fully accessing the taste system, and while sodium can block bitterness, it also seems capable not only of bringing its own flavor to the party but of boosting other flavors that might ordinarily be buried under bitterness. Now, some sensory scientists say that sodium may actually turn up the volume on flavors by electrically increasing the input of the flavors at the tongue or by altering the way the brain perceives them. Chefs, on the other hand, will simply insist that salt doesn't make things taste salty, it makes them taste good, and that includes sweets. In fact, I never make dessert without adding a little bit of salt.

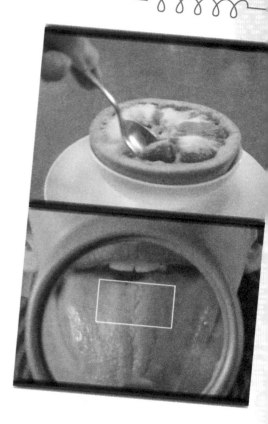

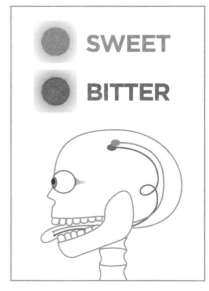

SWEET

BITTER

and the brain registers bitter.

When sweet foods

enter their receptors at the same time as bitter foods,

the brain registers them both.

GRAPEFRUIT BRÛLÉE

4 SERVINGS

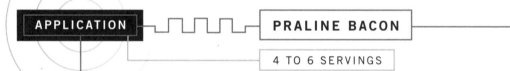

// **SOFTWARE** ///

2		red or pink grapefruits	chilled
2	tablespoons	coarse sugar	
¾	teaspoon	coarse sea salt	

// **SPECIAL HARDWARE** //

Blowtorch

// **PROCEDURE** //

1. Halve each grapefruit crosswise, and cut a thin slice off the bottom of each half to stabilize it. Remove the seeds from the grapefruit, and loosen segments with a **paring knife**.

2. Sprinkle each half evenly with the sugar. Using a **blowtorch**, melt the sugar to form a golden brown and crisp top. Sprinkle the hot sugar with the salt and serve immediately.

APPLICATION

PRALINE BACON

4 TO 6 SERVINGS

// **SOFTWARE** ///

1	pound	thick-sliced bacon	
2½	ounces	light brown sugar	
1½	ounces	pecan halves	

// **PROCEDURE** //

1. Heat the oven to 400°F.

2. Line a **half sheet pan** with **aluminum foil**. Arrange the bacon in a single layer on a **cooling rack** and set it in the prepared pan. Bake for 30 to 35 minutes, until the bacon browns and the fat is rendered and bubbly.

3. Meanwhile, combine the brown sugar and pecans in a **small food processor**. Pulse 15 times, or until the pecans are finely chopped.

4. Remove the bacon from the oven, sprinkle with the brown-sugar mixture, and pat down to adhere. Bake for 10 minutes, or until the bacon is crisp. Cool on the rack for 10 minutes before serving.

DARK SALTY CARAMELS

64 (1-INCH) CARAMELS

Invented by the French sometime after fire but before the airplane, the caramel has been married to salt for at least four hundred years. Caramels are amorphous candies like brittles, toffees, and taffies, but there's an extra challenge here, because the sugar is cooked to a point where many bitter compounds are created. Salt can tone down the bitterness while elevating the butter and coffee flavors the bitterness typically hides.

// **SOFTWARE** //

14½	ounces	sugar	
½	cup	H$_2$O	
½	cup	light corn syrup	
¼	teaspoon	cream of tartar	
1	cup	heavy cream	at room temperature
2	teaspoons	soy sauce	for saltiness, color, and funk
8	tablespoons	unsalted butter	cut into pieces, at room temperature
1	teaspoon	coarse sea salt	

// **PROCEDURE** //

(1) Line the bottom and sides of an **8-inch square pan** with **parchment paper**.

(2) Combine the sugar, water, corn syrup, and cream of tartar in a **heavy 4-quart saucepan** and place over high heat. Stir occasionally until the sugar has dissolved. Cover and continue to cook for 5 minutes.

(3) Meanwhile, combine the cream and soy sauce in a **liquid measuring cup**. Have this and the butter standing by.

(4) Remove the lid from the sugar mixture and attach a **candy thermometer** to the side of the pan. When the sugar mixture reaches 230°F, reduce the heat to medium and cook, without stirring, for 6 to 7 minutes, until the syrup is golden and is approaching 300°F. At this point there is less likelihood of crystallization, so gently swirl the pan to help break up any hot pockets.

(5) When the temperature reaches 350°F, the syrup will become deep amber. Remove the pan from the heat, gently swirl again to break up hot pockets, and cool for 2 minutes.

(6) Carefully pour in the cream mixture and add the butter. Stir to combine. Return the caramel to medium heat, stir until the butter is completely melted, and continue cooking until the mixture reaches 255°F. Remove from the heat and pour into the parchment-lined pan; tap the pan gently on the counter to release air bubbles.

(7) Cool on a **cooling rack** for 30 minutes, then sprinkle evenly with the salt. Continue cooling on the rack for an additional 3½ hours. Cut into 1-inch pieces and wrap individually in parchment. Store in an airtight container for up to 1 week.

CRYSTALLIZATION

As the sugar dissolves and the water starts to boil away, the sucrose molecules composed of a single glucose molecule bound to a single fructose molecule begin to tightly mingle, a habit that can lead to the formation of big, crusty crystals, which is bad. Cream of tartar, or tartaric acid, can hinder crystallization by snipping the bond holding the disaccharide together. Adding corn syrup further floods the party with other sugars capable of hindering any inconvenient hookups.

AMERICAN CLASSICS VII: CHICKEN AND DUMPLINGS

EPISODE 224 | SEASON 13 | GOOD EATS

The American culinary canon is rife with polarizing dishes, and by that I mean foods that folks feel so passionately about that they're willing to fuss and occasionally fight over their preparation as though their cultural, familial, and personal identities depended on it. Chili is such a dish, as is barbecue. Biscuits, cornbread, and gumbo are as well. And then there's chicken and dumplings. The conflict here concerns not the chicken, but the dumplings. And this is a very personal problem, because my mother belongs to the school of big, fluffy dumplings, referred to in some circles as "swimmers," while my mother-in-law is a proponent of the hard, flat, and slippery dumplings, a.k.a. "slickers." Choosing one over another always puts me in a dangerous position, like a vessel caught between the Scylla and Charybdis. And so one day I decided to discover the origins of this soupy species.

TIDBIT | Global dumplings:
Germany: *Konigsberger klops*
Italy: *Gnocchi*
France: *Quenelles*
Korea: *Mandoo*
Mexico: *Albondigas*

SLICKERS! VS. SWIMMERS!

298

When you ponder the fact that my mother's people hail from north Georgia and my mother-in-law sprouted a mere 146 miles away in neighboring North Carolina, you might be tempted to discount regional differences. Not so fast.

Diligent research revealed that my mom's dumplings originated not only from north of the Mason-Dixon line but ultimately from eastern and northern England. Norfolk is the exact location, where many references to such dumplings exist. Consider this example from Robert Armin, one of Lord Chamberlain's men, the theatrical troupe responsible for premiering so many of Shakespeare's plays. In his 1608 work, *A Nest of Ninnies* (great title), he describes someone as looking like a "Norfolk dumpling, thick and short." It doesn't take a professional historian to trace this edible track back through the Norman Conquest to northern France, where dumplings like my mom's are simmered in fish stews.

My mother-in-law's flat dumplings are more authentically Southern, as they descend from the "hard" dumplings of southern England, specifically Sussex, which was invaded in the year 477 by Germanic Saxons. Did I mention that my wife's family is of German extraction? Coincidence? Perhaps . . . not. What we have here is nothing less than a culinary extension of the Norman-Saxon Conflict, made immortal by popular stories such as those of Robin Hood and Ivanhoe. As these rifts are not about to be mended, we're just going to have to make both versions.

Which dumplings do I prefer? Since that question places me in a rather precarious position, suffice it to say I love them equally . . . depending on which mother is visiting.

Traditionally, chicken and dumplings are prepared with an old rooster, but the closest thing you're likely to find at your local megamart is a "stewing hen." This is a laying chicken that has exceeded her egg-laying usefulness. Unlike a young broiler, fryer, or even roaster, a stewing hen has lived long enough to develop real poultry flavor and connective tissue, which we can and will dissolve into gelatin, a process that can take hours—unless, of course, you have a time machine, otherwise known as a pressure cooker.

TIDBIT | On the twenty-ninth of every month, Argentines gather for a good-luck dumpling dinner called "night of the *ñoquis.*"

TIDBIT | Denis Papin, a French physicist, invented the pressure cooker. His "steam digestor" exploded on its first demonstration in 1679.

CHICKEN AND ROLLED DUMPLINGS

Flat or "slicker" dumplings require considerably more time to prep than "swimmers." Like most Southern baked goods, my mother-in-law's version is based on the biscuit method, wherein flour is mixed with leavening and seasoning, solid fat is cut in, cold liquid is added, and the dough is briefly kneaded. What's intriguing, however, is what comes after that.

// SOFTWARE

8	ounces	all-purpose flour	plus extra for rolling
2	teaspoons	baking powder	aluminum-free
4	teaspoons	kosher salt	or to taste
⅓	cup	vegetable shortening	at room temperature
½	cup	skim milk	chilled
1	5- to 5½-pound	stewing hen	giblets removed
7 to 9	cups	H_2O	to just under the max fill line
	to taste	black pepper	freshly ground

// SPECIAL HARDWARE

7-quart pressure cooker

// PROCEDURE

1. **Whisk** the flour, baking powder, and 1 teaspoon of the salt together in a **medium mixing bowl.** Rub the shortening into the flour mixture, using your fingertips, until it resembles coarse crumbs. Add the milk, a couple tablespoons at a time, just until you have a rough ball of workable dough. Knead the dough 3 or 4 times, until it is mostly smooth, but do not overwork.

2. Divide the dough into two equal pieces. Roll out each piece of dough, using a floured **rolling pin**, on floured **waxed paper or parchment paper** to about ¹⁄₁₆ inch thick. Cover the dough, still on the waxed paper, with a **tea towel**, and let dry for at least 8 hours. This can be done the night before or early in the morning.

3. Two to three hours before the dumplings are ready to cook, put the hen, water, and the remaining tablespoon of salt in a **7-quart pressure cooker**. Do not fill above the cooker's maximum fill line, or two-thirds full. Cover and lock the lid. Bring to pressure over high heat, about 20 minutes. Reduce the heat to low, so that you barely hear hissing from the pot. Cook for 45 minutes.

4. Release the pressure using the cooker's release device (read the manual!) or cool the cooker by running cold water over the lid for 5 minutes. Open carefully. Remove the hen from the broth and set aside to cool. The meat should be tender and falling away from the bone. Once the hen is cool enough to handle, pull the meat from the bones in small pieces, cover, and set aside. Discard the skin and bones.

5. Set a **cheesecloth-lined colander** in a **large container** and pour in the broth, discarding the solids. Taste and season the broth with additional salt, if desired. Return the broth to the pressure cooker, cover, and bring to a boil. Reduce the heat to medium to maintain a gentle boil.

6. Cut the dough into ½-inch-wide strips, break into 1½-inch-long pieces, and drop into the boiling broth. When all the dough has been used, gently push all of the dumplings down into the broth with a **slotted spoon**. Do not stir the dumplings. Cook for 10 minutes, or until the dumplings are cooked through, but not falling apart. Turn off the heat and add the meat. Serve in bowls with freshly ground pepper.

PRESSURE COOKERS

We've applied pressure on the show before, but let's review the principles.
1. The food goes in.
2. Water is added.
3. The vessel is sealed.
4. Heat is applied.
5. The pressure device, either a weight or "jiggler" set over a narrow steam port in older models or a spring-loaded piston in newer pots, maintains a pressure of fifteen pounds per square inch.

The pressure that is created typically raises the boiling point of the water inside from 212° to 252°F. How? The boiling point of water depends upon the atmospheric pressure. A pot of water sitting on the beach in Rio de Janeiro on a standard atmospheric day will be experiencing a pressure we represent barometrically as 29.92 inches of mercury. To reach a boil, enough heat energy must be poured into the pot to overcome that pressure. If we were to stack more sky on top of that vessel by placing it at the bottom of a very, very, very, very deep hole, a higher temperature would be required to hit the boil. Do the math and you'll see that cooking in a pressure cooker is equivalent to cooking in a twenty-thousand-foot-deep hole. All this means is that a pressure cooker can cook a whole roasting hen quickly and thoroughly.

Spring-loaded cookers have a pop-up disk that tells you when full pressure has been reached. If the disk is up, you won't be able to open the cooker.

Fluffy Northern drop-style dumplings, a.k.a. "swimmers", don't require very much time at all, because there's no drying phase involved, and so a typical procedure goes like this: Boil the butter and the liquid together, add the flour, beat until the mixture is cool, then work in the eggs. Remind you of anything? If you answered *pâte à choux* (or choux paste), give yourself a nice big hug, because that is exactly what my mama's dumplings really are, which means that they are as French as Chanel No. 5, only they taste good.

// SOFTWARE

1	5- to 5½-pound	stewing hen	giblets removed
3½	teaspoons	kosher salt	or to taste
7 to 9	cups	H₂O	to just under the max fill line
3	tablespoons	unsalted butter	
2¾	ounces	all-purpose flour	
2	large	eggs	at room temperature
	to taste	black pepper	freshly ground

// SPECIAL HARDWARE

7-quart pressure cooker

// PROCEDURE

1. Put the hen and 3 teaspoons of the salt in a **7-quart pressure cooker**. Add water just to cover the hen. Do not fill above the cooker's maximum fill line, or two-thirds full. Cover and lock the lid. Bring to pressure over high heat, about 20 minutes. Reduce the heat to low, so that you barely hear hissing from the pot. Cook for 45 minutes.

2. Release the pressure using the cooker's release device (read the manual!) or cool the cooker by running cold water over the lid for 5 minutes. Open carefully. Remove the hen from the broth and set aside to cool. The meat should be tender and falling away from the bone. Once the hen is cool enough to handle, pull the meat from the bones in small pieces, cover, and set aside. Discard the skin and bones.

3. Set a **cheesecloth-lined colander** in a **shallow, wide, 6-quart pot** and strain the broth, discarding the solids. Taste and season the broth with additional salt, if desired.

4. Place ½ cup of the broth, the butter, and the remaining ½ teaspoon salt in a **2-quart saucier**, set over high heat, and bring to a boil. As soon as it boils, add all of the flour at once and stir with a **wooden spoon** until the mixture starts to come together, about 1 minute. Decrease the heat to low and continue stirring until the mixture forms a ball and is no longer sticky, about 3 minutes. Transfer the mixture to a **medium bowl** and mix with an **electric hand mixer** on low speed for 5 minutes to cool until there is no more steam rising. Continue to mix on low and add the eggs, one at a time, making sure the first is completely incorporated before adding the second. You may need to stop occasionally and scrape down the sides of the bowl. Before adding the second egg, check the mixture for consistency: It should tear slightly as it falls from the beater, creating a "V" shape; add the remaining egg if it does not. Transfer to a **1-gallon zip-top bag**. Cut off one corner of the bag to make a quarter-size opening.

5. Bring the broth to a low simmer over medium heat. Pipe 1 inch of the dough and cut with **kitchen shears** directly over the broth, letting the dumpling drop into the broth. Repeat with the remaining dough. Cook, covered, for 8 to 10 minutes, or until the dumplings are cooked through. Remove from the heat, add the meat, and wait 2 to 3 minutes before serving. Serve in bowls with freshly ground pepper.

CURRY-OUS

During my time working on *Good Eats* I've come across many a curious case of food-related words whose connotations have been so contaminated through either cultural misappropriation or etymological foul play as to be nearly meaningless. So far the single most messed-up term I've come across is *curry*. I've reviewed a dozen different dictionaries, and it seems that *curry* derives from the ancient Tamil *khari*, meaning "a sauce or relish designed for service over rice." The modern definition is typically given as "a preparation of meat, fish, fruit, or vegetables cooked with a quantity of bruised spices and used as a relish or flavoring, especially for dishes composed of or served with rice." How very, completely, utterly nonspecific. Compounding the conundrum is the fact that the word *curry* is rarely, if ever, used in India. And that goes double for "curry powder," the spice blend most Americans think of when and if they think of curry.

KNOWLEDGE CONCENTRATE

To understand how curry powder happened, we must journey back to the thirteenth century, when Arab traders and Venetian merchants controlled the flow of spices from Asia to Europe and kept the prices so high that Indian black pepper was worth its weight in gold. Big spice-consuming countries such as Holland, England, Portugal, and Spain became so enraged that they finally struck out on their own in search of sea routes to the "Orient." Navigator Vasco da Gama managed to land in northeastern India and establish trade with the local rulers on behalf of Portugal.

By 1612 the British East India Company had turned their cannons on Portugal and relieved them of India, and by 1618 Sir Thomas Rowe was serving as the new English ambassador to the Mughal emperor. As it turns out, the kaleidoscopic flavors of the subcontinent blew the old boy's meat-and-potatoes palate right out of the water. When the English annexed all of India from 1857 to 1947, every soldier, merchant, and royal who made the trek returned to England jonesing for Indian flavors. Since English cooks lacked Indian skills, ingredients, and cookware, the best they could do was smother everything with a gravy or *khari* packed with ground spices, which were eventually mixed and sold as curry powder. And thus an entire multifaceted culture was reduced to dust.

CONSIDER THE TANDOOR

Walk into any Indian restaurant in America and I guarantee you will find tandoori chicken on the menu. *Tandoor* means "oven," and *tandoori* refers to foods that are cooked in a tandoor. Although its exact cultural origins are hazy, this vertical earthen oven rose to prominence in modern-day Punjab, in northern India. The device itself is cunningly simple. Air enters the bottom of the oven and feeds the open charcoal fire, which in turn loads the ceramic material with an excess of 800°F worth of heat. The tapered top focuses the convective heat. In other words, the tandoor is a big clay jet engine for cooking food.

Flat breads are typically slapped right onto the interior walls to bake, while meats are cooked on large skewers stuck down into the tandoor like umbrellas in a rack. The high heat of the tandoor, especially when combined with a yogurt-based marinade, creates a very distinctive flavor that is regrettably difficult to replicate in the home environment. Which is a good reason to make your own tandoor.

What you'll need:
▶ 20-inch-diameter terra-cotta pot (unglazed and free of cracks and blemishes; Italian models are the best)
▶ Angle grinder fitted with a masonry blade (available at your local hardware store)
▶ 1-inch-wide masking tape
▶ Pencil
▶ Surgical mask (for the dust)
▶ Safety goggles
▶ Common sense (always a good idea when dealing with power tools)

1. Find a nice open space to work outside, because there will be dust.
2. Turn the pot upside down on a stable surface and ring the bottom of the pot with the tape. Trace the bottom edge of the tape with the pencil, then remove the tape. You should now have a guide line that's 1 inch from the bottom of the pot.
3. Using the angle grinder, carefully cut the bottom off the pot. This takes some practice; just go slow and don't try to push through too quickly or the

blade will bind. You may want to practice on a smaller pot first.
4. Soak the pot in water for 8 to 12 hours before use to prevent cracks.
5. Allow the tandoor to dry for at least an hour before heating.
6. Slowly heat the tandoor. Begin with a pound of lit charcoal (use the chimney procedure on pages 306–7).
7. Add a pound of unlit charcoal every 10 minutes until you have a total of 4 pounds of charcoal and the tandoor is approximately 900°F.
8. Prepare the lamb as you would in the application on page 306: roast in the tandoor for 3 to 4 minutes, or until charred, rotating every minute or so.

When choosing skewers for even a small tandoor, consider how they will be used, which is like this:

This means we need to supersize our skewers: ³⁄₁₆-inch-wide, 27-inch-long nickel-plated steel is what I'm talking about. They're excellent for performing tandoor chores, for general grilling, or for repelling the occasional home invader.

ADVANCED TANDOOR HACK

- Fireplace mortar
- Perlite insulation (loose)
- 50-gallon drum cut in half
- Really big flowerpot
- Air vent
- Casters

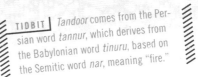

TIDBIT *Tandoor* comes from the Persian word *tannur*, which derives from the Babylonian word *tinuru*, based on the Semitic word *nar*, meaning "fire."

TIDBIT While wooden or bamboo skewers are fine for the grill, don't use them in your tandoor, lest they be reduced to ashes.

──┐┌─┐┌─┐┌─┐┌── **LAMB TIKKA MASALA**

6 SERVINGS

// SOFTWARE ///

2	tablespoons	Garam Masala (see sidebar)	
2	teaspoons	kosher salt	
½	teaspoon	whole cumin seeds	toasted and ground
½	teaspoon	whole coriander seeds	toasted and ground
¼	teaspoon	black pepper	freshly ground
1½	pounds	lamb leg sirloin	trimmed and cut into 1-inch cubes
1	cup	plain whole-milk yogurt	
¼	cup	vegetable oil	
1	large	onion	chopped
4	cloves	garlic	minced
1	tablespoon	grated fresh ginger	
1	medium	serrano chile	seeded and minced
1	28-ounce can	diced tomatoes	
1	cup	coconut milk	
	to taste	fresh mint or cilantro	chopped

// SPECIAL HARDWARE ///

Chimney starter, newspaper, vegetable oil in a spritz bottle, 4 pounds natural lump charcoal, and metal skewers

// PROCEDURE ///

1. Combine 1 tablespoon of the garam masala, 1 teaspoon of the salt, the cumin, coriander, and pepper in a **1-gallon zip-top bag**. Seal and shake to combine. Add the lamb and shake to coat. Add the yogurt to the bag, seal, and squish to coat. Refrigerate the bag in a **leakproof container** for 30 minutes or up to 1 hour.

2. **Spritz** 4 or 5 pieces of newspaper with oil and place in the bottom of a **chimney charcoal starter**. Fill the chimney with half of the **charcoal** and light the newspaper.

3. When the charcoal is lightly covered with gray ash, carefully pour it onto the bottom grate of a **kettle grill** and spread evenly. Top with the remaining unlit charcoal, spreading evenly so as not to suffocate the lit charcoal. Set the second grate in the kettle and cover until ready to cook.

4. Meanwhile, heat the oil in a **12-inch straight-sided sauté pan** over medium-high heat until it shimmers and almost begins to smoke. Add the onion and remaining 1 teaspoon salt and cook, stirring occasionally, until the onion is browned around the edges, 11 to 12 minutes. Reduce the heat to medium-low and add the garlic, ginger, and chile. Cook, stirring constantly, until the onion has softened and browned completely, about 7 minutes. Sprinkle with the remaining 1 tablespoon garam masala and stir several times to coat.

5. Add the tomatoes and cook, stirring occasionally, until they have reduced slightly and deepened in color, 15 to 20 minutes.

6. Remove the lamb from the yogurt mixture, leaving as much yogurt on the meat as possible. Thread the pieces of lamb ¼ inch apart onto the **skewers**. Grill 2 minutes on each side, or until the yogurt has slightly charred or blackened. Remove the lamb from the skewers. Add the lamb and coconut milk to the sauté pan, stir to combine, and heat through. Garnish with mint and serve over basmati rice.

GARAM MASALA

Although "curry powder" doesn't actually exist in India, spice mixtures most certainly do. The word for such a mixture is *masala*, which is always assembled from freshly toasted spices and can be either wet or dry. The most famous masala of them all, garam masala, is a dry one that serves as a primer for a great many dishes. It rarely appears alone but rather as the foundation for additional spices.

To make approximately ¾ cup or 2½ ounces of garam masala, combine in an 8-inch cast-iron skillet over medium-high heat: 2 tablespoons each of whole cardamom seeds, whole coriander seeds, and whole black peppercorns; 1 tablespoon each of whole cumin seeds and black mustard seeds; 20 cloves; 1 dried arbol chile, stemmed, seeded, and crumbled; and 1 (2-inch) piece of cinnamon stick, broken in half.

Cook, moving the pan constantly, until you smell the cumin toasting, 3 to 4 minutes. Remove the mixture to a plate and spread it out to cool for 5 minutes. Once cool, place the toasted mixture and 1 teaspoon of freshly grated nutmeg in a spice grinder. Process until a fine powder is formed, about 1 minute. Use immediately or store in an airtight container for up to 1 month.

TIDBIT | Whole spices stored in an airtight container in a cool, dark, dry place will keep for several years.

MASALA

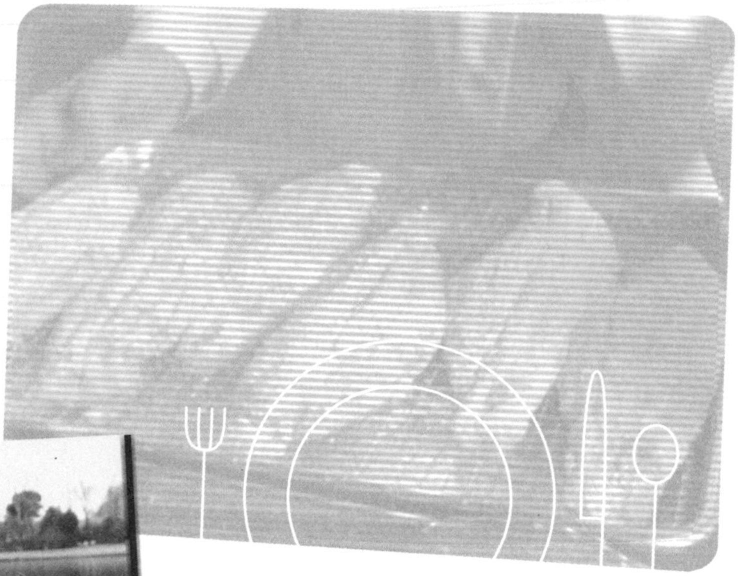

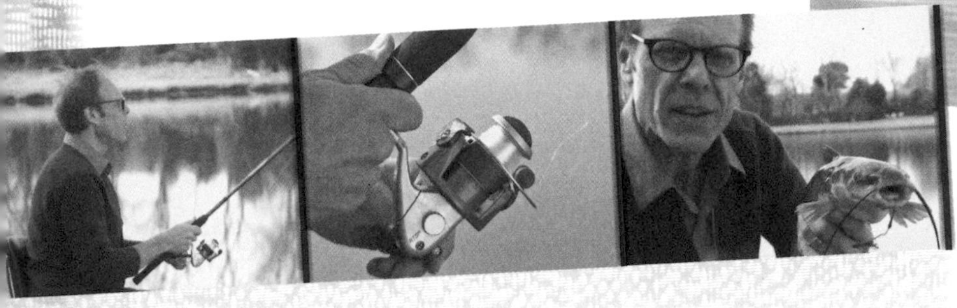

When I was a kid, I kept a fishing rod out in the carport so that when I got home from school I could dump the books and head off to the fishing hole. I'd dig up a few worms along the way, plop down on the bank, and in a couple of hours I'd have myself a few juicy *Ictalurus punctatus*, or channel catfish. Of course, when I was a kid, there were really only three words to describe the proper cooking procedure for a catfish: *deep*, *fat*, and *fried*. But as I matured and did a bit of traveling, I learned that the humble catfish of my youth is in fact a culinary sophisticate that, with subtle coaxing from the cook, can be converted to a global buffet of . . .

TIDBIT | The largest catfish on record weighed over six hundred pounds.

TIDBIT | Humphreys County, Mississippi, claims the title of "Catfish Capital of the World."

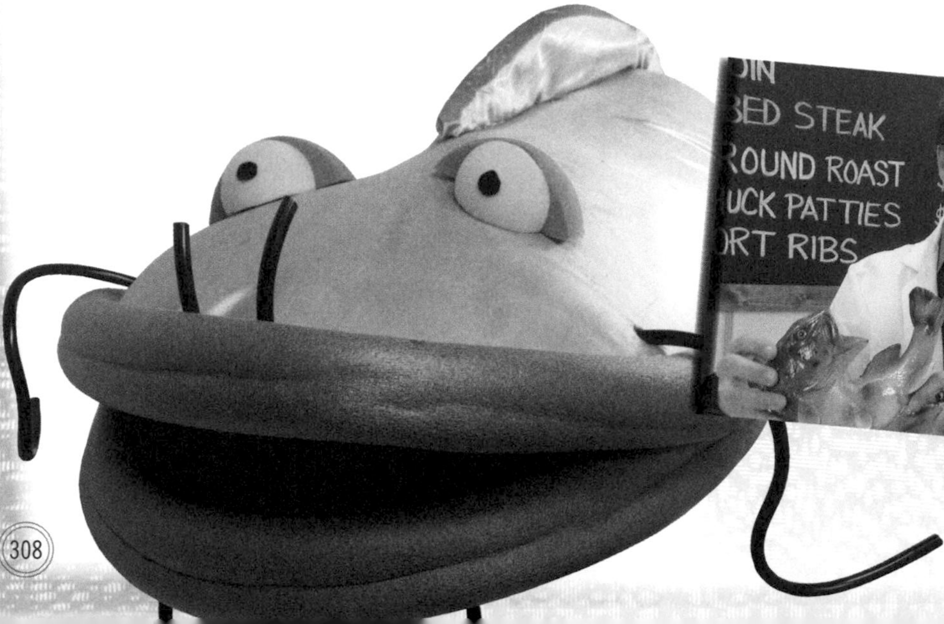

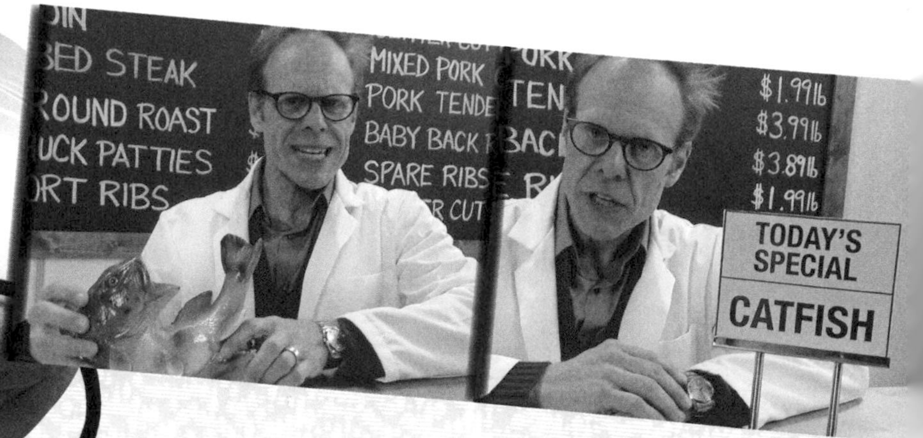

TODAY'S
SPECIAL

CATFISH

▷○ The catfish is a unique critter compared to other freshwater fish. For one thing, it's got whiskers (or, technically speaking, barbules) that function not only as feelers but as antennae, tuning in various signals from the surrounding environment. The skin is coated not with scales but with a slick slime that protects thousands of taste buds. That's right, the entire exterior of a catfish is a tasting surface. The skin is also interesting, because catfish drink through it, which is why wild catfish, caught from muddy little holes taste like . . . muddy little holes. These days, the catfish that come to American markets are raised via aquaculture and no longer convey the muddiness that some of us actually miss. Catfish aquaculture is that rare case in which good economics, good ecology, and good eats all align.

▷○ American farm-raised catfish are considered sustainable for a host of reasons. For one, they grow in scientifically controlled ponds on scientifically designed feed, which they convert at a very respectable 1.8 to 1. That means it only takes 1.8 pounds of feed to grow a pound of fish, and unlike, say, salmon or tuna, which require a lot of open water to thrive, catfish dig pond living, which means they don't have to be loaded up on a bunch of meds just to make it to market weight. Best of all, farmed catfish are sweet, firm, and versatile, a lot like, well, chicken. In fact, I think we ought to call them chicken of the pond.

▷○ When channel cats reach one to one and a half pounds, they are ready for harvest. After being rounded up in a pen, the fish are simply scooped up a thousand pounds at a time and moved into what's called a live-haul truck, which functions as kind of a big rolling aquarium that takes them directly to the processing plant.

▷○ Farmed catfish come in many market forms, including whole, with the skin on, heads and guts gone; whole, skin off; and then fillets in several sizes: 3 to 5 ounces, 5 to 7 ounces, 7 to 13 ounces, and 9 to 11 ounces, though I have to say the 7 to 9 are the ones I typically reach for. I should point out that while I have absolutely nothing against purchasing IQF—individually quick frozen—catfish in the water-glazed flash-frozen state, I do not like buying thawed fish, because I want to be able to control that process myself. Above all, when shopping for catfish you want to see "Country of Origin: U.S.A." on the sticker, because catfish imported from Asia are not the same species, and the way they're raised is, well, let's just say it would make the hair on the back of your neck stand up. So eat American.

HERE, KITTY KITTY!

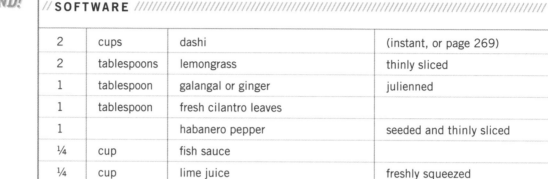

You can walk into just about any restaurant in Thailand and order up a cup of *tom kha pladuk*, or catfish coconut soup. *Tom* means "boil," *pladuk* "catfish," and *kha* refers to galangal, which is also called "blue" ginger and is available in most Asian markets and even some modern megamarts. If you can't find it, go ahead and use regular ginger, but know that results will not be quite the same.

THE MEKONG GIANT CATFISH IS AMAZINGLY FAST, EVEN ON LAND!

// SOFTWARE //

2	cups	dashi	(instant, or page 269)
2	tablespoons	lemongrass	thinly sliced
1	tablespoon	galangal or ginger	julienned
1	tablespoon	fresh cilantro leaves	
1		habanero pepper	seeded and thinly sliced
¼	cup	fish sauce	
¼	cup	lime juice	freshly squeezed
1	pound	U.S. farm-raised catfish fillets	cut into 1-inch pieces
14	ounces	coconut milk	

// PROCEDURE //

Bring the dashi to a simmer in a **4-quart saucepan** over medium heat. Add the lemongrass, galangal, cilantro, habanero, fish sauce, and lime juice and return to a simmer. Add the catfish and coconut milk and cook for 4 to 5 minutes, until the fish is just cooked through. Remove from the heat and serve immediately.

SOUTHERN FRIED CATFISH

6 CATFISH FILLETS

What all the Southerners have been waiting for. And believe you me when I tell you this is my favorite *Good Eats* fish application of all time.

// SOFTWARE

1	quart	peanut oil	
1	cup	stone-ground cornmeal	
1	cup	all-purpose flour	
1	teaspoon	Old Bay seasoning	
½	teaspoon	kosher salt	
¼	teaspoon	hot smoked paprika	
¼	teaspoon	black pepper	freshly ground
6	7- to 9-ounce	U.S. farm-raised catfish fillets	rinsed and thoroughly patted dry
¾	cup	low-fat buttermilk	

// PROCEDURE

1. Heat the oil in a **5-quart Dutch oven** over high heat until it reaches 350°F on a **deep-frying thermometer**. Adjust the heat to maintain the temperature.

2. **Whisk** the cornmeal and flour together in a **shallow dish**. Combine the Old Bay, salt, paprika, and pepper in a **small bowl**. Season the catfish fillets evenly on both sides with the spice mixture. Pour the buttermilk into another **shallow dish**. Dip each fillet into the buttermilk, flip once to coat both sides, hold over the pan, and allow the excess to drip off. Coat both sides of the fillets in the cornmeal mixture. Set the coated fillets on a **cooling rack** and let rest for 5 minutes.

3. Gently add the fillets, two at a time, to the hot oil and fry for 5 to 6 minutes, until golden brown. Remove to a **cooling rack** set over a **half sheet pan lined with newspaper**. Repeat with the remaining fillets. Serve right away—as in immediately.

FRY THAT CATFISH!

THE CATFISH SHALL RISE AGAIN

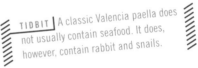

I'm the first to admit that paella falls well outside the generally accepted jurisdiction of *Good Eats*. Not only are specialized hardware, software, and skills required in order to properly prepare one, but most of us have never even tasted an honest-to-goodness specimen. So why bother? Because if you do bother to acquire the hardware, the software, and the skills, paella is just about the tastiest and easiest kitchen trick you can turn.

TIDBIT | A classic Valencia paella does not usually contain seafood. It does, however, contain rabbit and snails.

KNOWLEDGE CONCENTRATE

▷○ Besides advanced road-building techniques, aqueducts, and the like, Romans, who also conquered and ruled most of the Iberian peninsula between 218 and 17 B.C., introduced a woklike vessel called a *patella*, which had a curved rather than flat bottom and was intended for frying. Eventually Rome receded, only to be replaced by the Moors, a mixture of Islamic peoples from northern Africa, including some of Arab and Berber descent. The Moors brought sophisticated agricultural practices to the region, including irrigation, and a host of new crops, from oranges to saffron to rice, which was planted all around Valencia, where it grows to this day. Eventually Christian armies hoping to spread the smelly medievalism of the Dark Ages over Spain's culture of science, education, art, and enlightenment, ran the Moors slap out of town, but the rice and the paella (the dish and the pan) remained.

Paella comes from the Latin *patella*, meaning "plate." It's also where we get our word for kneecap, patella, which looks a little like a paella—from a distance. I only mention this because calling a paella a "paella pan" would be like calling it a "pan pan." The paella is unique in several ways:

1. It's made of high-carbon steel, so it's a very speedy conductor of heat, much faster than stainless steel, but like cast iron it will rust if it's not cared for properly.

2. Unlike most quality cookware, the paella is extremely light, almost flimsy in construction, and it won't heat evenly unless it's placed over a very wide, even heat source.

3. Paella come in sixteen standard sizes ranging from a Lilliputian eight inches up to fifty-two inches, which is seven inches wider than the gong John Bonham whomped on during Zeppelin's '77 tour, and I know because I was there. What's more, paella always have two wide loop handles, but never a lid. It's an oddball, and yet not a unitasker.

Most Americans are familiar with long-grain or indica rices, which are much longer than they are wide and have the habit of cooking up light, fluffy, and separate due to a very specific ratio of amylopectin and amylose starch molecules. The rice the Moors planted in Spain was a medium-grain, japonica rice, which contains a much higher percentage of amylopectin. This allows the rice to remain firm even when cooked, and it promotes stickiness to boot.

Thanks to the Internet, American cooks can choose from a wide range of authentic European rices for their paella, starting with Spanish rices. Although the famed Arroz Bomba from Murcia is considered *the* boutique paella rice of Spain, it's technically short-grain rice and is, to my taste, too darned sticky for paella.

Arroz de Valencia isn't a variety per se, but rather a mixture of Senia and Bahia rices—and fine paella fodder it is.

My favorite, however, is Calasparra, which is easily identified by the distinctive cloth sack it comes in.

If you can't lay in Spanish rice, you can squeeze by with an Italian Arborio, but keep in mind, these can be very, very sticky to work with, so hedge your bets with Vialone Nano from the Veneto region, which I would argue is the least sticky of all Italian varieties.

As previously noted, the paella—the pan—is thin carbon steel and must be positioned over a very even heat source if it is to perform properly. That's actually tough to pull off in the modern American kitchen, which is why I make all my paella in the Spanish style: outside, over fire. In Spain orange tree trimmings and grape vines are the fuel of choice, but if you're out, lump charcoal will do just fine. Have a gas grill? Crank your grill to high and keep it there. It may take a little longer, but your patience will be rewarded.

All paella begin with a sofrito, which like the Creole trinity or the French mirepoix is actually a mixture of aromatic vegetables. In this case, both green and red bell peppers are chopped and cooked down in the presence of garlic and grated tomatoes.

15 INCHES OF PURE CARBON STEEL

TIDBIT The largest paella in the world was made with a twenty-one-meter pan, and it fed 110,000 people.

6 TO 8 SERVINGS

// SOFTWARE

1	pound	tomatoes	
9	cups	low-sodium chicken broth	
3	cups	short- or medium-grain rice	
20	threads	saffron	
2	sprigs	fresh rosemary	leaves stripped from sprigs
3	teaspoons	kosher salt	
1	teaspoon	smoked sweet paprika	
2	tablespoons	olive oil	
3	pounds	chicken thighs and legs	bone-in, skin on
½	pound	fresh green beans	trimmed and broken in half
1	cup	red bell pepper	chopped
½	cup	green bell pepper	chopped
2	cloves	garlic	minced

TIP | Grating whole tomatoes may seem odd, but it's actually a fine method for reducing the pulp to a fine puree while leaving the skin behind.

// SPECIAL HARDWARE

Chimney starter, newspaper, vegetable oil in a spritz bottle, 4 pounds natural lump charcoal, 15-inch carbon-steel paella pan

// PROCEDURE

1. **Spritz** 4 or 5 pieces of **newspaper** with oil and place in the bottom of a **chimney charcoal starter**. Fill the chimney with half of the **charcoal** and light the newspaper.

2. When the charcoal is lightly covered with gray ash, carefully pour it onto the bottom grate of a **kettle grill** and spread evenly. Top with the remaining unlit charcoal, spreading evenly so as not to suffocate the lit charcoal. Set the second grate in the kettle and cover until ready to cook.

3. Meanwhile, halve the tomatoes and remove the seeds to a **fine-mesh sieve** set over a **small bowl** to catch the juice. Grate the seeded halves on the large holes of a **box grater** and discard the skins. Combine the reserved juice and grated tomato and set aside.

4. Warm the broth in a **kettle or 4-quart saucepan** over high heat until it reaches 200°F. Remove from the heat and cover to keep warm.

5. Combine the rice, saffron, rosemary, 1 teaspoon of the salt, and the paprika in a **small bowl** and stir.

6. Heat the oil in the **paella pan** on the prepared grill. Season the chicken on all sides with the remaining 2 teaspoons salt. Once the oil shimmers, add the chicken and cook until golden brown on both sides, 5 to 6 minutes per side. Move the chicken to the outer edges of the pan. Add the beans, red bell pepper, green bell pepper, and garlic to the center of the pan and cook until they begin to soften and darken in color, 2 to 3 minutes. Add the tomatoes and their juice and cook until most of the liquid has dissipated and the tomatoes thicken and darken, 4 to 5 minutes.

7. Add the rice mixture to the center of the pan and cook, stirring constantly, for 1 minute. Redistribute the chicken pieces on top of the rice. Add 4 cups of the warm broth and stir to distribute the rice evenly in the pan, making sure that all the rice is completely submerged in liquid. From this point forward do not stir the paella.

8. After 8 to 9 minutes, when all of the liquid is absorbed and the rice appears dry, add an additional 4 cups broth. Continue to cook for another 8 to 9 minutes, without stirring, until the liquid is absorbed, the rice is just firm to the bite, and the grains have a tiny white dot in the center. Add the remaining cup of broth, as needed, until the rice is cooked through. Watch the fire to make sure it is heating evenly and adjust the pan to prevent uneven cooking.

9. Remove the pan from the heat, cover with a **tea towel**, and rest for 15 minutes before serving.

TIDBIT True paella fans cherish the crust, or *socarrat*, that forms on the bottom of the pan.

TIDBIT A special tribunal called the Safranschau was formed to "deal" with shady saffron dealers in fifteenth-century Germany.

SAFFRON

A paella is just rice in a paella with at least twenty stigmas of the fall-flowering crocus, which the Moors called *sahafarn*, a mash-up of their words for "thread" and "yellow." The more popular name is *saffron*, and it just happens to be the most expensive food on earth.

These little stigmas are essentially the bits of botanical plumbing that pollen goes down for reproductive purposes. They contain a curious and powerful aromatic compound called safranal; a pungent, woodsy, bittersweet flavorant called picrocrocin; and a potent pigment, which has been used to dye the robes of kings and high priestesses for millennia. Getting at these stigmas is a laborious process, and since each flower has only three of them, it takes about seventy thousand flowers to produce a finished pound of saffron. It's no surprise that saffron has a long history of adulteration, so it helps to know what you're looking for and at. In Spanish *mancha* or Iranian *pashol* grades, the stigma will be connected to the yellow style, a kind of tube that holds up the stigma. Although the style is flavorless, its presence in the saffron is a sure sign that it hasn't been dyed. The styles have been picked away in Spanish and Kashmiri *coupé* grades and in Iranian *sargols*, which means they will cost more and, unfortunately, are easier to fake. How do you avoid being ripped off? Remember that the real stuff will always be expensive and fragrant, and it quickly turns hot water bright yellow after only a few minutes while the stigmas themselves remain very distinct. If the stigmas fall apart or turn mushy, the quality is . . . not so good. It may even be fake. My advice: Buy small portions, say half a gram at a time, of Spanish or Iranian saffron. Those are usually the most controlled. Buy from a reliable Internet source. Once you take possession, keep saffron in cool, dry, dark, airtight containment.

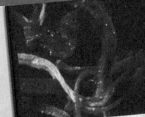

THE PORTERHOUSE RULES

There's a scene at the beginning of *Raiders of the Lost Ark* where Indiana Jones and the treacherous (and short-lived) porter Sapito are standing in the vestibule to the Hovitos Idol chamber. They're looking down this long, open hall at an amazing gold figure just sitting on an altar, waiting for them. Sapito starts forward, saying, "We must hurry. There is nothing to fear here." Jones, knowing better, pushes the other man against the wall, eyes the prize, and utters, "That's what scares me." Turns out the entire chamber is booby-trapped, and Jones barely makes it out alive.

This is exactly how I feel about steak. It's so simple; it's right there, and it's an American right—no, an American *rite*. And yet obtaining that shiny idol can be very tricky indeed, particularly when the steak in question is a porterhouse. I suspect that's why most folks choose to leave its care and cooking to professionals who charge up to a hundred bucks a slab.

Can the perfect porterhouse be attained by the home cook? Oh, yes, my friends. But you're going to have to go outside and you're going to have to obtain one special piece of equipment. But don't worry, it's small and cheap and oh so worth it.

KNOWLEDGE CONCENTRATE

▷○ **To unravel the mystery of the porterhouse we need only examine the factors that are often the big sell points for top-drawer steakhouses, namely:**

Prime beef	Dry aged
Grass fed	Seared "to perfection" under a 1600° to 1800°F broiler.

▷○ **The porterhouse itself is precious in large part because of its location, the short loin, which is as far from hoof and horn as you can get. This cushy neighborhood is home to the large loin, or back muscle, and the coveted tenderloin, which does about zero work all day and is therefore exquisitely tender due to an utter lack of connective tissue. Besides the T-shaped spine bone arrangement, there is very little connective tissue to complicate the meatscape, and yet not all the steaks cut from this area are the same. One must consider the fact that the tenderloin is a tapering muscle. Small in the front and big in the back, and the loin, although consistent in size and shape, is completely clear of connective tissue at one end, but not quite at the other.**

To be graded as "prime," the steer in question must be relatively young, between eighteen and twenty-four months, and the flesh must be deeply marbled, meaning that the meat itself contains a fair amount of intramuscular fat—that is, flecks and streaks of fat within the meat tissue that when cooked delivers a very succulent mouthfeel. Although some top-end butcher shops occasionally offer prime beef, most of it goes directly to high-end steakhouses, which is fine by me because I prefer choice-grade cuts, which contain less fat and taste even beefier.

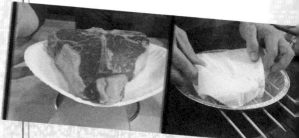

The U.S. government says: "In the porterhouse, the minimum width of the tenderloin shall be at least one point two five inches when measured parallel to the length of the back bone."

Do not be seduced by a porterhouse with a gigantor slab of tenderloin, because the loin section will no doubt contain considerable connective tissue. Go for a cut from the middle of the short loin with a clear-looking strip and a medium-size tenderloin.

What's in a name?

NATURAL means that the beef has been minimally processed and contains no additives, such as artificial flavors, colors, and preservatives. There is no reason on earth for any steak to not be "natural."

BRANDED BEEF, e.g. "certified red longhorn," may have to live up to stringent guidelines, but that doesn't mean it's better.

CERTIFIED ORGANIC beef comes from cows that have been raised on organic feed. They cannot be treated with antibiotics, and they must be certified as organic by the government. This means you're going to pay more for it. Will it be better? Not necessarily.

GRASS FINISHED doesn't really mean anything to the government or anyone else.

GRASS FED means that once the animal is weaned off of mother's milk, it eats only grass—which, by the way, is what God designed cattle to eat. Most of the beef cattle raised in the United States are indeed raised on grass, but they're then finished in feed lots, where they spend their last weeks—or months even—being fattened up on corn, which also "standardizes" the flavor. I call this the blandification of beef, which most of us have been trained to like.

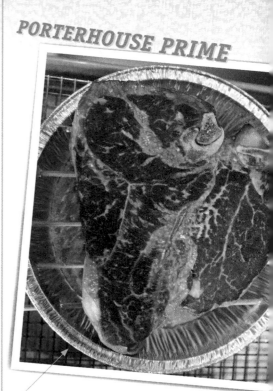

PORTERHOUSE PRIME

Top-drawer steakhouses have special climate-controlled rooms dedicated to aging primals and sub-primals that are then cut into steaks as needed. Why? For one thing, drying concentrates flavors by removing a fair amount of moisture from the meat. Enzymatic action is also brought to bear. Can you dry-age at home? Yes, but only if you're vewwy, vewwy careful.

My drying rig is constructed thusly: Stash your steak/drying rig in the bottom of your fridge, where it's the coldest and where it will remain isolated from other foods. Leave in place for twenty-four hours, then change out the paper towel, which will be wet and gooey. Store for another three days. Your patience will be rewarded.

High-end steakhouses don't use grills. They use powerful broilers. A simple device, really: Gas flames superheat ceramic elements capable of generating radiant energy in the 2500°F range. The drawer comes out, steak goes on the drawer, steak goes under the broiler, and in no time at all you have yourself a beautifully seared piece of meat. Such ordinance is heavy and expensive, but luckily we can fake it for about twenty bucks.

RESTAURANT BROILER

VERY HOT...BUT PRICEY

DRY-AGING

Consider the inner workings of living muscle. It's complex machinery that, upon expiration of the animal, grinds to a halt. For a short while, immediately following the critter's demise, the meat remains loose and tender, but then rigor mortis sets in and things get pretty tough. However, over time, natural chemical catalysts called enzymes go to work. Like a wrench, enzymes have specific shapes that bond with specific molecules. Once in place, the enzyme can either unite unrelated molecules or dismantle certain structures, such as the ones that toughen meat. The more time you give the enzymes to work, the more tender the meat gets, but only, of course, if the proper temperature and moisture level are maintained.

The salt is going to pull moisture out of the meat. But it's not just moisture, it's protein-laden moisture that, when brought to the surface, will help to enhance the searing process.

// **SOFTWARE** //

1	1¼-inch-thick	porterhouse steak	preferably grass fed
¾	teaspoon	kosher salt	

// **SPECIAL HARDWARE** //

Newspaper, vegetable oil in a spritz bottle, natural lump charcoal, chimney charcoal starter

// **PROCEDURE** ///

1. Wrap the steak in a single layer of **paper towel** and place on a **cooling rack** set inside a **half sheet pan**. Refrigerate in the coldest part of your refrigerator for 24 hours.

2. Discard the paper towel, rewrap, and return to the refrigerator, on the rack, for 3 days. Change the paper towel again if it becomes damp and sticks to the steak.

3. Remove the steak from the refrigerator 1 hour before cooking. Unwrap, and discard the paper towel. Thirty minutes before cooking, sprinkle the steak on both sides with the salt.

4. **Spritz** 2 pieces of **newspaper** lightly with oil and place in the bottom of a **chimney charcoal starter**. Place a pound of **natural lump charcoal** in the chimney starter and set it on the grate of a charcoal grill. Burn the coals for 11 to 15 minutes, or until all the pieces are ashen and have decreased to a single layer of charcoal with several holes through which you can see.

TIDBIT │ One of Mark Twain's favorite meals was pan-fried porterhouse steak with mushrooms and peas.

PHASE 1

Hot coals

Porterhouse steak

Fireproof material

5. Carefully shake the chimney to knock any ash off the coals. Pick up the chimney and brush away any coals or ash that have fallen onto the grate. Lay the steak on the grate where the chimney was. Place the chimney over the steak and cook for 1½ minutes. Watch for coals that may fall out of the chimney onto the steak and remove immediately.

6. Remove the chimney, flip the steak, and replace the chimney for another 1½ minutes. Place a second **grill grate or a cooling rack** on top of the chimney to heat during this time.

7. Carefully remove the steak from under the chimney and place on the second grate or cooling rack. Cover with a **medium metal bowl** and cook for 1 minute. Flip the steak, re-cover with the bowl, and cook for an additional 1 minute, or until the steak reaches an internal temperature of 120° to 125°F. Remove the steak from the chimney and rest on the cooling rack set inside a clean **half sheet pan**, uncovered, for 5 minutes. Slice and serve.

PHASE 2

Almost-finished porterhouse steak

Grill grate

Dying coals

Fireproof material

WHO THE HECK WAS "PORTER" AND WHAT'S WITH HIS "HOUSE"?

In the eighteenth century, a peculiarly dark and particularly strong beer became so popular with street and river porters in London that it eventually took their name: porter! A sixteen-ounce glass of this stuff was, at the time, the safest, fastest, most nutritious drink you could down. In fact, porter was really kind of the energy drink of its age. The establishments that catered to porters were called porterhouses, and such establishments sprang up along the waterways of London, and eventually New York. Porterhouses were equally popular with sailors, river pilots, and the like, who often dropped by after docking for a pint and a roasted hunk of critter. According to the respected New York author, historian, and "prince of butchers," Colonel Thomas F. Devaeux, once upon a time (in 1814), a crusty old river pilot entered a porterhouse owned by one Martin Morrison on Pearl Street in New York City.

Having sold out of the evening joint (that's what they used to call the big hunk of meat), Morrison hastily cut a slab from the back of a large loin roast, meant for the next day, a hunk that probably included a goodly portion of short loin, tenderloin, and whatnot. He fried it up, he served it up, and from that night on, Morrison asked his butcher to cut all his roasts into steaks for the "porterhouse."

GRILLUS DOMESTICUS

EPISODE 229 | SEASON 14 | GOOD EATS

If you own and operate a grill, sooner or later you're gonna attempt to grill a chicken. For red, white, and blue-blooded American cooks, it is simply inevitable. And yet, despite whatever firepower you may have amassed or skills you think you have attained, the meeting of *Gallus domesticus* and *Grillus americanus* can—and often does—result in culinary disaster. This is because the chicken, intact or in parts, is simply not grill friendly.

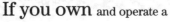

KNOWLEDGE CONCENTRATE

Grill-friendly foods are flat and uniformly shaped, which aids even cooking. They are lean. Although fat can lubricate meat fibers, it's a carbon-based energy-storage medium, and as such is highly flammable, which is why fatty grilled foods often arrive at table covered in soot. Grill-friendly foods are moist. Moisture is important, as it prevents burning while helping to conduct heat inward. At the same time, it can also push outward, taking sear-producing proteins with it, and this means that the food in question also needs to be at least somewhat porous for that moisture to move around. Now consider the chicken.

There are bones and joints everywhere. It's a griller's nightmare, because no matter how or where you cut it, uniformity and flatness are not to be achieved. And although the meat is moist, around 66 percent water, you just know that with all those bones and joints the meat is shot through with connective tissue, some of which will never soften . . . ever. And let's not forget the meat inside the breast. This anaerobic, fast-twitch musculature is suited to brief periods of wing flapping—ergo, it cooks at a very different rate than the leg muscles, which are composed of aerobic slow-twitch fibers meant for meandering. Oh, lest we forget, the whole package is wrapped up in a layer of skin, under which is housed a powerful accelerant: fat.

Since I like cutting things up, I typically opt for a whole chicken, which gives me the right parts at the right price, but if you just want breasts or thighs or legs or wings, buying piece by piece is an okay way to go. (Although in most cases you will pay for the fact that someone else is doing the cutting.)

"Roasting" chickens in the 5- to 7-pound range are, to my mind, too hefty for the grill because even with careful heat management the exterior tends to burn before the interior hits a safe temp. At 2½ to 4½ pounds, the "broiler" is just right for grilling.

This procedure produces 6 pieces: 2 legs (drumsticks), 2 thighs, and 2 "airline" breasts.[1]

Lay the chicken on a plastic cutting board breast side up, with the neck facing you. Remove both wings at the joint between the wing and drummette. Remove the thigh quarters by slicing down on either side of the back end of the breast. Grab both legs, pop the joints that connect to the back, and turn the bird over. Remove the thighs and legs by slicing where they attach to the backbone. Hold the thigh and leg together, feel for the slight indentation where the joints meet, and make an incision at this joint. Set the leg and thigh down and slice to separate. Repeat with the other leg piece. Turn the bird back over, breast side up, place your knife against the breastbone, and slice down along the rib cage, cutting the breast meat away from the bone. Follow the meat down along the ribs. Be sure to include the drummette when removing the breast. Repeat on the other breast.

Raw muscle, such as that in our chicken, is about 20 percent protein. In their raw state, proteins, which are just long chains of amino acids, appear as tight little bundles or balls, signified by these ball bearings. Sixty-six percent, give or take a few points, of **the muscle is actually water, into which a candy box of carbohydrates and minerals are dissolved. (Standing in for that moisture here is motor oil.) When we apply heat to the chicken, the meat fibers contract, heat energy excites the moisture, and it starts to push outward, toward the surface of the meat. On the one hand this is a good thing, because it can bring sear-worthy carbs and proteins to the surface of the meat. But if we're not careful, we push too hard and out goes the moisture, leaving us with dry, gritty fibers. In this first example, the protein didn't really do us any great favors. Soaking the meat in a brine, however, unfurls—or denatures—some of the proteins, so that instead of separate balls we have a tangled mesh (here being played by steel wool).**

When you cook this piece of meat, the mesh acts as a barrier, trapping some of that moisture inside, where we want it. And don't forget that the honey we add to the brine is hygroscopic, which means it will hold on to water tightly. By brining meat, we get our juiciness insurance policy and a nice little hit of flavor to boot.

If we're to overcome irregular shapes, connective tissue, and flammable fat, we must embrace bi-level cookery—that is, a method by which we cook over high direct heat and then either low direct or indirect heat. Since this type of fire is a real pain to work with on a small grill, I developed the "ring of fire," which employs a ring of aluminum foil and a couple of pie pans to create two very different zones of heat that are especially easy to manage on a circular grill such as my Weber Kettle.[2]

[1] A breast that has been cut clear of the ribs and keel bone but that still has the first wing bone (drummette) intact is referred to as an "airline" breast because it was once popular with airline chefs back in the day, when first-class meals were actually edible.

[2] And no, they don't pay me to say that. I'm just a fan.

RING OF FIRE GRILLED CHICKEN

4 SERVINGS

// SOFTWARE //

1	4- to 5-pound	broiler/fryer chicken	cut into 6 pieces
1	quart	H_2O	
½	cup	honey	
3½	ounces	kosher salt	about ¾ cup
1	tablespoon	curry powder	
1	tablespoon	chili powder	
2	teaspoons	cocoa powder	Dutch process
1	teaspoon	adobo powder without pepper	
1	teaspoon	ground cumin	
1	teaspoon	hot smoked paprika	

// SPECIAL HARDWARE //

Newspaper, vegetable oil in a spritz bottle, 2 to 3 pounds natural lump charcoal, chimney charcoal starter, 8 feet heavy-duty aluminum foil, 2 aluminum pie pans

// PROCEDURE ///

(1) Put the chicken pieces in a **1-gallon zip-top bag** with the water, honey, and salt. Seal the bag and move it around vigorously for 1 to 2 minutes to distribute the honey and dissolve the salt. Set the bag in a **leakproof container** and refrigerate for 1½ hours.

(2) Meanwhile, combine the curry powder, chili powder, cocoa powder, adobo powder, cumin, and paprika in **another 1-gallon zip-top bag**.

(3) Thoroughly drain the chicken, and pat very dry with **paper towels**. Do not rinse.

(4) Put the chicken in the bag with the spice mixture and shake to thoroughly coat the chicken. Lay the pieces on a **cooling rack** set inside a **half sheet pan**. Rest for 30 minutes.

(5) **Spritz** 2 pieces of **newspaper** lightly with oil and place in the bottom of a **chimney charcoal starter**. Fill the **chimney starter** with **natural lump charcoal**, 2 to 3 pounds, and set on the **bottom grate** of a **kettle grill**. Light the paper and heat until the coals are hot and ashy, 15 to 20 minutes. Prepare a ring of **heavy-duty aluminum foil** with the center 9 inches in diameter. Place this ring over the chimney starter and lay it on the charcoal grate.

6. Carefully and evenly distribute the hot charcoal outside the ring. Set an **aluminum pie pan** in the center of the ring to catch any drippings. Set the **cooking grate** in place and heat for 2 to 3 minutes.

7. Lightly oil the cooking grate. Arrange the chicken pieces, skin side down, on the grate over the hot coals. Turn the legs a quarter-turn every 3 to 4 minutes. Turn the thighs, wings, and breasts after 4 to 5 minutes. The skin should blister and darken in color. Adjust the intensity of heat by turning the grill grate to expose chicken pieces to cooler or hotter coals as needed and to avoid flare-ups.[3]

8. After 9 to 10 minutes total, move the breast to the center of the grill and cover with a **second aluminum pie pan**. After 10 to 11 minutes total, place the wings on top of the pie pan and lean the thighs and legs against the side of the aluminum pie pan away from the direct heat of the coals. Turn every 2 minutes. Place any pieces that finish cooking on top of the pie pan. After 18 to 20 minutes total, check the temperature with a probe thermometer inserted in the deepest part of each piece. The pieces should reach 155°F.

9. Remove the chicken to a **clean medium bowl**. Cover with a **tea towel** and rest for 5 minutes.

10. To serve, place the breast on a cutting board with the narrow end facing you and slice, leaving a small piece of meat connected at the wing end so that the meat can be fanned thusly on the plate:

    Or, simply pick it up with your fingers and dig in.

[3] The grill spin is a great maneuver but can be achieved only on a round grill—something to think about when purchasing.

TRIVIA | Yes, my grilling chair is made from an old grill that I couldn't bear to part with.

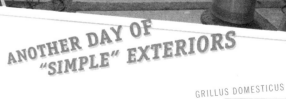

ANOTHER DAY OF "SIMPLE" EXTERIORS

SPEAR OF INFLUENCE

EPISODE 230 | SEASON 14 | GOOD EATS

There are a few things that I accept as part of everyday life that, if I didn't know better, I would assume had been dropped off by visiting aliens. The list includes: Surinam pipa toads, Prince (or the artist formerly known as), and *Asparagus officinalis*, the curious fernlike member of the lily family that seems to just jump out of the ground the first day of spring.

I speak of the king of vegetables and the vegetable of kings: asparagus. Although I myself am no king, after a long winter of root vegetables and hard squashes, I am seriously ready for the fresh green flavor of . . .

TIDBIT | California, Washington, and Michigan are the top asparagus growers in the United States.

TIDBIT | The Chinese used asparagus to treat arthritis, because asparagusic acid is a diuretic and can ease swelling.

NUTRITION

The Lady of the Refrigerator (LOTR) says: Besides potassium and thiamin and vitamins A and C and fiber, asparagus is a super source of folate, a water-soluble B-complex vitamin that plays a crucial role in RNA and DNA. Folate coenzymes are also very important for the synthesis of methionine, which, in turn, contributes to the synthesis of s-adenosyl methionine—a major player in methylation, which helps prevent cardiovascular disease and fight cancers. This is especially important for mommies-to-be because it can help prevent birth defects.

TIDBIT | In Belgium and France, they use etiolation, or light deprivation, to create chlorophyll-free white asparagus, which to my palate is so unbearably bitter and so outrageously expensive that I don't even want to talk about it.

324

The name *asparagus* comes from an ancient Persian word, *asparag*, which means "sprout," an apt title, seeing as how each of the shoots emanates from an underground root mass called a "crown." The root can live for up to twenty years and, in its prime, can push up shoots at an amazing rate of six to eight inches a day. At the start of the season, very thin shoots will come up. They're called sprue, and if you ask me they are watery and without substance, kinda like supermodels. The sprue are typically culled to make room for the thicker sprouts. The big, strong, stout stalks are vastly superior to the "pencil" asparagus spears that flood the markets in late spring.

You might wonder how something so juicy and delicious comes rocketing up out of the ground without a long growing season. This is possible because the very last of the season's sprouts are allowed to grow to a height of several feet. They then put out airy yellow fronds and turn themselves into carbohydrate engines, which reload the crown with the fuel it will need to make it through the winter and send up its goodness next spring.

As soon as a sprout is cut, it begins converting its sugars into fibers to reinforce the damaged end as the tip continues its ballistic growth. Even deeply chilled asparagus must be moved to market as quickly as possible, because the flavor goes downhill quickly. As an added challenge, the asparagus has to be shipped upright because it's negatively geotropic, meaning that the tips will bend to face whatever direction is up. So if you ever see bunches with bent tips, it means the asparagus was shipped or stored sideways. Nothing wrong with it other than that it looks kinda funny.

When purchasing bundles of asparagus (which can contain twelve to twenty-four stalks), always examine a core sample from the middle of the bundle. It should be bright green. The cut end may be a little fibrous, but should not be dry or cracked. The tip should be tight and compact, with no mushiness. Asparagus dries from the bottom and rots from the top. Examine the bunch for short stalks, which always seem to migrate mysteriously to the middle. Also beware of floppiness, a sure sign of age.

If you hope to store your asparagus for more than a few hours, treat the spears as the flowers they pretty much are. Take off any rubber bands, trim the bottoms by about half an inch, and place them in some form of vertical vessel with an inch of water. Set a plastic bag over the tops to prevent drying. But make sure there's room for air flow, as condensation will leave you with mushy tips—and mushy tips are never good eats.

Typically, asparagus must be trimmed of its woody lower stem. The problem is that the amount of material that needs pruning depends on the specific specimens under consideration. Traditionalists will tell you each spear will signal where it wants to be severed if you simply bend it to the break point. The problem is, I want my asparagus to be uniform in length. So, I rebundle it with a rubber band, measure the overall length, divide that by five, and that's how much I trim off. So if you have ten-inch spears, trim off two inches.

If the next inch is still a little on the woody side, I slice it into very, very thin rounds, for use in salads, soups, stocks, and so on. That leaves seven inches of asparagus for whatever the prime application might be.

TIDBIT | The ancient Greeks used asparagus to treat bee stings and toothaches.

TIDBIT | The ancient Roman emperor Augustus demanded that executions take place "quicker than you can cook asparagus."

Tip: Tight & Compact
Stalk: Bright & Stiff→
Cut End: ←Not Cracked Or Dry

TIP | Try to avail yourself of one of the many "pick your own" asparagus patches that spring up every year across this great country. Believe you me, asparagus doesn't get any better.

APPLICATION		STEAMED ASPARAGUS	

4 SERVINGS

// SOFTWARE //

¼	cup	H$_2$O	
1	pound	fresh asparagus	rinsed, 1 to 2 inches trimmed off the bottom
½	teaspoon	kosher salt	

// PROCEDURE //

Pour or **spritz** the water onto **4 paper towels**. Spread out the paper towels and lay the asparagus on top of the dampened towels. Sprinkle with the salt. Roll up the asparagus in the dampened towels. Lay the bundle, seam side down, in the **microwave**. Microwave on high power for 3 to 4 minutes, until the asparagus is just crisp tender. Remove from the microwave using **tongs** and carefully unwrap. Serve immediately.

APPLICATION		ROASTED ASPARAGUS	

4 SERVINGS

// SOFTWARE //

1	pound	fresh asparagus	rinsed, 1 to 2 inches trimmed off the bottom
1	tablespoon	olive oil	not extra virgin
1	medium	lemon	zested
½	teaspoon	kosher salt	
½	teaspoon	nutmeg	freshly grated
	to taste	black pepper	freshly ground

// PROCEDURE //

1. Heat the oven to 500°F.

2. Lay the asparagus on a long double layer of **heavy-duty aluminum foil**. Drizzle with the oil and toss to coat. Spread the spears into a single layer. Fold the edges of the foil to make a tray. Roast for 5 minutes. Carefully toss the spears with tongs and roast for another 5 minutes, or just until tender and the tips begin to brown. Sprinkle with the lemon zest, salt, nutmeg, and pepper and toss to evenly distribute. Serve immediately.

// SOFTWARE

2	teaspoons	unflavored gelatin	
2	tablespoons	cold water	
8	ounces	farmer's cheese or quark	at room temperature
8	ounces	cream cheese	at room temperature
3 to 5		jarred anchovies in olive oil	best quality, drained
7		fresh chives	chopped
½	teaspoon	black pepper	freshly ground
¼	cup	fresh flat-leaf parsley	roughly chopped
		Steamed Asparagus (opposite)	cooled

// PROCEDURE

(1) **Spritz** a **9-by-5-inch loaf pan** with water and line with **plastic wrap**, leaving enough excess to fold over the top when filled.

(2) Combine the gelatin and water in a **1-quart saucepan** and set aside to bloom for 5 minutes.

(3) Place the farmer's cheese, cream cheese, anchovies, chives, and pepper in a **food processor** and process for 1 minute. Stop and scrape down the sides of the bowl.

(4) Heat the bloomed gelatin over low heat for 1 minute, or until melted. Remove from the heat. With the food processor running, slowly pour the melted gelatin into the cheese mixture and process for 30 seconds.

(5) Sprinkle the parsley evenly across the bottom of the prepared loaf pan. Pour one-quarter of the cheese mixture over the parsley. Top with one-third of the asparagus in a single layer, alternating the direction of the tips. Repeat with the remaining cheese mixture and asparagus, ending with the cheese mixture. Fold the excess plastic wrap over the filling. Set a second loaf pan on top of the plastic wrap and press down to compact. Refrigerate for 2 hours, or until firm.

(6) Serve chilled, cut into 1-inch slices, along with crackers or toasted French bread slices. To store, wrap in plastic wrap and refrigerate for up to 2 days.

WHAT'S THAT SMELL?

If you've enjoyed asparagus as recently as half an hour prior to . . . uh . . . recycling your daily beverages, you will notice a peculiar and potentially potent aroma—or rather, some of you will. Despite significant scientific attempts to unravel the melodious mysteries of asparagus, confusion persists for two main reasons:

One: No one's been able to ascertain exactly which of the many complex compounds in asparagus is responsible for the job, so to speak. Two: Genetics seem to determine whether you are a smelly . . . excreter or not and whether you are a detector or a nondetector, in which case you don't even know what this conversation is about, which is probably a good thing.

Cutout One: I know what that smells like: methanethiol.

Cutout Two: No, you moron, that's asparagusic acid.

TIDBIT | The first commercially available powdered gelatin was introduced in 1890 by Charles B. Knox.

LITTLE BIG LUNCH: EGGS BENEDICT

EPISODE 231 | SEASON 14 | GOOD EATS

The history of food is fat with names we all know, like Clarence Birdseye, Milton Hershey, and Dr. Salisbury, but for each of these, a thousand unsung heroes languish in obscurity. Consider, for instance, Guy Beringer, who in 1895, while working for a curious little English magazine called *Hunter's Weekly*, penned this provocation: "Instead of England's early Sunday dinner, a post church ordeal of heavy meats and savory pies, why not a new meal, served around noon, beginning with tea or coffee. By eliminating the need to get up early on Sunday, brunch would make life brighter for Saturday night carousers." The essay was titled "Brunch: A Plea," and with it Beringer coined the term *brunch*, a portmanteau of "breakfast" and "lunch," and gave rise to our culture's last truly civilized meal. He went on: "Brunch is talk compelling. It puts you in a good temper. It makes you satisfied with yourself and your fellow beings. It sweeps away the worries and cob webs of the week."

Clearly Beringer intended for brunch to be prepared at home, and I, for one, agree. It's time we took brunch back from restaurants who have bushwhacked it with platters of pasty pastries, sticky steam-table Belgium waffles, and dried-up, grainy eggs Benedict. Speaking of, isn't it ironic that such an iconic dish, named for an infamous traitor, should suffer so at our hands? Well, I say the treachery stops here, because with just a few quality ingredients, a small smattering of science, and a mere dram of technical technique, eggs Benedict won't just be what's for brunch, it'll be . . .

ENGLISH MUFFINS

The English muffin is actually kin to the griddle-baked crumpet and was invented in 1880 by an English baker named Samuel Thomas in Chelsea—not London Chelsea, but New York City Chelsea. Yes, English muffins are technically American muffins. The muffins caught on quickly in fancy hotels, because they were so much easier to portion and toast than regular bread, which was still awaiting the invention of the mechanical bread slicer.

▷○ **Actually Benedict Arnold did not invent eggs Benedict, nor were they named for him. Truth is, no one's really sure where the dish got its name. The legendary food critic Craig Claiborne gave the cred to banker and yachtsman Commodore E.C. Benedict, who died in 1920 at the ripe old age of eighty-six, but not before inventing eggs Benedict. A likely story.**

Food scholar Evan Jones reports that back in the Gay Nineties, a hungover Wall Street stockbroker name of Lemuel Benedict had a habit of staggering into the Waldorf and ordering toast stacked with bacon, poached eggs, and a "gooseneck" of hollandaise, whatever that is. The Waldorf's chef at the time, Oscar Tschirky, supposedly changed the toast to an English muffin and put it on the menu.

And then there's the tale of Mrs. LeGrand Benedict, who, when unable to find anything she wanted on the menu at New York's Delmonico's, summoned Chef Charles Ranhofer. After a brief consultation, he whipped up the very first eggs Benedict just for her. In his 1894 tome, *The Epicurean*, Ranhofer does include a recipe for eggs "à la benedick": "Slice muffins crosswise, toast without browning, place round of ham on each, top with poached egg, sauce with hollandaise." Sounds like eggs Benedict to me.

▷○ **Any fan of this show will no doubt notice that on various occasions we have dabbled with, well, three of the four components listed here. That said, when attempting to align them together on the same plate at the same time, adaptation and innovation are required, starting, of course, with the muffins.**

Although the original griddle-cooked English muffins are more authentic, the baked ones are a lot easier to work with.

YEAST-BASED EGGS BENEDICT FOUNDATION PLATFORMS

8 MUFFINS

// SOFTWARE ///

12	ounces	all-purpose flour	
1½	ounces	nonfat dry milk	
1	tablespoon	sugar	
1	envelope	active dry yeast	
1	teaspoon	kosher salt	
10	ounces	H_2O	
1	tablespoon	vegetable shortening	
8	teaspoons	quick-cooking rolled oats	

// SPECIAL HARDWARE ///

8 (3¾-inch-diameter by 2-inch-tall) cans with tops and bottoms removed or 8 English muffin rings

// PROCEDURE ///

1. Combine the flour, dry milk, sugar, yeast, and salt in the bowl of a **stand mixer fitted with the paddle attachment**. Mix on low speed for 10 seconds.

2. Put the water and shortening in a **microwavable container** and heat to 120° to 130°F, about 2 minutes. Stir until the shortening is thoroughly melted. Add the water mixture to the dry ingredients and mix on medium speed for 3 minutes, or until well combined, stopping to scrape down the bowl halfway through mixing. Cover the bowl with **plastic wrap** and refrigerate overnight.

3. Remove the dough from the refrigerator, uncover, and mix on medium speed, using the paddle attachment, for 3 minutes.

4. Position the 8 cans on a **half sheet pan** and generously spray the rings and pan with **nonstick cooking spray**. Sprinkle ½ teaspoon of the oats in the bottom of each ring. Scoop the dough with a **2-ounce disher** into the rings, dividing the dough evenly among the rings. Sprinkle each top with ½ teaspoon oats. Cover with **parchment paper** and set in a warm place for 60 minutes.

5. Heat the oven to 400°F.

6. Leave the parchment in place and set a **second half sheet pan** on top. Bake for 20 minutes, then remove the top half sheet pan. Continue to bake for an additional 5 to 10 minutes, or until the muffins reach an internal temperature of 210°F and are lightly browned.

7. Remove the pan, with the muffins still in the rings, to a cooling rack for 10 minutes. Slide a **small offset spatula or paring knife** around the perimeter of the ring to loosen. Cool completely before splitting with a **fork**.

Let's say it's the morning of your brunch, and you have an hour to prep. You've made the English muffins; what are you going to do next? It depends on how many people we're talking about. If you're making brunch for two, then I'd probably make the hollandaise and then poach the eggs right before service. If you have six, eight, ten people, do you really want to poach twelve, sixteen, or even twenty eggs at the last minute? Luckily there is a way to perfectly poach a mess of eggs.

// SOFTWARE //

4	quarts	H_2O	
¼	cup	distilled white vinegar	
1	teaspoon	kosher salt	
8	large	eggs	

// PROCEDURE //

(1) Place **4 (6-ounce) custard cups** in a **deep 6-quart straight-sided sauté pan or rondeau**. Add 4 quarts water or enough to cover the cups by at least ¼ inch. Add the vinegar and salt to the water and place the pan over high heat. Heat just until the water begins to boil and the cups clatter against the bottom of the pan, 20 to 25 minutes.

(2) Adjust the heat to maintain a water temperature of 205°F outside the cups. Break the eggs one at a time into another **custard cup or ladle**. Pour the eggs slowly into each of the cups, timing them about 10 seconds apart. Cook for 5 minutes each.

(3) Serve immediately or remove the eggs from the cups and transfer them to an **ice-water bath** to stop the cooking. Refrigerate for up to 6 hours in the ice bath.

WHEN IT COMES TO POACHING EGGS, TIME AND TEMPERATURE ARE EVERYTHING.

HOLLANDAISE SAUCE

1¼ CUPS

Of course, eggs B isn't eggs B without hollandaise, a rich, savory stirred custard probably created in France in the eighteenth century. The original name was probably sauce à la hollandaise and referred to the high-quality butters of Holland. Why the French, who typically ignore any ingredient from outside their own borders, would make such a nomenclatural allowance is beyond me, but I'm betting it had to do with visiting dignitaries or a big, fat business deal.

You'll notice that this procedure is more akin to that of a lemon curd than a typical hollandaise, but I find that it gives me better texture with almost zero chance of breaking.

// SOFTWARE ///

3	large	egg yolks	
1	tablespoon	H$_2$O	
¼	teaspoon	kosher salt	plus extra to taste
½	teaspoon	ground cayenne	
8	ounces	unsalted butter	cut into 16 pieces and chilled
3 to 4	tablespoons	lemon juice	freshly squeezed and strained
¼	teaspoon	sugar	

// PROCEDURE ///

1. **Whisk** together the egg yolks, water, salt, and ¼ teaspoon of the cayenne in a **2-quart saucier** for 1 minute.

2. Place the saucier over low heat and whisk vigorously, moving the pan on and off the heat every 10 to 15 seconds, until the mixture reaches 140° to 145°F, about 3 minutes. Add one piece of butter at a time every 30 seconds, while continually whisking and moving the saucier on and off the heat. Maintain the temperature at 120° to 130°F throughout the remainder of the cooking process. When half of the butter, or 8 pieces, have been added, add 1 tablespoon of the lemon juice. Add the remaining 8 pieces of butter, one every 30 seconds, while continuing to move the saucier on and off the heat and maintaining 120° to 130°F. After the last piece of butter has been added, add 1 tablespoon lemon juice, the remaining ¼ teaspoon cayenne, and the sugar and whisk for 1 to 2 minutes.

3. Taste and add more lemon juice as desired. Move immediately to a **short, wide-mouthed Thermos** to hold for up to 2 hours. Reheat over low heat for 45 seconds.

A good Thermos will keep hollandaise hot for hours.

4 SERVINGS

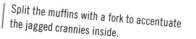

Split the muffins with a fork to accentuate the jagged crannies inside.

// SOFTWARE ///

8	slices	Canadian bacon	julienned
4		Yeast-Based Eggs Benedict Foundation Platforms (page 330)	split
8		Poached Eggs (page 331)	
		Hollandaise Sauce (left)	

// PROCEDURE //

1. Put the Canadian bacon in a **10-inch sauté pan** over medium heat. Cook, stirring frequently, until heated through and beginning to turn lightly brown around the edges, 4 to 5 minutes. Remove from the heat, but leave the bacon in the pan to keep warm until serving.

2. Toast the platforms under the **broiler** for 3 to 4 minutes.

3. To reheat the poached eggs, return the water to a simmer, remove from the heat, and add the eggs. Wait 1 to 2 minutes or until warmed through.

4. For each serving, place two small drops of hollandaise on a plate and set one half of a platform on top of each. Put a small amount of bacon on top of each half. Top each half with 1 warm poached egg and a spoonful of hollandaise. Serve immediately.

Use a steamer basket to lower and retrieve reheated eggs.

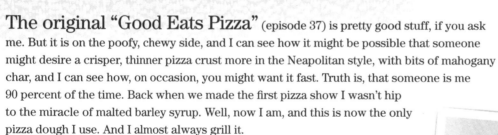

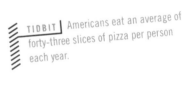

The original "Good Eats Pizza" (episode 37) is pretty good stuff, if you ask me. But it is on the poofy, chewy side, and I can see how it might be possible that someone might desire a crisper, thinner pizza crust more in the Neapolitan style, with bits of mahogany char, and I can see how, on occasion, you might want it fast. Truth is, that someone is me 90 percent of the time. Back when we made the first pizza show I wasn't hip to the miracle of malted barley syrup. Well, now I am, and this is now the only pizza dough I use. And I almost always grill it.

TIDBIT | Americans eat an average of forty-three slices of pizza per person each year.

TIDBIT | Al Fomo, a restaurant in Providence, Rhode Island, is credited with serving the first grilled pizza in the United States.

KNOWLEDGE CONCENTRATE

When it comes to yeast-leavened breads, like pizza dough, a long, cold rise always produces better flavor and texture because cold decelerates the life cycle of yeast so that they produce flavor compounds and CO_2 at a slower rate, allowing the dough time to absorb the goodness. That said, there might just be one particular ingredient that we can invite to the party that might grant us slow-rise flavors at fast-rise rates, not to mention temperatures.

Barley syrup is produced according to these simple steps:

1. Barley grain is allowed to sprout, or germinate, in water. Germination sets enzymes into motion, which converts the grain's starch reserves into a double-glucose sugar, maltose.

2. The grain is then kiln-dried and mixed with water as well as other cooked grain products, which are gobbled up by the enzyme.[1]

3. A slurry is extracted and then boiled down into a syrup.

The really important thing about maltose is that, unlike sucrose and glucose, yeasts can break it down very slowly, which means that when we lead our dough into its second rise, the little boogers will still have plenty to eat, and that means they'll still produce CO_2.

Nine times out of ten, when I'm making a yeast-risen dough I reach for bread flour because it contains more gluten-forming protein and will therefore create a more elastic dough. But what I want here is pliancy and speed, so I use all-purpose flour because its protein content is a little lower.

The words "instant" or "rapid rise" on a container of yeast refer to the speed at which the yeasts get to work. A great majority of the yeasts in packets of "active dry" are actually flat-out dead. Instant and rapid-rise specimens are processed in such a way that more yeasts are "not quite dead yet" and they're packaged with a shot of ascorbic acid (vitamin C), which gives them a little boost as they wake up. Instant/rapid yeasts do not have to be soaked or "proofed" before they go into a dough, which is nice.

Why the grill? The problem with home ovens is that they're calibrated to heat only to 550°F. You could potentially file off the door lock and bake during the self-clean cycle, when temperatures top 800°F, but that particular modification would void your warranty and quite possibly your homeowner's insurance. Besides, 800°F is just medium-warm for a real pizza oven. Now, when I say "real," I mean, of course, an old-school, Old World wood-fired oven with a soapstone floor and thick walls capable of capturing 1200°F of crust-searing heat. Alas, I do not possess such a device, and so to the grill I must go.

TRIVIA We made this "earthen oven" out of a plastic dog "igloo."

[1] All the operations up to this point are considered "malting."

GRILLED PIZZA, TWO WAYS

DOUGH YIELDS 3 PIZZAS,
TOPPINGS YIELD 1 PIZZA EACH

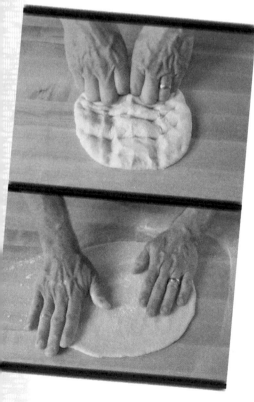

// SOFTWARE

FOR THE DOUGH

16	ounces	all-purpose flour	plus extra for the peel and rolling
1	envelope	instant or rapid-rise yeast	
1	tablespoon	kosher salt	
10	ounces	warm H$_2$O	approximately 105°F
2	tablespoons	olive oil	plus 2 teaspoons for the bowl
1	tablespoon	malted barley syrup	

OPTION 1: FOR THE MARGHERITA PIZZA

1	large	tomato	cut into ⅓-inch-thick slices
5 to 7	teaspoons	olive oil	divided
2	cloves	garlic	minced
½	teaspoon	kosher salt	
¼	teaspoon	red pepper flakes	
½	ounce	Parmesan cheese	grated
1½	ounces	part-skim mozzarella	shredded
4 to 6	large	basil leaves	shredded

OPTION 2: FOR THE DATE-AND-PROSCIUTTO PIZZA

3½	ounces	fresh mozzarella	cut into ¼-inch-thick slices
3 to 6	teaspoons	olive oil	divided
½	ounce	Parmesan cheese	grated
1	ounce	prosciutto	approximately 3 slices, coarsely chopped
4	whole	dried dates	pitted and finely chopped
1	teaspoon	fresh thyme leaves	

// PROCEDURE

1. Combine the flour and yeast in the work bowl of a **stand mixer fitted with the dough hook attachment**. Add the salt, water, 2 tablespoons oil, and malted barley syrup. Start the mixer on low and mix until the dough just comes together, about 1½ minutes. Increase the speed to medium and knead for 15 minutes.

(2) Tear off a small piece of dough and flatten it into a disk. Gently stretch the dough until it is very thin. The dough will be quite sticky, but manageable. Hold it up to the light and look to see if the baker's windowpane, a taut, see-through membrane, has formed. If you can see through the dough, it's ready; if you can't, continue to knead. Fold the dough onto itself and shape it into a smooth ball. Oil the bowl of the stand mixer or other large container with the 2 teaspoons oil. Put the dough in the bowl and roll it around to coat with the oil. Cover with a **tea towel or plastic wrap** and leave at room temperature until doubled in size, about 1 hour.

(3) Split the dough into 3 equal parts using a **knife or dough scraper**. Flatten each piece into a disk on the countertop. Fold each piece into a ball, then roll the balls on the counter until they tighten into rounds. Cover with a tea towel and let rest for 45 minutes.

(4) Heat a **gas grill** to high and make sure the grill's grates are clean and free of debris. Proceed with one or both of the pizza options below.

(5) MAKE THE MARGHERITA PIZZA: Toss the tomato with 1 tablespoon of the oil, the garlic, salt, and red pepper flakes in a **medium mixing bowl** and set aside.

(6) Lightly flour the countertop and flatten one of the dough balls. Use a **rolling pin** to roll the dough into a 16-inch round, rotating and stretching the dough as you go. Transfer the dough to a lightly floured **pizza peel** and stretch to reshape if necessary.

(7) Oil the grill grates and decrease the heat to medium. **Brush** the dough with 1 to 2 teaspoons of the oil and flip it onto one end of the hot grill, leaving room for the tomatoes. Place the prepared tomatoes on the grill, close the lid, and cook for 1 to 2 minutes, or until the bottom of the crust is golden brown and the tomatoes are softened. Brush the raw side of the dough with 1 to 2 teaspoons of the oil, then flip using the peel. Top with the grilled tomatoes, smashing and spreading them to create a sauce. Sprinkle with the Parmesan, mozzarella, and basil. Close the lid and cook for another 1 to 2 minutes, until the bottom of the crust is golden brown and the cheese has melted. Using the peel, remove the pizza to a **cooling rack** and let rest for 3 minutes before slicing.

(5) MAKE THE DATE-AND-PROSCIUTTO PIZZA: Layer **2 paper towels** on a **plate** and arrange the mozzarella slices on top in a single layer. Top with **2 more paper towels**, a **second plate**, and a **2-pound weight**. Set aside at room temperature for 20 minutes.

(6) Meanwhile, lightly flour the countertop and flatten one of the dough balls. Use a **rolling pin** to roll the dough into a 16-inch round, rotating and stretching the dough as you go. Transfer the dough to a lightly floured **pizza peel** and stretch to reshape if necessary.

(7) Oil the grill grates and decrease the heat to medium. **Brush** the dough with 1 to 2 teaspoons of the oil and flip it onto the hot grill. Close the lid and cook for 1 to 2 minutes, until the bottom of the crust is golden brown. Brush the raw side of the dough with 1 to 2 teaspoons of the oil, then flip using the peel, brush with the remaining 1 to 2 teaspoons oil, and top with the Parmesan, prepared mozzarella, prosciutto, dates, and thyme. Close the lid and cook for another 1 to 2 minutes, until the bottom of the crust is golden brown and the cheese has melted. Using the peel, transfer the pizza to a **cooling rack** and let rest for 3 minutes before slicing.

TIDBIT | The toppings of the margherita pizza—basil, fresh mozzarella, and tomatoes—are said to represent the colors of the Italian flag.

Some of you are sitting there all grumpy-dumpy because you live in a fifth-floor walkup in the middle of the city and cannot gain access to any kind of grill. Well, chins up, New York, London, Paris, Munich. If you've got a gas cooktop, a cooling rack, and a pair of vise grips, then the thinnest pizza on earth is closer than right around the corner. Although you could certainly dress this giant cracker up in pizza trimmings, I find it better suited to dipping in hummus, salsa, or other dips.

// SOFTWARE ///

1	ball	pizza dough (page 336)	
2 to 4	teaspoons	olive oil	
	kosher salt	to taste	
	black pepper	to taste	freshly ground

// SPECIAL HARDWARE ///

Vise grips

// PROCEDURE //

1. Lightly flour the countertop and flatten the dough ball. Use a **rolling pin** to roll the dough into an 11-by-17-inch rectangle to fit a **stainless-steel cooling rack**.

2. Lay the dough sheet on the rack and gently stretch it around the edges, pinching to hold the dough in place.

3. **Brush** the dough with 1 to 2 teaspoons of the oil and season with salt and pepper. Attach **vice grips** to one end of the cooling rack to use as a handle.

4. Turn a gas burner on high and hold the rack about 2 inches above the flame. Move back and forth constantly for 3 to 4 minutes, until the bottom is golden brown.

5. Carefully turn the dough over, brush with 1 to 2 teaspoons oil, and season with additional salt and pepper if desired. Cook, as before, for an additional 2 to 3 minutes, until golden brown.

YES, WE HAVE NO BANANA PUDDING

EPISODE 233 | SEASON 14 | GOOD EATS

Banana pudding rocks, or at least it used to. Most of us grew up on the pudding our moms made from the recipe on the yellow box of vanilla wafers or some variation thereof. And you know what? They were all good. Most of us kind of drift away from 'nana pudding as we age—but then we have kids, and the circle of life repeats. Only, I could swear the quality of these puddings has seriously slipped in just one or two generations and I feel pretty certain the problem isn't the pudding. It's the wafers. Perhaps the corporation most famous for producing them decided to cut back on the vanilla, or maybe the composition of the fats. But one thing's for sure: if we're going to make puddingdom safe for coming generations we're going to have to make our own wafers. Only then will we be able to confidently proclaim banana pudding as . . .

TIDBIT | Bananas in space? Banana pudding was served aboard *Apollo 12.*

TIDBIT | Bananas are by far the most popular fruit in the United States.

TIP | Bananas with a few dark spots are best for pudding.

339

A SELECTION OF "VICTORIAN PUDDINGS"

KNOWLEDGE CONCENTRATE

When Americans say banana pudding, we're not just talking about a bowl of creamy yellow goo, but rather a bowl of creamy yellow goo layered with sliced ripe bananas and vanilla-flavored wafers. Such constructs come to us courtesy of the Victorians, who were fairly crazy about "puddings," which to a Brit means any form of dessert. If one could travel back to that age, say Christmas 1893, one might very well find on any sideboard the entire banana pudding family tree.

FOOL: Pureed fruit folded into whipped cream, popular since the sixteenth century.

SILIBA: A very old froth of sorts, composed of sweet wine and cream.

TIPSY CAKE: Slightly stale sponge cake, hollowed out and filled with booze.

HEDGEHOG CAKE: Cake carved into the shape of a hedgehog, with some jam in front of it.

TRIFLE: The evolutionary next step, stale cake cubes saturated with spirits and stratified with custard, fruit, and whipped cream.

Bananas were strictly an American phenomenon, but even then they didn't enter the dessert picture until shipments from the Caribbean began showing up at the Port of New Orleans around 1900. Then they became so plentiful that folks just didn't know what to do with them, so they followed the English model and made 'em into trifle. Although I'd love to tell you to search out some obscure banana, the good old Cavendish is pretty much the right banana for the job. Ripeness, however, matters, so go with slightly under-ripe specimens free of big brown bruises, and with just a kiss of green at either end.

TIDBIT The first printed recipe for pastry cream dates back to *Le pâtissier français*, published in France in 1690.

TRIVIA My favorite scene in the show is the North/South pudding style battle waged by Generals Lee and Grant. We wanted to give the figures a kind of wax-museum feel, so we placed both on small platforms mounted on skateboard wheels canted at an angle so that they would glide up and down two long pieces of pipe. The floats were operated via long pipe handles on either side of the frame. Riding on the floats is a lot harder than it looks.

WHEN IT COMES TO BANANA PUDDING, THE NORTH AND SOUTH ARE STILL SOMEWHAT AT ODDS.

// SOFTWARE

7	ounces	all-purpose flour	
¾	teaspoon	baking powder	aluminum free
½	teaspoon	kosher salt	
4	ounces	unsalted butter	at room temperature
3½	ounces	vanilla sugar	
1	large	egg	
4	teaspoons	vanilla extract	
1	tablespoon	whole milk	

// PROCEDURE

1. Position one rack in the top third of the oven and another in the bottom third. Heat the oven to 350°F. Line **2 half sheet pans** with **parchment paper**.

2. Sift together the flour, baking powder, and salt in a **small bowl** and set aside. Cream the butter and vanilla sugar in a **stand mixer fitted with the paddle attachment** on medium speed for 2 minutes, stopping to scrape down the sides of the bowl after 1 minute. Add the egg and incorporate on medium speed for 30 seconds. Scrape down the sides of the bowl. Add the vanilla and milk and blend on low speed for 15 seconds. Add the flour mixture and mix on low speed just to incorporate. Chill the batter in the refrigerator for at least 10 minutes before scooping.

3. Scoop the batter in 1-teaspoon balls onto the prepared pans, about 35 cookies per pan. Use the heel of your hand to slightly flatten each ball. Bake for 15 to 20 minutes, rotating the pans halfway through baking, until golden brown. Remove to a **cooling rack** to cool completely before removing from the pan.

8 TO 10 SERVINGS

BAKED OR NOT?

It's generally held that triflelike banana puddings assembled from a cooked then chilled custard and topped with whipped cream are favored by those living in the northern United States, a fact that testifies to the strong British influence in our hearty hardworking cuisine. And yet, in the South, 'nana puddings are baked, usually with a meringue top, and served warm, reflecting a French sensibility. This begs the question: Why is it that a box of wafers historically produced by a factory in New York City has printed on its side a baked pudding recipe? Because a vast majority of said boxes are actually sold in the South. Yankees, it would seem, have no use for vanilla wafers. My own house is divided on the bake/no bake issue; I prefer the former, while my wife and daughter salivate copiously over the latter. And so, I make both. (More for everyone.)

YES, WE HAVE NO
BANANA PUDDING

// SOFTWARE

¾	cup plus 2 tablespoons	sugar	
3	tablespoons	cornstarch	
¼	teaspoon	kosher salt	
2	large	eggs	
1	large	egg yolk	
2	cups	whole milk	
3	tablespoons	unsalted butter	cut into 6 pieces and chilled
½	teaspoon	vanilla extract	
45		Vanilla Wafers (page 341)	
4	ounces	banana liqueur	
3	ripe	bananas	peeled and cut into ¼-inch rounds
1	tablespoon	freshly squeezed lemon juice	
1	cup	heavy whipping cream	very cold

// PROCEDURE

1. Combine ¾ cup of the sugar, the cornstarch, and salt in a **3-quart saucier**. Add the eggs and egg yolk and whisk to combine. Add the milk and **whisk** for 30 seconds, or until well combined. Cook over medium-low heat, stirring constantly, until the mixture reaches 172° to 180°F, 5 to 10 minutes; the mixture will begin to thicken and bubble around the edges. Remove from the heat and whisk in the butter, one piece at a time, being sure each piece is fully incorporated before adding the next. Whisk in the vanilla. Cover the surface of the pudding with a **round piece of parchment paper** and refrigerate until the pudding reaches 45°F, about 2 hours.

2. Lay the vanilla wafers on a **half sheet pan**. Slowly and evenly pour the banana liqueur over the cookies. Set aside for 10 minutes.

3. Toss the bananas in the lemon juice in a **small bowl** and set aside.

4. Spread a small amount of pudding in the bottom of a **1½-quart glass bowl**. Cover with a layer of vanilla wafers, followed by a layer of banana slices. Spoon one-third of the remaining pudding on top of the bananas and repeat, ending with a layer of pudding.

5. Put the cream in a **stand mixer fitted with the whisk attachment**, add the remaining 2 tablespoons sugar, and whisk just until stiff peaks form. Spoon the whipped cream over the cooled pudding and spread to cover completely. Top with any remaining soaked cookies. Refrigerate for 30 minutes before serving. Store, covered, in the refrigerator for up to 3 days.

BAKED BANANA PUDDING

8 TO 10 SERVINGS

// SOFTWARE

3		ripe bananas	peeled and cut into ¼-inch rounds
1	tablespoon	lemon juice	freshly squeezed
½	cup plus 2 tablespoons	sugar	
⅓	cup	all-purpose flour	
¼	teaspoon	kosher salt	
4	large	eggs	separated
2	cups	half-and-half	
½	teaspoon	vanilla extract	
45		Vanilla Wafers (page 341)	
1	pinch	cream of tartar	

// PROCEDURE

1. Heat the oven to 400°F.

2. Toss the bananas in the lemon juice in a **small bowl** and set aside.

3. Combine ½ cup of the sugar, the flour, and salt in a **3-quart saucier**. Add the egg yolks and whisk to combine. Add the half-and-half and carefully whisk to combine. Cook over medium-low heat, stirring constantly, until the mixture reaches 172° to 180°F, 5 to 10 minutes; the mixture will begin to thicken and bubble around the edges. Remove from the heat and whisk in the vanilla.

4. Spread a small amount of the pudding in the bottom of an **ovenproof 1½-quart glass bowl**. Cover with a layer of vanilla wafers, followed by a layer of banana slices. Pour one third of the remaining pudding on top of the bananas and repeat, ending with a layer of pudding.

5. Put the egg whites and cream of tartar in a **stand mixer fitted with the whisk attachment** and beat on medium speed until soft peaks form. Gradually add the remaining 2 tablespoons sugar and continue whisking until stiff peaks form. Spoon the meringue over the warm pudding, being sure to cover the edges. Bake for 8 to 10 minutes, until the meringue is evenly browned. Cool for 15 minutes before serving, and cool completely before refrigerating. Refrigerate for up to 3 days.

Why include a distinctly Mexican food form in an "American Classics" episode? Because the taco is essentially a sandwich, a distinctly American food form. I would argue that due to its ingenious architecture and balanced bread: filling ratio, the taco is perhaps the ultimate expression of the sandwich paradigm. With that in mind, I say it's only right that we examine the taco through the red, white, and blue lens of . . .

The "American" taco style of my youth

I'VE ALWAYS WANTED TO OPERATE MY OWN TACO TRUCK.

Since a comprehensive list of taco types and styles would fill this entire tome, I'll list here only my absolute favorites:

TACOS AL PASTOR, or shepherd's-style tacos, actually have their origins in the Lebanese *shawarma*, in which thin pork steaks are wrapped around a spit and then fire roasted and served up with vegetables, especially potatoes.

TACOS DE ASADOR are composed of grilled meats served on two small overlapping tortillas and finished with either guac or salsa.

TACOS DE CARNITAS are tacos filled with fresh herbage and lots of lovely, long-cooked pork that's been chopped or shredded (stop drooling).

TACOS DE LENGUA are filled with tongue, salsa, and cilantro. Very tasty.

TACOS DE CHICHARRONE: Three words: *crisp, pork, skin*.

TACOS DE PESCADO are fish tacos.

TACOS DORADOS, or fried golden tacos, came out of New Mexico in the late 1940s. This was most likely the dish that inspired the development of the worst thing to ever happen to tacos: the prefried, "crispy" (read: hard) taco shell. It was an attempt by a New York restaurateur, Juvencio Maldonado, to speed the production of hand-fried taco shells that led to his invention: a fried taco shell mold.

Although I feel certain he meant no harm, when Mr. Maldonado filed for patent protection for his invention on July 21, 1947, he was laying the unfortunate groundwork for the hard, flavorless, shatters-when-you-take-a-bite American taco shell. Luckily, with a little aluminum foil you can make your own mold and take back the *tacos dorados*.

The American taco meat of choice is ground sirloin. Legally speaking, *hamburger* can come from any beef primal or trimmings and may even have fat added to it, up to 30 percent of its total weight. Depending on how it's labeled, *ground meat* may differ from hamburger only by virtue of the fact that fat cannot be added to get it up to 30 percent, which isn't to say it wasn't already 30 percent fat. *Ground chuck* contains an awful lot of connective tissue, and *ground round* is typically dry and mealy when cooked. Ground sirloin, on the other hand, is the perfect mixture of a beefy goodness and moisture that hails from between the rather dry round and the juicy but expensive short loin. If your megamart does not have ground sirloin already in the case, then simply choose an appropriate-size steak or roast and ask your butcher to grind it for you. That's what they're there for.

Mexican cheeses can all be filed into five categories: fresh, soft, semisoft, semifirm, and firm. Since they tend to crumble rather than melt, fresh cheeses are most typically applied to tacos. Most folks in the United States are familiar with queso fresco, a mixture of cow's and goat's milk that has a spongy, crumbly texture, and queso blanco, a cow's-milk cheese with a texture somewhere between cottage cheese and fresh mozzarella. My favorite is *panela*, easily identified by its outer basketweave relief, which in authentic versions is created by an actual basket, betraying the cheese's Greek pedigree. *Panela* absolutely will not melt, even if you put a flamethrower to it.

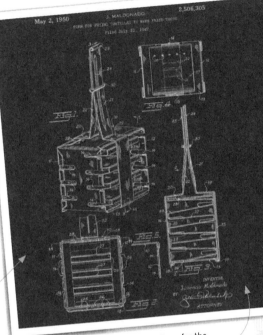

Patent drawings for the first taco-shell fryer

TIDBIT The first visual record of the taco is a photo from the 1920s showing a woman selling *tacos de canasta*, or "tacos from a basket."

AMERICAN CLASSICS VIII

⎍⎍⎍ **TACO POTION #19**

¼ CUP PLUS 2 TABLESPOONS

// SOFTWARE ///

2	tablespoons	chili powder	
1	tablespoon	whole cumin seeds	freshly toasted and ground
2	teaspoons	cornstarch	
2	teaspoons	kosher salt	
1½	teaspoons	hot smoked paprika	
1	teaspoon	ground coriander	
½	teaspoon	cayenne pepper	

// PROCEDURE //

Put all the ingredients in a **small jar** and shake to combine. Store in an airtight container for up to 1 month.

APPLICATION ⎍⎍⎍ **CREMA**

APPROXIMATELY 1 CUP

// SOFTWARE ///

1	cup	heavy cream	
1	tablespoon	low-fat buttermilk	
1		chipotle chile in adobo sauce	
¼	teaspoon	kosher salt	

// PROCEDURE //

1. Put the cream in a **microwave-safe 16-ounce glass jar**. Microwave on high power for 30 to 40 seconds, until the cream is just under 100°F. Add the buttermilk, close the jar, and store in a warm place for 24 hours. The cream will have thickened to the consistency of thin yogurt.

2. Add the chipotle and salt and blend with an **immersion blender**, in the jar, until smooth, about 20 seconds. Refrigerate until ready to use.

FLOUR TORTILLAS

8 TORTILLAS

SOFTWARE

9	ounces	all-purpose flour	plus extra for kneading and rolling
1	teaspoon	kosher salt	
⅓	cup	lard	(see sidebar, page 224)
½	cup	cool H$_2$O	

PROCEDURE

(1) Combine the flour and salt in a **food processor** by pulsing 2 or 3 times.

(2) Add the lard in 4 or 5 chunks and pulse 10 to 15 times, until the mixture resembles coarse crumbs. With the processor running, add the water in a steady stream just until a ball of dough begins to form, about 30 seconds.

(3) Sprinkle ¼ cup flour on a clean surface, remove the dough from the bowl of the processor, and knead for 2 to 3 minutes, or until well incorporated, and not as sticky. Wrap the dough ball in **plastic wrap** and rest at room temperature for 1 hour.

(4) Evenly divide the dough into 8 pieces and, using your hands, form into round balls. Keep the dough balls covered with a **tea towel**. Roll the balls into 7-inch rounds with a **rolling pin** on a lightly floured surface.

(5) Heat an **electric nonstick griddle** to 375°F.

(6) Put the tortillas, 2 or 3 at a time, on the griddle and cook for 4 minutes per side, or until light golden. Hold for up to 2 hours at room temperature wrapped in a barely damp tea towel. Repeat with the remaining tortillas. Microwave for 1 minute in the damp tea towel to reheat.

TIDBIT In early Spanish dictionaries, the word *taco* was defined as either a ramrod, a billiard cue, or a gulp of wine.

The electric griddle is by far the best tool for cooking tortillas.

ALL-AMERICAN BEEF TACOS[1]

6 SERVINGS

// SOFTWARE ///

¾	cup	peanut oil	
12	6-inch	yellow corn tortillas	
	to taste	kosher salt	plus 1 teaspoon for seasoning beef
1	medium	onion	chopped
1	pound	ground sirloin	
2	cloves	garlic	minced
1	recipe	Taco Potion #19 (page 346)	
⅔	cup	low-sodium beef broth	
6	ounces	panela cheese	crumbled
12	slices	pickled jalapeño	
1	cup	shredded iceberg lettuce	optional
1	large	tomato	seeded and chopped; optional
½	cup	fresh cilantro leaves	optional

// PROCEDURE ///

(1) Make a taco mold by folding a **5-foot-long piece of heavy-duty aluminum foil** into a block that is approximately 8 inches long, 4 inches high, and 2 inches deep. Set aside.

(2) Heat the oven to 250°F.

(3) Heat the oil in a **12-inch cast-iron skillet** over medium heat for 5 minutes, or until it reaches 350°F. Adjust the heat to maintain the temperature.

(4) Shape 1 tortilla around the foil mold, forming it into a taco shape. Use **tongs** to hold up the sides against the mold, place the bottom of the tortilla in the hot oil, and fry for 20 seconds. Lay one side of the tortilla down in the hot oil and fry for 30 seconds. Flip the tortilla over and fry the last side for 30 seconds. Remove the taco shell to a **cooling rack** set over a **newspaper-lined half sheet pan** and cool for 30 seconds before removing the mold. Sprinkle the hot tortilla with salt to taste. Repeat with the remaining tortillas. Keep the taco shells warm in the oven while preparing the filling.

(5) Drain all but 2 tablespoons of the oil from the skillet and return it to medium heat. When the oil shimmers, add the onion and cook for 3 to 4 minutes, or until softened and lightly browned around the edges. Add the sirloin, 1 teaspoon salt, and the garlic. Cook for 3 to 4 minutes, or until browned, stirring occasionally to break up the meat. Add the taco seasoning and broth. Bring to a simmer and cook, uncovered, for 2 to 3 minutes, or until the sauce is slightly thickened.

(6) Assemble each taco with meat mixture, cheese, and jalapeño slices, and lettuce, tomato, and cilantro, if desired. Serve immediately.

WHEN HOSTING A TACO PARTY, KEEP THE MEAT MIX IN A SLOW COOKER!

[1] Essentially a north-of-the-border version of the original Tex-Mex *tacos dorados*.

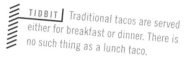

4 TO 6 SERVINGS

Although the fish taco was probably born in Ensenada, Mexico, around the turn of the century, in the early 1980s it migrated north and annexed San Diego, California, where it currently serves as that city's unofficially official dish. As Mexican restaurants around the country have fought to make *tacos de pescado* their own, terrible mutations have been designed. It's time to clean the slate and get back to basics.

// SOFTWARE ///

3	cloves	garlic	
1	cup	packed fresh cilantro leaves	
2		limes	zested, cut into wedges for serving
2	teaspoons	whole cumin seeds	toasted and ground
1½	teaspoons	kosher salt	
1	teaspoon	black pepper	freshly ground
¼	cup	tequila	
1	pound	tilapia fillets	
1	tablespoon	olive oil	
8	7-inch round	warm Flour Tortillas (page 347)	
		Crema (page 346)	
		red cabbage	shredded

TIDBIT | Traditional tacos are served either for breakfast or dinner. There is no such thing as a lunch taco.

// PROCEDURE ///

1. Put the garlic, cilantro, lime zest, cumin, salt, and pepper in a **small food processor** and pulse until combined, about 20 seconds. With the processor running, add the tequila. Put the tilapia in a **1-gallon zip-top bag**, add the cilantro mixture, seal the bag, and move it around to coat each fillet. Set aside at room temperature for 15 to 20 minutes.

2. Heat an **electric nonstick griddle** to 375°F.

3. **Brush** the griddle with the oil. Cook the fillets for 3 to 4 minutes per side, or until just cooked through and opaque. Cut into strips and serve in warm tortillas with the crema, cabbage, and lime wedges.

FRY HARD III:
FRY, TEMPURA, FRY!

EPISODE 235 | SEASON 14 | GOOD EATS

On this program we've done our fair share of frying, both pan-frying and deep-fat satis-frying, if you know what I mean. We even dedicated two entire episodes to the attainment of golden-brown deliciousness. Alas, that was child's play compared to . . . tempura!

In the show, we portrayed tempura as a giant Japanese monster, or *kaiju*, capable of shaking houses and eating cooks whole. In other words: Tempura can be scary. Even most Japanese don't dare attempt it at home. When they want tempura they go to special tempura restaurants. And yet, if we stand up and fight our irrational fears with sound science, some simple everyday ingredients, well-tuned technique, and basic-issue hardware, tempura can magically morph from monster to, well . . . you know.

Our best
Lucky Yates
puppet ever

KNOWLEDGE CONCENTRATE

▷○ **In Japanese cuisine there are several forms of deep-fried foods, or *agemono*, one of which is *koromo-age* or "batter-fried" foods. The most typical *koromo-age* is tempura, which is typically composed of lightly battered vegetables and/or fish that are quickly fried.**

▷○ **The way I see it, if we are to be victorious over tempura, three conditions must coexist:**

1. The food must be perfectly prepped.

2. The oil must be carefully chosen and heated to an exact temperature.

3. And as for the batter, it must fry up light, crisp, and flavorful but not greasy.

▷○ **Traditionally, tempura is a method for cooking vegetation and mild white seafood. My favorite target foods include:**

— Slender, fresh green beans   — Tilapia   — Sweet potatoes (called *satsumaimo* in Japan)

— Flat-leaf parsley   — Shrimp

As for prep, little is necessary for the beans (snap off the ends if you like), parsley (wash and dry), or the shrimp (peel but don't decapitate). The sweet potatoes should be peeled and cut ⅛ inch thick with a mandoline or other slicer. Consistency is key, so don't try to pull this off with a knife.

350

The modern cook has access to dozens of different cooking oils, harvested from nuts, seeds, various vegetation, and fruits, each with its own individual temperature range and flavor characteristics. But when it comes to tempura I depend on good old vegetable oil, which is cheap, plentiful, and comfortable in tempura's thermal happy zone. And, if you're careful with it, you can recycle it for a second fry session another day.

The Japanese characters for *tempura* translate to "flour like gauze" or "batter like revealing dress," depending on how you read them. When the Portuguese first unleashed tempura upon Nippon (see sidebar, page 357), the batter was simply water, flour, and egg. I've tried about every possible combination thereof and have not (ever) been able to come up with anything but greasy, gloppy nastiness. The problem, as I see it, is gluten.

Any time wheat flour and water are agitated together, two wheat molecules, glutenin and gliadin, unwind and intertwine, forming a resilient elastic matrix. Gluten is springy, gluten is tough, and what's worse, gluten holds on to both water and fat. This translates to gummy, greasy tempura—not a gauzelike, revealing dress.

Therefore, if we are to make decent tempura, we must minimize gluten. That means avoiding ingredients containing water, glutenin, and gliadin, as well as prolonged mixing. And since gluten can form over time as the batter just sits, we also need to wait and assemble it in the moments immediately prior to cooking. Instead of all-purpose wheat flour, use a combination of rice flour and unbleached cake flour. Rice flour, easily obtainable at most megamarts and certainly Asian markets, contains no gluten-forming molecules; cake flour is finely milled so that it integrates into batters very quickly. Why unbleached? Consider a starch granule:

The process of bleaching isn't just about making the flour white, though that is a factor. Bleaching cracks open the starch structure, making it much more fat friendly, which is a good thing if you're making a cake batter but not so much a tempura. By utilizing unbleached cake flour you can avoid this overfriendliness. If you can't procure unbleached product, go ahead with regular cake flour but know that it will make a subtle difference and tempura success is all about subtle differences.

As for the liquid, instead of simply using water, go with seltzer water or club soda, which introduces batter-lightening bubbles as well as a slight acidity that can help to limit gluten formation. I also replace some of the water in the recipe with vodka. Unlike water, alcohol doesn't tend to soak into flour, it doesn't contribute to the formation of gluten, and since it evaporates at a relatively low temperature—around 70°F—any batter containing it should, technically speaking, cook faster than one that's water based.

Last but not least, we require the services of an egg, which will provide some fat for flavor, some color, and some protein for binding.

JAPAN VIA HOLLAND

Every couple of years we try out the current crop of electric countertop fryers, which all claim to take oil up to 375°F—pretty much my deep-fry minimum—but I have yet to see a machine that can actually deliver on this. And even if they could, such devices would qualify as hard-to-clean unitaskers. And so we stick with traditional vessels.

When choosing a pot for stove-top frying, you could reach for an iron tempura pot, which is a wide vessel with a bottom that rounds out gradually to a flat bottom. But they're expensive and hard to find, which is why I stick with a good old cast-iron Dutch oven. And despite the fact that tempura pros just "know" what the temperature of the oil is by reading the way bubbles trickle off the end of a submerged chopstick, I need a thermometer, and it's much easier to deploy on a Dutch oven than on a tempura pot.

6 TO 8 SERVINGS

// SOFTWARE //

5	ounces	unbleached cake flour	
5	ounces	white rice flour	
1½	quarts	vegetable oil	
1	large	egg	beaten
½	cup	vodka	
1½	cups	cold seltzer water	
5 to 6	ounces	sweet potato	peeled and cut into ⅛-inch-thick slices
	to taste	kosher salt	
¼	pound	fresh green beans	trimmed
8	stems	hearty flat-leaf parsley	
½	pound 31- to 35-count	shrimp	head and tail on, peeled and deveined
½	pound	tilapia fillets	cut into 1-inch pieces

// PROCEDURE ///

1. **Whisk** the cake flour and rice flour together in a **medium glass bowl** and divide in half. Set aside.

2. Heat the oil in a **5-quart Dutch oven** over high heat until it reaches 375°F on a **deep-fry thermometer**.

3. When the temperature reaches 365°F, whisk the egg, vodka, and seltzer water in a **medium mixing bowl** and divide in half. Place half of the mixture in the refrigerator and reserve. Pour half of the liquid mixture into half of the flour mixture and whisk to combine for 10 to 15 seconds. Some lumps may remain. Set the bowl in a **larger bowl** filled with **ice**.

4. Dip the sweet potatoes in the batter using **tongs**, drain for 2 to 3 seconds over the bowl, then add to the hot oil. Adjust the heat to maintain a temperature between 375° and 400°F. Fry 6 to 8 pieces at a time for 1 to 2 minutes, until puffy and very light golden. Transfer to a **cooling rack** lined with **3 layers of paper towels** set over a **half sheet pan**. Sprinkle with salt if desired. Repeat the dipping-and-frying procedure with the green beans and parsley leaves. Serve the vegetables as an appetizer while preparing the seafood.

5. Whisk together the remaining halves of dry and liquid batter ingredients as above and repeat dipping and frying with the shrimp and fish. Sprinkle with salt, if desired, and serve immediately.

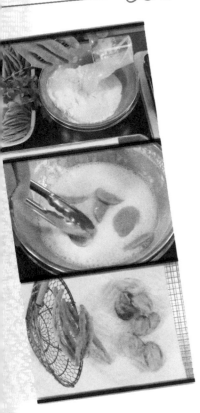

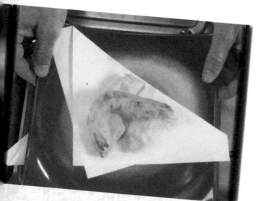

NOTE: Always serve tempura pieces on plain white paper, folded but never straight across. Always go for an off angle.

APPLICATION — SOY GINGER DIPPING SAUCE

1 CUP

// SOFTWARE //

½	cup	low-sodium soy sauce	
¼	cup	rice vinegar	
2	tablespoons	fresh ginger	finely grated
2	tablespoons	scallion	chopped
2	cloves	garlic	minced
2	teaspoons	sugar	
1	teaspoon	sesame oil	

// PROCEDURE //

Put all of the ingredients in a **lidded jar** and shake well to combine. Serve as dipping sauce for tempura.

TIP | Regardless of what kind of sauce you serve for tempura dipping, it won't be close to authentic unless you serve some freshly grated daikon alongside. This ubiquitous Japanese radish is formidable in appearance but quite mild in flavor.

TEMPURA HISTORY

It is interesting to note that like so many technologies perfected by the Japanese—transistor radios, trains, cell phones, peaches, coffee—tempura is actually a Western import.

In 1494 Spain and Portugal signed the Treaty of Tordesillas, which divided all newly discovered lands, meaning most of the planet, between them for the purpose of bringing Catholicism—and, of course, trade—to the unwashed heathens of the world, a mission for which they had the blessing of the pope (if not the Dutch, English, or French, who also had their sights set on global domination). Japan became Portugal's territory and in 1549 a Jesuit name of Frances Xavier landed there and began the good work.

By converting the nobility first, Xavier met with considerable success initially and even taught them a few culinary tricks to help them navigate all those fasting days, such as the Quatuor Tempora, which took place each quarter of the year. During this time the clergy consumed mostly fish, which they typically batter-fried. Christianity was eventually outlawed in Japan in 1587, but the cooking method, whose name morphed from *tempora* to "tempura," stuck, and over time the Japanese have refined it to a high art.

TRIVIA | Believe it or not, these characters mean "batter like revealing dress" or something like that.

FRY HARD III

353

I eat oats almost every day, usually for breakfast but not always. Sometimes I eat them for dinner, sometimes lunch, sometimes for a snack. I believe that their considerable nutritional power has greatly assisted me in essentially de-aging my body by nearly twenty years. Despite what I led you all to believe in our first Oat Cuisine episode, most of the oats I eat are rolled oats. I feel so strongly about the rolled oat as a culinary partner that I felt the subject deserved a second episode. And so, read on, gentle reader, and marvel at the lowly oat.

ME, IN THE SMALL INTESTINE!

Just pretend for a moment that this lump of pasta dough is actually a whole oat grain or groat, the fruit of the *Avena sativa* plant, if you like. The process of making rolled oats begins by hulling this grain and then steaming it to make it pliable:

To make a standard old-fashioned oat, the groat is simply rolled, like this:

It's kept a little on the thick side. Then it's dried. Some companies toast them afterward in order to bump up the flavor, something you could easily do at home. To make quick-cooking oats, you take the same groat and you cut it into pieces and then each one of these pieces is in turn rolled very thin, much thinner than the original rolled oat in most cases, and that looks something like this:

To make instant oats, of course, you would start with an even thinner slice and roll it even thinner, if you can imagine that. Now, I do not care for this type of oats because they tend to fall apart, and they don't deliver much in the way of flavor or texture. The process also tends to damage some of the soluble fibers, and that's a bad thing. All the applications from here on out will call for and rely on standard old-fashioned rolled oats. They may not be instant, they may not even be quick, but they are darned good.[1]

So what's the deal with oats and cholesterol? Cholesterol is a waxy compound that is a naturally occurring steroid produced in the liver, which assists in the formation of cell membranes, production of bile salts (key to digestion), vitamin D conversion, and the production of sex hormones. The liver makes most of the cholesterol we need, but 25 percent of what's in our blood comes from the foods we eat—animal fat, eggs, and such. Since it's a fat, cholesterol can't mix with blood, so your body produces carriers in the form of two proteins: low-density lipoproteins, or LDLs, and high-density lipoproteins, or HDLs. LDLs deliver cholesterol to cells. But if a cell already has enough, the delivery is essentially rejected. Problem is, LDLs outnumber HDLs three to one, and LDLs are lazy, so if they can't deliver their waxy load they just stick it on the walls of your arteries. This can be a really big problem leading to atherosclerosis, and that is a very bad thing indeed. Oats can help because they contain a soluble fiber called beta glucan, which can bind in the intestines to bile, which is made, in part, of cholesterol. The oat gel then ushers the cholesterol *out of the building*, if you get my drift. Once this cholesterol is gone, your system will replace it with more cholesterol that might have ended up on your arteries had you not made room for it down below. Eat more oats, and this cholesterol will exit as well.[2]

Now, I'm not saying that a couple of oatmeal cookies will fix what ails ya, but enough research has been done to convince the FDA to allow cholesterol-lowering health claims to be made on packages of oatmeal. So now you know, and as GI Joe says, "Knowing is half the battle."

Avena Sativa Imagined

TIDBIT | Rolled oats were invented as a way to speed cooking, making it one of the first American "fast" foods.

[1] I very rarely suggest or endorse actual brands, but I have to say that Bob's Red Mill thick rolled oats pretty much rock. And no, Bob doesn't pay me to say that.

[2] Thus it is more healthful to eat small doses of oats several times a day rather than a big bowl once a day.

1 LOAF

Making a yeast-risen oat bread is tricky because the gaseous emissions of yeast cannot be captured without gluten, the molecular mesh created when wheat proteins are agitated with water. Since oats contain zip for gluten, if we hope to make a risen oat-based loaf we must compensate by adding a wheat flour containing as much gluten as possible—and that means "bread" flour.

// SOFTWARE //

1	package	active dry yeast	
11	ounces	bread flour	plus extra for kneading
¼	cup plus 1 tablespoon	toasted uncooked old-fashioned rolled oats	
1	teaspoon	kosher salt	
12	ounces	leftover cooked old-fashioned rolled oats	at room temperature
¼	cup	warm H_2O	
2	tablespoons	agave syrup	
1	tablespoon	olive oil	plus extra for the pan
1	large	egg yolk	
1	tablespoon	H_2O	

// PROCEDURE //

1. Combine the yeast, bread flour, uncooked oats, and salt in a **small bowl** and set aside.

2. Combine the leftover cooked oatmeal, warm water, agave syrup, and oil in a **large bowl**. Add the dry mixture to the cooked oatmeal mixture in 3 installments and mix thoroughly with a **wooden spoon** after each addition.

3. Turn the dough onto a lightly floured surface and knead by hand for 10 minutes, incorporating more flour if needed. The dough will be sticky. Lightly oil a **bowl or container** and put the dough inside. Cover with **plastic wrap** and set in a warm place to rise for 1 hour, or until the dough has doubled in size.

4. Punch down the dough, shape into a loaf, and place in a lightly oiled **9-by-5-inch loaf pan**. Cover with plastic wrap and place in the refrigerator overnight.

5. Heat the oven to 350°F.

6. Combine the egg yolk and water in a **small bowl**. Lightly **brush** the top of the loaf with egg wash and sprinkle with the remaining 1 tablespoon uncooked oats. Bake for 55 to 60 minutes, until the bread reaches an internal temperature of 210°F. Remove the loaf from the pan to a cooling rack for 30 minutes before slicing and serving.

THE OATIEST OATMEAL COOKIES EVER

ABOUT 3 DOZEN COOKIES

I have baked hundreds of different "oatmeal" cookies, and 98.358 percent of them called for gobs of wheat flour. Now, why would you make an oatmeal cookie with wheat flour when you could use oat flour and produce a cookie that is gluten free? Consider, too, the fact that such a cookie tastes more oaty and feels more crunchy and chewy than a cookie that relies on wheat—which obviously has no place in an oatmeal cookie.

// SOFTWARE

16	ounces	old-fashioned rolled oats	
1	teaspoon	baking powder	
1	teaspoon	ground cinnamon	
	pinch	kosher salt	
10	ounces	unsalted butter	at room temperature
6	ounces	dark brown sugar	
3½	ounces	granulated sugar	
1	large	egg	
1	teaspoon	vanilla extract	
4	ounces	raisins	optional

// PROCEDURE

1. Heat the oven to 375°F.

2. Spread the oats in a single layer on a **half sheet pan**. Bake for 20 minutes, or until lightly toasted. Cool the oats on the pan for 2 to 3 minutes.

3. Grind 8 ounces of the oats in a **food processor** for 3 minutes, or until they have the consistency of whole-wheat flour. Add the baking powder, cinnamon, and salt to the food processor and pulse 2 or 3 times to combine. Set aside.

4. Combine the butter and sugars in a **stand mixer fitted with the paddle attachment** and mix on medium speed for 3 minutes, or until light in color. Stop once to scrape down the sides of the bowl. Slow the mixer to the lowest speed and add the egg and vanilla. Mix to combine. Slowly add the ground-oats mixture until just combined. Stop once to scrape down the sides of the bowl. Add the remaining toasted oats and the raisins, if using. Stir to combine.

5. Scoop the dough with a **1½-ounce disher** onto **half sheet pans** lined with **parchment paper**, leaving 2 inches between mounds. Bake for 12 to 14 minutes, until the cookies begin to brown around the edges. Rotate the pan halfway through baking. Cool on the pans for 2 minutes, then move to a cooling rack to cool completely.

ALL HALLOWS EATS

EPISODE 237 | SEASON 14 | GOOD EATS

Halloween has always been the Brown family holiday. I'm proud to say that no member of my clan has ever handed out a store-bought candy to a trick-or-treater. In fact, each year when the black cats hiss and the goblins gobble, we Browns crack open our ancient codex of All Hallows Eve treats and get to cooking.

TRICK OR TREAT?

TIDBIT | Over 85 percent of U.S. homes hand out candy on All Hallows Eve.

This kid totally doesn't trust me.

358

The groovy thing about candy making is that dozens—nay, hundreds—of different products can be produced from the exact same pot of ingredients, namely water, sugar, and corn syrup, simply by cooking the mixture to different concentrations. In the days before reliable thermometers, these concentrations were detected by the way a small amount of the cooking syrup reacted to being dropped into a container of ice water. The denser the concentration, the harder the resulting ball of goo would be. This reality gave way to the system of "ball stages."

Luckily, we do have reliable thermometers today and can use temperature as our guide. The general rule is that the lower the temperature of the syrup, the lower the sugar concentration, and the softer the candy.

Stage	Temperature	Use
Thread	230°–235°F	syrup, preserves
Soft ball	235°–240°F	fudge, pralines
Firm ball	245°–250°F	chewy candies
Hard ball	250°–265°F	nougat, marshmallow
Soft crack	270°–290°F	taffy, butterscotch
Hard crack	300°–310°F	brittle, lollipops
Caramel	320°–360°F	caramel sauce

KIDS ON RED DYE?

Although digital thermometers rule the marketplace these days, when it comes to candy I prefer an old-school analog model, because you can witness the acceleration of the temperature. In other words, an analog (liquid in a tube) thermometer functions as a "trend" instrument, which gives you a better idea of how you need to control your heat.

Why put nonfat dry milk in a candy? Because besides milk sugars, dry milk contains a goodly number of milk proteins, which can absorb liquid and coagulate into a kind of gel. This happens in the presence of enzymes and acids, like the ones that are found, albeit in small amounts, in corn syrup.

About that food coloring. Although the federal government insists that the highly regulated food, drug, and cosmetic (FD&C) dyes are safe, there is some research that suggests that some food dyes, especially reds, can cause kids to go, well, bonkers. If this worries you, just skip the food coloring in these treats (but let me remind you that kids get more than enough food coloring from manufactured foods to turn them into a swarming hoard of rabid zombies).

If you do go for the color, there are options besides the usual liquid stuff you get at the megamart, including gel pastes, plain old gels, and dry food colorings, which are very powerful. I tend to use pastes in soft candies, which are already fairly wet, and liquid colors when I know high temperatures will be attained and the extra liquid will be cooked off.

TIDBIT | Samhain was a sacred festival held by Celtic cultures to celebrate summer's end.

60 TO 80 PIECES

// **SOFTWARE** //

4½	ounces	confectioners' sugar	about 1¼ cups
½	ounce	nonfat dry milk	about 6½ teaspoons
¼	teaspoon	kosher salt	
3½	ounces	granulated sugar	about ½ cup
3¾	ounces	light corn syrup	about ⅓ cup
2½	tablespoons	H₂O	
2	tablespoons	unsalted butter	at room temperature
½	teaspoon	vanilla extract	
2 or 3	drops	yellow and orange gel paste food coloring	

TIDBIT October 30 is National Candy Corn Day.

// **PROCEDURE** //

1. Combine the confectioners' sugar, dry milk, and salt in a **food processor**. Pulse 4 or 5 times, until the mixture is smooth and well combined. Set aside.

2. Combine the granulated sugar, corn syrup, and water in a **2-quart pot**. Place over medium heat, cover, and cook for 4 minutes. Add the butter, clip on a **candy thermometer**, and bring the mixture to 230°F, 1 to 2 minutes. When the sugar syrup reaches 230°F, remove from the heat and remove the thermometer.

3. Add the vanilla and the dry mixture and stir continuously with a **silicone spatula** until well combined. Pour onto a **half sheet pan** lined with a **silicone baking mat**. Cool for 10 to 15 minutes, until the mixture is cool enough to handle.

4. Divide the dough into 3 equal pieces. Add 2 drops of yellow food coloring to one piece and knead the dough until the color is consistent throughout. Add 2 drops of orange to the second piece and knead until the color is consistent throughout. Leave the third piece white.

5. Roll each piece of dough into a strand about 18 inches long. Cut each strand in half. Roll one of the white pieces into a strand that is about ½ inch thick and about 22 inches long. Repeat with a yellow piece and an orange piece. Lay the strands side by side and press them together using your fingers. Cut the strand into 4-inch pieces. Lay the cut strands, one at a time, onto the **silicone mat** and press each into a wedge shape, like a triangle. Use a **wire butter slicer** to cut the candies into pieces. If you don't have a wire butter slicer, use a **knife, metal bench scraper, or pizza cutter** to slice the dough into small pieces. Repeat with the remaining dough.

6. Lay the finished pieces on a piece of **parchment or waxed paper** to dry for 1 hour. Store in an **airtight container with parchment paper** between each layer.

HOMEMADE CANDY—
SO WORTH THE TROUBLE

6 CANDY APPLES

TIDBIT | William Kolb, a New Jersey candy maker, produced his first batch of candied apples in 1908.

Having witnessed how a sugar syrup can become a soft yet toothsome paste, we will now see what can happen when the temperature is elevated and the resulting elixir applied to the most symbolic food of the harvest season.

// SOFTWARE ///

6	small	apples (Pink Lady, Gala, or McIntosh)	at room temperature
14	ounces	sugar	about 2 cups
15	ounces	light corn syrup	about 1⅓ cups
⅔	cup	H₂O	
1	teaspoon	cayenne pepper	
½	teaspoon	cinnamon oil	
15 to 20	drops	red liquid food coloring	

// SPECIAL HARDWARE //

6 sets of chopsticks

// PROCEDURE //

1. Pour 3 inches of water into a **3½-quart saucepan** and bring to a boil over high heat.

2. Insert the narrow end of a **chopstick** into the bottom (blossom end) of each apple.

3. Dip the apples, one at a time, into the boiling water for 20 seconds to remove the wax coating. Wipe dry with a **paper towel**.

4. Transfer the apples to a **half sheet pan** lined with **parchment paper or a silicone baking mat** and set aside.

5. Combine the sugar, corn syrup, and the ⅔ cup water in a **2-quart saucepan** and set over medium heat. Cover and bring to a boil, 4 to 6 minutes. Remove the lid and clip on a **candy thermometer**. Continue cooking the syrup until it reaches 300°F, about 15 minutes. When the syrup reaches 300°F, remove from the heat and remove the thermometer. Add the cayenne, cinnamon oil, and food coloring and stir thoroughly to combine. Cool for 3 minutes, or until the bubbles calm and begin to subside.

6. Dip each apple in the warm syrup, turning slowly to coat. Continue to turn, allowing the excess to drip back into the pot.

7. Cool the apples completely on the prepared half sheet pan. Wrap individually in **waxed paper and plastic wrap** or store for 2 to 3 days in an **airtight container**.

WHY CORN SYRUP?

Let's say you construct a syrup of only sugar (that is, the disaccharide sucrose) and water. As the water is heated, the sucrose will dissolve and all will be well. But as the water boils out of the pan, the sucrose molecules will become more and more compacted. If they group tightly enough, they'll join together in a uniform pattern. In other words, they will crystallize. If this happens, your syrup will turn into a big, pretty rock sitting in a puddle of water. Although this can be prevented if extra care is taken not to agitate the syrup as it cooks, a better solution is to take out anti-crystallization insurance by adding nonsucrose molecules, such as those in corn syrup, which is high in fructose. These molecules can get between the sucrose molecules, thus keeping them from crystallizing.

NO CRYSTALS HERE

"**Summer squash are *not* good eats.**" Or so I said a few years back when someone asked me about making this very episode. It was my belief at the time that regardless of shape, size, or color, summer squash were nutrient-negative, water-logged cousins of melons, which simple country folk (like my immediate ancestors) stewed with onions just before starving to death. But when a farmer my family buys food from during the summer delivered a few as part of our weekly basket, I felt duty bound to cook and consume the wretched things. Not having much faith in the possibilities, I put very little effort into them, and you know what? That was all it took. Now I know that the key to summer squash is to purchase them in season, from a local source, and to cook them as soon as possible and as quickly as possible, if at all. Then and only then are their subtly sublime flavors tantamount to . . .

TIDBIT | Georgia and Florida are the leading producers of summer squash in the United States.

TIDBIT | Squash as we know it was introduced to Europe by Columbus at the end of the fifteenth century.

CONCERNING ZUCCHINI

We all know zucchini is as Italian as Sophia Loren, and yet all squash are New World plants, American in origin. So what gives? Cultural cross pollination, that's what. Spanish explorers brought squash seeds back to the Old World, and various characteristics were encouraged through generations of selective cross breeding. If you are an art enthusiast, you might argue that zucchini must have been born prior to 1580, when Vicenzo Campi completed his *Fruittivendola*, which clearly depicts a basket of zucchini with blossoms, but upon closer examination you see these are actually *cocozelle*, a close ancestor of the modern zucchini, which did not emerge until the twentieth century. Nice painting, though.

Botanically speaking, all squashes are berries, seed-bearing bodies, and they're closely related to winter squashes, melons, and gourds, which are often turned into bird houses and other crafty things. The word *squash* **comes from** *askoot asquash*, **which is Algonquin for "eaten green," an obvious reference to the fact that summer squash are best when they're harvested just a week after their flower fully opens.**[1]

Let us now review a few garden versions of *Cucurbita pepo* **that are commonly found in farmers' markets and megamarts alike:**

Here, of course, we have the YELLOW CROOKNECK, a classic.

And the Italian variation, the ZUCCHINI.

Here's the GLOBE SQUASH, also called "apple" squash. They come in various sizes and colors.

As do the PATTYPAN SQUASHES, which resemble edible flying saucers.

This is a new hybrid called the ZEPHYR, which is a cross between the yellow crookneck and the delicata, which is actually a cold-weather variety.

Regardless of type, the bigger they get, the more fibrous and unpalatable they become. So try to pick or purchase smallish or medium specimens with smooth, shiny skins. Scratches or little gouges are not a big deal, but avoid soft spots and browning.

When it comes to storage, tender little squashes are like time bombs, and the clock is ticking away. Sure, if you wrap them in paper towels to prevent surface condensation and then stash them in a zip-top and suck out all the air before sealing and storing in the warmest part of the fridge, which is up top, not down in the crisper drawer, you'll get two or three days of optimum freshness, but truth is when the season hits, the best thing you can do is arm yourself with a wide range of anticipatory applications that can be implemented at a moments' notice. And this doesn't necessarily require cooking.

YELLOW CROOKNECK

GLOBE OR APPLE

PATTYPAN

ZEPHYR

[1] This means, of course, that by the time 90 percent of summer squash arrive at your megamart they're no longer worth eating.

TURNING A STRIP OF SQUASH INTO A "NOODLE"

Let's say for a moment that this stack of boxes is a piece of zucchini fresh from the garden. In its fresh, growing state, it is stiff, what plant people call "turgid." That's because each cell contains a kind of bag called a cell membrane, which is packed with all the structures the cell needs to do its business. It's also chock-full of water

that's actually under pressure. If we cut into the plant and add salt, the salt will dissolve into a saturated brine, which will then pull moisture out of the membrane. It's only a matter of time before that inner bag simply collapses, attaining

what's called a "hypertonic state." The cell will eventually plasmolyze and pull away from the cell wall. The structure then collapses. If managed properly, this will result not in mushiness, but rather a dense yet floppy structure, kind of like a cooked noodle.

MANDOLINES

Mandoline is a pretty French word for any device designed to slice food by means of sliding it up and down an adjustable plane into which a fixed blade has been set. Now, two types predominate the market. First you have the traditional stand model, which is like a factory, capable of fabricating many different cuts, various forms of slices, juliennes, matchsticks, even waffle cuts if you know what you're doing. It's expensive. It's got a lot of parts that you have to keep up with. Maintaining everything and adjusting everything is a chore, and cleaning it is . . . well, nine times out of ten I just leave it in the drawer and use a knife. If I want to use a mandoline, it's going to be a hand model. My favorite is a lightweight plastic model. It's capable of only four different thicknesses of cuts, but I don't really need more. It has a sharp ceramic blade that never needs sharpening, it's easy to clean, and because the blade is set at an angle, it's great for slicing softer items like tomatoes.

// SOFTWARE

2	pounds	zucchini	trimmed
1	teaspoon	kosher salt	
3	tablespoons	extra virgin olive oil	
2	tablespoons	lemon juice	freshly squeezed
2	teaspoons	whole-grain mustard	
½	teaspoon	black pepper	freshly ground
½	small	red onion	thinly sliced
1	cup	frisée lettuce	torn into pieces
⅓	cup	radishes	thinly sliced
⅓	cup	toasted almonds	chopped
⅓	cup	fresh basil leaves	cut into chiffonade
1	ounce	Manchego cheese	shaved

// PROCEDURE

1. Shave the zucchini into long wide ribbons using a **vegetable peeler or mandoline**, turning the squash, if necessary, to ease shaving. Discard the seedy core.

2. Put the zucchini in a **colander** set inside a **bowl**, sprinkle with salt, toss, and drain for 30 minutes. Discard the liquid.

3. **Whisk** together the oil, lemon juice, mustard, and pepper in a **medium bowl**. Add the zucchini, onion, frisée, and radishes. Toss to combine. Sprinkle with the almonds, basil, and cheese and serve. Store, covered, in the refrigerator for up to 3 days.

TIDBIT | *Zucchini* is the diminutive of *zucca,* or "gourd."

MY FAVORITE SLICER

OVERSTUFFED PATTYPAN SQUASH

4 SERVINGS

TIDBIT | Pattypan squash are also known as scallop, custard, or cymling squash.

// **SOFTWARE** //

4	6-ounce	pattypan squash	
2	tablespoons	olive oil	
1	teaspoon	kosher salt	
½	teaspoon	black pepper	freshly ground
1	large	shallot	diced
1	clove	garlic	minced
½	cup	fresh corn kernels	about 1 ear
½	cup	lima beans	cooked
2	ounces	toasted pecans	chopped
1	tablespoon	fresh thyme leaves	

THE THREE SISTERS

Native Americans learned to grow corn, squash, and beans together, not only because they represent a complete protein when served together but because they form a perfect agricultural community. Traditionally, the corn was planted first, and when it was about six inches tall the beans and squash were planted around it. The beans used the corn stalks for support, and the squash hogged all the sunlight around the base of the mound, thus choking out weeds. The beans also fixed nitrogen in the soil and the squash provided mulch.

// **PROCEDURE** //

1. Heat the oven to 400°F. Place a **half sheet pan** in the oven to heat for 15 minutes.

2. Trim the woody ends from the squash and split them in half horizontally. Scoop out the squash seeds, leaving a ½-inch shell. Reserve the flesh.

3. Brush the cut sides of the squash with 1 tablespoon of the oil and season with ½ teaspoon of the salt and ¼ teaspoon of the pepper. Place the squash, cut sides down, on the preheated pan and roast for 15 minutes, or until the squash is tender and the flesh side is browned.

4. Meanwhile, finely chop the reserved squash flesh. Heat a **10-inch cast-iron skillet** over medium heat and add the remaining 1 tablespoon oil. When the oil shimmers, add the chopped squash, shallot, garlic, and the remaining ½ teaspoon salt and ¼ teaspoon pepper. Cook, stirring occasionally, for 2 to 3 minutes, until tender and browned. Add the corn, lima beans, pecans, and thyme. Cook until heated through, about 1 minute.

5. Divide the stuffing evenly among the cooked squash shells and serve immediately.

TIDBIT Pumpkins were so common in early America that Boston's port was known as Pumpkinshire.

TRIVIA Shooting pumpkins in summertime isn't easy. We found someone to grow an early batch for us. They came early and pretty much filled the building.

They say that Benjamin Franklin hated the idea of making the carrion-munching eagle our national bird, a post he would have preferred to fill with the wily yet noble turkey, which I admit would look pretty funny on a quarter. When it comes to the American notion of apple pie being an edible symbol of our culture, I am utterly simpatico with Ben. Apple? Really? They're from Kazakhstan, don't you know? Instead I would elect the pie made with pumpkin, which just so happens to be 100 percent North American. Problem is, like so much edible Americana, we've allowed convenience to supplant flavor. Ninety-nine point nine percent of pumpkin pies produced in this country issue forth from a can. And cans aren't American, my friends, they're French—not that there's anything wrong with that. I say it's about time we took back our pie and made it into some seriously . . .

The word *pumpkin* was morphed by early American colonists from the English *pumpion*, which was itself an adaptation of the French *pompon*, which came from the Greek *pepon*, meaning "large melon," which makes sense because pumpkin, squash, and melons are all members of the *Cucurbitacea* family, and as such are fruits—that is, flesh-encased seed packets born of flowers. Pumpkins are highly nutritious and, due to their meaty flesh and tough skin, long keeping, which is why they were valuable winter staples. In fact, once local natives taught the settlers to grow pumpkins, Governor Bradford of the Plymouth Colony ordered the settlers to grow them to avert starvation. So crucial were pumpkins to life that one pilgrim penned these lines:

"For pottage and puddings and custards and pies, our parsnips and pumpkins are common supplies. We have pumpkins at morning and pumpkins at noon. If it were not for pumpkins we should be undoon."[1]

There are many different varieties of pumpkins, yet of the millions grown in the United States each year, most aren't worth eating. That's because as soon as Americans traded in their root cellars for refrigerators, these old nutrition bombs were relegated to nonculinary duties, including but not limited to accessorizing headless horsemen, transporting girls with glass shoes, and "chucking" across fields via trebuchet. These days, most pumpkins are grown not for their flavor but rather their ability to stand up to knife, saw, and candle, and all for one night of glory in late October—but that's another show.

If taste rather than shape is truly your goal, I strongly suggest you either grow or seek out a classic baking variety, three of which immediately leap to mind:

The big old DICKINSON is the pumpkin that's most often found in cans of pumpkin puree. Regrettably, I find that the canning process is not kind to the distinct flavor of the Dickinson—and, let's face it, it's kind of big and unruly to work with at home.

The JARRAHDALE is a very nice choice indeed. Its pale exterior conceals a bright orange flesh with a strong melon aroma. It's from New Zealand, and kind of hard to find here.

Here we have my favorite, the beautiful and diminutive SUGAR PIE PUMPKIN, which possesses a very smooth flesh, a very high concentration of sugar, and a size that's perfect for the home culinarian. If you cannot find one of these, skip the jack-o'-lanterns altogether and go with butternut squash, which is easily found, almost identical in flavor, and easy to work with in the home kitchen environment.

WILL THIS FIT MY HAT?

[1] Our source is a dissertation by Cynthia Ott (*Squashed Myths*, p. 160), 2002. The original source is *The Poets and Poetry of America*, collected by Rufus Wilmont Griswold (1856). The poet's name is unknown.

TIDBIT If stored at an optimum 50° to 60°F at 50 to 70 percent humidity, most pumpkins will remain culinarily viable for up to three months.

Dickinson   Jarrahdale   Sugar "Pie"

WHOLE PUMPKIN PIE SOUP

4 TO 6 SERVINGS

Ironically, the very factors that render the pumpkin something of a symbolic anachronism made it doubly valuable in the colonial kitchen. Consider, if you will, the only oven housed in the early American home. It was the hearth. What few pots the cook had access to would be placed either over the fire, in front of it, or down in the dying embers. A traditional pie—that is, a crust in a pan with a filling—would have been pretty much impossible to make in a hearth. But keep in mind that the crust of most early pies served only as a vessel. It wasn't typically intended for consumption, and that means, technically speaking, the only thing we need to do to a pumpkin to make it into a pie is to fill it with something and park it by the fire, and that's exactly what the early colonists did. I realize this is not what most of us would think of as a pie, but keep in mind that from a flavor and texture standpoint, it was probably as close to a pumpkin pie as the early colonists ever got.

// SOFTWARE

1	whole	baking pumpkin	about 4 pounds, rinsed
2	teaspoons	vegetable oil	
1	tablespoon	unsalted butter	
½	small	yellow onion	diced
1	teaspoon	kosher salt	
1	clove	garlic	minced
1	small	apple	peeled, cored, and diced
1	cup	low-sodium chicken broth	
½	cup	heavy cream	
2	ounces	goat cheese	
1	teaspoon	fresh thyme leaves	

// PROCEDURE

1. Heat the oven to 375°F.

2. Make a lid from the top of the pumpkin by cutting around the stem at a 45-degree angle. Make sure the opening is large enough to work within. Remove the seeds and fibers with a **metal spoon or ice cream scoop** and **kitchen shears**. Reserve the seeds for another use. Brush the exterior of the pumpkin and lid with oil. Oil a **round casserole dish** large enough to hold the pumpkin and put the pumpkin inside.

3. Combine the butter, onion, salt, garlic, apple, broth, and cream in the hollow pumpkin. Replace the lid of the pumpkin to cover. Bake for 1½ hours.

4. Remove the lid. Add the cheese and thyme and bake for an additional 30 minutes, uncovered. Remove the pumpkin from the oven and gently scrape some of the flesh into the soup mixture. Puree with an **immersion blender** to desired consistency, being careful to avoid the sides and bottom of the pumpkin. Serve immediately.

PUMPKIN PUREE

2 TO 2½ POUNDS PUREE

To make a pumpkin pie that modern Americans would actually recognize will require some pumpkin puree, and no, we're not going to open a can.

Heavy butcher's cleaver—note hole for hanging

// SOFTWARE //

1	4- to 6-pound	baking pumpkin	rinsed and dried
	to taste	kosher salt	

// PROCEDURE //

1. Heat the oven to 400°F.

2. Slice a small piece of skin off one side of the pumpkin so when laid on its side the pumpkin won't roll. Remove the stem and split the pumpkin in half from top to bottom, using a large **cleaver** and a **mallet**. Scoop out the seeds and fiber with a **large metal spoon or ice cream scoop** and **kitchen shears**. Reserve the seeds for another use.

3. Sprinkle the flesh with salt and lay the halves, flesh side down, on a **half sheet pan** lined with **parchment paper**. Roast for 30 to 45 minutes, or until a **paring knife** can be easily inserted and removed from the pumpkin. Test in several places to ensure doneness.

4. Remove the sheet pan to a **cooling rack** and cool the pumpkin for 1 hour. Using a large spoon, remove the roasted flesh of the pumpkin from the skin and transfer to a **food processor**. Process for 3 to 4 minutes, until very smooth. Store in the refrigerator for up to 1 week or freeze for up to 3 months.

DO NOT TRY THIS AT HOME!

PUMPKIN PIE

1 (9-INCH) PIE OR 5 (5-INCH) MINI-PIES

// SOFTWARE //

FOR THE CRUST

6	ounces	gingersnap cookies	
1	tablespoon	dark brown sugar	
1	teaspoon	ground ginger	
1	ounce	unsalted butter	melted

FOR THE FILLING

16	ounces	Pumpkin Puree (page 369)	
1	cup	half-and-half	
½	teaspoon	nutmeg	freshly grated
½	teaspoon	kosher salt	
¾	cup	dark brown sugar	
2	large	eggs	
1	large	egg yolk	

FOR THE BRÛLÉE FOR MINI-PIES

5	teaspoons	light brown sugar	

// PROCEDURE ///

1. Heat the oven to 350°F.

— MAKE THE CRUST:

2. Combine the gingersnaps, brown sugar, and ginger in a **food processor**. Process until the cookies are fine crumbs. Drizzle the butter into the crumb mixture. Pulse 8 to 10 times to combine.

3. Press the gingersnap mixture into the bottom, up the sides, and just over the lip of a **9-inch glass pie dish**. Place on a **half sheet pan** and bake for 10 to 12 minutes, until lightly browned. Cool the crust at least 10 minutes before filling. For mini-pies: Evenly divide the crust mixture among **5 (5-inch) pie tins** and bake on a half sheet pan for 5 minutes. Cool for 10 minutes.

TIDBIT | Americans consume around 50 million pumpkin pies a year, most of them in November and December.

MAKE THE FILLING:

(4) Bring the pumpkin puree to a simmer over medium heat in a **2-quart saucepan**. Cook, stirring occasionally, for 2 to 3 minutes, or until slightly thickened. Add the half-and-half, nutmeg, and salt. Stir and return the mixture to a simmer. Remove from the heat and cool for 10 minutes.

(5) **Whisk** the brown sugar, eggs, and egg yolk in a **large bowl** until smooth. Add the pumpkin mixture and whisk until thoroughly combined. Pour the filling into the warm pie crust and bake on the same half sheet pan for 45 to 50 minutes, until the center jiggles slightly but the sides of the filling are set. Cool on a **cooling rack** for at least 2 hours before slicing. The pie can be made and refrigerated up to 2 days in advance and is best the day after it is made.

FOR MINI-PIES:

Divide the filling evenly among the pans; bake on the same half sheet pan for 25 minutes, or until the center juggles slightly but the sides of the filling are set. Cool on a **cooling rack** for 2 hours. Spread 1 teaspoon of the brown sugar on the top of each pie. Melt the sugar using a **blowtorch** to form a crisp top. Cool for 5 minutes before serving.

CONCERNING PUMPKIN NUTRITION

Besides the vegetable protein and the fiber, calcium, and potassium, the really big news here is the alpha and beta carotenes that break down in the small intestine to make vitamin A. This means that both alpha and beta carotene are what we call vitamin A precursors. Vitamin A keeps your skin and your mucus membranes healthy and it's a powerful antioxidant. It's also critical for eyesight, especially night vision.

ONCE AGAIN, I MUST COAX CAROLYN INTO AN UNCOMFORTABLE POSITION.

American cuisine has come a long way in the last twenty years, but if you want to experience true elegance, sophistication, and subtlety on the dessert side of the plate, you'd better charge up the old time machine, my friend, because we've done missed the boat. These days it's all death by chocolate this and chile, caramel, bacon sundae that, but back in the '20s and '30s, swank dessert carts offered swells the likes of baked Alaska, *oeufs à la neige*, and pavlova, each an elegant artifact from a more genteel age, each based upon a meringue—and each, sadly, all but extinct. That's a shame, because the magical marriage of egg white, sugar, and air known as meringue goes by yet another name, and that's . . .

▷○ **A meringue is an egg foam into which sugar has been worked, but it should be noted that if you were to remove the sugar the egg whites would still create a foam. A foam being, of course, nothing but a very large collection of very, very small bubbles. How do you produce bubbles from an egg white? Consider the gumball machine.**

Just stick with me here a minute. Let's say that this is a microscopic view of an egg white. The air spaces represent water, and the capsules are balled-up proteins, which take up only 10 percent of the mass.

Here's the cool part. As we all know, proteins are really just long chains of amino acids that are balled up on themselves in their natural state, as portrayed by the pipe cleaners. What's captivating about this is that not all of the amino acids are the same. Some are hydrophilic—that is, water loving—while others are hydrophobic, or water strongly disliking.[1] In the wadded-up form, the hydrophilics are on the outsides while the hydrophobics are deep within. When we denature the structure by beating the tar out of it with a whisk or similar appliance, many of the molecular bonds that hold the chains into a wad will be broken, and the mass will kind of spread out. The proteins, with continued beating, will tangle up in a process we call coagulation. What in the world does this have to do with bubbles? Just because the proteins have denatured and coagulated doesn't mean that their hydrophilic or hydrophobic characteristics have been lost. Some parts of this structure still like being stuck in water and others would much prefer to be stuck out into the air. The only shape that makes everyone happy is a hollow sphere known as a "bubble."

Problem is, this structure isn't very stable, and baking makes it even worse, because once the water cooks out, there aren't enough proteins behind to keep the form together. Luckily, there is a substance that will strengthen this structure, lending considerable flavor at the same time. I speak, of course, of the disaccharide sucrose: sugar. Sugar is hygroscopic, so it holds water inside the bubble structure even when cooked. Sugar also provides adhesion, literally holding the foam together. How much sugar we integrate and how we invite it to the party greatly affect the nature of the final foam, and its culinary viability.

▷○ **The baking world generally recognizes the existence of three basic meringues:**

— FRENCH: Uncooked

— ITALIAN: Syrup cooked

— SWISS: Cooked

We will examine each in situ.

[1] That's a technical term.

H_2O

A gumball machine is like an egg white.

GRADE A EGG · PROTEIN APLENTY · 25¢ 25¢

Balled-up proteins

Amino chains unravel and retangle with others.

Hydrophobic
Hydrophilic

When a bubble is created, hydrophilic aminos touch the H_2O and hydrophobics face the air both outside and inside.

TIDBIT | Meringue was called "sugar puff" in the seventeenth century.

6 SERVINGS

CONCERNING PASSION FRUIT

When it comes time to serve the pavlova, I'm a traditionalist, so I reach for the discouragingly ugly but undeniably delicious purple passion fruit. The passion fruit is technically South American, but the purple variety has been commercially grown around Auckland in New Zealand since the 1930s.

Although it's considered to be the national dessert of Australia, pavlova was actually concocted in New Zealand, Wellington in fact, where the famed Russian ballerina Anna Pavlova toured in 1926. Historians say that a popular fruit-filled meringue cake, developed during colonial days when eggs were plentiful but flour was not, was rechristened in Pavlova's honor. A proper pavlova is characterized by a crisp, crunchy exterior, and a spongy, marshmallowy interior. To achieve these ends, we employ a light French-style meringue and a relatively cool oven.

// SOFTWARE

4	ounces	(pasteurized) egg whites	at room temperature (3 to 4 large egg whites)
	pinch	kosher salt	
6	ounces	sugar	
½	teaspoon	vanilla extract	
½	teaspoon	distilled white vinegar	
1	teaspoon	cornstarch	
1	cup	whipped cream	
4	whole	passion fruit	cut in half and fruit pulp scooped out

// PROCEDURE

1. Heat the oven to 250°F. Line a **half sheet pan** with **parchment paper**. Use a **9-inch round plate** to trace a circle in the middle of the parchment. Turn the parchment over.

2. Put the egg whites and salt in a **stand mixer fitted with the whisk attachment** and beat on high speed until stiff peaks form, 4 to 5 minutes. Reduce the speed to medium and slowly add the sugar over 2 minutes. Stop and scrape down the sides of the bowl. Increase the speed to high and beat until the mixture is smooth and glossy and stiff peaks form, 6 to 7 minutes. Decrease the speed to low and add the vanilla, vinegar, and cornstarch. Mix just to combine.

3. Gently **spoon** the meringue onto the parchment and spread to fit the shape of the circle, forming a slight well in the center. Bake for 45 minutes. Turn off the oven and leave the meringue inside for 3 hours, or until it is crisp and dry on the outside. Open the oven door and cool completely before removing from the oven, about 30 minutes.

4. Just before serving, combine the whipped cream and the passion fruit pulp and spread in the center of the meringue. Serve immediately.

BAKED ALASKA

6 TO 8 SERVINGS

On October 18, 1867, a bill was signed finalizing the purchase of the Alaska territory from Russia. The deal was negotiated by New York senator William H. Seward, and to honor him, Delmonico's restaurant served up a dish called Seward's Folly, which was later redubbed Alaska Florida, and finally baked Alaska. It features the candylike yet highly durable cooked Italian meringue.

// SOFTWARE

1½	quarts	strawberry ice cream	softened
1	9-by-5-by-½-inch piece	chiffon cake (see tip)	cooled completely
8	ounces	sugar	
4	ounces	light corn syrup	
2	ounces	H₂O	
4	ounces	egg whites	at room temperature (3 to 4 large egg whites)
	pinch	kosher salt	
½	teaspoon	vanilla extract	

TIP The cake can be made by baking the cupcake batter on page 129 in a half sheet pan lined with parchment paper at 325°F for 20 to 25 minutes.

// PROCEDURE

1. Line a **9-by-5-inch loaf pan** with **plastic wrap**.

2. Put the ice cream in the pan and spread it evenly. Place the piece of cake on top of the ice cream, press down gently, and put the pan in the freezer for 1 hour.

3. Combine the sugar, corn syrup, and water in a **2-quart saucepan** and place over high heat. Stir just until the sugar dissolves, about 5 minutes. Clip on a **candy thermometer** and bring the mixture to 240°F.

4. While the syrup is cooking, put the egg whites, salt, and vanilla in a **stand mixer fitted with the whisk attachment** and whisk the eggs on high speed until they hold medium peaks, 4 to 5 minutes.

5. When the sugar syrup reaches 240°F, remove from the heat and, with the stand mixer on low speed, slowly and carefully pour the syrup in a thin, steady stream into the egg-white mixture, being careful not to let the syrup come in contact with the whisk. When all of the syrup has been added, increase the mixer speed to high and beat until stiff peaks form and the mixture has cooled, 8 to 10 minutes.

6. Remove the loaf pan from the freezer, turn upside down onto a **heatproof serving platter**, and remove the plastic wrap. Completely cover the ice cream–cake combo with a 1-inch layer of meringue all around, sealing the meringue to the platter around the bottom edge.

7. Use a **blowtorch** to brown the meringue all over. Serve immediately. The dessert may be frozen after the meringue has been browned.

OEUFS À LA NEIGE

We move now to "eggs on snow," a French concoction wherein poached egg–shaped meringues float serenely upon a pool of classic crème anglaise. Here we use a cooked or Swiss meringue, which differs from our first meringue in two significant ways:

1. The sugar is mixed with the egg whites before whipping.

2. The mixture is gently cooked to 140°F, allowing it to take advantage of two scientific facts. One, hot water can hold more sugar in solution than cold, and two, egg whites containing dissolved sugar can be whipped into firmer, more finely textured foams.

HOW TO HACK MERINGUE

This is a blow-dryer bonnet, available for ten bucks at any beauty store. And if you happen to have a crank-up-style stand mixer, it'll slide right on. So place your hair dryer someplace safe and secure (like a banana hanger, which up to this moment was a unitasker poster child). Connect the bonnet, turn the hair dryer to low heat, and boom: instant meringue cooker. I've actually scrambled French-style eggs this way (meaning eggs and cream) with the dryer on medium and the mixer on low. But I never ever walk away with the dryer on.

// SOFTWARE ///

FOR THE MERINGUE

8	ounces	sugar	
4	ounces	egg whites	at room temperature (3 to 4 large egg whites) (reserve the yolks)

FOR THE CRÈME ANGLAISE

3	cups	whole milk	
4	tablespoons	sugar	
1		vanilla bean	split and seeds scraped
4	ounces	egg yolks	(5 to 6 large egg yolks)
	pinch	kosher salt	
⅓	cup	chopped pistachios	optional

// PROCEDURE ///

MAKE THE MERINGUE:

1. Heat 1 inch of water in a **4-quart saucepan**, covered, over high heat until it simmers, about 8 minutes. Lower the heat to maintain a simmer.

2. Combine the sugar and egg whites in the **bowl of a stand mixer** and set the bowl over the simmering water. **Whisk** continually until the sugar has dissolved and the mixture lightens in color, doubles in volume, and reaches 140°F, 3 to 4 minutes.

3. Place the bowl on the stand mixer fitted with the **whisk attachment** and whisk on high speed until stiff peaks form and the meringue has cooled slightly, about 7 minutes. Set aside.

MAKE THE CRÈME ANGLAISE:

(4) Put the milk, 2 tablespoons of the sugar, and the vanilla bean in a **2-quart saucier**, cover, and place over high heat. Bring just to a simmer, about 5 minutes, Uncover, reduce the heat to low, and maintain a temperature of 180° to 190°F.

(5) Use a **1½-ounce disher** to scoop the meringue, 4 scoops at a time, into the milk mixture and poach for 3 minutes. Gently flip with a **slotted spoon** and cook for another 3 minutes, or until firm to the touch. Transfer to a **half sheet pan** lined with a **tea towel**. Repeat with the remaining meringue mixture, maintaining the temperature of the milk mixture to make sure it does not boil. Hold the meringues at room temperature until ready to serve or store in an airtight container up to overnight.

(6) Reduce the heat to low and keep the milk mixture warm in the pan.

(7) Whisk together the egg yolks, salt, and remaining 2 tablespoons sugar in a **medium bowl** until well combined and slightly lightened in color, about 2 minutes. Slowly add half of the milk mixture, whisking constantly. Return the entire mixture to the saucepan over low heat and cook, stirring frequently with a **spatula or wooden spoon**, until the sauce has thickened slightly and coats the back of the spatula or spoon, 8 to 9 minutes. You should be able to draw a line on the back of the utensil with your finger.

(8) Strain the sauce through a **fine-mesh sieve** into a bowl set over an ice-water bath and stir until chilled. The sauce can be made a day ahead and stored, covered, in the refrigerator.

(9) Spoon a small amount of sauce into the center of each of 6 shallow serving bowls and top with 2 *oeufs*. Sprinkle with pistachios, if desired, and serve.

TIDBIT | Early European cooks beat egg whites with birch twigs and created a dish they called "snow."

TIDBIT | *Oeufs à la neige* is often misidentified as "Floating Islands."

I love to travel but rarely have the time, which is one reason I keep my pantry well stocked. Through it I can venture far and wide without ever leaving home. Consider the chickpea. Not only is it ridiculously nutritious, and vise-grip versatile, no ingredient save the chickpea better sums up the Near and Middle Eastern cuisines that I'll probably never get to taste firsthand. And that, my friends, is reason enough to award the chickpea the title . . .

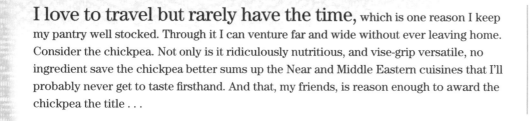

EACH "CECI BEAN" CONCEALS A RAM'S HEAD.

▷◦ Say hello to *Cicer arietinum*, which, nomenclatural issues notwithstanding, is a bean, not a pea. The *arietinum* part of the name derives from *aries*, "ram," since the seed does resemble a ram's head . . . sorta. It has long been held that the *cicer* part was adapted from the family name of the Roman orator Cicero, whose great-great-great-grandfather supposedly adopted the name "Cicero" because he somehow knew that one of his de-scendents would have a wart on his nose. If you doubt the veracity of the story (as I do), it may be enough of an explanation to accept that Romans called any round, hard seed a *cicer*, the way the English called anything of that general size and shape a "corn."

▷◦ By the time Cicero sprouted his famous nose wart, the chickpea was already several millennia old. Born in Egypt, the chickpea wasted no time spreading through the Middle East to Northern Africa and east to India. The Moors were responsible for taking it to Spain, where the name "garbanzo" was applied. Although India grows about 64 percent of the world crop, mostly of the smaller *desi* variety, other producers include Turkey, Iran, Iraq, Myanmar, Australia, Ethiopia, Canada, Mexico, and other countries here and there, including the United States.

▷◦ There are two distinct varieties of chickpea. *Desi* are smallish and typically possess thick, pigmented seed covers, many of which are split or ground into a flour called besan. In the West, most chickpeas are the larger and more common *kabuli* type, which are larger than *desi* chickpeas and sport a thinner seed coat. Although canned *kabuli* chickpeas are available, I do not think they profit a lick from the canning procedure (convenience aside) and would much rather cook them myself.

▷◦ Why has the chickpea become so important to so many? Protein and lots of it, and zinc and iron, which means that chickpeas are a very good plant-based replacement for meat, especially if it's married to certain other ingredients.

▷◦ To soak or not to soak. Like most dried beans and peas, chickpeas are rock hard. Soften-ing them can be achieved by long cooking or soaking for up to 8 hours before cooking. Why so long? In most culinary cases we need to soften and cook that starch as well as soften the tough outer skin, which are in fact separate operations. When you place a chickpea in liquid to soak, the water doesn't just go through the skin. It passes through a structure called the hilum, which is like a spigot where the seed was connected to its pod. If the liquid moving inside is really hot, the starch will swell or gelatinize before the outer shell softens and the chickpea will blow itself to bits, which is another reason to presoak. With soaking, the inner starch has time to hydrate and the outer skin softens and becomes more elastic. And depending on the final destination, sometimes that soak is all the little *cicers* need.

SLOW-COOKER CHICKPEAS

Chickpeas can be easily cooked using a slow cooker. Just sort and rinse 1 pound of dried chickpeas, then combine them with 7 cups of water and ¼ teaspoon of baking soda in a 2½-quart slow cooker. Cover and cook on high for 4 hours or low for 8 to 9 hours, until tender. Drain and use in hummus or any other desired application. Makes 6 cups, or about 2 pounds, of cooked chickpeas.

SALT AND VINEGAR ROASTED CHICKPEAS

4 TO 6 APPETIZER SERVINGS

In the region around Corum in Turkey, young and old alike munch a curiously crunchable concoction called *leblebi*, the recipe for which goes something like this:

Build a roasting stove out of fire bricks.

Roast fresh chickpeas and while they're hot, seal them in cloth sacks.

Wait two days.

Repeat, then spread the chickpeas in a cool, dry place and leave for two weeks.

Moisten, seal in sacks, and wait a day.

Roast again, then wait two days.

Roast them a final time, then remove the skins and enjoy.

Luckily there is a faster and easier way.

BEANS AND PROTEIN

Protein molecules are constructed of smaller structures called amino acids. Some of these our bodies can actually produce, but there are eight that adult humans need that we can't make, namely phenylalanine, valine, threonine, tryptophan, isoleucine, methionine, leucine, and lysine. These we must consume in food form, and any food that contains them all is referred to as a complete protein. Meat, fish, and eggs are all complete proteins, as are soybeans, the only vegetable on the list. Chickpeas are missing sufficient levels of tryptophan, methionine, and cystine. Luckily, most nuts and seeds can complete the equation, which may explain why traditional chickpea dishes from the Near East so often contain sesame seeds, or more specifically the sesame-seed paste known as tahini, a key ingredient in the ubiquitous puree known as hummus.

// SOFTWARE

1	pound	dried chickpeas	
¼	cup plus 1 teaspoon	red wine vinegar	
1	teaspoon	Dijon mustard	
1	teaspoon plus ½ teaspoon	kosher salt	
1	tablespoon	olive oil	

// PROCEDURE

1. Put the chickpeas in a **medium bowl** and add enough **cold water** to cover by 2 inches. Soak overnight.

2. Heat the oven to 400°F.

3. Drain the chickpeas, return them to the bowl, and set aside.

4. Put ¼ cup of the vinegar, the mustard, and 1 teaspoon salt in a **small lidded container** and shake vigorously to combine. Add the oil and shake to combine.

5. Pour the dressing over the chickpeas and toss to combine. Spread the chickpeas on a **half sheet pan** and roast for 60 to 65 minutes, tossing every 15 minutes, or until the chickpeas are deep golden brown and crunchy. Remove from the oven, return to the mixing bowl, add the remaining vinegar and salt, and toss to combine.

6. Transfer back to the sheet pan and spread out to cool completely before serving.

TIDBIT The chickpea is the most widely consumed legume in the world.

TIDBIT Chickpeas were grown in the hanging gardens of Babylon.

// SOFTWARE

1	pound	cooked chickpeas	
2	cloves	garlic	minced
1½	teaspoons	kosher salt	
5	tablespoons	lemon juice	freshly squeezed
¼	cup	H$_2$O	
⅓	cup	tahini	stirred well
¼	cup	extra virgin olive oil	plus extra for serving
	to taste	ground sumac[1]	

// PROCEDURE

1. Combine the chickpeas, garlic, and salt in a **food processor**. Process for 15 to 20 seconds. Stop, scrape down the sides of the bowl, and process for another 15 to 20 seconds.

2. Add the lemon juice and water. Process for 20 seconds.

3. Add the tahini. Process for 20 seconds, then scrape down the sides of the bowl.

4. With the processor running, drizzle in the oil.

5. Transfer the hummus to a **serving bowl** and drizzle with additional oil and sprinkle with sumac.

LIKE THE HAT?

[1] The berry of the Middle Eastern shrub *Rhus coriaria*, not to be confused with its American cousin, poison sumac. Ground into a spice that is earthy, sweet, and sour at the same time, sumac is easily obtained from specialty spice vendors via the Internet.

15 TO 20 FALAFEL

If you ever stroll the streets of Lebanon, Israel, and Jordan, you'll encounter many a cart selling balls or patties of fried, ground chickpeas called falafel, which are typically served inside a warm pita with some form of salad and dressing. If you remember these as beany hush puppies from your low-rent college days, we're about to erase that memory.

// SOFTWARE ///

1	pound	dried chickpeas	sorted and rinsed
1	teaspoon	whole cumin seeds	
1	teaspoon	whole coriander seeds	
2	cloves	garlic	coarsely chopped
4		scallions	trimmed and finely chopped
2	teaspoons	kosher salt	
½	teaspoon	black pepper	freshly ground
1	teaspoon	baking powder	aluminum-free
½	teaspoon	cayenne pepper	
2	tablespoons	fresh parsley leaves	finely chopped
2	quarts	peanut oil	

// PROCEDURE //

(1) Put the chickpeas in a **medium bowl** and add enough cold water to cover by 2 inches. Soak overnight.

(2) Put the cumin and coriander in an **8-inch cast-iron skillet** and place over medium-high heat. Cook, shaking the pan frequently, until the seeds give off an aroma and just begin to brown. Transfer to a spice grinder and process until finely ground. Set aside.

(3) Drain the chickpeas. Combine the soaked chickpeas, cumin, coriander, garlic, scallions, salt, black pepper, baking powder, cayenne pepper, and parsley in a medium bowl.

(4) Pass this mixture through a **meat grinder or stand mixer grinder attachment fitted with the smallest die**. (Alternatively, you can divide the mixture in half and process one half at a time in a food processor, pulsing 10 to 20 times.)

(5) Scoop the mixture into 1½- to 2-ounce portions using a **2-inch disher**. Place on a **half sheet pan** lined with **parchment paper**.

6. Heat the oil in a **5-quart Dutch oven** over high heat until it reaches 350°F. Adjust the heat to maintain the temperature.

7. Gently place the falafel, one at a time, in the hot oil. Fry 4 at a time for 5 to 7 minutes, until deep golden brown. Remove to a **half sheet pan** lined with a **cooling rack** and topped with a **paper towel** to drain. Repeat until all falafel have been cooked. Serve with yogurt sauce, if desired.

TIDBIT | Falafel are sometimes called "Israeli hot dogs".

10 MINUTES MORE	YOGURT SAUCE FOR FALAFEL

1½ CUPS

// SOFTWARE

8	ounces	plain yogurt	
4	ounces	feta cheese	crumbled
2	tablespoons	fresh parsley	chopped
1	tablespoon	fresh mint	chopped
2	cloves	garlic	minced
1	tablespoon	lemon juice	freshly squeezed
1	tablespoon	harissa	
½	teaspoon	kosher salt	

// PROCEDURE

Whisk all the ingredients together in a **medium bowl**. Serve as sauce for falafel. Store in an **airtight container** in the refrigerator for up to 3 days.

Although I've heard

the tales of Faustian deals made between desperate bakers and a certain black-clad gentleman under midnight moons on the prairie, I somewhat doubt that the first recipe for the deep, moist, chocolaty cake known as devil's food was handed over in exchange for eternal rights to an equally tasty soul. The moniker "devil's food" is simply a testament to the cake's sinfully rich nature, jet-black chocolatiness, and the fact that that it is diametrically opposed to the angel food cake, which is neither rich nor chocolaty nor sinful. And yet by today's standards, most devil's food cakes aren't exactly decadent, which is why the devil has taken refuge in box cakes packed with highly specialized industrial ingredients assembled via scientifically calculated formulae. I for one will not succumb to the siren song of the box, not as long as the shining light of science can deliver the dark, dense delight that goes by the name of . . .

TIDBIT | Some early devil's food cake recipes called for unorthodox additions such as mashed potatoes, cinnamon, and cloves.

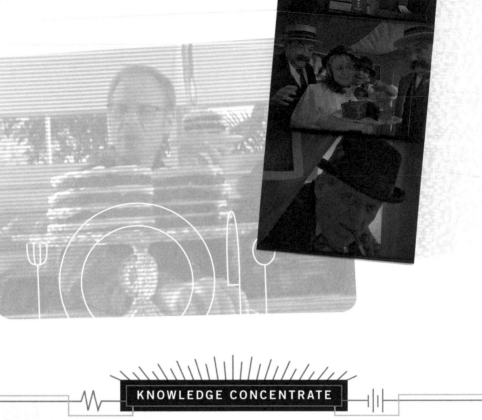

KNOWLEDGE CONCENTRATE

▷○ **If you look at the devil's food recipes that were passed around among bakers in the early to mid-1950s you can see that they were little more than layer cakes with chocolate added to them. Most call for solid chocolate, solid fat, and milk and for assembly via the creaming method, wherein the solid fat and sugar are beaten together before the dry and wet components are added. All technicalities, I admit, and yet collectively they lead a cake away from the valley of moistness and into a kind of dessert desert. We can repair the situation, starting with cocoa powder.**

▷○ **Devil's food isn't so much chocolate cake as chocolate-flavored cake, and when it comes to baked goods, strange though it sounds, chocolate doesn't deliver nearly as much flavor as cocoa powder. Once the cocoa bean or nib is aged, roasted, and ground, the resulting substance, chocolate liquor, can with minimal processing be turned into unsweetened or baking chocolate, which contains about 50 percent cocoa solids and between 35 and 50 percent cocoa butter, the fat portion of the seed. Not only is cocoa butter relatively lacking in flavor, it is also solid at room temperature, which means it will harden any cake it's in to some degree.**

If the cocoa liquor is squeezed in a press such as the one invented by Dutchman Conrad Van Houten, the fat can be removed from the equation, leaving a solid disk that, when ground, yields a reddish-brown powder possessing a rather acidic and fruity flavor. The acidity of this "natural" cocoa powder makes it fairly insoluble in water. Van Houten corrected this by treating a batch of nibs with an alkaline solution before pressing. The resulting powder was very dark, very flavorful, and dispersed easily in water. Dubbed "Dutch process cocoa," this powder is my choice for devil's food because its flavor is focused (not fruity), and when worked into a batter it is black as night.

Having settled upon the appropriate cocoa powder, we must consider integration. Many recipes call for simply sifting it into the dry ingredients, but, like coffee, cocoa is a bean—and beans should be brewed in order to fully give up their goodness, which is why I always soak or "bloom" my cocoa in boiling liquid (typically water) before building my batter.

I always use oil rather than butter because oil is liquid at room temperature and will therefore deliver a moister mouthfeel than butter. Besides, with all this cocoa, you'd never taste butter, so why waste it? Also, I never use milk in a devil's food cake because it tends to cover up the sharper edges of the chocolate flavor—and those edges, which could be construed as bitterness, I do so love.

Since we've gotten rid of the butter, there is no reason to employ the creaming method and we can instead assemble via the muffin method, which is easy, requires no special machinery, and can be derailed only by overmixing.[1]

Most American cakes are robed either in a boiled "seven-minute" frosting or some form of buttercream, the main ingredients of which are butter and confectioners' sugar. The sugar is fine enough to dissolve in the small amount of water found in the butter and it contains cornstarch, which helps keep the frosting stable. It is essentially an emulsion, after all. Since it easily integrates with fats, this is the perfect vehicle for solid chocolate. I know I said not to use it in the cake, because we want the cake moist and tender. The frosting, however, needs to be a little on the stiff side or it'll just ooze right off. Not good eats.

Many modern bakers don't realize that red velvet cake is nothing more than a devil's food cake hacked for a finer texture and a different pigment. Red velvet cake is, in the South at least, considered to be more refined than devil's food and thus it's finer and more uniform in texture. To achieve this, we must trade our oil in for butter and return to the creaming method, wherein sugar granules perforate solid fat, giving birth to tiny bubbles that provide the cake's "tooth."

Then, of course, there's red velvet cake's distinctive hue. Trading Dutch process for natural cocoa powder and upping the acidity of the batter with buttermilk and a shot of vinegar, we can affect the anthocyanin compounds in the cocoa. These pigments belong to a family of antioxidants also found in red cabbage. As you may recall from our "Head Games" episode (see volume 1), cooking red cabbage in water with baking soda turns the cabbage blue, while adding an acid keeps the reds bright. This same effect, granted on a smaller scale, works in a cocoa-flavored cake, rendering dark red what was once dark brown. This condition can be augmented by the use of beets in the batter, but if you want your cake really, really red, you're going to have to reach for food coloring.

| Basic cocoa press

[1] Unlike the creaming method, which often runs aground due to underbeating.

DEVIL OF A CAKE

385

1 (9-BY-13-INCH) CAKE, 15 TO 20 SERVINGS

// SOFTWARE

1	cup	boiling H$_2$O	
4	ounces	Dutch process cocoa powder	
10½	ounces	dark brown sugar	
5½	ounces	all-purpose flour	
4	ounces	cake flour	
1	teaspoon	baking soda	
½	teaspoon	kosher salt	
1	cup	canola oil	
4½	ounces	sour cream	at room temperature
2	large	eggs	at room temperature
2	large	eggs yolks	at room temperature
2	cups	Chocolate Frosting (page 388)	

// PROCEDURE

1. Set a rack in the center of the oven and heat the oven to 325°F. Spray a **9-by-13-inch metal pan** with **nonstick cooking spray**, line it with **parchment paper** so it hangs over the sides of the pan, spray the parchment with nonstick spray, and set aside.

2. **Whisk** the boiling water and cocoa powder together in a **small bowl** and set aside.

3. Combine the brown sugar, flours, baking soda, and salt in a **stand mixer fitted with the paddle attachment**.

4. Whisk the oil, sour cream, eggs, and egg yolks in a **large vessel with a pouring spout** (like a large measuring cup). Add to the cocoa-and-water mixture and gradually whisk to combine.

5. With the mixer on low speed, add the liquid mixture to the dry mixture over 30 seconds. Continue to beat on low speed for another 30 seconds. Stop and scrape down the sides of the bowl. Continue to beat on low speed until the batter is smooth. Pour the batter into the prepared pan and bake for 30 to 35 minutes, until the cake springs back when pressed and reaches an internal temperature of 205°F. Cool in the pan on a **rack** for 30 minutes, then remove the cake from the pan and cool completely before frosting.

DEVIL OF A CAKE

TIP | I've always thought of devil's food as a single-layer type of cake, so I typically bake it in a 9-by-13-inch metal pan lubed with nonstick cooking spray and lined with parchment paper.

TIDBIT | Unlike wax paper, parchment paper is impregnated with heat-resistant silicone.

TIDBIT | Before the advent of cocoa powder, the Aztecs ground cacao beans to create a grainy, bitter chocolate drink.

RED VELVET CAKE

2 (9-INCH) ROUND LAYERS;
10 TO 12 SERVINGS

// SOFTWARE ///

5½	ounces	all-purpose flour	
4	ounces	cake flour	
½	ounce	natural cocoa powder	not Dutch process
1	teaspoon	baking soda	
½	teaspoon	kosher salt	
1	cup	low-fat buttermilk	at room temperature
1	fluid ounce	red liquid food coloring	
1	tablespoon	distilled white vinegar	
1	teaspoon	vanilla extract	
10½	ounces	dark brown sugar	
4	ounces	unsalted butter	at room temperature
2	large	eggs	at room temperature
3	cups	Cream Cheese Frosting (page 388)	

// PROCEDURE //

1. Set a rack in the middle of the oven and heat the oven to 325°F.

2. Spray **2 (9-inch) round cake pans** with **nonstick cooking spray**, line them with **parchment paper rounds**, spray the parchment with nonstick spray, and set aside.

3. **Whisk** the flours, cocoa powder, baking soda, and salt together in a **bowl** and set aside.

4. Whisk the buttermilk, food coloring, vinegar, and vanilla together in a **small bowl** and set aside.

5. Combine the brown sugar and butter in a **stand mixer fitted with the paddle attachment** and cream on medium speed for 2 minutes, or until lightened in color. Scrape down the sides of the bowl with a **spatula**. Return the mixer to medium speed and add the eggs one at a time, beating until they are fully incorporated.

6. With the mixer on low, add the flour mixture in three installments, alternating with the buttermilk mixture (in two installments), beginning and ending with the flour mixture. Scrape down the sides of the bowl between installments. Mix on low speed until smooth.

7. Divide the batter evenly between the prepared pans and bake for 30 to 35 minutes, until the cake springs back when pressed or reaches an internal temperature of 205°F. Cool in the pans on a **rack** for 10 minutes, then remove the cakes from the pans and cool completely before frosting.

TIP For parchment origami (that is, pan lining), turn to page 59.

TIDBIT Beets were once used as both a sweetener and a colorant in red velvet cake.

Leave the sides unfrosted for visual contrast!

DEVIL OF A CAKE

APPLICATION ⎍⎍⎍ CHOCOLATE FROSTING

2 CUPS

// SOFTWARE ///

5½	ounces	unsalted butter	at room temperature
1	ounce	mayonnaise	
3	ounces	semisweet chocolate	melted and cooled
8	ounces	confectioners' sugar	
	pinch	kosher salt	

// PROCEDURE ///

1. Beat the butter and mayonnaise in a **stand mixer fitted with the paddle attachment** on high speed until light and fluffy, 3 to 4 minutes. With the mixer on low, slowly pour in the melted chocolate. Continue mixing until all the chocolate is incorporated, stopping to scrape down the sides of the bowl as needed. Turn off the mixer and add one-third of the confectioners' sugar. Mix on low to combine. Stop to scrape down the sides of the bowl. Repeat until all of the sugar has been incorporated. Add the salt and continue to beat until the frosting is smooth and lightens slightly in color, 2 to 3 minutes.

2. Use immediately or store in an **airtight container** at room temperature for up to 4 hours or refrigerate for up to 1 week. Bring to room temperature before using chilled frosting.

APPLICATION ⎍⎍⎍ CREAM CHEESE FROSTING

3 CUPS

CREAM CHEESE

Unlike butter, which melts at a relatively low 90°F, cream cheese can hold its own until it reaches well above 200°F. That means butter cream–style frostings can be prepared and kept in hot summer months. Two Southern specialties are strongly associated with cream cheese frosting: the carrot cake and the red velvet cake. You'll need a 12-ounce block—and make sure it's never been frozen, as that will result in a repulsive runniness.

// SOFTWARE ///

12	ounces	cream cheese	at room temperature
3	ounces	unsalted butter	at room temperature
1½	teaspoons	vanilla extract	
13½	ounces	confectioners' sugar	
	pinch	kosher salt	

// PROCEDURE ///

Combine the cream cheese and butter in a **stand mixer fitted with the paddle attachment** on medium speed just until blended. Add the vanilla and beat until combined. With the speed on low, add the confectioners' sugar in 4 batches, beating until smooth between additions. Add the salt and mix to combine. Refrigerate for 5 to 10 minutes before using.

If you're a fan of this program you've probably noticed that we have made more pie in the last decade than any other single dish. Why pie? Besides the fact that it tastes good, I believe pie is quite possibly the strongest link to our edible past. This is especially true of the pie we call chicken pot pie, a pie I hereby certify and qualify as . . .

HEY, ISN'T THAT MY WHISK?

KNOWLEDGE CONCENTRATE

Although pot pies flourished in ancient Greece and Rome, where salted pastry crusts were used as a means of preservation, the golden age of pot pies didn't dawn till the Middle Ages, when meat pies including those enclosing fowl were all the rage. Sometimes such pastry crusts, which were also called "coffins," held surprising entertainments within. Consider the nursery rhyme: "Sing a song of sixpence, a pocket full of rye, four and twenty blackbirds baked in a pie. When the pie was opened the birds began to sing. Oh, wasn't that a dainty dish to set before the king?"

Confining live birds required a strong dough constructed with hot water. A relatively high amount of fat was also melted into that hot liquid to provide flavor, limited gluten production, and a bit of waterproofing. I've made several such pies from ancient recipes, and although I find eating them kinda fun, most modern mouths would consider them . . . inedible. My favorite dough for building a "standing pie" is a puff pastry. We dedicated an entire episode to the subject of store-bought puff pastry in Volume 1, but I've found I vastly prefer making my own.

WORD IN A PIE

Until the Middle Ages, the word *pie* still meant a bird, specifically the European magpie, which was called "pie" because it is "pied" (meaning variegated black and white) and because back then "pie" referred to a hastily assembled pile, which is what this bird is famous for making in its nest (typically of purloined shinies). When *pie* came to mean "pie," *mag* was added to the bird's name because it means "to chatter," which this bird does plenty of.

MOVING BEYOND THE FROZEN PIE

In 1951 the C.A. Swanson & Sons company unleashed the first frozen, reheatable meal, and its name was "chicken pot pie." Many of us remember such pies fondly because back then our moms didn't know any better than to feed us meals containing 23 grams of fat and 690 mg of sodium. Now we know better and have the means to do something about it.

Most modern chicken pot pies are wrapped or topped in a French-style puff pastry, a laminate dough composed of hundreds if not thousands of layers of strong, high-gluten dough alternating with solid strata of butter. Creating it is an amazingly labor-intensive venture and frankly, in the words of my grandmother, "I'manottagonnadoit." Luckily there is another method, one that can produce about 70 percent of the lift with all the flavor in a fraction of the time. It is the "Scotch" or "blitz" method, and it's the only puff pastry you need to know.

// **SOFTWARE** ///

FOR THE PASTRY

10	ounces	bread flour	
2	ounces	whole-wheat flour	
1	teaspoon	fine kosher salt	
10	ounces	butter	cubed and frozen
6	ounces	ice water	

FOR THE FILLING

2	tablespoons	vegetable oil	
1½	pounds	chicken thighs and/or breasts	skin and bone removed and cut into ½-inch cubes
2½	teaspoons	kosher salt	
1	large	yellow onion	chopped
8	ounces	cremini mushrooms	cut into ¼-inch-thick slices
2	medium	carrots	peeled and cut into ¼-inch-thick rounds
2	medium	celery stalks	cut into ¼-inch-thick slices
2	cloves	garlic	minced
½	teaspoon	black pepper	freshly ground
½	teaspoon	dried thyme	
½	teaspoon	dried tarragon	
2	ounces	unsalted butter	
3	ounces	all-purpose flour	
2	cups	low-sodium chicken broth	
1½	cups	2% milk	at room temperature
8	ounces	frozen green peas	
1	teaspoon	fresh thyme	chopped
1	teaspoon	fresh tarragon	chopped

FOR THE EGG WASH

1	large	egg yolk	beaten
1	tablespoon	H_2O	

// PROCEDURE

MAKE THE PASTRY:

1. Combine the bread flour, whole-wheat flour, and salt in a **medium bowl**. Place in the freezer until very cold.

2. Place the flour mixture and butter in a mound on a clean work surface. Use a **bench scraper** to cut the butter into the flour until the mixture is crumbly and the butter pieces are about the size of almonds. Add the ice water, 2 tablespoons at a time, and mix into the dough, using the bench scraper, until it just barely comes together. Do not add too much water; it will come together.

3. Shape into a rectangle and pound with a **rolling pin** until it is about the size of a sheet of paper (8½ by 11 inches). Use the bench scraper to fold the dough into thirds, like a letter. Pound with the rolling pin, then rotate 90 degrees.

4. Repeat step 3 three more times, for a total of 4 turns of the dough. Pound with the rolling pin and fold the shorter sides of the rectangle in toward the center, from top to bottom, and then fold in half, like a book.

5. Wrap in **parchment paper** and refrigerate for 60 minutes.

6. Set a rack in the center of the oven and heat the oven to 425°F.

MAKE THE FILLING:

7. Put 1 tablespoon of the oil in a **10-inch cast-iron skillet** and place over high heat until it shimmers. Add the chicken, season with 1 teaspoon of the salt, and cook, turning occasionally, until the chicken is no longer pink on the outside but not dry, 4 to 6 minutes. Remove the chicken from the skillet and set aside in a **medium bowl**.

8. Lower the heat to medium and add the remaining 1 tablespoon oil to the skillet; heat until it shimmers. Add the onion, mushrooms, carrots, celery, garlic, remaining 1½ teaspoons salt, the pepper, and dried herbs and stir to combine. Cook, stirring occasionally, until the onion has softened, about 5 minutes. Add the butter and cook until it has melted. Stir in the flour and cook for 1 to 2 minutes. Gradually stir in the broth and milk. Bring to a simmer, stirring constantly, and cook until the sauce thickens, about 3 minutes. Remove from the heat and stir in the peas, fresh herbs, and chicken. Set aside.

MAKE THE EGG WASH:

9. Combine the egg and water in a **small dish** and set aside.

10. Divide the warm filling among **4 (16-ounce) ramekins** and place on a **half sheet pan** lined with **parchment paper**.

11. Remove the pastry from the refrigerator. Divide in half. Return one half to the refrigerator. Sprinkle lightly with flour and roll to ¼ inch thick. Using your ramekins as a guide, cut the pastry into 2 circles that are ½ inch wider than the rim, using a **sharp knife or pizza cutter**. Repeat with the other half of the dough.

12. Brush each dough round with egg wash and place, egg-washed side down, on the top of each filled ramekin. Brush the top of the pastry with egg wash. Bake for 15 minutes. Lower the temperature to 400°F and bake for another 15 to 20 minutes, until the crust is puffed and golden brown and the filling is bubbly. Cool for 10 minutes before serving.

A BIRD IN THE PIE IS
WORTH TWO IN THE BUSH

A very hearty breakfast . . . or dinner, for that matter.

// SOFTWARE ///

FOR THE FILLING

1	pound	chicken sausage	bulk or link
3	tablespoons	unsalted butter	
3	ounces	all-purpose flour	
2	cups	whole milk	
1½	cups	low-sodium chicken broth	
1		rotisserie chicken	meat removed from skin and bone, shredded, and finely chopped
1½	teaspoons	kosher salt	
1½	teaspoons	fresh sage	chopped
½	teaspoon	black pepper	freshly ground

FOR THE CHEESY HERBALICIOUS BISCUITS

12	ounces	all-purpose flour	plus extra for rolling
2	teaspoons	baking powder	aluminum-free
½	teaspoon	baking soda	
1	teaspoon	kosher salt	
1	teaspoon	fresh thyme	chopped
1	teaspoon	fresh sage	chopped
¼	teaspoon	cayenne pepper	
4	ounces	extra sharp white cheddar cheese	
4	ounces	unsalted butter	frozen
7	ounces	low-fat buttermilk	

A BIRD IN THE PIE IS
WORTH TWO IN THE BUSH

// PROCEDURE //

(1) Heat the oven to 400°F.

MAKE THE FILLING:

(2) Set a **10-inch cast-iron skillet** over medium heat. Crumble the sausage into the pan and cook, stirring occasionally, until no longer pink, about 6 minutes. Add the butter and cook until it melts, stirring to coat the sausage. Sprinkle in the flour and cook for 2 minutes, stirring frequently. Add the milk and broth and scrape any browned bits off the bottom of the pan. Bring to a simmer and cook until the sauce thickens, about 2 minutes.

(3) Add the chicken, salt, sage, and pepper and stir to combine. Set aside while preparing the biscuits.

MAKE THE CHEESY HERBALICIOUS BISCUITS AND BUILD THE PIE:

(4) Combine the flour, baking powder, baking soda, salt, thyme, sage, and cayenne in a **medium bowl** and set aside.

(5) Grate the cheese and butter using the **large disk of a food processor or the large holes of a box grater**. Immediately add the cheese and butter to the flour mixture. Stir to combine. Pour in the buttermilk and stir just to combine. Dump the dough onto a floured work surface and start folding the dough over on itself, gently kneading for 30 seconds, or until the dough is soft and smooth. Press the dough out to ½ inch thick. Use a **3-inch round cutter** to cut out biscuits, being sure to push the cutter straight down through the dough to the work surface. Make your cuts as close together as possible to limit waste. Gather together any remaining dough, pat out again, and cut out as many biscuits as you can in order to get 8 or 9 total. Set the biscuits atop the filling in the skillet, being careful to leave at least ½ inch of space between them. Bake until the biscuits are tall and golden, 15 to 20 minutes. Cool on a cooling rack for 10 minutes before serving.

My favorite biscuit cutter is 3 inches in diameter and came in a set of 5 nesting cutters.

TIDBIT | The world's largest lasagna was made in 2008 and weighed in at 8,800 pounds.

TIDBIT | The earliest references to combining pasta and tomato sauce date back only to the 1830s.

If there is a watchword in twenty-first-century marketing

it isn't *luxury* or *economy* or *beauty* or *efficiency*, it's *comfort*. Don't believe me? Just flip through your TV channels sometime and count the "comforts." You'll be impressed, believe you me. Needless to say, the "comfort" concept extends to food, as in comfort food, which is defined, since 1977 at least, as "foods consumed to achieve some level of improved emotional status, whether to relieve negative psychological affect or to increase the positive." While pondering the comfort continuum a while back I started wondering what food—what actual ingredient—is the most comforting of all. After considerable canoodling, I now feel confident that the answer is clear:

Lasagna: both the noodle and the famous dish that bears its name.
Anything containing either is firmly established in
the pantheon of . . .

TIDBIT | The last king of Naples, Francesco II, was nicknamed *Lasa* due to his father's love of lasagna.

Lasagna is one of the oldest forms of pasta. The word itself is ancient and comes from either the Arabic *lawzinaj*, meaning a "thin cake," or the Greek *lasanon*, or "chamber pot," which then evolved into the Latin *lasanum* or "cooking pot," which is considerably more appetizing. In either case, *lasagne* later evolved into thin, wide noodles, which were often fried in ancient Rome. Fast forward to the thirteenth century, and people are floating boiled *laganum* in broth as dumplings. In the fourteenth century, the first lasagna-style recipe appears, and it includes cheese, cinnamon, and saffron. By the seventeenth century, baked lasagna dishes are common in southern Italy and quickly migrate north. Another century passes and the migration continues to a new land, America, which welcomes Italian cuisine and its curious noodle because it is delicious and economical, and because you could buy homemade wine in Little Italy even during Prohibition. After the war, convenience became this country's culinary cry, and the casserole its champion. And no casserole outshined lasagna and the frilly, flat noodles that called it home.

Like most pastas, lasagna is made from protein-laden semolina wheat, water, and little else. And by the way, if it's a single noodle the word ends in an "a." If plural, it's an "e." Although fresh lasagna is certainly lasagna, the flavor and texture of this noodle is, I believe, best delivered by the dry, factory-made version. But not all are alike. I find that American versions, whether flat or frilled, are quite thick and produce too much chew, while Italian versions tend to be thinner and more delicate. There are also no-boil lasagnas, which are precooked then dried so that they can be added to various applications in their mummified state. I've tried them and gosh darn it I don't like them.

A great majority of lasagna recipes call for cooking the noodles through in a copious amount of boiling water. Why? I haven't the faintest. After all, I don't need the noodles cooked, I just need them to be flexible enough to construct the dish—and that state is easily achieved with a quick soak in hot water.

The only liquid I add to my lasagna comes from a 14½-ounce can of tomatoes, and I don't use all of it. Why? Most American-made lasagna suffers from way too much liquid. This is due in part to the fact that so many recipes call for boiling the noodles. Still more wateriness comes from the introduction of factory-fresh ricotta cheese, which lends almost no flavor, a bit of grittiness, and a lot of moisture. And then there's the sauce. Most classically prepared restaurant lasagna is constructed with not one but two sauces, a Bolognese-style ragu or meat sauce, and a white dairy-based *balsamella*, which is the Italian version of a béchamel. The way I see it, my lasagna will already have enough moisture in it from cooking meat and vegetation. All I need to do is introduce some starch and some milk proteins and sugars. I can get the first from all-purpose flour and the second from powdered milk. I like goat's-milk powder because it's got a bit of funk in the flavor, but any powdered milk will do in a pinch.

As far as I'm concerned lasagna—the dish, not the noodle—has relatively few components: meat, vegetable, noodle, sauce. For the first two, I religiously observe a 3:3 ratio, meaning three meats and three veggies. Cheese is utterly optional. That's right . . . cheese does not the lasagna make. Just wanted to go ahead and say that. (Sorry, Garfield.)

TIDBIT | Italian-American food was the first "ethnic" food to gain widespread acceptance in the U.S.

MY LASAGNA PAN: THE SLOW COOKER

The ubiquitous slow cooker was conceived by some revolutionary thinker at Chicago's Naxon Utilities Corporation sometime before 1964. Called the "bean pot," the device was little more than a pot with a built-in low-wattage electrical coil. The revolutionary device went all but unnoticed when the Rival Corporation purchased Naxon in 1970 primarily to get at their lucrative sun lamps and laundry equipment business. The head of home economics at Rival discovered the diamond in the rough, the product was gussied up, and it hit the market in 1971 as the Crock-Pot. By '75, sales were up to 93 million. Then came the microwave, and the need for speed overtook the culinary collective. Luckily, cooks are starting to rediscover the long-lost ingredient that is time, and the Crock-Pot is back in style. (Though I have to say I much prefer the old-school, three-setting analog model to modern, programmable digital ones.) I keep mine plugged into a hardware store–issue lamp/appliance timer so that I can turn it on and off without having to be in the house.

// SOFTWARE

1	pound	lasagna noodles	
1	small	eggplant	quartered lengthwise and sliced on mandoline
1	small	zucchini	sliced lengthwise on mandoline
2	tablespoons	kosher salt	
1	pound	hot and mild beef sausage links	preferably grass fed
14½	ounces	canned whole tomatoes	
2	teaspoons	Italian seasoning	
½	ounce	all-purpose flour	
½	ounce	goat's-milk powder	
2	large	portobello mushroom caps	cut into ³⁄₁₆-inch-thick strips
½	pound	ground pork	
4	ounces	part-skim mozzarella	grated

// PROCEDURE

1. Put the noodles in a **9-by-13-inch metal pan** and pour enough **hot water** over to cover. Set aside for 30 minutes, or until pliable. Drain the noodles, separate them, and set aside.

2. Put the eggplant and zucchini in the bowl of a **salad spinner**. Sprinkle with the salt and purge for 20 minutes, tossing after the first 10 minutes.

3. Remove the sausage from its casing and chop or pinch into ½-inch pieces. Set aside.

4. Rinse the eggplant and zucchini under running water and spin until mostly dry.

5. Use 4 noodles to line the sides of a **2½- to 3-quart slow cooker**. Overlap the noodles slightly and press against the sides so they stick.

6. Crush 1 tomato with your hand into the bottom of the slow cooker.

7. Cover with half of the sausage.

8. Sprinkle with ½ teaspoon of the Italian seasoning, one-fourth of the flour, and one-fourth of the milk powder. Add one-fourth of the purged vegetables in a layer, slightly overlapping the pieces. Add one-fourth of the mushrooms in a layer. Add one-fourth of the remaining noodles in a layer, cut to fit any gaps, slightly overlapping the pieces. Gently press down on the noodles before building next layer.

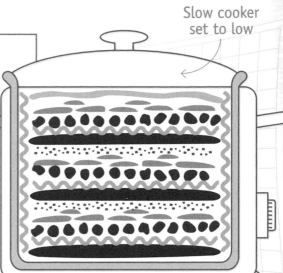

Slow cooker set to low

9. Repeat steps 7 and 8, substituting half of the pork for the sausage.

10. Repeat steps 7 and 8, using the remaining sausage.

11. Repeat steps 7 and 8, using the remaining pork.

12. Spread 2 tablespoons of the tomato juice from the can on the top of the last layer of noodles.

13. Cook on low for 4 hours, or until a knife easily slides through the layers. Degrease according to note below.

14. Turn off the slow cooker, top with the cheese, cover, and leave for 15 minutes before serving.

NOTE: Degreasing: One of the most common lasagna-centric complaints is that it's often greasy, what with all that sausage. This is indeed a difficult issue to wrangle when a rectangular vessel is involved. Cooking deep and round presents far more effective options. Simply place a lid (with a lip) from a 2-quart saucepan on top of the cooked dish and press gently downward. The fat will gurgle up the sides and into the top of the lid pretty as you please. When full, simply lift up and discard as you wish. Repeat until you're happy with your grease content.

LAYER KEY:

	Tomatoes
	Noodles
	Meat
	Vegetables
	Seasoning
	Cheese

NOTE: If you want your cheese browned, hit it with your blowtorch or a hardware-store heat gun.

AS THE KUGEL TURNS

In German the word *kugel* means "sphere." It's also the name of what many Yiddish cooks would no doubt consider Jewish lasagna. Although savory kugels are often made with layers of potatoes, many Jews and Gentiles alike agree that the most comforting kugel of all are *lokshn kugel*: noodle kugel. And although fresh egg noodles are traditional, dry lasagna does the job even better, if you ask a goyem like me.

// SOFTWARE

FOR THE TOPPING

| 2 | tablespoons | sugar | |
| 1 | teaspoon | nutmeg | freshly grated |

FOR THE PUDDING

8	ounces	lasagna noodles	(9 or 10 noodles)
4	tablespoons	unsalted butter	melted and cooled slightly
8	ounces	cream cheese	at room temperature
8	ounces	sour cream	at room temperature
4	whole	eggs	at room temperature
⅓	cup	sugar	
1	teaspoon	vanilla extract	
½	teaspoon	kosher salt	
6	ounces	dried apricots	coarsely chopped
4	ounces	golden raisins	

// PROCEDURE

MAKE THE TOPPING:

1. Combine the sugar and nutmeg in a **small bowl** and set aside.

MAKE THE PUDDING:

2. Spray an **8-inch square glass baking dish** with **nonstick cooking spray** and set aside.

3. Heat the oven to 350°F.

4. Cook the noodles to al dente according to the package directions and drain. Arrange the noodles in a single layer on **2 pieces of parchment paper**. Use a **pizza cutter** to cut into 1-inch-wide strips.

5. Using your hands, toss the noodles and 1 tablespoon of the butter together in a **medium bowl**.

6. Puree the remaining butter, the cream cheese, sour cream, eggs, sugar, vanilla, and salt in a **blender** until thoroughly combined. Pour the cream cheese mixture over the noodles, add the apricots and raisins, and stir to combine. Transfer the noodle mixture to the prepared pan and sprinkle with the sugar-nutmeg topping. Cover with **aluminum foil** and bake for 35 minutes. Uncover and continue to bake for 15 to 20 minutes, until the pudding is set, slightly puffed, and golden around the edges. Cool for 15 minutes before serving.

Sooner or later most people who cook for a living have some sort of epiphany. Mine came in the summer of 1981. I was nineteen, and having been denied entry to several colleges—not to mention the army due to my asthma—I set off to backpack in Europe on ten dollars a day. I made my way from England to Amsterdam, over to Berlin, back through Belgium, then down through France to the Mediterranean. I hit the docks of Marseille broke, tired, and very hungry. In a dingy café I ordered a cheeseburger and was served a strange bowl of stew called (near as I could tell) "boil your face." I tasted it, and saw the light. This was flavor like nothing I'd ever tasted. A mélange of seafood, a rich, red, luxurious liquid redolent of citrus and spice, and, there in the middle, a huge toasted crouton which had been smeared with a creamy goodness that tasted like mayo made from roasted peppers. By the third bite I knew I had found my . . .

SHOOTING THE VIEWMASTER
UNDERWORLD SEQUENCE

Although few dishes are considered to be more French than bouillabaisse, some have suggested the dish is actually Greek. According to Thucydides, Greeks from Phocaea founded Marseille in 600 B.C. The Greeks go on to claim that bouillabaisse was first concocted by none other than the goddess Aphrodite, who, despite being married to the short and unattractive Hephaestus, god of fire and forge, was chronically running around with Ares, the god of war. One day, Aphrodite concocted a seafood soup, heavily seasoned with saffron, which was long thought to possess soporific powers. Hephaestus drank the soup but instead of falling asleep he went down to his shop and crafted a fine iron net in which he captured the naughty duo in the act.

It's a romantic tale, to be sure, but the simple truth is that fisherman stews tend to happen wherever fisherman fish—and bouillabaisse is no exception. And, like so many other of its ilk, the bouillabaisse parts list is highly adaptable. The only real challenge is figuring out the seafood.

Meet the classic denizens of the classic bouillabaisse: the *rascasse*, a member of the scorpion fish family (like the *chapon*); the *baudroie*; a variety of anglerfish; the red mullet; the *daurade*, a member of the bream family; *John Dory*; *gallinette*; and conger eel. And the lobster. These are trash fish, which is why fishermen eat them: They can't easily sell them. Typically at least four different members of this roster appear in bouillabaisse, but the only one that seems a requirement is the *rascasse*, which is unique to the area. The scorpion fish are a big family, though, and if you fish, you can catch Pacific scorpion right off of Los Angeles harbors, but they rarely show up in markets because sushi bars grab them up. But guess what: It doesn't really matter. The way I look at it you want a firm white fish, a flaky white fish, a crustacean, and a bivalve, and you want them as fresh as possible. And that Americans can easily manage. My favorites, which are also considered sustainable by the Monterey Bay Aquarium's Seafood Watch, are:

FIRM: Cobia and black sea bass (a.k.a. black rockfish)

FLAKY: Halibut and black cod

CRUSTACEAN: Frozen spiny lobster tails (available raw)

BLUE MUSSELS: Rope grown, live in the shell

And FISH HEADS AND BONES, preferably from cold-water fish.

Why fish heads and bones? Because, just as the soul of chicken soup is chicken stock, the heart of a bouillabaisse is fish stock. In either case, a stock is typified by the extraction of gelatin from connective tissues, and there's no better place to get that than bones and heads. Cold-water fish usually contain more gelatin than warm-water specimens.

Having procured your seafood, be sure to keep the fish and lobster on ice that can drain without waterlogging the meat. The mussels should be stashed in a deep container topped with moist newspaper. Remember, they're alive in there and nothing will kill them quicker than fresh water.

WAITER, THERE'S A FISH IN MY STEW!

400

ROUILLE[1]

1 CUP

NOTE: If you don't have a gas cooktop, use a blowtorch . . . or your broiler.

// **SOFTWARE** ///

1	medium	red bell pepper	
3	large cloves	garlic	peeled
1		fresh red chile (for example, Fresno)	stem removed and seeded
1	teaspoon	lemon juice	freshly squeezed
¼	teaspoon	coarse sea salt	
½	cup	olive oil	

// **PROCEDURE** ///

1. Cook the pepper over a gas burner set to medium-high, turning with **tongs** every few minutes, until the skin blackens and is thoroughly charred.

2. Remove the pepper to a **metal bowl**, cover with a **spare pot lid** (one that fits just inside the bowl, but above the peppers), and cool for 5 minutes.

3. Remove the blackened skin from the pepper by rubbing with a **clean kitchen towel**. Pull out the stem and seed cluster and discard, along with the skin.

4. Put the roasted pepper, garlic, chile, lemon juice, and salt in the bowl of a **mini food processor**. Process for 1 to 2 minutes, until smooth. Stop and scrape down the sides of the bowl once or twice.

5. With the food processor running, slowly drizzle in the oil and process until thick.

6. Serve with fish stew.

[1] *Rouille* is French for "rust," and that's a pretty fair descriptor of the color. Some versions contain bread crumbs, others saffron, others eggs. This version is straightforward, flavorful, and long keeping if refrigerated.

WAITER, THERE'S A
FISH IN MY STEW!

| APPLICATION | | "AB"OUILLABAISSE |

6 TO 8 SERVINGS

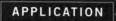

// SOFTWARE //

FOR THE FISH STOCK

16	ounces	raw fish heads, bones, tails, and lobster tail shell	
4	whole	fresh bay leaves	
1	teaspoon	coarse sea salt	
½	teaspoon	whole black peppercorns	
6	cups	H_2O	

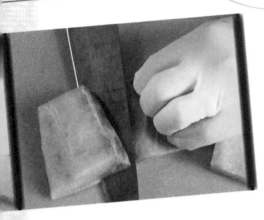

FOR THE STEW

½	cup	olive oil	
6	ounces	onion	coarsely chopped
3	ounces	fennel bulb	coarsely chopped
1	teaspoon	coarse sea salt	
½	cup	dry white wine	
1	(14½-ounce) can	diced tomatoes	undrained
¼	cup	fresh flat-leaf parsley	chopped
1	3-inch piece	orange peel	optional
	pinch	saffron	about 20 threads; optional
8	ounces	firm fish fillets, such as farmed cobia, wild striped bass; 1 or 2 types	cut into 1-inch pieces; at room temperature
8	ounces	flaky fish fillets, such as black cod or wild halibut (1 or 2 types)	cut into 1-inch pieces; at room temperature
2	cloves	garlic	crushed
¼	teaspoon	cayenne pepper	
8	ounces	mussels	cleaned, beards trimmed; at room temperature
1	large (8-ounce)	raw lobster tail	shell removed and meat cut into 1-inch pieces; at room temperature

TO SERVE

1	clove	garlic	cut in half
1		baguette	sliced
		Rouille (page 401)	optional

TIDBIT Bouillabaise is so revered, the French created a standard: "La Charte de la Bouillabaise Marseillaise."

WAITER, THERE'S A FISH IN MY STEW!

// PROCEDURE //

MAKE THE FISH STOCK:

1. Rinse the fish heads and place them in a tall **6-quart saucepot** with the tails, bones, lobster shell, bay leaves, salt, peppercorns, and water. Place over medium-high heat, cover, and bring to a simmer. Lower the heat to maintain a simmer, and cook for 25 minutes.

2. **Strain** into a **large bowl**, discard the solids, and set aside. Clean the saucepot.

MAKE THE STEW:

3. Put ¼ cup of the oil in the saucepot and place over medium heat. When the oil shimmers, add the onion, fennel, and ½ teaspoon of the salt. Sauté for 10 minutes or until semitranslucent, stirring frequently. Deglaze the pan with the wine, scraping any bits from the bottom of the pan. Add the reserved stock, tomatoes, parsley, orange peel, and saffron, if using. Place over high heat, cover, and bring to a boil. Lower the heat to maintain a simmer and cook for 15 minutes.

4. Increase the heat to high. Add the remaining ¼ cup oil, the remaining ½ teaspoon salt, the fish, garlic, and cayenne and boil rapidly, uncovered, for 5 to 7 minutes, stirring occasionally. Remove from the heat, add the mussels and lobster, cover, and let stand for 2 to 4 minutes, until the fish is cooked through and the mussels open. Discard any unopened mussels.

TO SERVE:

5. Set the broiler to high.

6. Lightly rub the baguette slices on both sides with the garlic. Place the prepared bread slices on a **half sheet pan** and broil, 1 inch away from the broiler, for 1 to 2 minutes. Turn the slices over and broil for another 1 to 2 minutes. Top with Rouille (page 401), if desired, and serve with the fish stew.

TIDBIT | Go to www.seafoodwatch.org for a list of sustainable seafood available in your region.

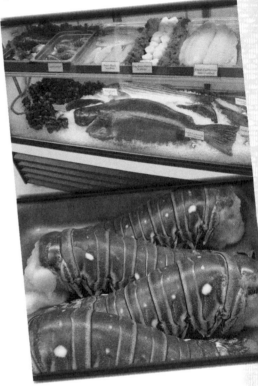

PUTTING THE "BOIL" IN BOUILLABAISE

Remember my little malapropism from back in '81, "boil your face"? It was only partly wrong. *Bouillir* does in fact mean "boil," while *baisse* translates to "lower." So obviously there is reducing and boiling going on here. Why is this necessary? Science.

Let's say that this liquid represents the liquid phase of the soup: the stock and wine, and the tomato liquid. On top we have the oil. Anyone who's made vinaigrette knows that these two do not work and play well with each other and, if you're going to bring them into an even semistable union, agitation will be required. And that would be pretty tough to do with a whisk, since our soup's got a bunch of bits and pieces in it.

The answer: the convective action of boiling, a fine agitator indeed. But when the bubbles stop, you ask, won't the mixture just separate again? No, it won't. Remember the stock? Well, we use water to extract a considerable amount of gelatin from those fish bones, and fish gelatin is very sticky stuff due to the molecular weight of the proteins concerned, proteins that make excellent emulsifiers, which can and will keep your boiled bouillabaisse together even after the heat is gone.

WAITER, THERE'S A FISH IN MY STEW!

THE PROOF IS IN THE BREAD PUDDING

Bread pudding has been my favorite dessert ever since my favorite stepfather, a "coonass" from way back, first made me his special New Orleans bread pudding with whiskey sauce. The attraction, besides flavor, texture, and heady, warm aroma, is that there's something noble about bread pudding, about worn-out, stale old bread rising up from its crumbs, to be reborn, phoenixlike, as dessert. Problem is, there's a lot of bad bread pudding out there. That's because it's simple but not exactly easy. But if you get it right, it certainly is . . .

KNOWLEDGE CONCENTRATE

▷ If bread pudding doesn't seem very puddinglike by American standards, keep in mind we're dealing with an English dessert here, and over in that country "pudding" is synonymous with dessert. Although boiled and steamed "puddings" are certainly ubiquitous, those based on leftover bread are much older, reaching back to at least the Middle Ages and a dish called "sop," composed of various edible bits and pieces moistened and cooked inside a hollow bread crust. Such classic bread "puddings" such as "Poor Knights of Windsor," "Wet Nellie," "Summer Pudding," and "Whitepot" all descend from the humble sop.

▷ Despite the fact that American recipe writers have spent the better part of a century trying to gourmet-up bread pudding, thus concealing its fearful symmetry, we can make sense of the madness as long as we think "car."

The bread is the body; a standard custard—that is, a balanced combination of eggs and dairy—is the engine. Any and all flavorants, as well as various hunks and chunks, are but accessories—wheel covers, mud flaps, satellite radios, sunroofs, fuzzy dice, and so on. Such adjuncts can sweeten the pot, but they do not a bread pudding make. With so many power plants available and so many body styles and accessories, it helps to have a formula, and here's mine: 10–12, 5, 3, 3, 1, 2.

That is: 10 to 12 cups of bread, 5 of dairy in the form of half-and-half, 3 eggs, 3 egg yolks, 1 cup of sugar, which can be of mixed varieties, and 2 ounces of user-defined liquid flavorants—a spirit, extract, or the like.

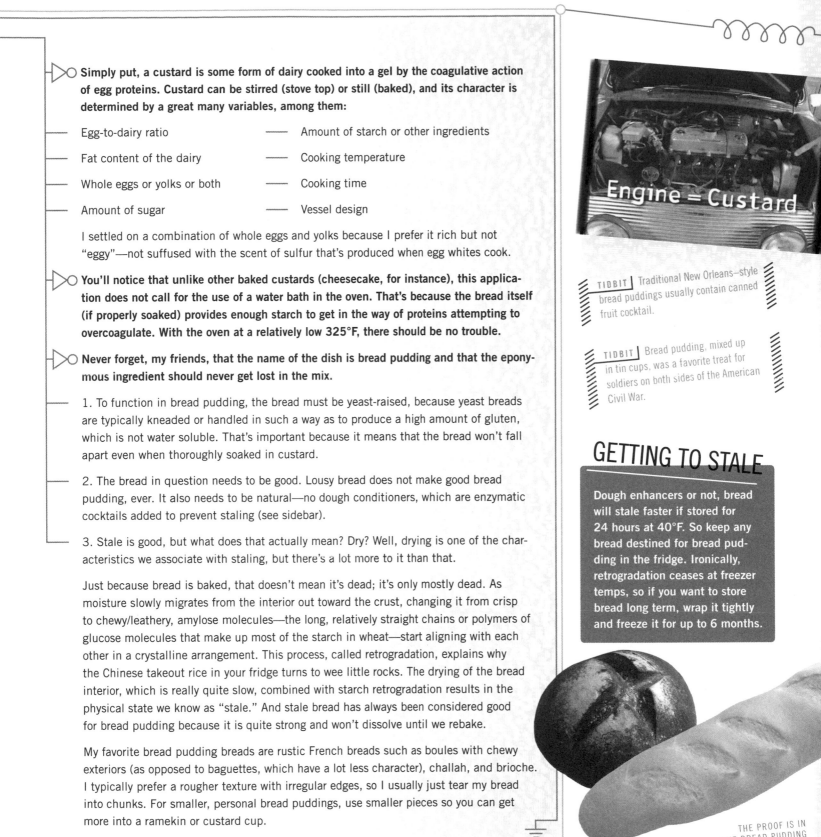

Simply put, a custard is some form of dairy cooked into a gel by the coagulative action of egg proteins. Custard can be stirred (stove top) or still (baked), and its character is determined by a great many variables, among them:

— Egg-to-dairy ratio

— Fat content of the dairy

— Whole eggs or yolks or both

— Amount of sugar

— Amount of starch or other ingredients

— Cooking temperature

— Cooking time

— Vessel design

I settled on a combination of whole eggs and yolks because I prefer it rich but not "eggy"—not suffused with the scent of sulfur that's produced when egg whites cook.

You'll notice that unlike other baked custards (cheesecake, for instance), this application does not call for the use of a water bath in the oven. That's because the bread itself (if properly soaked) provides enough starch to get in the way of proteins attempting to overcoagulate. With the oven at a relatively low 325°F, there should be no trouble.

Never forget, my friends, that the name of the dish is bread pudding and that the eponymous ingredient should never get lost in the mix.

1. To function in bread pudding, the bread must be yeast-raised, because yeast breads are typically kneaded or handled in such a way as to produce a high amount of gluten, which is not water soluble. That's important because it means that the bread won't fall apart even when thoroughly soaked in custard.

2. The bread in question needs to be good. Lousy bread does not make good bread pudding, ever. It also needs to be natural—no dough conditioners, which are enzymatic cocktails added to prevent staling (see sidebar).

3. Stale is good, but what does that actually mean? Dry? Well, drying is one of the characteristics we associate with staling, but there's a lot more to it than that.

Just because bread is baked, that doesn't mean it's dead; it's only mostly dead. As moisture slowly migrates from the interior out toward the crust, changing it from crisp to chewy/leathery, amylose molecules—the long, relatively straight chains or polymers of glucose molecules that make up most of the starch in wheat—start aligning with each other in a crystalline arrangement. This process, called retrogradation, explains why the Chinese takeout rice in your fridge turns to wee little rocks. The drying of the bread interior, which is really quite slow, combined with starch retrogradation results in the physical state we know as "stale." And stale bread has always been considered good for bread pudding because it is quite strong and won't dissolve until we rebake.

My favorite bread pudding breads are rustic French breads such as boules with chewy exteriors (as opposed to baguettes, which have a lot less character), challah, and brioche. I typically prefer a rougher texture with irregular edges, so I usually just tear my bread into chunks. For smaller, personal bread puddings, use smaller pieces so you can get more into a ramekin or custard cup.

Engine = Custard

TIDBIT | Traditional New Orleans–style bread puddings usually contain canned fruit cocktail.

TIDBIT | Bread pudding, mixed up in tin cups, was a favorite treat for soldiers on both sides of the American Civil War.

GETTING TO STALE

Dough enhancers or not, bread will stale faster if stored for 24 hours at 40°F. So keep any bread destined for bread pudding in the fridge. Ironically, retrogradation ceases at freezer temps, so if you want to store bread long term, wrap it tightly and freeze it for up to 6 months.

CONCERNING HALF-AND-HALF

Why buy half-and-half when you can simply mix your own milk and cream? Keep in mind that while milk contains at least 3¼ percent fat by law, various versions of cream contain anywhere from 18 to 36 percent fat. So if you do choose to mix your own, you'll have a bit of number crunching to do to hit the 12 to 18 percent butterfat delivered by most half-and-half. If you find yourself in a dessert emergency, then improvise by combining whatever dairies you have on hand, as long as half of the final elixir is cream of some sort. But if your pudding is premeditated, I'd say buy half-and-half and call it a day.

// SOFTWARE

1	2- to 3-inch	cinnamon stick	
1	teaspoon	nutmeg	freshly grated
1	teaspoon	dried orange peel	
15	whole	cloves	
15	whole	black peppercorns	
2 to 3	pieces	crystallized ginger	chopped
5	cups	half-and-half	
3	large	eggs	
3	large	egg yolks	
½	cup	granulated sugar	
½	cup	dark brown sugar	
¼	cup	spiced rum	such as Kraken
1	10-inch	French boule	2½ pounds, or 10 to 12 cups cubes
½	cup	golden raisins	
½	cup	dried cherries	
1 to 2	tablespoons	unsalted butter	melted

// PROCEDURE

1. Place the cinnamon, nutmeg, orange peel, cloves, peppercorns, and ginger into 3 cups of half-and-half in a **microwavable container** and microwave on high for 3 minutes. Check the temperature of the mixture and microwave it in 30-second increments until it reaches 180°F. Cover and steep for 15 minutes.

2. Place the eggs and yolks in a **blender with an 8-cup carafe**. Blend on low speed for 30 seconds. Increase the speed to one-quarter power and slowly add the sugars; blend until slightly thickened, about 1 minute. Add the remaining 2 cups half-and-half. With the machine still running, pour in the spiced half-and-half through a **small hand strainer**, then add the rum. Use immediately or store, covered, in the refrigerator for up to 72 hours.

3. Heat the oven to the lowest setting—warm if possible.

4. Cut a 7-inch round disk off the top of the boule using a **long bread knife or serrated slicer**. Tear the disk into pieces and scatter them in a **large roasting pan**. Cut all the way around the inside of the boule just inside the outer wall. Leaving the outer shell intact, cut the interior of the bread first in a downward direction, then in a perpendicular direction to create a grid, the way you would cube mango flesh to remove it from the skin.

Remove the plugs of bread and tear them into hunks about the size of an egg. Add the hunks to the roasting pan and bake for 1½ to 2 hours, or until the bread is dry. Remove the pan from the oven.

(5) Sprinkle the raisins and cherries over the bread, pour in the custard, and press the bread to submerge all the pieces. Cover and soak for 2 hours at room temperature or up to 8 hours in the refrigerator.

(6) Heat the oven to 325°F.

(7) Pour the melted butter into a **spray bottle** and spritz the inside of the bread shell. Be sure to cover the bottom with a thin layer to prevent the custard from soaking through. Put the bread shell in a **10-inch cast-iron skillet** and place it in the oven to toast the interior for 30 minutes.

(8) Remove the bread shell from the oven and transfer the soaked bread mixture into the shell. Bake for 1½ to 2 hours, or until the bread pudding puffs up and reaches an internal temperature of 165° to 170°F. Remove from the oven and cool for 30 minutes before slicing or scooping to serve.

| 10 MINUTES MORE | ⌐⌐ | MARSHALL'S[1] WHISKEY SAUCE |

| 1 CUP |

This is great with bread pudding, but also very good over ice cream . . . or cereal . . . or broccoli.

TIP | If you need to hold the sauce for service, store it in a tightly sealed, preheated Thermos. Don't reheat.

// SOFTWARE ///

2	cups	whole milk	
2	large	eggs	
¾	cup	sugar	
3	tablespoons	cornstarch	
2	teaspoons	unsalted buller	
2	teaspoons	vanilla extract	
½	ounce	brandy or bourbon	

// PROCEDURE ///

(1) Bring the milk to a simmer in a **small saucepan** over medium heat

(2) **Whisk** together the eggs, sugar, cornstarch, and butter in a **metal bowl** set up double boiler–style over a **saucepan** of simmering water.

(3) Slowly pour the milk into the egg mixture, then continue cooking, whisking continuously, until thickened. Remove from the heat and whisk in the vanilla and booze before serving warm.

[1] My late stepfather—a "coonass" from way back.

THE PROOF IS IN
THE BREAD PUDDING

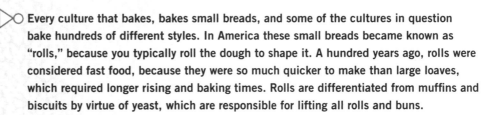

I have long suspected that the maelstrom of mediocrity in which our culture currently finds itself spastically spinning was somehow set in motion by an event that took place right here at the very epicenter of our civilization: the dinner table. Furthermore, I propose that the actual tipping point, if you will, concerned one particular edible: the dinner roll, which according to my calculations made its last regular appearance at the family supper table on April 20, 1964. Once that soft, aromatic, warm, yeasty, ever-so-slightly-sweet edible hug vanished, our civilization began to quietly crumble. Is it too late to get our hug back? Of course not. But we're all going to have to bake tall and answer the roll call of . . .

[1] Technically speaking, yeast don't consume flour; they consume sugar made available as enzymes in the flour, typically provided by the miller in the form of miniscule amounts of malted barley flour, break down the large starch polymers into easy-to-ferment bits.

KNOWLEDGE CONCENTRATE

▷○ **Every culture that bakes, bakes small breads, and some of the cultures in question bake hundreds of different styles. In America these small breads became known as "rolls," because you typically roll the dough to shape it. A hundred years ago, rolls were considered fast food, because they were so much quicker to make than large loaves, which required longer rising and baking times. Rolls are differentiated from muffins and biscuits by virtue of yeast, which are responsible for lifting all rolls and buns.**

▷○ **All rolls fit into one of two basic categories: "lean" and "rich." While our cultural fore-fathers, the English, tend toward lean, hard rolls, here in America the influence of Germanic cultures steered our roll toward the rich side of the spectrum by introducing milk, butter, and a bit of sugar to the equation.**

▷○ **Consider the fantastic four of bread-dom: flour, water, yeast, and salt.**

— The starch and protein of the *flour* provide the structure, and it should be noted that unless you're making a very crusty, rustic loaf, bread flour—with its few extra percentage points of protein—just isn't necessary. All-purpose flour will do fine.

— Then there's *water*, which hydrates the flour components and provides the moisture the yeast need to spring to life and consume the flour,[1] thus producing CO_2, complex flavors, and more yeast. When it comes to yeast baking, water quality matters. Tap water is iffy at best because many municipalities add a fairly high amount of chlorine, which kills microbes—including yeast. The other issue is that yeast do not thrive in soft water—that is, water that doesn't contain much in the way of dissolved minerals. Hard waters tend to be loaded up with magnesium and calcium ions, which yeast love. After all, they're more plant than animal, and plants like to be in soil, and what is soil if not minerals?

Many recipes these days call for "rapid-rise" or "instant" *yeast*, and in past episodes I myself have extolled the virtues of these speedy, supercharged microbes that get to fermenting faster than active dry yeast because the granules contain more yeast that are actually alive and they're packaged with "stimulants" like vitamin C. And yet, I have found that with proper treatment, active dry yeast are just as effective and may actually be superior, especially when sugar is added to the equation, because when instant yeast hit that sugar they kinda burn themselves out.

Recipe writers these days are fond of saying that *salt* is "optional," but in bread making that is not the case. Without at least a little salt, bread tastes utterly dead, unpalatable no matter how much butter you smear on it. Salt also strengthens gluten molecules and helps to prevent staling by holding onto water.

Although flour, water, yeast, and salt can indeed produce a tasty loaf, *milk*, *butter*, *sugar*, and *eggs* can enhance both the flavor and texture of rolls. Sugars, including sucrose and lactose in the milk, caramelize to create complex flavors. Sugar is also hygroscopic, so it clings to water tenaciously, preventing the final bread from drying out. Fat in the form of butter and egg yolks also lubricates gluten structures and, of course, it adds considerable flavor. Egg yolks also contain emulsifiers that can help integrate the fat into the dough. Best of all, we don't need a lot of any of these to effect big changes.

Having considered software, we now turn to assembly. The following steps constitute what is called the "straight dough" method:

Mix	Rise	Shape	Bake
Knead	Punch down	Proof	Cool

I've hacked both the stages and the nomenclature to more accurately (in my opinion) represent the steps:

Integrate	Align	Configure
Hydrate	Double	Double
Integrate (part deux)	Redistribute	Bake
Stretch	Portion	Cure

It's a tough list to memorize, which is why I prefer this handy mnemonic phrase: "I Have Imagined Seeing a Demented, Rabid Platypus Carelessly Drinking Blue Cocktails." How easy is that?

One of the nice things about roll dough is that it can be crafted into a wide array of shapes. These include but are not limited to pan loaves, knots, cloverleafs, butterflakes (which are cooked in muffin tins), and, of course, the Parker House Roll.

ROLL CALL

The Parker House roll, named for the Boston hotel where it was invented, is the quintessential American roll, easily recognized by its folded top, which conceals a pat of butter. When I was a kid I had an aunt who made butterflake rolls, which I think are even easier to configure than Parker House and a lot more fun to eat, as the layers tear off for individual buttering (not that you would actually ever do such a thing). You can shape this same dough into any number of nifty forms.

// SOFTWARE ///

8	ounces	warm whole milk	100°F
2¼	ounces	sugar	
1	tablespoon plus 1 teaspoon	active dry yeast	
15	ounces	all-purpose flour	
2		egg yolks	
2½	teaspoons	kosher salt	
4	ounces	unsalted butter	at room temperature

// PROCEDURE ///

1. Combine the milk, sugar, yeast, flour, egg yolks, and salt in a **stand mixer fitted with the paddle attachment**. Combine on low speed for 5 minutes. Let rest for 10 to 15 minutes and switch out the paddle attachment for the **dough hook**.

2. Add 2 ounces of the butter on low speed. Increase the speed to medium and mix for 5 to 8 minutes, until the dough pulls away from the sides of the bowl and you're able to gently pull the dough into a thin sheet that light will pass through. Turn the dough out onto a lightly floured work surface and roll and shape with your hands to form a large ball. Return the dough to the bowl, cover with **plastic wrap**, and set aside in a warm, dry place to rise until doubled in size, about 1 hour.

— TO MAKE PARKER HOUSE ROLLS:

3. Remove the dough from the bowl and roll it into a 16-by-3-inch log. Use a **bench knife** to cut the dough into 16 portions. Roll each portion on the counter until it tightens into a small round. Flatten each round with the palm of your hand into a 3-inch circle. Put a thin pat of butter in the center of the circle, then fold in half and gently press to seal the edges. Place the rounds on a **half sheet pan** sprayed with **nonstick cooking spray**, spacing them evenly.

4. Melt the remaining 1 ounce butter and **brush** the tops of the rolls with the butter. Cover with **plastic wrap** and set aside in a warm, dry place to rise until doubled in size, about 30 minutes.

TIDBIT | Before commercial yeast hit the market, home bakers had to use suds from local brewers.

5) Heat the oven to 400°F.

6) Remove the plastic wrap and bake for 8 to 10 minutes, until the internal temperature of the rolls is 200°F, rotating the pan halfway through baking.

— TO MAKE BUTTERFLAKE ROLLS:

3) Remove the dough from the bowl and **roll** out into a 12-inch square about ½ inch thick. Melt the remaining 2 ounces butter and **brush** the top of the dough with the butter. Let cool and solidify.

4) Use a **pizza cutter** to cut the dough into 12 (12-by-1-inch) strips. Line 6 of the strips up, cut side up so the buttered sides alternate, gently press together, and cut into 6 (2-inch) pieces. Place the pieces in a **12-cup muffin tin** sprayed with **nonstick cooking spray**. Cover with **plastic wrap** and set aside in a warm, dry place to rise until doubled in size, about 30 minutes.

5) Heat the oven to 400°F.

6) Remove the plastic wrap and bake for 8 to 10 minutes, until the internal temperature of the rolls is 200°F, rotating the pan halfway through baking. (Alternatively, cover with plastic wrap and place in the refrigerator for 12 to 16 hours. Bring to room temperature, about 90 minutes, then bake at 400°F for 8 to 10 minutes, rotating the pan halfway through baking.)

— TO MAKE BROWN-'N'-SERVE ROLLS:

3) Coat a **9-by-13-inch metal pan** with **nonstick cooking spray**.

4) Remove the dough from the bowl and use a **bench knife** to cut the dough into 2-ounce portions. You should have 14 or 15 portions. **Roll** each portion on the counter until it tightens into a small round. Place in the prepared pan, spacing them evenly. Cover with **plastic wrap** and set aside in a warm, dry place to rise until the rolls have doubled in size, 30 to 45 minutes.

5) Heat the oven to 275°F.

6) Melt the remaining 2 ounces butter. **Brush** the tops of the rolls with the butter. Bake for 30 minutes, or until the rolls are set and reach an internal temperature of 185° to 190°F but are still pale. Place the pan on a **cooling rack** and cool for 10 minutes. Remove the rolls from the pan and cool to room temperature, 30 to 45 minutes. Wrap the rolls tightly in **plastic wrap** and freeze.

7) When ready to bake, bring the rolls to room temperature, 60 to 90 minutes. Heat the oven to 400°F. Bake for 10 to 12 minutes, until deeply browned, rotating the pan halfway through baking.

TIDBIT Parker House rolls are sometimes called pocketbook rolls due to their purselike appearance.

PARKER HOUSE

BROWN-'N'-SERVE

In the annals of bakery there is a special page for Joseph Gregor, who in 1949 was a baker and volunteer fireman in Avon Park, Florida. One day Gregor had just parked a pan of Parker House rolls in the oven when the alarm sounded. Not wanting to set yet another fire while he was gone, Gregor pulled the rolls from the oven and left them on the counter. He was gone for some hours and upon his return saw that the rolls had in fact kept their shape. Figuring he had nothing to lose, he finished baking them. The results: amazing. After perfecting the process, Gregor began selling his Pop-n-Oven rolls. Eventually General Mills traded him a bucket of money for the secret.

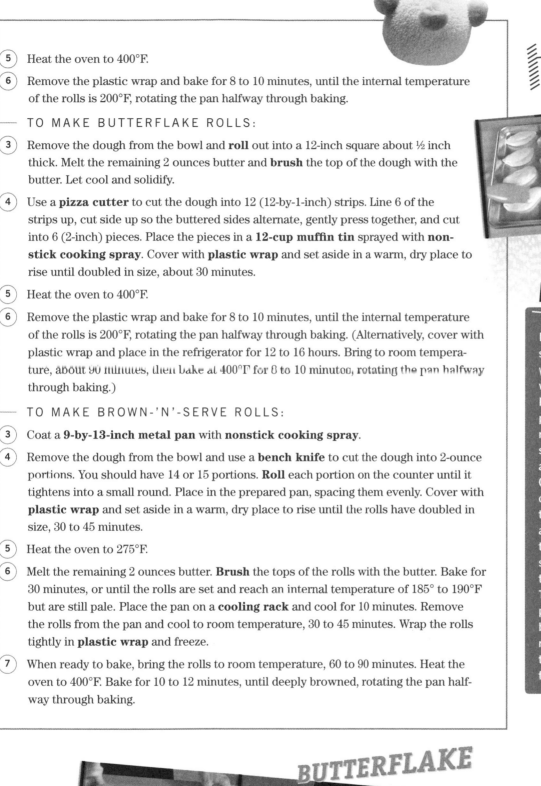

BUTTERFLAKE

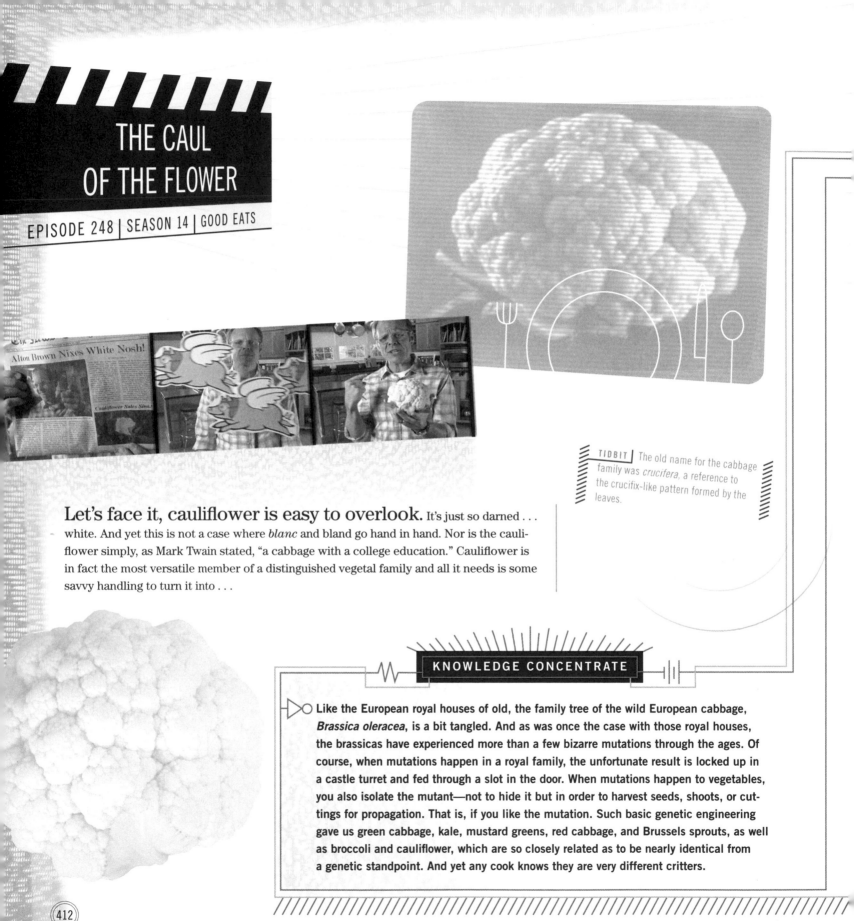

Alton Brown Nixes White Nosh!

Cauliflower Sales Sink!

TIDBIT | The old name for the cabbage family was *crucifera*, a reference to the crucifix-like pattern formed by the leaves.

Let's face it, cauliflower is easy to overlook. It's just so darned . . . white. And yet this is not a case where *blanc* and bland go hand in hand. Nor is the cauliflower simply, as Mark Twain stated, "a cabbage with a college education." Cauliflower is in fact the most versatile member of a distinguished vegetal family and all it needs is some savvy handling to turn it into . . .

KNOWLEDGE CONCENTRATE

Like the European royal houses of old, the family tree of the wild European cabbage, *Brassica oleracea*, is a bit tangled. And as was once the case with those royal houses, the brassicas have experienced more than a few bizarre mutations through the ages. Of course, when mutations happen in a royal family, the unfortunate result is locked up in a castle turret and fed through a slot in the door. When mutations happen to vegetables, you also isolate the mutant—not to hide it but in order to harvest seeds, shoots, or cuttings for propagation. That is, if you like the mutation. Such basic genetic engineering gave us green cabbage, kale, mustard greens, red cabbage, and Brussels sprouts, as well as broccoli and cauliflower, which are so closely related as to be nearly identical from a genetic standpoint. And yet any cook knows they are very different critters.

TIDBIT | Cauliflower was first brought to England by Flemish weavers escaping the sixteenth-century Spanish occupation of the Netherlands.

The biggest difference between broccoli and cauliflower is that broccoli is continuously pouring its energy and resources into the production of hundreds of tiny yellow flowers. This results in an assertive, fibrous plant that prefers to be cooked fast and moist lest its emerald hue fade and its up-front flavors turn sulfury. The crown of the cauliflower is also a tightly formed cluster of buds, but in this case they are blanks—auto aborted, in a sense, which means that the nutrients meant for the flowers remain down in the stems and that the buds remain dormant in tight clumps or "curds." Bad news for the cauliflower, perhaps, but good news for the cook.

The standard cauliflower crown gets its alabaster complexion from the giant leaves that sprout right below the head. In many varieties these leaves remain wrapped around the head, blocking sunlight. No sunlight, no chlorophyll. No chlorophyll, no green. Although many varieties, such as the popular Ravella, are "self-wrappers," many others, like the equally popular Snow Crowns and Snow Peaks, require assistance from growers, who tie the large outer leaves over the heads by hand. Pigmented varieties such as the Purple Cape and Romanesco require no coverage, but then their flavors are stronger than that of their white kin.

Cauliflowers come in three main types, depending on when they ripen: early, fall, or overwinter. I prefer early varieties for their sweetness, but am grateful that the others are there to allow for a year-round U.S. harvest.

Unless you buy directly from a farmstand, odds are the cauliflower you face will be trimmed of leaves and stems and wrapped tightly in plastic, which will allow cursory examination. If you see any black or gray spots, put it down and walk away. Same for soft or mushy spots. If a thorough exam is desired, you must breach this flimsy containment and sniff. There should be no sulfury "cabbage" stinkiness. Lastly, bend the leaves at the bottom. If they're floppy, walk away.

TIDBIT | In every European language the name for cauliflower translates to "flowering cabbage," despite the fact that it almost never does.

I make every effort to cook cauliflower the same day I bring it home, but if such hasty culinary action is not in your cards, keep your curds in a layer of paper towel, or even a couple of big cabbage leaves, to prevent condensation from settling on the curd, then wrap in plastic, then put the whole thing in the coldest part of the fridge, which will always be the bottom, most likely in the crisper drawer.

When it comes to cooking cauliflower, I prefer dry heat or a combination of dry and steam. The longer exposure to heat develops its nutty flavor compounds while softening the higher concentrations of plant pectins and other carbohydrates, creating an almost custardlike consistency. And since cauliflower contains 3.6 times more naturally occurring salt than broccoli, it doesn't need to be cooked in salted water. In fact I never cook cauliflower in water because water does nothing but wash away flavor and make things mushy.

THE CAUL OF THE FLOWER

HOMEMADE BREAD CRUMB HOW-TO

So, you've got half a baguette staling from some dinner last week. Instead of trashing the poor thing, tear it into 1-inch pieces. Heat your oven to 300°F. In a blender, pulse the bread pieces into coarse crumbs. Spread the crumbs evenly on two half sheet pans and bake for 5 minutes, or until the crumbs just begin to brown and are crisped. Cool the crumbs on the pans for 15 to 20 minutes, then transfer them to an airtight container, where they can be stored at room temperature for up to 2 weeks.

// SOFTWARE

1	tablespoon	unsalted butter	
1	large (2-pound) head	cauliflower	
½	cup	heavy cream	
4½	ounces	cheddar cheese	shredded on the small holes of a box grater
½	cup	homemade coarse bread crumbs	not panko and not canned
1	large	egg	beaten
1	teaspoon	kosher salt	
1	teaspoon	dry mustard powder	
½	teaspoon	smoked paprika	
6	grinds	black pepper	
¼	teaspoon	cayenne pepper	

// PROCEDURE

1. Position one oven rack in the middle position and one in the top position and heat the oven to 400°F. Coat a **7-by-11-inch baking dish** with the butter and set aside.

2. Put the cauliflower in a **small glass bowl**, stalk end up. Use a paring knife to remove the lower leaves. Trim the curds off the stem, keeping them as intact as possible. Try to keep the size uniformly large and make as few cuts as possible. Cover tightly with **plastic wrap** and microwave on high power for 4 minutes. Rest, still covered in plastic, for another 4 minutes.

3. Meanwhile, combine 4 ounces of the cheese, the bread crumbs, egg, salt, mustard powder, paprika, black pepper, and cayenne in a **large bowl**.

4. When 1 minute remains on the cauliflower rest period, microwave the cream on high power for 30 seconds. Pour the cream into the cheese mixture and stir to combine.

5. Unwrap the cauliflower and, working quickly, using a **tea towel**, crush and rub the large florets between your hands to break up the curds. Add the curds to the cream mixture and stir until the cheese is thoroughly melted and combined.

6. Spread the cauliflower mixture in the prepared baking dish and bake for 20 minutes on the middle rack. Remove the dish and turn the broiler to high. Sprinkle the remaining cheese atop the cauliflower. Broil, with the door ajar, on the top rack, 6 to 8 minutes, or until the top is bubbly and appropriately brown. Rest for 10 minutes before serving.

TABOULEH

6 TO 8 SERVINGS

Although I cannot abide raw cauliflower being served on a crudités platter or in a salad, there is one application where raw is good. The trick is to make it very, very small—small enough to stand in for bulgur in tabouleh.

// SOFTWARE

1	large (2-pound) head	cauliflower	separated into florets
2	tablespoons	lime juice	freshly squeezed
2	teaspoons	kosher salt	
1	tablespoon	extra virgin olive oil	
¾	cup	golden raisins	
½	cup	tomatoes	finely chopped
½	cup	fresh parsley	chopped
2	tablespoons	fresh mint	chopped
¼	teaspoon	black pepper	freshly ground
½	cup	pine nuts	

// PROCEDURE

1. Process all of the florets in a **food processor** using the **largest grating disk**.

2. **Whisk** the lime juice, 1 teaspoon of the salt, and the oil together in a **large bowl**. Add the cauliflower, raisins, tomatoes, parsley, mint, and pepper and toss to combine.

3. Put the pine nuts in a small **fine-mesh sieve** and rinse under cold water. Toss with the remaining 1 teaspoon salt. Transfer to a **small brown paper bag**, folded over, and microwave on high power for 1 to 1½ minutes. Remove from the microwave and set aside for 1 minute. When the nuts are cool, add them to the cauliflower mixture and toss to combine. Cover and refrigerate for 1 hour or up to overnight before serving. Refrigerate, covered, for up to 2 days.

PINE NUTS

Pine nuts are extracted from the mature cones of several varieties of *Pinaceae Pinus*, a.k.a. pine trees. Once extracted, the outer shell must also be removed. It's a labor-intensive process, which is one reason pine nuts cost so darned much. Although nuts from the European stone pine *Pinus pinea* are considered the pièce de résistance, I prefer those of the pinyon pines grown in the western United States. There are also several Asian varieties, but I'd steer clear of nuts from Chinese white and red pines as they have been linked to cases of "pine mouth," the only symptom of which is a strange metallic taste in the mouth that strikes within a day or two of consumption. The cause remains a mystery, but we have top men on it . . . top men. Once quality nuts have been procured, you may want to salt and roast them in order to fully realize their potential. But take care. Pine nuts are the number one most often burned ingredient in professional kitchens.

THE CAUL OF THE FLOWER

If you're a fan of this program

you've probably noticed that we've committed several episodes to exploiting the culinary virtues of pasta, specifically Italian pastas, which come in every conceivable size and shape even though they're almost all composed of the exact same stuff: hard wheat flour, water, and maybe an egg yolk. When contemplating the noodles of Southeast Asia, however, the situation is reversed. Most of the noodles are either medium or fine strands, or flat sheets. The real variety is in ingredients. Asian noodles are made from just about every starch-bearing plant you can imagine. Although many are on the bland side, Asian noodles are highly absorbent, which means they can soak up plenty of whatever sauce you throw at them. They also deliver an astonishingly wide array of textures, can be served hot or cold, and (best of all) most don't have to be boiled—and that virtue alone is enough to nominate them as . . .

TIDBIT | In a 2000 poll, the Japanese people rated instant noodles as the country's top technical innovation of the twentieth century. Karaoke came in second, and the Walkman third.

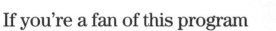

THE PANTRY AT THE OTHER SIDE OF THE EARTH

The first time you face a well-stocked Asian noodle aisle, things can be a little overwhelming. There are Japanese noodles like soba and udon, Chinese noodles like lo mein, ramen, and bean threads, Thai noodles, and Korean noodles. The situation is complicated by the fact that the very same noodle can be given different names in different cultures. Japanese noodles are usually easy to identify because names like *udon*, *soba*, and *shiratake* are simple to spot and have standard definitions and even packaging. When dealing with noodles from the rest of the region, I'd suggest you forget names and shop by shape and starch type, which is usually printed in English. The big starches are:

— Rice

— Tapioca

— Sweet potato

— Bean

Before diving into these fine noodle products, let's consider the molecular matter that makes them possible. All noodles are formed by a paste (that's *pasta* in Italian, by the way) composed of water and a flour. If the flour is wheat, the resulting noodle, whether rolled or extracted, is held together by that plastic and elastic protein matrix known far and wide as gluten. However, the pastes that produce Asian noodles (with the exception of wheat and egg noodles) contain no proteins whatsoever and therefore zero gluten. What holds them together? The same stuff that makes bread stale: amylose.

Amylose is a polymer, a long, mostly straight chain of glucose molecules, represented by these batteries, that, like glucose, store energy. When this paste is first created, these molecules are highly disordered. But after the noodles are extruded and cooked, the molecules go through a process called retrogradation, which we investigated in semi-depth just a few pages ago (as it related to bread pudding). Retrogradation refers to the realignment of amylose molecules into a uniform, crystalline order after cooking, an order that is highly stable until it's rehydrated in warm water.

While most Asian noodles are extruded, rice pastes can also be spread thinly on mats, steamed, and dried to create a parchmentlike sheet that can be rehydrated and wrapped around a wide array of ingredients.

Sailors have long been fans of mung beans because their high-protein sprouts can be easily and quickly grown in small plastic tubs, thus delivering considerable nutrition with little care or space. Noodles made from mung bean starch are often marketed as "cellophane" noodles because in their dry state they're translucent, due to the fact that they're composed of nothing but starch granules with no protein or other molecular matter to block light.

2 COMMON STARCHES

Amylose   Amylopectin

STARCHES ARE JUST LONG CHAINS OF GLUCOSE MOLECULES, STORING ENERGY LIKE D-BATTERIES.

TIDBIT | Up until recently, Asian noodles could not be sold as "noodles" in the United States because they didn't contain eggs.

14 ROLLS

This application utilizes both rice wrappers and thin rice noodles or "sticks" to produce a much-loved appetizer or salad course that's rarely presented in the home environment.

// SOFTWARE ///

FOR THE SPRING ROLLS

5	ounces	rice sticks	
2	tablespoons	soy sauce	
1	pound	unpeeled large shrimp	
3	tablespoons	lime juice	freshly squeezed (2 limes)
1	tablespoon	sambal chile paste	
2	teaspoons	sugar	
1	large	cucumber	unpeeled
1	large	carrot	peeled and grated
¾	cup	fresh cilantro	chopped
¾	cup	fresh mint or Thai basil	chopped
14	8½-inch	round rice paper wrappers	
14	leaves	Bibb, Boston, or other soft lettuce	

FOR THE SAUCE

½	cup	soy sauce	
¼	cup	rice vinegar	
2	tablespoons	fresh ginger	grated
2	tablespoons	scallions	chopped
2	cloves	garlic	minced
2	teaspoons	sugar	
1	teaspoon	toasted sesame oil	

// PROCEDURE ///

MAKE THE SPRING ROLLS:

(1) Soak the rice sticks in a **large bowl** in enough hot water (110°F) to cover by 1 inch for 15 minutes, or until the brittleness is gone and the noodles begin to be more pliable.

(2) Bring 2 quarts water and 1 tablespoon of the soy sauce to a boil in a **4½-quart saucepan**. Add the shrimp and cook until just firm, 1 to 2 minutes. Use a **spider or slotted spoon** to remove the cooked shrimp to a **cutting board** and cool for 3 minutes. When cool enough to handle, peel, coarsely chop, and set aside.

3. Return the water–soy sauce mixture to a boil. Drain the noodles and add them to the hot water. Cook until tender, about 3 minutes.

4. Meanwhile, **whisk** the lime juice, the remaining 1 tablespoon soy sauce, sambal, and sugar together in a **medium bowl**.

5. Drain the noodles in a **colander** and rinse under cold water. When the noodles have thoroughly drained, add them to the lime juice mixture, toss, and set aside while preparing the vegetables.

6. Roll-cut the cucumber: Trim the ends, then cut into thirds. Insert the blade of the knife into the cucumber just to the start of the seeds. Slowly rotate the cucumber so that the flesh cuts away from the seed core (you should end up with a sheet of seedless cucumber; it is okay if it cracks). Discard the inner core and seeds. Cut the cucumber sheet into 2-inch pieces, then cross-cut into very thin matchsticks. Toss the cucumber, carrot, and herbs together in a **small bowl**. Transfer any unabsorbed liquid from the noodles to the cucumber mixture and toss to combine.

7. Cut the noodles into small, 1- to 2-inch pieces with **kitchen shears**.

8. Fill a **pie dish** with 1 inch (3 cups) warm water (100° to 110°F). Dip one rice paper wrapper into the water for 10 seconds, then transfer to a cutting board and let sit until the wrapper is pliable and slightly tacky, about 1 minute. Put ¼ cup of the vegetable mixture on the bottom third of the wrapper nearest to you. Spoon 2 tablespoons chopped shrimp on top of the vegetables. Top with ¼ cup of the noodles. Bring the bottom edge of the wrap tightly over the filling, then fold in the two sides. Finish rolling from bottom to top until the entire wrapper is rolled. Be careful not to tear the rice paper. Place on a **half sheet pan** lined with **parchment paper** and cover with a **damp tea towel**. Repeat with remaining wrappers until the filling is gone.

MAKE THE SAUCE:

9. Combine all of the sauce ingredients in a **lidded jar** and shake well to combine. To serve, pick up each spring roll with a lettuce leaf and dip in the sauce.

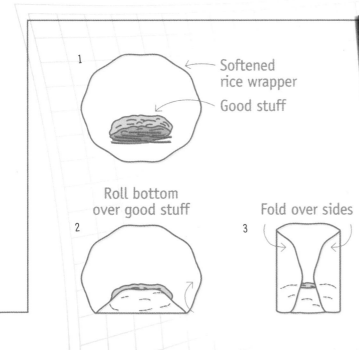

1. Softened rice wrapper ← / Good stuff ←

Roll bottom over good stuff

2.

Fold over sides

3.

4. Roll

5. Roll and moisten flap to seal, and stack, seam down

MAYI SHANG SHIU

4 ENTRÉE OR 6 APPETIZER SERVINGS

Szechuan, a region in southwestern China, is known for its flagrant use of chiles, garlic, and sesame products, three of my favorite things, which explains why two of this episode's dishes are influenced by the area, beginning with *mayi shang shiu*, which translates roughly to "ants climbing in trees"—for reasons that will become obvious when you make the dish.

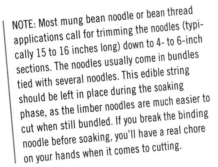

// SOFTWARE

5	ounces	mung bean threads	3 bundles
2	ounces	soy sauce	
1	tablespoon	rice wine (mirin)	
1	tablespoon	sambal chile paste	
1	teaspoon	cornstarch	
10	ounces	ground pork	
1	tablespoon	canola oil	
4		scallions	sliced on the bias
½	cup	chicken broth	

// PROCEDURE

1. Soak the noodles in a **large bowl** in enough hot water (120° to 150°F) to cover by 1 inch for 20 minutes (if the bundles are tied, leave the tie in place), then cut with **shears** into thirds or into 4- to 6-inch pieces and drain thoroughly in a **colander** for 10 minutes.

2. Combine the soy sauce, rice wine, and sambal in a **medium bowl**. **Whisk** until smooth. Whisk in the cornstarch. Add the pork and mix until thoroughly integrated. Set aside for 30 minutes.

3. Place a **12-inch sauté pan** over high heat for 1 minute. Add the oil and swirl to coat the bottom and sides of the pan. When the oil shimmers (it needs to be very hot), add the meat mixture. Cook, stirring constantly, for 2 minutes, breaking the meat up into *very* small pieces. Add two-thirds of the scallions and continue cooking and stirring until the meat is well browned and in very small pieces, about 2 minutes. Lower the heat to medium-high and add the broth. Cook until reduced, about 3 minutes.

4. Gradually add handfuls of noodles to the pan, tossing with the meat mixture until they are combined, the pieces of meat cling to the noodles, and no liquid remains.

5. Serve immediately with the remaining green onions.

NOTE: Most mung bean noodle or bean thread applications call for trimming the noodles (typically 15 to 16 inches long) down to 4- to 6-inch sections. The noodles usually come in bundles tied with several noodles. This edible string should be left in place during the soaking phase, as the limber noodles are much easier to cut when still bundled. If you break the binding noodle before soaking, you'll have a real chore on your hands when it comes to cutting.

NOTE: When dealing with either bean or rice threads, I don't just drain the soaked noodles, I give 'em a good squeeze to eliminate as much excess moisture as possible.

ANTS IN TREES!!

FINAL THOUGHTS

I've always said that when the time came, I would be the one to open the gate and lead *Good Eats* out to pasture. Well . . . it's time. I feel very torn about this. *Good Eats* has been my life's work up to this point. It has defined me as a craftsman and an artist, and I am both thrilled and terrified to discover what comes next.

I hope that *Good Eats* has entertained and educated in equal measure. If it hasn't, I have no one but myself to blame. Food Network has always supported me creatively and has, through the years, allowed me unparalleled freedom. I have valued their trust in me and have worked hard to re-earn it in half-hour installments. I thank my fans and my crew for making this dream a reality. I especially thank my wife and partner, DeAnna, for essentially making my dream her life's work as well. I hope I have the opportunity and the courage to return the favor one day.

I've learned enough about food over the last dozen years to know that I barely know anything at all. I still could not snatch a pebble out of Julia Child's hand even though she's . . . well, you know. I do know that we have some pretty big problems in this country, and I think at least a few of them could be solved if we concentrated as much on cooking as we do on eating. Food is fabulous stuff, to be sure, but cooking can also be its own reward. Cooking is an action, and it's time for more action and a little less consumption.

And it wouldn't hurt us to be a little thankful every now and then.

// WEIGHT EQUIVALENTS ////////////////////////////////////

The metric weights given in this chart are not exact equivalents, but have been rounded up or down slightly to make measuring easier.

Avoirdupois	Metric
¼ ounce	7 grams
½ ounce	15 grams
1 ounce	30 grams
2 ounces	60 grams
3 ounces	90 grams
4 ounces	115 grams
5 ounces	150 grams
6 ounces	175 grams
7 ounces	200 grams
8 ounces (½ pound)	225 grams
9 ounces	250 grams
10 ounces	300 grams
11 ounces	325 grams
12 ounces	350 grams
13 ounces	375 grams
14 ounces	400 grams
15 ounces	425 grams
16 ounces (1 pound)	450 grams
1½ pounds	750 grams
2 pounds	900 grams
2¼ pounds	1 kilogram
3 pounds	1.4 kilograms
4 pounds	1.8 kilograms

// VOLUME EQUIVALENTS //

These are not exact equivalents for American cups and spoons, but have been rounded up or down slightly to make measuring easier.

American	Metric	Imperial
¼ teaspoon	1.2 milliliters	—
½ teaspoon	2.5 milliliters	—
1 teaspoon	5.0 milliliters	—
½ tablespoon (1½ teaspoons)	7.5 milliliters	—
1 tablespoon (3 teaspoons)	15 milliliters	—
¼ cup (4 tablespoons)	60 milliliters	2 fluid ounces
⅓ cup (5 tablespoons)	75 milliliters	2½ fluid ounces
½ cup (8 tablespoons)	125 milliliters	4 fluid ounces
⅔ cup (10 tablespoons)	150 milliliters	5 fluid ounces
¾ cup (12 tablespoons)	175 milliliters	6 fluid ounces
1 cup (16 tablespoons)	250 milliliters	8 fluid ounces
1¼ cups	300 milliliters	10 fluid ounces (½ pint)
1½ cups	350 milliliters	12 fluid ounces
2 cups (1 pint)	500 milliliters	16 fluid ounces
2½ cups	625 milliliters	20 fluid ounces (1 pint)
1 quart	1 liter	32 fluid ounces

// OVEN TEMPERATURE EQUIVALENTS ///

Oven Mark	°F	°C	Gas
very cool	250–275	130–140	½–1
cool	300	150	2
warm	325	170	3
moderate	350	180	4
moderately hot	375–400	190–200	5–6
hot	425–450	220–230	7–8
very hot	475	250	9

INDEX

COPYRIGHT

Published in 2011 by Stewart, Tabori & Chang
An imprint of ABRAMS

Library of Congress Cataloging-in-Publication Data

Brown, Alton, 1962-
 Good eats 3 : the later years / Alton Brown.
     p. cm.
  title: Good eats three
 Includes index.
 ISBN 978-1-58479-903-0
 1. Cooking. 2. Cookbooks. 3. Good eats (Television program) I. Good eats (Television program) II. Title. III. Title: Good eats three.
 TX651.B7273 2011
 641.5–dc23

                            2011012300

Editors: Kate Norment and Liana Krissoff
Designers: Galen Smith and Danielle Young
Production Manager: Tina Cameron

The text of this book was composed in ITC Century, Trade Gothic, Vintage Typewriter, and ITC Officina Serif.

Printed and bound in the United States
10 9 8 7 6 5 4 3 2 1

Stewart, Tabori & Chang books are available at special discounts when purchased in quantity for premiums and promotions as well as fundraising or educational use. Special editions can also be created to specification. For details, contact specialsales@abramsbooks.com or the address below.

THE ART OF BOOKS SINCE 1949
115 West 18th Street
New York, NY 10011
www.abramsbooks.com

SOCK PUPPET BLUEPRINT

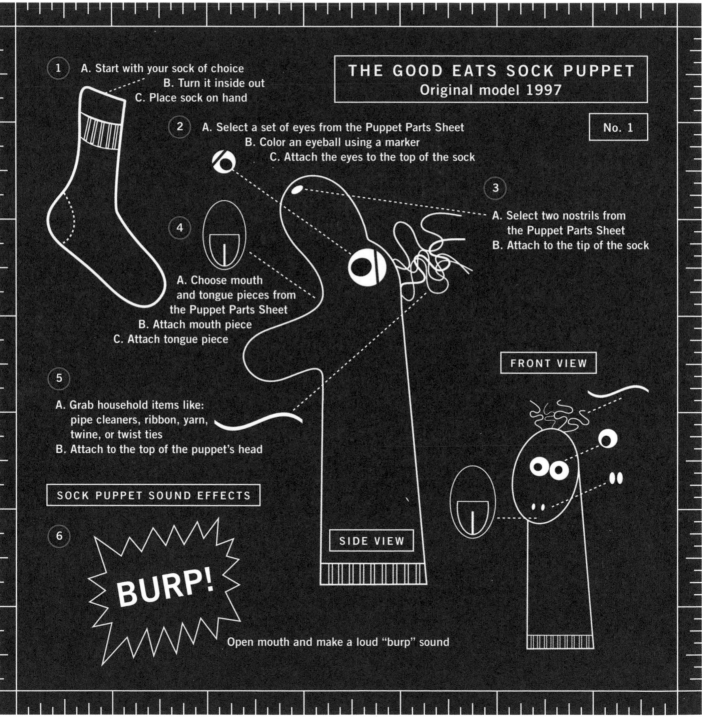

1
A. Start with your sock of choice
B. Turn it inside out
C. Place sock on hand

THE GOOD EATS SOCK PUPPET
Original model 1997

No. 1

2
A. Select a set of eyes from the Puppet Parts Sheet
B. Color an eyeball using a marker
C. Attach the eyes to the top of the sock

3
A. Select two nostrils from the Puppet Parts Sheet
B. Attach to the tip of the sock

4
A. Choose mouth and tongue pieces from the Puppet Parts Sheet
B. Attach mouth piece
C. Attach tongue piece

5
A. Grab household items like: pipe cleaners, ribbon, yarn, twine, or twist ties
B. Attach to the top of the puppet's head

FRONT VIEW

SIDE VIEW

SOCK PUPPET SOUND EFFECTS

6

BURP!

Open mouth and make a loud "burp" sound

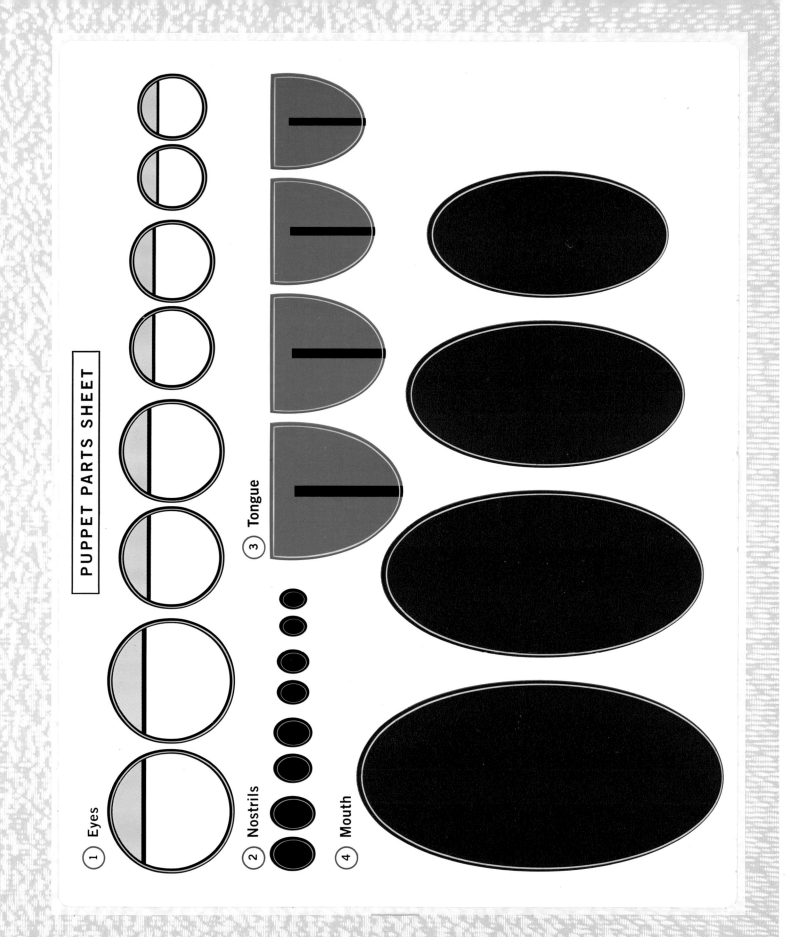